Y0-BXH-053

Reference Sources in
Library and Information Services

Reference Sources in
Library and Information Services:
A Guide to the Literature

Gary R. Purcell

with

Gail Ann Schlachter

Foreword by Charles A. Bunge

ABC-Clio Information Services
Santa Barbara, California
Oxford, England

Library of Congress Cataloging in Publication Data

Purcell, Gary R.
　　Reference sources in library and information services.

　　Includes indexes.
　　1. Reference books—Library science.　2. Reference books—Information science.　3. Library science—Bibliography.　4. Information science—Bibliography.
I. Schlachter, Gail A.　II. Title.
Z666.P96　　　1983　　　011'.02　　　83-19700

ISBN 0-87436-355-1

10　9　8　7　6　5　4　3　2　1

ABC-Clio Information Services
2040 Alameda Padre Serra, Box 4397
Santa Barbara, California 93103

Clio Press Ltd.
55 St. Thomas Street
Oxford, OX1 1JG, England

Manufactured in the United States of America

CONTENTS

PART TWO: Subject-Related Reference Works

INDEXES

FOREWORD

If there is truth in the maxim "Him that makes shoes goes barefoot himself," it is perhaps not surprising that, until now, the field of library and information science has had no comprehensive guide to its own reference literature. Surprising or not, it has not been a desirable state of affairs. For too long, we have been in the ironic position of being impoverished in a land of bibliographic riches. While guides to the reference literature of other disciplines abound, many of them prepared by librarians, until now there has been no single source to which librarians and library educators could turn that would identify the hundreds of encyclopedias, dictionaries, almanacs, handbooks, manuals, directories, biographical compilations, statistical sources, bibliographies, indexes, and abstracting services in the library field. Now, with the publication of *Reference sources in library and information services*, Purcell and Schlachter have laid out for us the multitude of English- and foreign-language reference sources available to provide information and citations to materials of interest to our profession.

At least four groups should find this work especially valuable. First, practicing librarians who need to help their clients find information about libraries, librarianship, and related fields, or who need to find such information for their own professional and educational uses, will welcome the savings in time and the increased access offered here. Second, library and information science educators and researchers will find this volume very useful in developing their courses and reading lists and in supporting their own research and scholarly activities. Library and information science students will also be important beneficiaries. I hope that all such students are introduced to this volume early in their studies, for I know that if they are, they will use it again and again. Finally, this work will be helpful to library collection developers, whether they are responsible for professional collections in various libraries or for building general reference collections, as they attempt to make available to their clientele the most useful reference sources.

As the first user of this guide, I was struck with the care and thoroughness of the authors. Drawing on insights and skills developed during their years of using, teaching, and reviewing reference works, Purcell and Schlachter spent over three years identifying, examining, culling, and describing reference works, from the obvious to the obscure, in library and information science. The result is a remarkably current and comprehensive guide to a very diverse group of materials. I suspect even the authors were surprised to find over 1,000 titles that met their well-chosen selection criteria. Each of these titles is carefully annotated with notes that, for some users, will be as important and helpful as the range and diversity of the reference works listed.

In my own work as student, reference librarian, and library educator, I have been frequently frustrated in my attempts to identify potentially helpful reference works. In fact, there are questions I have had about the field in the past that have gone unanswered, not because the information was unavailable, but because I was unable to determine the appropriate source. As I reviewed the listings in this guide, I repeatedly discovered "new" publications I might have used in these earlier quests.

Whether it is intellectual curiosity or professional need that prompts you to delve into the library literature, you will find Purcell and Schlachter's *Reference sources in library and information services* invaluable in starting and continuing your search.

—*Charles A. Bunge*
Professor, Library School,
University of Wisconsin-Madison

ACKNOWLEDGMENTS

The cooperation of numerous individuals and access to the resources of several major libraries were instrumental in the creation of this reference work. The university libraries whose staffs and collections were particularly helpful in identifying and locating materials cited here include Columbia University; the University of Tennessee; Peabody College of Vanderbilt University; the Universities of California at Berkeley, Los Angeles, Santa Barbara, and Davis; the University of Southern California; and the University of Michigan. The Library of Congress, the New York Public Library, and the Los Angeles Public Library also offered assistance.

Special thanks go to staff members who tracked down information in response to requests by mail or telephone, especially Joel M. Lee, Headquarters Librarian at the American Library Association in Chicago; Beryl L. Anderson, Director of the Library Documentation Centre at the National Library of Canada in Ottawa; Nancy D. Lane, Head of the Centre for Library and Information Studies at Canberra College of Advanced Education in Belconnen, Australia; Frank L. Schick, at the National Center for Educational Statistics' Learning Resources Branch in Washington, D.C.; and Celia Leyte-Vidal at Duke University's Perkins Library in Durham, North Carolina.

A number of individuals provided unique information about reference resources on specific subject areas or geographic regions. In particular, we wish to acknowledge the contributions of Thomas J. Galvin, Dean of the School of Library and Information Science at the University of Pittsburgh; Linda Phillips, Head of the Undergraduate Reference Department at the University of Tennessee; Pauline Bayne, Head of the Music Library at the University of Tennessee; Edwin S. Gleaves, Chair of the Department of Library and Information Science at Peabody College of Vanderbilt University in Nashville; Bernard Kreissman, University Librarian at the University of California at Davis; and Wiley Williams, on the faculty of the School of Library Science at Kent State University. In addition, we would like to note the invaluable assistance of the state and provincial librarians in the United States and Canada who supplied previously unrecorded information about their library directories and statistical compilations.

Many colleagues well acquainted with reference publications and the literature of librarianship were asked to assist in the development of the *Guide*. Of this group, we would especially like to recognize the contributions of June Engle, of the Division of Library and Information Management at Emory University, and Professor Charles Bunge, of the Library School at the University of Wisconsin-

Madison, both of whom evaluated the manuscript in its early stages and made numerous recommendations for improvement.

During the more than three years that work on the *Guide* proceeded, three graduate assistants at the University of Tennessee's Graduate School of Library and Information Science assisted the authors by verifying bibliographic entries, locating reviews and summaries in various bibliographic resources, entering data into the word processor, and performing countless other useful tasks. Our thanks for this work go to Abbey Landrey, Larry Creider, and Michael Hicks.

Special acknowledgment is due to the following persons who contributed significantly in different yet important ways. Darrell and Sallie Purcell along with Larry Earl Bone opened up their homes during frequent research trips. John D. Murray, Director of the Voskuyl Library at Westmont College in Santa Barbara, California, allowed the authors unlimited use of the Library's facilities at a critical point in the completion of the manuscript. His generosity to the authors is greatly appreciated. Virginia Murray typed the final manuscript of the work, retyping numerous changes and additions as needed. Her highly competent work has been an important factor in the timely completion of this book. Similarly, Barbara Pope, Clio Books Editor, provided invaluable editorial counsel and review, often above and beyond the call of duty.

Even with the assistance of all these people, we would not have been able to complete the *Guide* without the constant support and understanding of our families. Carolyn, Kay, Kristen, Beth, Ronald, and Benjamin Purcell willingly relinquished the presence of a husband and father during weekends, evenings, and vacations for a long period of time to see this work through to completion. Sandy and Eric Schlachter likewise gave up the companionship of their mother for many evenings and weekends to enable her to work on the manuscript. To these members of our families and to all others who contributed in any way to this book, we extend our heartfelt thanks.

INTRODUCTION

During the past twenty-five years, the library science field has been characterized by dynamic growth and change. With the onset of new information delivery systems, the rising interest in information-seeking behavior, and the concern for improved library and information services, librarians increasingly recognize the need for accurate, thorough control over the professional literature—control that will enable them to analyze, measure, and evaluate current services. Given the rapid technological advances in the information industry, the growing sophistication of users, and the abundance of reference literature devoted to library and information services, the need for a source that brings together this broad body of knowledge for easy access has become ever more evident.

Until now, no single guide has provided thorough coverage of the vast array of reference publications dealing with library services and issues. Earlier attempts to provide access to this important professional literature have restricted their coverage in substantive ways. *American reference books annual*, for example, has provided reviews of the professional literature on an annual basis for more than 10 years, but only for materials published in the United States and Canada. Both Walford's *Guide to reference material* and Sheehy's *Guide to reference books* offer international coverage, but the number of listings are limited to less than 300 library-related reference citations in each edition. Similarly, none of the bibliographic guides that focus solely on library science cover the reference literature as a whole. Besterman's *Bibliography: library science and reference books*, for example, offers international coverage but includes only bibliographic citations. Despite the general nature of its title, Lilley and Badough's *Library and information science: a guide to information sources* focuses only on bibliographic works, and citations are limited to publications that emphasize English-language materials. Consequently, librarians have had difficulty in determining appropriate sources to add to their professional collections or to use in answering questions about their own field. Students and researchers interested in library science also have had little guidance in identifying relevant sources to consult in their data collection.

In an effort to fill this bibliographic gap, we have spent the last three years researching, reviewing, describing, and indexing the wealth of reference literature related to librarianship. The result is *Reference sources in library and information services*, a guide to the literature that is both international and extensive in its coverage of reference materials.

The *Guide* has been prepared to assist librarians, library school students, library educators, library researchers, and other library and information personnel interested in library issues and services. Over 1,000 reference sources are described, providing access to the people, places, events, organizations, terminology, statistics, laws, manuscripts, dissertations, books, articles, manuals, media, data bases, and other materials related to the library field.

SCOPE

The following criteria were established to determine which library-related materials to include.

Library-related sources: Works that deal primarily, extensively, or exclusively with the operations, terminology, personalities, history, techniques, issues, or institutions related to library and information services are included. General publications covering librarianship indirectly or secondarily are omitted, since numerous other guides to the literature describe these sources in depth. Subject bibliographies and guides to the literature of specific fields (e.g., history, economics, sociology), which are important tools for librarians but are not library-related reference works, are also excluded. Other types of reference works—such as classification systems and schedules, library standards (since most are issued as articles and are not available in a separately-published form), and state- and provincial-level materials (except when they were issued as directories or statistical sources)—were viewed as outside the scope of this guide.

Reference materials: The major types of reference publications are covered in this guide. Bibliographies, indexes and abstracts, annual reviews, current contents services, online data bases, glossaries and other dictionaries, encyclopedias, annuals, handbooks, yearbooks, biographical directories, library directories, and sources of library statistics fall into this category. The emphasis is on separately-published material; therefore, very few journal articles containing reference information are cited. Studies, reports, functional works, journals, general histories, individual biographies, textbooks, and other monographs are excluded.

Materials of interest to English-language users: The *Guide* is intended primarily for an English-language audience; consequently, most of the items listed are English-language publications. The focus is on titles issued in the United States, Canada, the United Kingdom, Australia, and New Zealand. Foreign-language titles are included—particularly in the chapters covering bibliographies, dictionaries, and directories—if they are perceived to have value for English-language users.

Cataloged materials: Only sources that have been commercially available and would tend to be cataloged in larger libraries are identified in the *Guide*. Processed materials (such as holdings lists of libraries) and pamphlet-like publications (fifty pages or less) are generally omitted.

Twentieth-century publications: In general, the time period covered by the library-related reference materials cited in the *Guide* extends from the early 1900s through the first half of 1983. However, specific time coverage varies by type and subject of publication. For example, all relevant abstracting and indexing services are described, regardless of the publication date. On the other hand, most of the titles identified in the subject chapter were issued within the past ten years; titles released earlier have been included there only if they provide information that is still of value but unavailable in the other sources listed.

ARRANGEMENT

The *Guide* is divided into two major parts, further subdivided into chapters. Part I is arranged by type of publication. Nearly 700 sources that deal with library and information services as a whole, not focusing on any one aspect of the field, are included. Bibliographic works, dictionaries and other terminologies, encyclopedias, yearbooks, handbooks, biographical compilations, library directories, and sources of library statistics are described. Some of the chapters are further subdivided by format or geographic coverage, and entries are arranged alphabetically by title within these subdivisions. Part II identifies approximately 500 reference works that concentrate on one or more library-related issues, developments, processes, institutions, or techniques. The titles are grouped by subject. There are 103 subject sections in all, ranging from acquisitions to micrographics to women in librarianship, and subdivided by format.

In all cases, entries are listed alphabetically by title, but the specific order in which the titles are listed varies from chapter to chapter. For example, the sources in Chapter 1, "Bibliography," are divided by format (e.g., indexing and abstracting services, current contents services, online data bases) and subdivided (where appropriate) by place of publication. In Chapter 5, directories of libraries and other information agencies are grouped by region and subdivided by country of coverage. The subject-related sources described in Chapter 7 are arranged by topic and subdivided by format. For additional information on the arrangement of titles followed in individual sections of the *Guide*, see the introductions that precede each chapter and section.

We have attempted to provide as complete a bibliographic citation as possible, identifying (where relevant) title, author, edition, place, publisher, date, number of pages or frequency, series, Library of Congress (LC) card number, International Standard Book Number (ISBN), and/or International Standard Serial Number (ISSN). In a number of cases, however, it was not possible to supply all bibliographic components. First of all, many items lacked ISBN, ISSN, and/or LC numbers. Data were not always available on a serial's initial publication date. (We used question marks when the dates could not be ascertained or were in question.) In addition, although a serial or series may have gone through a number of publishers or frequencies of publication, the publication history may not have been recorded anywhere. Further, we frequently found contradictory bibilographic information in standard sources and even in the publications themselves. Where bibliographical records were at variance, we generally accepted the information presented in OCLC records, particularly if those records had been prepared by the Library of Congress or the National Library of Canada.

All *Guide* entries are annotated. These annotations are descriptive and, when appropriate, evaluative in nature. The emphasis is on purpose, scope, arrangement, limitations, unique features, and usefulness. Special care has been taken to trace the publication history, including title changes, of the sources covered in the *Guide*. Also, numerous cross-references are provided to tie together these related publications.

Generous use of cross-listing is employed throughout the *Guide*. Titles are listed in all relevant sections; however, a full description of a title is provided only once, in the section that seemed most appropriate. The reader is always directed to the annotation containing the most complete information.

Three indexes have been prepared. The title index refers to all materials cited as separate entries or listed in the annotations. Similary, an author index identifies all personal authors, corporate authors, compilers, editors, and translators listed in the citations or annotations. The geographic index provides access to both the place of publication and the geographic coverage of works cited in the *Guide*. Because all subject-oriented reference works are listed and cross-listed by topic in Chapter 7, no other subject access is provided.

COMPILATION OF THE GUIDE

The *Guide* was compiled after an extensive search through a variety of resources: major bibliographic sources and review publications covering library and information science literature; catalogs of collections with major library and information science holdings; current publishers' catalogs; on-site visits to a number of major libraries, including the Library of Congress, Columbia University's School of Library Service, the University of Tennessee, and the Universities of California at Berkeley, Davis, Santa Barbara, and Los Angeles; selected bibliographic data bases; and personal contact or correspondence with individuals in several locations, both in the United States and abroad. Initially, we developed an extensive file of titles for possible inclusion. Following this, we located and examined each of the titles, making notes for subsequent description. Through these various processes, titles judged to fall within the scope of this work and to have utilitarian value were identified, reviewed, and included in the *Guide*.

As in any bibliographic project, this compilation has its limitations. In spite of all of the efforts noted, there are a few titles we were unable to locate. In those instances, the information given was culled from secondary sources, primarily from reviews or from verbal descriptions provided by librarians we contacted. Some titles, particularly directories published outside of the United States, appeared by title to be appropriate for inclusion. If, however, we could not locate either a review or a contact person to describe the source, the title was excluded. Similarly, because the bibliographic control and availability in the United States of statistical materials from non-English-speaking countries is so erratic, they were omitted from this edition of the *Guide*.

Regardless of the care that is taken when collecting data and editing a work, errors inevitably occur or changes will take place between the day the manuscript is completed and the time the book reaches the shelves. Users of this reference tool are encouraged to render a service to fellow scholars and librarians by notifying the editors of any information that should be changed or added to future editions of the *Guide*.

LIST OF ABBREVIATIONS

AACR   *Anglo-american cataloguing rules*
AALL   American Association of Law Libraries
AALS   Association of American Library Schools
ABHA   *Annual bibliography of the history of the printed book and libraries*
A.C.T., ACT   Australian Capital Territory
Acad.   Acedemia; Académie; Academy
ACRL   Association of College and Research Libraries
AD   Prefix for series codes assigned to technical reports distributed by the Defense Technical Information Center
ADBS   Association Française des Documentalistes et des Bibliothécaires Spécialistes
A.D.I., ADI   American Documentation Institute
AECT   Association for Educational Communications and Technology
AGARD   Advisory Group for Aerospace Research and Development, NATO
AIDS   Automated Informatics Documentation System
AIESI   Association International des Ecoles des Sciences de l'Information
AK   Alaska
Akad.   Akademiai; Akademi; Akademie; Akademy
AL   Alabama
ALA   American Library Association
ALISE   Association of Library and Information Science Educators
ALSC   Association for Library Service to Children
ANABAD   Asociación Nacional de Archiveros Bibliotecorios Arquedogos y Documentalistas (Spain)
AR   Arkansas
ARBA   *American reference books annual*
ARL   Association of Research Libraries
ARLIS/NA   Art Libraries Society of North America
ASIS   American Society for Information Science
Aslib   Association of Special Libraries and Information Bureaux (formerly ASLIB)
Assn.   Asociación; Association; Associazone
Assoc.   Associates
AUSLOAN   Australian interlibrary loans manual
AZ   Arizona

BBK	Bibliotechno-Bibliograficheskaia Klassifikaciia (A Russian classification system)
BID-Indeks	An online bibliographic data base available from Norsk Senter for Informatik
BL	British Library
BRS	Bibliographic Retrieval Services (an information retrieval service located in Scotia, NY)
BT	broader term
CALL	*Current awareness—library literature*
CCM	Crowell-Collier Macmillan Information Corporation
CLA	California Library Association; Canadian Library Association
CLAIM	Centre for Library and Information Management
CLENE	Continuing Library Education Network and Exchange
CLSA	Church and Synagogue Library Association
CO	Colorado
cols.	columns
COM	computer-output microfilm
comp.	compiled
CONICYT/CENID	Comisión Nacional de Investigación Científica y Tecnologica, Dirección de Información y Documentación, Centro Nacional de Informacion y Documentación
COSTI	Center of Scientific and Technical Information
CPL	Council of Planning Librarians
CRG	Classification Research Group
CSG	Capital Systems Group
CSIR	A unit of the Central Reference and Research Library (Ghana)
CT	Connecticut
DATEX-P	The German Federal Post Office telecommunication network
DC	District of Columbia
DDC	Defense Documentation Center; Dewey Decimal Classification system
DDR	Deutschen Demokratischen Republik
DE	Delaware
Dept.	Department; Departamento
DGD	Deutschen Gesellschaft für Dokumentation
DIALOG	Information retrieval service from Lockheed (Palo Alto, CA)
DISSIS	*Design of information in the social sciences*
distr.	distributor; distributed
ed.	editor; edition; edited
ED	ERIC document number
EDP	electronic data processing
enl.	enlarged
ERIC	Educational Resources Information Center

ERIC-IR	ERIC Clearinghouse on Information Resources
EURONET	European telecommunications network
exp.	expanded
FIC-II	FID Study Committee/Information for Industry
FID	International Federation for Documentation
FLA	Fellowship of the Library Association
GA	Georgia
GPO	Government Printing Office
GPO S/N	GPO Stock Number
GSLIS	Graduate School of Library and Information Science(s)/Service(s)
GU	Guam
HI	Hawaii
IA	Iowa
IBE	International Bureau of Education
IBGE	Instituto Brasileiro de Geografia e Estatística
ID	Idaho
IFLA	International Federation of Library Associations
IFLAI	International Federation of Library Associations and Institutions
IL	Illinois
IN	Indiana
Indeks IOD	Former name for BID-Indeks
INFODATA	Online data base available from Informationzentrum, Gessellschaft für Information und Dokumentation
Inst.	Institut; Institute; Instituto; Institution; Instytut
IREBI	*Índices de revistas de bibliotecología*
Irreg.	Irregular
IS	Indian Standard
ISBN	International Standard Book Number
ISO	International Organization for Standardization
ISSN	International Standard Serial Number
JAL	*Journal of academic librarianship*
JICST	Japan Information Centre of Science and Technology (Nihon Kagaku Gijutsu Jōhō Senta)
JLA	Japan Library Association
KDSz	*Könyvtári és dokumentációs szakirodalom*
KS	Kansas
KTS	Komitee Terminologie und Sprachfragen der Deutschen Gesellschaft für Dokumentation
KWIC	key-word-in-context
KWOC	key-word-out-of-context
KY	Kentucky
LA	Louisiana
LC	Library of Congress
LIBGIS	Library General Information Survey

LISA	*Library and information science abstracts*
LIST	*Library and information services today*
LMTA	Library Media Technical Assistants
LRMP	*Library resources market place*
LTP	Library Technology Program
MA	Massachusetts
MD	Maryland
ME	Maine
MEDLARS	Medical Literature Analysis and Retrieval System
MEDLINE	MEDLARS Online
METRO	Metropolitan Reference and Research Library Agency (New York)
MI	Michigan
MKSzB	*Magyar Könyvtári szakirodalom bibliográfiaja*
MLA	Medical Library Association; Music Library Association
MN	Minnesota
MS	Mississippi
MT	Montana
NATO	North Atlantic Treaty Organization
NB	Nebraska
NBLC	Nederlands Biblioteek en Lektuur Centrum
NC	North Carolina
NCES	National Center for Education Statistics
ND	North Dakota
NFAIS	National Federation of Abstracting and Indexing Services
NH	New Hampshire
NJ	New Jersey
NLS	National Library Service for the Blind and Physically Handicapped
NM	New Mexico
n.p.	not paged
no.	number
NOVI	Studiecentrum NOVI
N.S.W., NSW	New South Wales
NT	narrower term
NTIS	National Technical Information Service
NUC	*National union catalog*
NV	Nevada
NY	New York
NYPL	New York Public Library
OH	Ohio
OK	Oklahoma
OR	Oregon
ORBIT	On-line, Real Time, Branch Information, Oracle Binary Internal Translator (an information retrieval system from SDC)

OSTI	Office of Scientific and Technical Information
OSzK	Országos Széchényi Könyvtár
p.	page; pages
PA	Pennsylvania
Ph.D.	Philosophiae Doctor (Doctor of Philosophy)
PLRG	Public Libraries Research Group
pp.	pages (spanned)
PPZI	*Przegląd pismiennictwa zagadnień informacji*
Pr.	Press
PR	Puerto Rico
prelim.	preliminary
prep.	prepared
prov.	provisional
pt.	part
pub.	publication
PX	partial refer from
rev.	revised
RI	Rhode Island
RIE	*Resources in education*
RISM	*Répertoire international des sources musicales*
RSFSR	Russian Soviet Federated Socialist Republic
RT	related term
RZI	*Referativnyi zhurnal, 59: informatika*
SBN	Standard Book Number
SC	South Carolina
SCANNET	Scandinavian telecommunications network
SD	South Dakota
SDC	System Development Corporation
2d	second
SERMLP	Southeastern Regional Medical Library Program
SHARE	*Sisters have resources everywhere*
SLA	Special Libraries Association
SN	Standard Number (GPO)
SPEL	*Selected publications in european languages*
SSSR	Soiuz Sovetskikh Sotsialisticheskikh Respublik
3d	third
TN	Tennessee
trans.	translated; translation
TX	Texas
U.K., UK	United Kingdom
U.S.	United States
U.S.S.R., USSR	Union of Soviet Socialist Republics
UDC	Universal Decimal Classification (system)

Unesco	United Nations Educational, Scientific, and Cultural Organization (formerly UNESCO)
Univ.	Universidad, University
UT	Utah
UVTEI	Ustředié Vědeckých, Technických a Ekonomických Informací
v.	volume; volumes
v.p.	various paging
VA	Virginia
VALA	Victorian Association for Library Automation
VEB	Volkseigener Betrieb (public companies in the German Democratic Republic)
VI	Virgin Islands
VINITI	Vsesoiuznyi Institut Nauchnoi i Teknicheskoi Informatsii
WA	Washington
WI	Wisconsin
WV	West Virginia
WVLC	West Virginia Library Commission
WY	Wyoming
Wydawn.	Wydawnictwo (Polish word for press)
X	refer from
Z.f.B.	Zentralinstitut für Bibliothekswesen
ZIID	Zentralinstitut für Information und Dokumentation

PART ONE:

General Reference Works

1.

Bibliography

INTRODUCTION

This chapter cites an array of bibliographic sources which, as a whole, provide coverage from the nineteenth century to the present. These sources access all forms of materials—archives, journals, research reports, and online data bases—and are issued in over fifteen languages and twenty-five countries by professional organizations, governmental units, commercial publishers, and individuals. Sources are conveniently divided into six sections: indexing and abstracting services; bibliographies and library catalogs; current contents services; review publications; online data bases; and dissertations and theses.

Indexing and Abstracting Services: This section includes over sixty indexing and abstracting publications that list and/or describe 100 or more library-related publications per year. Of these, more than half (forty-one) are published in languages other than English (only thirteen are or have been issued in the United States). Generally, these services cite a publication in the original language and supply a translation in the language of the country in which the service is published. With few exceptions, abstracts are also presented in the language of the country of publication.

The services covered in this section vary in the number of entries and length of abstracts. Some services list only 100 titles per year. Others, such as *Library literature* (entry no. 52), identify 8,000 entries annually. Abstracting services, like *Referativnyi zhurnol, 59: informatika* (entry no. 62), *Information science abstracts* (entry no. 48), and *Library and information science abstracts* (entry no. 38), describe up to 4,000 items each year. Some annotations of the abstracting services contain only one sentence; in others, the abstracts may contain several paragraphs. The services also vary in their extent of international and domestic coverage. However, most cite at least some items not found in any other secondary service and, for this reason, each makes a unique contribution to the bibliographic control of the literature.

Bibliographies and Library Catalogs: Over the years, numerous separately-published bibliographies on library-related topics have been issued. While most of these are subject specific and are covered in Chapter 7 of the *Guide*, nearly forty are general in nature and are provided here. Unlike indexing and abstracting services, the majority of these titles have been published in English and one-third in the United States. The most comprehensive of these sources are catalogs covering such major collections as the School of Library Service at Columbia University (entry no. 69) and England's Library Association Library (entry no. 92). The remaining items identified consist of either monographs or bibliographic articles included in journals. Emphasis is placed on current materials. General bibliographies and library catalogs published before 1960 are omitted unless they represent significant bibliographic contributions.

Current Contents Services: Current contents services offer the opportunity to scan reproductions of the contents pages of current journals in the field. Numerous services exist for various disciplines. The most widely known of these, *Current contents*, provides minimal coverage of the literature of library and information service. *IREBI: índices de revistas de bibliotecología* (entry no. 106) is the only separately-published current contents service that currently focuses on library-related journals. The other three library-related contents services ceased publication in 1980 or earlier. Nevertheless, they are listed here because they may be useful for retrospective searching through library literature. *CALL* (entry no. 103), for example, reproduced the tables of contents of more than 200 library-related journals from 1972 to 1980.

Review Publications: Among the most valuable of bibliographic resources are the "review" or "state of the art" publications. Typically, these publications take the form of a bibliographic essay that identifies major contributions to the literature of a topic for a specific period of time and are augmented by a lengthy list of papers or monographs. Review publications are most commonly found in the scientific and medical fields, where it is estimated that more than 20,000 reviews are published annually. There are only seven journals and monographs that provide general "state of the art" reviews for the library and information fields in English or Western European languages. (For subject-specific review publications, see appropriate sections of Chapter 7.) While most library-related review articles appear in the journal literature, there are two important separately-published sources that provide state of the art coverage on a systematic or continuing basis—*Annual review of information science and technology* (entry no. 114) and *Advances in librarianship* (entry no. 113).

Online Data Bases: Numerous online bibliographic data bases include citations to library-related monographs, journal articles, and report literature. However, only six of these sources focus primarily, exclusively, or extensively on materials in the library field. Of these, the most important is *LISA* (entry no. 118), which currently provides over 48,000 entries online, adding approximately 6,000 new items each year.

Dissertations and Theses: The earliest dissertation concerned with librarianship was completed in 1925. Subsequently, over 1,000 library-related doctoral studies have been produced. The first attempt to provide bibliographic control over this segment of library literature was issued by Cohen, Dennison, and Boehlert in 1963 (entry no. 128). The most comprehensive coverage was provided by Schlachter and Thomison (entry nos. 126–127) in their two-volume annotated bibliography of library-related dissertations completed at U.S. and Canadian universities from 1923 through 1981.

A number of journals that currently identify dissertation topics accepted or dissertations completed, (e.g., *Journal of education for librarianship, Library quarterly*, and *Information hotline*) are not cited in this section. Only separately-published monographs concentrating exclusively on library-related dissertations are covered.

Master's theses (research papers associated with the master's level in the United States and with the Fellowship in the Library Association in the United Kingdom) are more uneven in quality than dissertations; consequently, their utility is more uncertain. Unlike dissertations, which can be obtained on microform or in photoduplicated copy from University Microfilms International in Ann Arbor, Michigan, most theses (at least in the United States) are available only in typescript from the university where the degree was awarded or, less frequently, from the Educational Resources Information Center (ERIC). Thus, accessing master's theses is more difficult than accessing doctoral dissertations.

Bibliographic access poses a similar problem. Since 1978, no separately-published bibliography has concentrated on library-related master's theses, and the two serials that currently list American theses, *Library quarterly* and *Library literature*, depend on library school graduates to submit notification of completed theses. As a result, their coverage is incomplete.

INDEXING AND ABSTRACTING SERVICES

Abstracting and indexing services that emphasize or specialize in bibliographic coverage of librarianship and/or information science are listed in alphabetical order by title under country of publication. Countries are arranged in alphabetical order by country name without regard to continental location. In some cases, publications are in languages other than the native language of the country in which they are published.

Argentina

1 "Bibliografía bibliotecológica Argentina." Appears in **Documentación bibliotecológica, 1968– .** Bahía Blanca: Centro de Documentación Bibliotecológica, Universidad del Sur, 1969– . Annual. LC 72–625104. ISSN 0070–6841.
This Spanish-language work indexes and provides brief abstracts for about 100 journal

articles per year. Included are articles published in Argentina and articles by Argentine authors published elsewhere. The arrangement is by Universal Decimal Classification system. Additional access is provided by an author index. The first volume of the indexing service covers the period 1853–1967 and was published in 1969. Subsequent volumes index literature from 1968–1969, 1970, 1971–1972, 1973, 1974–1975. The index is now published as part of the serial, *Documentación bibliotecológica*.

2 **IREBI: índices de revistas de bibliotecología.** Madrid: Oficina de Educación Iberoamericana; Bahía Blanca: Centro de Documentación Bibliotecológica; Madrid: Inst. Bibliográfico Hispanico, 1973– . Quarterly. LC 74–648263. ISSN 0378–746X.

The tables of contents of approximately 200 journals in library and information science are reproduced each year in this work. A particularly valuable feature of this work is its detailed subject index. For further information see entry **34**.

Bulgaria

3 **Bibliotekoznanie, bibliografiia, knigoznanie, nauchna informatsiia.** Sofia: Narodna Biblioteka "Kiril i Metodij," 1967– . Annual.

Approximately 400 citations, many with brief annotations, are listed each year. Written in Cyrillic, the work surveys the literature of librarianship, bibliography, informatics, and scientific information. Coverage is limited to about forty periodicals issued within Bulgaria. Arrangement is by the Universal Decimal Classification system; an author index appears in each volume.

Canada

4 **Canadian library literature index: a preliminary checklist.** By the Reference Section of the Association Canadienne des Bibliothèques. Ottawa: Canadian Library Assn., 1956. 79p. LC 58–41202.

The publications of Canadian provincial libraries and library associations are indexed in this work, which was designed to supplement existing indexes. Also included are government publications, books, newspapers, and pamphlets. The period covered is 1950–1956. The index has never been updated.

Cuba

5 **Revista referativa informática.** Havana: Inst. de Documentación e Información Científica y Técnica, Acad. de Ciencias de Cuba, 1974– . Irreg. LC 76–649765.

Approximately 800 abstracts of papers and articles in information science and informatics, from eighty periodicals, are published each year. Coverage is international. Titles are in Spanish, followed by the title in the original language; abstracts are in Spanish. Arrangement is classified, by broad subject categories. Author and subject indexes in Spanish provide additional access. A list of journals covered is included.

Czechoslovakia

6 **Bibliograficke přehledy z oblasti technického knihovnictví a vedeckotechnických informací.** Prague: UVTEI, 1969– . 6 per year.
Each year, this work lists approximately 2,500–3,000 journal articles and brief abstracts (usually only one sentence each). Emphasis is on writings concerned with special and technical libraries and with informatics. Coverage is international, but most items are European in origin. Arrangement is by broad subject categories, with additional access provided by a KWIC index to author, subject, country of publication, and journal. The work was formerly titled *Přehledy literatury v oblasti technického knihovnictvi.*

7 **Metodika a technika informací.** Prague: UVTEI, 1959–1970.
This title is continued by "Titulova bibliografie" in *Československa informatika.* For further information see entry **8**.

8 "Titulova bibliografie." Appears in **Československa informatika.** Prague: UVTEI, 1971– . Monthly. LC 71–613413.
This section of a Czechoslovak serial indexes approximately 1,200 items per year from the fields of library science, documentation, and information science. Coverage is international; titles of entries and some summaries appear in the original language followed by a Czech translation. Materials listed include books, journal articles, and conference proceedings. The serial, *Československa informatika,* was titled *Metodika a technika informaci* from 1959 to 1970 (entry **7**).

France

9 "Bibliographie de la littérature documentaire d'expression française, 1967–1972." Appears in **Documentaliste: revue d'information et de techniques documentaires.** Paris: ADBS, 1964– . Quarterly.
This work is continued by "Index des travaux d'auteurs français et francophones." For further information see entry **12**.

10 "Bulletin de documentation bibliographique." Appears in **Bulletin des bibliothèques de France.** Paris: Direction des Bibliothèques et de la Lecture Publique, 1956– . Monthly. LC 60–23187.
This French-language indexing and abstracting service, prepared by the Bibliothèque Nationale, indexes or abstracts approximately 2,000 items per year. Subject coverage includes librarianship, but extends to other aspects of documentation and includes items such as bibliographic guides or bibliographies for various disciplines. Materials indexed include monographs, journal articles, and reports. The service is divided into three parts: the first provides only the bibliographic entry for relevant titles; the second includes abstracts and reviews, some of considerable length; the third lists items received but not reviewed. Arrangement of the first two parts is by broad topic. Additional access is provided by annual author and subject indexes.

11   Bulletin signalétique 101: science de l'information: documentation. Paris: Centre de Documentation, Centre National de la Recherche Scientifique, 1972– . Monthly. LC 73–643943. ISSN 0301–0309.
This extensive abstracting service lists up to 4,000 items per year. Coverage is international, with particular emphasis on Western Europe. Materials indexed include journal articles, monographs, reports, proceedings, dissertations, theses, patents, and standards from librarianship, information science, and various other areas of technical information processing. Arrangement is by an alphanumeric classification scheme; entries are numbered. Titles appear in the original language, but abstracts are in French, and range from one to six sentences. Access is provided by author and subject indexes, in French and English, which appear in each issue and are cumulated annually. From 1970 to 1971, this publication was titled *Bulletin signalétique 101: information scientifique et technique.*

12   "Index des travaux d'auteurs français et francophones, 1973– ." Appears in **Documentaliste: revue d'information et de techniques documentaires.** Paris: ADBS, 1964– . Quarterly. LC 72–625305. ISSN 0012–4508.
This is an unannotated key-word-out-of-context (KWOC) index to the contributions of French authors in the fields of library science, information science, and documentation appearing in *Bulletin signalétique* (entry **11**). Materials covered include books, journal articles, monographs, technical reports, and reference works. The number of items indexed varies. From 1964 to 1967, the journal's title was *Documentaliste,* and from 1967 to 1972, the index section of the journal was known as "Bibliographie de la littérature documentaire d'expression française" (entry **9**).

German Democratic Republic

13   Bibliographische mitteilungen zum bibliothekswesen. Leipzig: Deutsche Bücherei; Berlin: Zentralinstitut für Bibliothekswesen, 1958–1964. 6 per year.
This title is continued by *Informationsdienst bibliothekswesen.* For further information see entry **15**.

14   Information und dokumentation: annotierte titelliste. Berlin: Zentralinstitut für Information und Dokumentation der DDR, 1975– . Monthly. LC 78–642874.
This German-language work provides brief abstracts of approximately 1,200 items annually from the international literature of documentation and information science. Articles, monographs, technical reports, some dissertations, and translations into German are indexed. Arrangement is by broad subject categories. From 1968 to 1974, this work was titled *Informationsdienst information: dokumentation: annotierte titelliste mit beilage ZIID-mitteilungen* (entry **16**).

15   Informationsdienst bibliothekswesen. Leipzig: Deutsche Bücherei; Berlin: Zentralinstitut für Bibliothekswesen, 1971– . 6 per year. LC 72–625651. ISSN 0044–1457.
Abstracts of approximately 1,600 items per year, taken from the domestic and foreign literature of librarianship, are provided here. Materials include journals, technical reports, and monographs; emphasis is on Eastern European materials. Arrangement is by Universal Decimal Classification system. Each issue has an author and subject index, and annual and quinquennial indexes are issued. Each entry is numbered. Formerly titled, from 1965 to

1970, *ZIID-referatekartei bibliothekswesen* (entry **17**); from 1958 to 1964, *Bibliographische mitteilungen zum bibliothekswesen* (entry **13**).

16 Informationsdienst information: dokumentation: annotierte titelliste mit beilage ZIID-mitteilungen. Berlin: Zentralinstitut für Information und Dokumentation der DDR, 1968–1974.
This title is continued by *Information und dokumentation: annotierte titelliste.* For further information see entry **14**.

17 ZIID-referatekartei bibliothekswesen. Leipzig: Deutsche Bücherei; Berlin: Zentralinstitut für Bibliothekswesen, 1965–1970. 6 per year.
This title is continued by *Informationsdienst bibliothekswesen.* For further information see entry **15**.

Germany, Federal Republic of

18 Dokumentation und arbeitstechnik. Frankfurt/Main: Deutsche Gesellschaft für Dokumentation. 19??–1949.
This title is superseded by *Nachrichten für dokumentation: zeitschrift für information und dokumentation.* For further information see entry **20**.

19 Fachbibliographischer dienst: bibliothekswesen. Berlin: Deutches Bibliotheks Inst., 1966– . Irreg. LC 73–644808. ISSN 0429–9655.
This annual bibliography of journal articles and monographs covers librarianship and information science. Although the number of items listed per year varies, it has been well over 5,000 entries annually. Coverage is international but tends to emphasize European, particularly German, publications. Entries are in the original language. Each volume covers the literature of the previous year or earlier, depending on how quickly the volumes are published. Arrangement is in classified order; author and subject indexes are provided. A list of periodicals indexed is included.

20 "Schrifttum zu den informationswissenschaften." Appears in **Nachrichten für dokumentation: zeitschrift für information und dokumentation.** Frankfurt/Main: Deutsche Gesellschaft für Dokumentation, 1950– . 5 per year. LC 56–17817. ISSN 0027–7436.
Bibliographic coverage of about 500 items per year is provided here. Journal articles from more than 100 German-language journals in the fields of librarianship, documentation, and information science are abstracted. Also included are summaries of conference proceedings and some monographs. A brief supplement provides abstracts, in German, for a few selected foreign titles. An annual subject index is arranged by Universal Decimal Classification and augmented by an index of institutions. The journal supersedes *Dokumentation und arbeitstechnik* (entry **18**).

Hungary

21 Express information of hungarian literature on library science and documentation/Gyorstájékoztató a magyar könyvtártudományi i irodalomrol. Budapest:

OSzK, Könyvtártudományi es Módszertani Központ, 1965–1972. Quarterly.
This title is continued by *Magyar könyvtári szakirodalom bibliográfiaja*. For further information see entry **24**.

22 Hungarian library and information science abstracts. Budapest: OSzK, Könyvtártudományi es Módszertan i Központ. 1972– . 2 per year. LC 72–626707. ISSN 0046–8304.
This work provides lengthy abstracts (300–350 words) of 120–130 journal articles and monographs per year. The Hungarian literature of librarianship and information science is covered. The title of each entry is in Hungarian and English, and the abstracts are in English. Arrangement is by broad subject areas. Each issue has an English-language subject index (cumulates annually).

23 Könyvtári es dokumentációs szakirodalom: referáló lap (KDSz). Budapest: OSzK, Könyvtártudományi es Módszertani Központ, 1963– . Quarterly. LC 41–4024. ISSN 0454–3491.
This Hungarian-language publication abstracts the literature of librarianship, documentation, and information science. The approximately 500 abstracts per year are arranged by broad subject category. Coverage is international and includes journal articles and monographs. A subject index, with an annual cumulation, provides access.

24 Magyar könyvtári szakirodalom bibliográfiaja (MKSzB). Budapest: OSzK, Könyvtártudományi es Modszertani Központ, 1973– . Quarterly. LC 74–645595. ISSN 0133–736X.
Journal, monograph, and report literature published in Hungary for librarianship and information science is covered here. Dissertations are also included. Each year, approximately 1,200 entries are listed; some are abstracted. Entries are in Hungarian, arranged in broad subject categories, and numbered, with the numbering sequence continuing from one volume year to the next. This work was titled *Express information of hungarian literature on library science and documentation/Gyorstájékoztató a magyar könyvtártudományi i irodalomrol* (entry **21**) from 1965 to 1972 and was issued by the same institution.

India

25 Indian library science abstracts. Calcutta: Indian Assn. of Special Libraries and Information Centres, 1967– . Quarterly. LC SA 68–10323. ISSN 0019–5790.
The 180 to 200 entries per issue, with brief annotations in English, are drawn from approximately fifteen Indian library and information science journals. Arrangement of entries is by colon classification with numbered entries. The work was published annually from 1967 to 1972 and quarterly since then. Each issue is indexed by author and subject.

Japan

26 "Current documentation literature." Appears in **Dokumêntesyon kenkyu.** Tokyo: Nihon Dokumenteshon Kyokai, 1950– . Monthly. ISSN 0012–5180.
This Japanese-language work abstracts about 350 journal articles per year from approximately sixty domestic and foreign journals. Emphasis is on documentation and information

science. Arrangement is in classified order using the Universal Decimal Classification system. The journal in which this abstracting service is published was known as *UDC Information* (entry **30**) from 1950 to 1958, when it assumed its present title.

27 **Gekkan.** Tokyo: JICST, 1958–1962. Monthly.
This title is continued by *Jōhō kanri*. For further information see entry **28**.

28 **Jōhō kanri.** Tokyo: JICST, 1963– . Monthly. ISSN 0021–7298.
A section of this journal carries about 250 abstracts per year of Japanese literature in information science and documentation. Entries are in Japanese; an index in Japanese and English is provided. From 1958 to 1962, the journal was titled *Gekkan* (entry **27**).

29 "Tosho-kan zasshi kiji sakuin." Appears in **Tosho-kan zasshi.** Tokyo: Nippon Tosho-kan Kyokai, 1907– . Monthly. ISSN 0385–4000.
Journal references appearing in roughly forty Japanese journals are indexed here. Approximately 1,300 references covering the fields of library science, information science and documentation appear per year. The work is published in Japanese by the Japan Library Association.

30 **UDC information.** Tokyo: Nihon Dokumenteshon Kyokai, 1950–1958. Monthly.
This title is continued by *Dokumentesyon kenkyu*. For further information see entry **26**.

Netherlands

31 **R & D projects in documentation and librarianship.** The Hague: International Federation for Documentation (FID), 1971– . Quarterly. ISSN 0301–4436.
This serial identifies and provides brief accounts of work in progress internationally in various facets of librarianship, information science, and documentation. The number of projects identified per year is between 250 and 300. Each entry includes a project title, a brief description of the nature of the work, the name of the principal investigator, the name and address of the sponsoring institution, and, where available, the amount of financial support awarded to the project. Arrangement is by country and then by project number. Entries and annotations are in English.

Poland

32 **Przeglad pismiennictwa zagadnien informacji (PPZI).** Warsaw: Inst. Informacji Naukowej, Technicznej i Ekonomicznej, 1962– . Monthly.
This work indexes and abstracts approximately 3,000 items per year from the international literature of library and information science. Materials covered include journals, books, technical reports, and conference proceedings. Titles are in the original language, with a Polish translation; abstracts are in Polish.

Romania

33 **Buletin de informare in bibliologie.** Bucharest: Biblioteca Centrala de stat a Republicii Socialiste Romania, 1960– . Monthly. ISSN 0007–3784.

Approximately 2,000 items are indexed and abstracted per year in this work. Coverage is international, with emphasis on European materials. Entries are in the original language, abstracts in Romanian. Arrangement is classified under broad topics.

Spain

34 IREBI: índices de revistas de bibliotecología. Madrid: Oficina de Educación Iberoamericana; Bahía Blanca: Centro de Documentación Bibliotecológica; Madrid: Inst. Bibliográfico Hispanico, 1973– . Quarterly. LC 74–648263. ISSN 0378–746X.

The tables of contents of approximately 200 journals in library and information science are reproduced each year in this work. Journal coverage is international, with emphasis on European-language publications. The contents pages, in the original language, are from major journals from the various countries represented. A complete list of the journals covered is also provided. A particularly valuable feature of this work is its detailed subject index.

Sweden

35 Nordisk bibliografi och bibliotekslitteratur. Lund: Bibliotekstjänst, 1957– . Irreg. This work reprints and cumulates the bibliography indexed in "Nordisk bibliografi och bibliotekslitteratur," a section of the *Scandinavian journal of libraries/Nordisk tidskrift for bok- och biblioteksväsen.* For further information see entry **36**.

36 "Nordisk bibliografi och bibliotekslitteratur." Appears in **Scandinavian journal of libraries/Nordisk tidskrift for bok- och biblioteksväsen.** Stockholm: Almqvist & Wiksel, 1914– . Quarterly. LC 15–22512. ISSN 0029–148X.

This work indexes approximately 1,300 references to library literature published in Denmark, Finland, Iceland, Norway, and Sweden. Subject headings appear in Swedish, with English translations. An author index is provided. The bibliography is reprinted and cumulated under the title, *Nordisk bibliografi och bibliotekslitteratur* (entry **35**).

United Kingdom

37 "Current awareness list." Appears in **Aslib information.** London: Aslib, 1973– . Monthly. ISSN 0305–0033.

Coverage of this abstracting service is international and includes nearly 1,500 titles per year. Emphasis is on documentation, special libraries, and information science. Monographs, journal articles, conference proceedings, technical reports, and library or documentation standards are abstracted. Entries are in the original language; abstracts are in English. Listings are arranged by broad subject categories.

38 Library and information science abstracts (LISA). London: Library Assn., 1969– . 6 per year. LC 78–228730. ISSN 0024–2179.

Formerly published as *Library science abstracts* (entry **39**), this abstracting service was initiated to assist students in the United Kingdom to prepare for Library Association examinations. In 1950, responsibility for publishing it was assumed by the Library Association. When the title was changed in 1969, the scope was increased to include information science, and Aslib agreed to supply related abstracts. Emphasis is on periodical articles, with less comprehensive treatment of monographs and technical reports. Currently about 6,000 items are abstracted and about 300 periodicals, selected pamphlets, and some conference proceedings are represented. Although coverage is international, priority is given to British and European journals. Titles are in the original language, with an English translation. Entries are arranged in classified order using the Classification Research Group system. Although not published in a separate thesaurus, a brief summary of the CRG scheme appears in each issue of *LISA*. Access to abstracts is through an author index and an alphabetical subject index compiled by means of a chain index procedure.

39 Library science abstracts. London: Library Assn., 1950–1968. Quarterly. LC 82–1259. ISSN 0459–262X.
This title is continued by *Library and information science abstracts (LISA)*. For further information see entry **38**.

40 Radials bulletin. London: Library Assn., 1974– . 2 per year. LC 77–648394. ISSN 0302–2706.
This serial identifies research projects (approximately 500 per year) in librarianship, information science, and documentation initiated in the United Kingdom. Abstracts are arranged by the Classification Research Group (CRG) system, the same used in *Library and information science abstracts* (entry **38**). Each issue is indexed by subject, researcher, and institution. This work is cumulative, so projects are identified even if referred to in an earlier issue. This was developed from the "Register of research" (entry **41**), which formerly appeared in the *Library Association; yearbook* from 1968 to 1973 (entry **265**).

41 "Register of research, 1968–1973." Appears in **Library Association: yearbook.** London: Library Assn., 1891– . Annual. ISSN 0075–9006.
This work has developed into an independent abstracting service, *Radials bulletin* (entry **40**). For further information about the *Yearbook* see entry **265**.

42 SPEL: selected publications in european languages. Aberystwyth, Wales: College of Librarianship, 1973– . Annual. LC 77–649505. ISSN 0307–5354.
This work lists and abstracts selected periodicals and books from other European countries likely to be of special interest to librarians in the United Kingdom. About 500 brief abstracts appear in each issue, featuring works from selected countries. Titles are arranged by country and then subject.

United States

43 American reference books annual (ARBA). Littleton, CO: Libraries Unlimited, 1970– . Annual. LC 75–120328. ISSN 0065–9959.
Although not limited to library and information science, this publication regularly reviews a substantial number of new books in this field. The reviews are descriptive, evaluative, and signed. Preference is given to English-language titles. Reviews of other subjects emphasize reference materials, but coverage of library and information science includes nonreference

materials as well. Approximately 200 library and information science titles are covered each year. Arrangement is by broad topic, with author, title, and subject access.

44 Bibliography of library economy: a classified index to the professional periodical literature in the english language relating to library economy, printing, methods of publishing, copyright, bibliography, etc., from 1876 to 1920. By H. G. T. Cannons. Chicago: American Library Assn., 1927. New York: Burt Franklin Reprint, 1970. 680p. LC 73–122221.

This is an index to the literature of librarianship from the landmark year 1876 until 1920. Selected U.S. and British journals and some monographs, including major reports, are covered. An earlier edition, published in 1910, provided access to articles in forty-eight periodicals. The 1927 edition is larger and indexes sixty-five periodicals. Organized using a classified arrangement, items appear under more than one subject heading. An alphabetical list of the subject headings used provides indirect alphabetical access by subject. There is no index by title or by author (for author access to this work, see entry **45**).

45 Cannons' bibliography of library economy, 1876–1920: an author index with citations. Ed. by Anne Harwell Jordan and Melbourne Jordan. Metuchen, NJ: Scarecrow, 1976. 473p. LC 76–3711. ISBN 0–8108–0918–4.

Articles that appeared in Cannons' *Bibliography of library economy* (entry **44**) are indexed by personal author. The editors indicate that they included all entries from Cannons' work that listed a personal author's name. Entries are arranged alphabetically by author's last name and then alphabetically by title. Each entry includes author's surname and initials, title of the article, title of the periodical where it appeared, volume number, and page number. For entries other than periodical articles, publication year is given. Because all essential bibliographic information is shown here, it is not necessary to refer to Cannons' bibliography.

46 Current index to journals in education. Phoenix: Oryx, 1969– . Monthly. LC 75–7582. ISSN 0011–3565.

Published for the Educational Resources Information Center in conjunction with the National Institute of Education, this title indexes nearly 800 journals in education, with an average of 1,800 articles covered in each monthly issue. About thirty of the journals are in library and information science and additional coverage of topics in these fields is available from articles appearing in other journals indexed by the service. Each entry contains full bibliographic information and a brief document resume (abstract) of the article. Monthly indexing by author and subject cumulates semiannually and annually. Subject descriptors are assigned from the *Thesaurus of ERIC descriptors* (see entry **207**). This work constitutes one of the two major components of the *ERIC* data base (entry **115**). The other major component is *Resources in education* (see entry **55**).

47 Documentation abstracts. Philadelphia: Documentation Abstracts, 1966–1968. Quarterly. LC 66–9894.

This title is continued by *Information science abstracts*. For further information see entry **48**.

48 Information science abstracts. Ed. by Documentation Abstracts, Inc. New York: Plenum, 1969– . 6 per year. LC 75–648959. ISSN 0020–0239.

Originally titled *Documentation abstracts* (entry **47**), this work abstracts approximately 6,000 items per year. Coverage of journal articles, books, conference proceedings, technical reports, and other materials is international, but emphasis is on English-language publications. Entries are arranged by broad subject topics, with consistent classification numbers in each issue. Not limited to librarianship and information science, this work includes materials in other disciplines that touch on documentation and information-related topics. Subject and author access is available through issue and annual indexes.

49 "JAL guide to new books and book reviews on library science, information science and educational administration." Appears in **Journal of academic librarianship.** Ann Arbor, MI: Mountainside, 1975– . 6 per year. LC 75–647252. ISSN 0099–1333.

Roughly 700 new monographs and journal articles in librarianship, information science, documentation, and higher education are listed and reviewed in this journal. Most are English-language publications; emphasis is on U.S. titles. Coverage, which follows publication of the item, is fairly prompt. Annotations are evaluative, and thus recommendations are given regarding the quality of the work.

50 Libraries in american periodicals before 1876: a bibliography with abstracts and an index. Comp. by Larry J. Barr, Haynes McMullen and Steven G. Leach. Ed. by Haynes McMullen. Jefferson, NC: McFarland, 1983. 444p. LC 83–780. ISBN 0–89950–066–8.

This is a retrospective bibliography of references to libraries appearing in American periodicals prior to 1876. The compilers used all available periodical indexes and in addition searched through issues of individual periodical titles that were not indexed. More than 1,500 entries are included, approximately 150 of which are abstracted. Articles with fewer than 150 words are quoted in their entirety. Index access is by author, types of libraries, cities, persons, and major ideas or events. Because this bibliography predates *Cannons*, (entry **45**), it should be used first in any historical literature search for library-related subjects.

51 Library and information sciences: weekly government abstracts. Springfield, VA: NTIS, 1972– . Weekly. LC 77–1300. ISSN 0364–6467.

Abstracts from *Government reports announcements and index* published by NTIS (available online through DIALOG, entry **120**) and *Resources in education* (entry **55**) are reprinted here. Approximately 1,000 items per year are abstracted. Most entries are technical reports produced by or on contract through U.S. government agencies, or are items submitted to the ERIC-IR Clearinghouse. Each entry includes standard bibliographic information plus document accession numbers and a price code for the cost of paper and microfiche copies. An annual subject index is available.

52 Library literature: index to library and information science. New York: Wilson, 1936– . 6 per year. LC 79–2556. ISSN 0024–2373.

This is an international, cumulative author/subject index to about 10,000 items issued annually in library and information science. The work indexes articles in more than 200 library and non-library journals, as well as monographs, pamphlets, films, filmstrips, microforms, theses, and dissertations. In addition, each issue has a separate list of selected items acquired by the ERIC-IR Clearinghouse and a checklist of monographs cited for the first time. Cross-references are used extensively throughout. Bibliographic entries include full author, title, date and place of publication, and pagination. Coverage of non-English-language publications (with titles translated into English) is extensive. *Library literature* began publication as a continuation of H. G. T. Cannons' *Bibliography of library economy 1876–1920* (entry **45**), published in 1927. Initially, it was published as a project of ALA's Junior Members' Round Table, but was later turned over to H. W. Wilson. The first volume published by H. W. Wilson was *Library literature 1933–35*. The first annual volume was published in 1936. In 1939, publication became semiannual; it was changed to quarterly in 1955 and to six issues per year in 1969. Currently, there are bound annual and biennial cumulative volumes.

53 Library work, cumulated, 1905–11: a bibliography and digest of library literature. Ed. by Anna Lorraine Guthrie. New York: Wilson, 1912. 409p.
A predecessor to *Library literature* (entry **52**), this bibliographical source cumulates approximately 2,500 subject entries that appeared in the quarterly issues of *Library work* from April, 1906 to October, 1911. The publication indexed thirty-two periodicals from the field of librarianship. Of these, twenty-four were in English and the remainder in Danish, Dutch, German, Italian, Norwegian, Spanish, and Swedish. Items are indexed by subject with cross references. Some entries carry brief notes about the contents.

54 Research in education. Washington, DC: National Inst. of Education, U.S. Dept. of Health, Education and Welfare, 1966–1974. Monthly.
This work is continued by *Resources in education*. For further information see entry **55**.

55 Resources in education. Washington, DC: National Inst. of Education, U.S. Dept. of Education, 1974– . Monthly. LC 75–644211. ISSN 0098–0897.
Formerly titled *Research in education* (entry **54**), this monthly abstracting journal announces report and other materials in education and related fields. Although only a small percentage of the items included in this service cover library and information science, the total volume is sufficient to make this one of the largest abstracting services in the English language for this field. Citations to library and information science materials focus on report literature generated by the U.S. Department of Education and other agencies of federal, state, and local governments; additional coverage is provided for unpublished papers, conference proceedings, course syllabi, and various other ephemeral resources. Specifically excluded are journal articles, monographs issued by trade book publishers, and most non-U.S. materials. Each issue consists of document resumes (abstracts) and indexes. The resumes contain full bibliographic information and are arranged by assigned ERIC accession number. Each of these entries is indexed by subject (descriptors taken from the ERIC *Thesaurus*; (entry **207**), personal author, institution, and publication type. These monthly indexes cumulate semiannually and annually. Microfiche copies of all ERIC documents are available, either from the ERIC Document Reproduction Service or from libraries which

subscribe to and maintain deposit collections of the documents. *Resources in education* forms a major part of the ERIC data base, which is also available online (entry **115**). The other major component of the ERIC data base is published under the title *Current index to journals in education* (entry **46**).

U.S.S.R.

56 Bibliograficheskaia informatiia: bibliotekovedenie i bibliografovedenie SSSR. Moscow: Ministerstvo Kul'tury SSSR, Informatsionnyi Tsentr po Problemam Kul'tury i Ickusstva, 1979– . Monthly. LC 77–648630.

This journal provides current bibliographic coverage of new Russian materials on librarianship and bibliography. *Novosti nauchnoi literatury: bibliotekovedenie i bibliografovedenie: inostrannaia literatura* (entry **60**) covers non-Russian materials and is published simultaneously. Combined, these two journals contain annotations for approximately 4,000 items per year. The types of materials covered include monographs, journal articles, and pamphlets. Foreign titles are in the original language with a Russian translation. The annotations are in Russian. Arrangement is classified by the BBK (bibliotechno-bibliograficheskaia klassifikatsiia), a Russian classification system and entries are indexed by subject and author. These works were formerly included in a single journal and from 1943–1973 this was titled *Bibliotekovedenie i bibliografiia: ukazatel' sovetskoj literatury* (entry **57**), and during 1974 was titled *Novaia sovetskaia i inostrannaia literatura po bibliotekovedeniiu i bibliografii* (entry **59**). From 1975 to 1979, the journal that covers Russian materials was titled *Novosti nauchnoi literatury; bibliotekovedenie i bibliografovedenie; sovetskaia literature* (entry **61**).

57 Bibliotekovedenie i bibliografiia: ukazatel' sovetskoj literatury. Moscow: Gosudarstvennaia Ordena Lenina Biblioteka SSSR im. V. I. Lenina, Informatsionnyi Tsentr po Problemam Kul'tury i Iskusstva, 1943–1973.

This title was continued by *Novaia sovetskaia i inostrannaia literatura po bibliotekovedeniiu i bibliografii* in 1974. From 1975, coverage is continued by two titles, *Novosti nauchnoi literatury: bibliotekovedenie i bibliografovedenie: sovetskaia literatura* and *Novosti nauchnoi literatury: bibliotekovedenie i bibliografovedenie: inostrannaia literatura*. For further information see entry **60**.

58 Informatics abstracts. Moscow: VINITI, 1963– . Monthly.

This is the English-language edition of *Referativnyi zhurnal 59: informatika: otdel'nyj vypusk*. For further information see entry **62**.

59 Novaia sovetskaia i inostrannaia literatura po bibliotekovedeniiu i bibliografii. Moscow: Gosudarstvennaia Ordena Lenina Biblioteka SSSR im. V. I. Lenina, Informatsionnyi Tsentr po Problemam Kul'tury i Iskusstva, 19??–1974. Monthly. LC 75–643490.

This title is continued by two separate journals, *Bibliograficheskaia informatiia: bibliotekovedenie i bibliografovedenie: v SSSR* and *Novosti nauchnoi literatury: bibliotekovedenie i bibliografovedenie: inostrannaia literatura*. For further information see entry **56**.

60 Novosti nauchnoi literatury: bibliotekovedenie i bibliografovedenie: inostrannaia literatura. Moscow: Ministerstvo Kul'tury SSSR, Informatsionnyi Tsentr po Problemam Kul'tury i Iskusstva, 1975– . Monthly. LC 77–640773.

This title provides current bibliographic coverage of new non-Russian materials on librarianship and bibliography. The companion journal, *Bibliograficheskaia informatiia: bibliotekovedenie i bibliografovedenie v SSSR,* provides the same coverage for Russian materials. For further information see entry **56**.

61 Novosti nauchnoi literatury: bibliotekovedenie i bibliografovedenie: sovetskaia literatura. Moscow: Ministerstvo Kul'tury SSSR, Informatsionnyi Tsentr po Problemam Kul'tury i Ickusstva, 1975–1979. Monthly. LC 77–648630.

This journal provides bibliographic coverage of new Russian materials on librarianship and bibliography. It is continued by *Bibliograficheskiia informatiia: bibliotekovedenie i bibliografovedenie v SSSR.* For further information see entry **56**.

62 Referativnyi zhurnal 59: informatika: otdel'nyi vypusk. Moscow: VINITI, 1971– . Monthly. LC 65–41719. ISSN 0486–235X.

This is the major abstracting journal for librarianship, information science, and informatics in the Soviet Union. As many as 4,800 items are abstracted per year. Coverage is international, with emphasis on Russian- and East European-language materials. Types of materials covered include journal articles, books, proceedings, and patents. Both entries and abstracts are in Russian. An English-language edition is also published. It is currently titled *Informatics abstracts* (entry **58**) and was formerly known as *Abstract journal referativnyi zhurnal: informatika.* The English-language edition lacks author and subject indexes. Entries are arranged by broad subject categories. The title of the Russian language journal from 1963 to 1970 was *Referativnyi zhurnal: nauchnaia i tekhnicheskaia informatsiia.*

63 Ukazatel' literatury po nauchno-tekhnicheskoi informatsii i bibliotekovedeniiu. Moscow: Gosudarstvennaia Publichnaia Nauchno-tekhnicheskaia Biblioteka SSSR, 1973– . Monthly.

Nearly 2,000 periodical articles per year in information science and librarianship are listed here. Each is abstracted, and both the entry and the abstract are in Russian. Each issue of the journal includes a list of periodicals and author and subject indexes.

Yugoslavia

64 Bibliotekarske novosti: referativni bilten. Novi Sad: Biblioteka Matice Srpske, 1971– . LC 72-624971. ISSN 0350-0462.

About 1,000 journal articles per year are abstracted here. Entries are in the original language, abstracts in Serbo-Croatian. Coverage is international; arrangement is by the Universal Decimal Classification system, and access is provided by an author index.

BIBLIOGRAPHIES AND LIBRARY CATALOGS

Bibliographies on librarianship and information science that are not limited to a single subject and catalogs to the holdings of some major library science collections are arranged alphabetically by title under country or geographical area of coverage. International bibliographies and library catalogs are listed first. These are followed by publications with coverage limited to national areas. Individual countries are arranged in alphabetical order without regard to continental location.

International

65 ABHA: annual bibliography of the history of the printed book and libraries. Ed. by Hendrik D. L. Vervliet. The Hague: Martinus Nijhoff, 1970– . Annual. LC 74–641084. ISSN 0303–5964.

This international bibliography, prepared under the auspices of the Committee on Rare and Precious Books and Documents of the International Federation of Library Associations, lists monographs, journal articles, exhibition catalogs, dissertations, and auction and booksellers catalogs dealing with various aspects of books and libraries. Emphasis is on the history of the printed book and on the art, craft, and technology of book production. In addition, one section is devoted to publications on aspects of libraries and librarianship. Histories of libraries and publications that characterize library collections are emphasized. The latest volume (8) covers the year 1977 and includes 3,200 bibliographic entries taken from 1,700 periodicals. More than twenty-five countries are represented. Entries are arranged by broad topic and then by geographical area covered. Entries are in the original language, with no English translation. There are author and geographical/personal name indexes.

66 Bibliographie des bibliotheks- und buchwesens. Leipzig: Harrassowitz, 1904–1925. (Pub. suspended 1912–1922).

From 1904 to 1912, *Internationale bibliographie des buch- und bibliothekswesens mit besonderer beruecksichtigung der bibliographie* was published as a supplement to this work. Beginning in 1922, the *Internationale bibliographie* was issued as a separate work. For further information see entry **74**.

67 Bibliography: library science and reference books: a bibliography of bibliographies. By Theodore Besterman. Totowa, NJ: Rowman & Littlefield, 1971. 271p. LC 70–29437.

A spin-off of Besterman's *World bibliography of bibliographies,* this presents a listing of separately published, library science-related bibliographies from all over the world and from various time periods. Entries are brief, but include title, publisher, place and date of publication, and number of entries.

68 A bibliography of librarianship: classified and annotated guide to the library literature of the world (excluding slavonic and oriental languages). By Margaret

19

Burton and Marion E. Vosburgh. New York: Burt Franklin Reprint, 1970. 176p. (Burt Franklin bibliography and reference series, no. 322). LC 75–118171.

This work, a selected, annotated bibliography of library literature from English and Western European languages, was compiled in 1934 to provide a basic list of materials for a professional library. Of the approximately 1,600 entries, most are monographs, although some reference materials are listed. Coverage extends back to the 19th century, but most materials date from the 20th. The range of topics is representative of library practice in the United States and Western Europe during the period covered. Arrangement is by broad topic; subject and author indexes provide further access.

69 Dictionary catalog of the Library of the School of Library Service, Columbia University. Boston: G. K. Hall, 1962. 7v. LC 63–2444 rev. ISBN 0–8161–0634–7. **First Supplement.** Boston: G. K. Hall, 1976. 4v. ISBN 0–8161–1166–9.

This is the largest published bibliography of materials in librarianship and information science. As a consequence, it is the premier bibliographic work for retrospective searching. The main set and the first supplement represent the holdings of one of the world's major libraries in this field up to 1975. The original catalog includes 127,000 cards, and 62,000 additional cards are found in the first supplement. A second supplement is in progress and will be published soon. The emphasis in the collection is in-depth coverage of librarianship, information science, and related fields for English-language materials; non-English materials are also covered. Monographs, journals, reports, pamphlets, and other publications from various countries and languages are found here. Arrangement is in dictionary form, with author, title, and subject entries included. This arrangement makes separate author, title, or subject indexes unnecessary. Subject designations are those used for Library of Congress subject headings, and about half of the cards reproduced in this work are Library of Congress cards.

70 Documentation source book. By Gertrude Schutze. New York: Scarecrow, 1965. LC 65–13551.

This work is supplemented by *Information and library science source book.* For further information see entry **72**.

71 FID publications: an 80 year bibliography, 1895–1975. The Hague: FID, 1975. 94p. LC 76–350239. ISBN 92–66–00531–2.

Publications of the International Federation for Documentation are inventoried in this bibliography. Although it does not include all publications for which FID has been responsible, the most significant are among the 587 numbered entries. The actual number of publications identified is considerably larger, however, since several items appear under the same publications number in the listing. The arrangement, titles listed within five-year periods in no particular order, is somewhat difficult to use. However, access is available through the following indexes: subject, personal author, and FID committee. Although most items are no longer available from FID, the current *FID publications catalogue* may be consulted to determine which can still be acquired.

72 Information and library science source book: a supplement to Documentation source book. By Gertrude Schutze. Metuchen, NJ: Scarecrow, 1972. 483p. LC 72–1157. ISBN 0–8108–0466–2.

Monographs, periodical articles, and technical reports concerned with various aspects of library and information science are included in this selected bibliography. Coverage is primarily of English-language materials, and although the criteria for selection are not indicated, one can infer that the compiler applied subjective judgment based on extensive experience to select those items she found to be most useful or enlightening. This supplements an earlier work titled *Documentation source book* (entry **70**). Both volumes emphasize specialized library or information work rather than the broad range of library service.

73 International bibliography of the book trade and librarianship/Fachliteratur zum buch- und bibliothekswesen, 1976–1979. Ed. by Helga Lengenfelde and Gitta Hauser. 12th ed. Munich: K. G. Saur, 1981. 692p. ISBN 3–598–20516–3.
The 12th edition of this work serves as an international review of monographic literature concerned with librarianship, publishing, book manufacturing, and the retail book trade. In addition, related fields such as archival work and information science are represented selectively. The bibliographic listing of library and book trade publications is cumulative and results in substantial coverage. For example, the 10th edition (1969–1973), the 11th edition (1973–1975), and the 12th edition combined list approximately 25,000 titles. The current edition lists 9,826 numbered entries. Although this work does not index the journal literature, it includes pamphlets and brochures, research reports, standards, and, of course, monographs. Emphasis is on European and U.S. materials, but some items are included from most countries of the world. Arrangement is first by continent and country of publication, and then by topic. Topic headings are in English, followed by the German term. Entries are in the original language, with titles from non-Roman alphabets transliterated. Access is through author/editor/compiler and subject indexes.

74 Internationale bibliographie des buch- und bibliothekswesens, mit besonderer berücksichtigung der bibliographie, 1904–12, 1922–39. Leipzig: Harrassowitz, 1905–1940. Nendeln: Kraus Reprint, 1969. 15v. in 7. LC 73–644457.
Initially a supplement to the *Bibliographie des bibliotheks- und buchwesens* (entry **66**), this work later was published independently and annually. It includes material related to librarianship and the book trade from all countries, with emphasis on European-language materials. Periodical articles and monographs are covered. Arrangement is by classified order.

75 Librarianship and the third world: an annotated bibliography of selected literature on developing nations, 1960–1975. By A. M. Abdul Huq and Mohammed M. Aman. New York: Garland, 1977. 372p. LC 76–30916. ISBN 0–8240–9897–8.
Journal articles and monographs dealing with librarianship and library development are listed and annotated here. A total of 1,475 numbered entries are included. Annotations vary from one to four sentences. Entries are arranged alphabetically by the English name of the country or region covered in the article or monograph. More than sixty countries are represented individually, and several more are represented through articles that deal with such regions as Latin America and the Middle East. The index is by personal or corporate author. Coverage is largely of recent materials.

76 LIST: library and information services today: an international registry of research and innovation. Ed. by Paul Wasserman. Detroit: Gale, 1971–1975.

Annual. LC 71–143963. ISSN 0075–9821.

This work (no longer published) identifies research projects in progress between 1971 and 1975 in various facets of library and information science throughout the world. Information solicited through questionnaires resulted in a substantial number of research activities being identified. For example, the 1975 volume includes 1,335 entries. Inclusion does not imply endorsement. In the time that has elapsed, many projects identified here have been completed, and some have resulted in publications that can be identified elsewhere. Each entry in the registry provides the name of the investigator, project name, institutional affiliation, and, when possible, a brief description of the project. Extensive indexing provides access by subject headings, classified subject categories, name of investigator, title, organization name, geographical location of the project, source of funding, and acronyms.

77 Wie finde ich bibliothekarische literatur? By Frank Heidtmann. Berlin: Berlin Verlag, 1978. 288p. LC 80–670025. ISBN 3–87061–188–X.

Although this bibliographic guide to the literature of library and information science is written in German and emphasizes German sources, it also lists selected examples of bibliographies, indexes, and other works from various countries and languages. One valuable feature is the inclusion of sample pages from some of the publications cited. The format is more that of a textbook than an annotated bibliography. Access to individual sources is by title and subject.

ARAB COUNTRIES

78 The arab world: libraries and librarianship, 1960–1976: a bibliography. By Veronica S. Pantelidis. London: Mansell, 1979. 100p. LC 79–308681. ISBN 0–7201–0821–7.

This work lists 1,047 items published between 1960 and 1976 that deal with librarianship in twenty-one countries of the Arab world. Materials listed include books, periodicals, conference and working papers, reports, abstracts, and audio-cassettes. A criterion for inclusion is accessibility to the general user: all items are either in English or accompanied by an English abstract or summary. Arrangement is by country, with a general section at the beginning which lists publications that cover several or all Arab countries. Subdivisions under each country are by topic. Entries are in the original language but are translated into English as well. Some entries have brief annotations. An author/title index to the numbered entries is provided.

79 Bibliographical guide to arabic literature in librarianship and documentation. By Mohammed Fathy Abdel Hady. Cairo: Documentation and Information Dept., Arab Educational, Cultural and Scientific Organization, 1976. n.p.

This is a guide to approximately 4,000 items in Arabic, plus a few in other languages. Entries appear in Arabic script. Periodical articles, monographs, pamphlets, theses, technical reports, and conference papers are covered. Materials date from the last quarter of the 19th century, but most were published since the second quarter of the 20th century. Each entry has a full bibliographic description based on the 1967 *Anglo-american cataloging rules* (AACR I), modified as necessary to suit Arabic publications. Arrangement is alphabetical by Arabic subject headings. Author and subject indexes and lists of periodicals and conferences from which papers were indexed are provided.

ASIA

80 **Asian libraries and librarianship: an annotated bibliography of selected books and periodicals and a draft syllabus.** By G. Raymond Nunn. Metuchen, NJ: Scarecrow, 1973. 137p. LC 73–6629. ISBN 0–8108–0633–9.

This is an annotated bibliography of 353 books and periodicals dealing with libraries and librarianship throughout Asia. No journal articles or other materials are included. The coverage is limited to works on bibliography, types of libraries, classification, publishing, and library associations. Also listed are some of the most important library periodicals for each country. Annotations (in English) range from one to four sentences. Entries are in a Romanized version of the original language, followed by an English translation of the title. Materials are arranged by region and then by country. There is an author/title index and an index to titles in Chinese, Japanese, Korean, and Thai using Chinese and Thai characters.

National

CANADA

81 **Library science periodicals in Canada: a list of titles current in 1981/Les périodiques en bibliothéconomie au Canada: liste des titres courants en 1981.** Comp. by Carolynn Robertson. Ottawa: Library Documentation Centre, National Library of Canada, 1981. 20p. ISSN 0226–4226.

This list identifies 126 library science journals published in Canada through August 1981. Titles with national, provincial, or regional interest are covered; excluded are journals with local interest only (e.g., staff newsletters and acquisitions lists). The list is arranged alphabetically by the title as it is printed on the publication. Entries contain the title, issuing body, address, ISSN number, frequency, subscription price, and abbreviations of any indexing or abstracting services covering the journal.

COLOMBIA

82 **Bibliografía bibliotecológica Colombiana 1966–1970.** Comp. by Luis Lozano Floren. Medellín: Univ. de Antioquia, 1971. 125p.

This volume covers 888 references to the literature of librarianship in Spanish, from Colombian authors. Earlier cumulations cover 1953–1955, 1956–1958, and 1961–1965. Arranged by broad topic headings, this bibliography also has a personal and corporate author index.

CZECHOSLOVAKIA

83 **Bibliography of library science and documentation: CSR 1968–1970/Bibliografie českého knihovnictví, bibliografi a VTI.** Comp. by Josef Straka. Prague: Statni Knihovni CSR, 1971. 231p. LC 79–414621.

This work is continued by *Library science and documentation: 1975–76/Bibliografie českého knihovnictví, bibliografi a VTI/Bibliografiia bibliotekovedeniia, bibliografii: nauchno-tekhnichesko informatsii.* For further information see entry **84.**

84 **Library science and documentation: 1975–1976/Bibliografie českého knihovnictví, bibliografi a VTI/Bibliografiia bibliotekovedeniia, bibliografii: nauchnotekhnichesko informatsii.** Prague: Sektor Vyzkumu a Metody Knihovnictvi, Statni Knihovni CSR, 1979. 192p. LC 80–513743.

This is a bibliography of titles published in Czech on librarianship, documentation, and information science, covering the years 1975–1976. An earlier work (see entry **83**) was published in 1971, covering the years 1968–1970.

GERMAN DEMOCRATIC REPUBLIC

85 **25 Jahre publizistische Tätigkeit des Zentralinstituts für Bibliothekswesen und seiner Mitarbeiter, 1950–1974: Auswahlbibliographie.** Ed. by Fritz Kunz. Berlin: Zentralinstitut für Bibliothekswesen, 1975. 106p. LC 76–459672.

This is a complete list of publications of the Zentralinstitut für Bibliothekswesen issued between 1950 and 1974. A variety of library and bibliographic topics are covered. The work is indexed by title and subject.

86 **Zehn jahre bibliotheksverband der Deutschen Demokratischen Republik: chronik, bibliographie, verzeichnis der veröffentlichungen.** Ed. by Wilfried Kern. Berlin: Bibliotheksverband der DDR, 1974. 88p. LC 75–404232.

This selected, ten-year bibliography lists contributions to the field of library and information science from the German Democratic Republic.

GERMANY, FEDERAL REPUBLIC OF

87 **Bibliographie zum bibliotheks- und buchereiwesen.** Comp. by Ursula von Dietze. Wiesbaden: Harrassowitz, 1966. 223p. LC 67–112742.

This is a selected bibliography of monographs about libraries and librarianship in the German Federal Republic.

INDIA

88 **Indian library literature: an annotated bibliography.** By Ram Gopal Prasher. New Delhi: Today and Tomorrow, 1971. 504p. LC 74–926208.

Intended to identify Indian contributions to librarianship, this work covers 3,550 items from the monograph and journal literature of the field from 1955 to 1971. Also cited are bibliographical sources and Indian indexing and abstracting services. Materials on the book trade, as it pertains to librarianship, are also included. Some entries have brief annotations, but most have none. Entries are in English and provide sufficient bibliographic information to locate the publication. Arrangement is by Dewey Decimal Classification. Topics include the full range of library, information science, and documentation subject matter. Subject and author indexes are provided.

PAKISTAN

89 **Fifteen years' work in librarianship in Pakistan: 1947–62.** By Anis Khurshid and Syed Irshad Ali. Karachi: Dept. of Library Science, Univ. of Karachi, 1965. 65p. LC 65–8298.

This work is supplemented by *Librarianship in Pakistan: ten years' work: 1963–1973*. For further information see entry **90**.

90 Librarianship in Pakistan: ten years' work: 1963–1973. Comp. By Zahirruddin Khurshid. Karachi: Dept. of Library Science, Univ. of Karachi, 1974. 214p. LC 74–930309.

This bibliography of contributions to library literature published in Pakistan covers 1963–1973. Arranged by author and subject, the entries are in English for the most part, but some are in other languages, e.g., Bengali, Urdu, and Sindhi. This work supplements an earlier, similar work titled, *Fifteen years' work in librarianship in Pakistan: 1947–62* (entry **89**).

UNITED KINGDOM

91 British and irish library resources: a bibliographic guide. By Robert B. Downs with Elizabeth C. Downs. 2d ed. London: Mansell, 1981. 427p. ISBN 0–7201–1604–X.

More than 6,700 catalogs, guides, and articles that describe or analyze the holdings of British and Irish libraries are identified in this bibliography. The scope extends to all subjects, types of libraries, and types of library materials. Entries are numbered and each entry is listed one time under the Dewey Decimal Classification category deemed most appropriate. There are author, editor, compiler, institution, and subject indexes. The first edition of this work was published in 1973.

92 Catalogue of the library. London: Library Assn., 1958. 519p. LC 58–40138.

The *Catalogue* is a bibliographic record of all books held by the library of the Library Association as of March 1, 1956. Subsequent accessions are listed in *The Library Association record*. At the time of publication, more than 19,000 books, pamphlets, and volumes of periodicals were in the collection. Although coverage is international, a substantial proportion of the titles are from the United Kingdom. Arrangement is by Universal Decimal Classification system.

93 Complete list of OSTI and BL R&D reports, 1965–78: report numbers 5001–5442. London: Research and Development Dept., British Library, 1978. 36p. LC 79–318380. ISBN 0–905984–24–2.

Reports published by the Office of Scientific and Technical Information and by the British Library, from 1965 to 1978, are listed here. Numerous technical reports significant to the development of information systems in the United Kingdom during the time period are among the 442 reports identified. Full bibliographic information, sufficient to obtain copies if desired, is provided.

UNITED STATES

94 ALA publications checklist, 1979– : a list of materials currently available from the American Library Association. Comp. by the Staff of the ALA Headquarters Library. Chicago: American Library Assn., 1979– . Annual. LC 79–643470. ISSN 0193–810X.

This publication provides "bibliographic data on every publication currently available from the association and its units. It includes not only books, pamphlets and journals, but also membership materials, journal reprints, working documents of ALA, and such audiovisual materials as the cassette programs from the Annual Conferences." Coverage is comprehensive; approximately 500 entries are included in each annual volume. Information is provided on how to order items from the publishing units. Arrangement is alphabetical by title. Index access is by author, issuing units, and subject. Publication is scheduled for the beginning of each calendar year.

95 **American library resources: a bibliographical guide.** By Robert B. Downs. Chicago: American Library Assn., 1951. 428p. LC 51–11156. **Supplement, 1950–1961.** By Robert B. Downs. Chicago: American Library Assn., 1962. 226p. **Supplement, 1961–1970.** By Robert B. Downs. Chicago: American Library Assn., 1972. 256p. ISBN 8389–0116–6. **Supplement, 1971–1980.** By Robert B. Downs. Chicago: American Library Assn., 1981. 210p. LC 81–203055. ISBN 0–8389–0342–8.

The primary volume and the supplements to this work identify and provide brief annotations for bibliographical works that describe or facilitate access to the holdings of American library collections. Among the types of works covered are catalogs and bibliographies of individual library holdings, union lists, checklists, guides to special collections, and library surveys. The basic volume includes approximately 6,000 entries and the supplements contain 2,818 entries, 3,421 entries, and more than 4,200 entries, respectively. The works are cumulative; entries found in the earlier volumes are not repeated unless a new edition has been published. Each of the volumes is arranged by subject and indexed by subject, author, compiler, editor, types of materials, and some titles. There is also a *Cumulative index, 1870–1970* (entry **96**).

96 **American library resources: cumulative index, 1870–1970.** Comp. by Clara D. Keller. Chicago: American Library Assn., 1981. 89p. LC 81–12788. ISBN 0–8389–0341–X.

This work serves as an index to the basic volume and the first two supplements of *American library resources* (entry **95**). It provides cumulative author, compiler, and subject access to the annotated entries in the main volume and first two supplements. Entries in the index are noted with a Roman numeral to indicate the volume and an Arabic number to indicate the entry number. The third supplement is not covered in this index.

97 **Library and information science: a guide to information sources.** By Dorothy B. Lilley and Rose Marie Badough. Detroit: Gale, 1982. 151p. (Books, libraries and publishing information guide series, v.5) LC 82–962. ISBN 0–8103–1501–7.

This work focuses on bibliographic sources in library and information science and general bibliographic works that cover library and information science materials. The citations are limited to publications that emphasize English-language materials. Specifically excluded are non-bibliographic reference works, including dictionaries and encyclopedias, directories, statistical compilations, and biographical sources. Entries are descriptively annotated, with the text varying in length from a few words to half a page. The main body of the volume consists of two sections, one listing bibliographic publications by the forms of information sources to which they provide access (dissertations, periodicals, books, etc.) and the other listing publications by type of information sources, (indexing and abstracting services, reviewing sources, etc.). This arrangement results in some duplication in the coverage of titles that fall into both categories. Completing the volume are two brief sections that deal with bibliography and bibliographic searching and that provide index access by author, title and subject.

98 Library and information science cumindex. By Frederick G. Kilgour. Los Altos, CA: R&D Pr., 1975. 722p. LC 72–86076. ISBN 0–88274–006–7.
This work is an effort to cumulate "back-of-the-book index entries" from ninety-six titles in librarianship. A total of 90,000 index entries are included. The titles to which they refer are all English-language monographs selected to represent various facets of librarianship. Several selected out-of-print titles were included because of their quality. Books without indexes were omitted from consideration. The index is alphabetical and has numerous *see* and *see also* references.

99 Library and information sciences: an ERIC bibliography. By ERIC Clearinghouse on Library and Information Science. New York: CCM, 1972. 487p. LC 72–82741. ISBN 0–8409–0334–0.
Compiled here are approximately, 3,200 citations and abstracts of documents in the ERIC system, from its beginning to 1972, that cover library and information science topics. The full ERIC entries are reproduced and arranged by accession number. Additional access is provided through an author/subject index. Other ERIC bibliographies dealing with specific subjects in library and information science are found in the subject section of this guide.

U.S.S.R.

100 Bibliothekswesen und bibliographie in der Sowjetunion 1945–1975: eine bibliographie. Ed. by Friedhilde Krause, Nikolaj A. Laskeev and Gennadi Wasilewitsch. Leipzig: VEB Bibliographisches Inst., 1978. 248p. LC 79–350009.
This classified list of 1,755 publications from the U.S.S.R. covers various topics in librarianship from 1945 to 1975. Entries are in transliterated Russian. Brief annotations are in German. Author and title indexes provide access. This bibliography is based on an earlier work, *Sowjetisches bibliotheks- und buchwesen: bibliographie 1945–1972* (entry **101**).

101 Sowjetisches bibliotheks- und buchwesen: bibliographie 1945–1972. By Friedhilde Krause, Nikolaj Alesandrovic Laskeev and Gennadi Wasilewitsch. Berlin: Deutsche Staatsbibliothek, 1975. 293p. (Deutsche staatsbibliothek, bibliographische mitteilungen, no. 26) LC 76–462209.
This work is superseded by *Bibliothekswesen und bibliographie in der Sowjetunion 1945–1975: eine bibliographie.* For further information see entry **100**.

102 A survey of soviet literature in library science, 1948–1952. By Raissa Bloch Maurin. Washington, DC: Catholic Univ. Pr., 1954. 149 leaves.
A master's thesis from Catholic University of America, this work identifies major contributions to the literature of librarianship produced during the period 1948–1952. Entries are in transliterated Russian, but are not annotated. Publications include monographs, significant periodical articles, reports, and conference proceedings.

CURRENT CONTENTS SERVICES

Current contents services that include fifty or more journals in library and information science are arranged alphabetically by title without regard to geographic coverage or place of publication.

103 CALL: current awareness—library literature. Framingham, MA: Goldstein, 1972–1980. 6 per year. LC 72–622347. ISSN 0091–5270.
The tables of contents of more than 230 library and library-related journals are printed here bimonthly. Contents pages are not reproduced directly, but are reset, listing only major articles. Emphasis is on English-language journals; coverage includes U.S. state journals and Canadian provincial journals. Each issue also carries articles about aspects of the library field that are indexed in *Library literature* (entry **52**) and *Library and information science abstracts* (entry **38**). However, no index access to the articles listed in the contents service is provided. Instead journals are arranged by broad categories. This contents service ceased publication in 1980.

104 Contents in advance: union list of library periodicals. Philadelphia: Prometheus Pr., 1955–1959. Irreg. LC 55–8731.
One of the earliest current contents publications, this work provides international coverage of librarianship, documentation, archival, and bibliographical periodicals. Contents pages are reproduced exactly, but reduced. About 120 periodicals are covered per issue. Because it has long since ceased publication, this work is primarily of historical interest—its publisher, Eugene Garfield, is also the publisher of *Current contents* (entry **105**).

105 Current contents: social and behavioral sciences. Philadelphia: Inst. for Scientific Information, 1974– . Weekly. LC 79–3415. ISSN 0092–6361.
This is one of several issues of *Current contents* published simultaneously. Each provides reproductions of tables of contents from journals in a variety of subject disciplines. The social and behavioral sciences issue reproduces the tables of contents of approximately fifty journals in librarianship, information science, and archives. Most are English-language journals, although several European-language journals are included. English translations of the foreign-language titles are provided. The original contents pages are reduced, but are otherwise reproduced exactly. A subject index appears weekly. A cumulative journal index and complete list of journals covered are published three times a year. A particularly valuable feature of this service is the timeliness of its weekly publication schedule.

106 IREBI: índices de revistas de bibliotecología. Madrid: Oficina de Educación Iberoamericana; Bahía Blanca: Centro de Documentación Bibliotecológica; Madrid: Inst. Bibliográfico Hispánico, 1973– . Quarterly. LC 74–648263. ISSN 0378–746X.
Contents pages from more than 200 journals in librarianship, information science, documentation, and archives are reproduced in full. Coverage is international, and many significant journals in languages other than English are included. Especially useful is the subject index, which gives the user subject access to all journal articles found in the contents pages. For further information see entry **34**.

107 New contents librarianship. Munich: K. G. Saur, 1979. Quarterly. ISSN 0171–9122.

Originally intended to be a quarterly and to cover 322 current periodicals from throughout the world, this journal ceased publication after the first issue.

REVIEW PUBLICATIONS

Journals and monographs devoted specifically to library and information science review articles are arranged alphabetically by title under country of publication.

United Kingdom

108 British librarianship and information science, 1971–1975. Ed. by H. A. Whatley. London: Library Assn., 1977. 379p. NUC 80–228549. ISBN 0–85365–099–3. ISSN 0071–5662.

This work is continued by *British librarianship and information work 1976–1980*. For further information see **109**.

109 British librarianship and information science, 1966–1970. Ed. by H. A. Whatley. London: Library Assn., 1972. 712p. LC 73–157654. ISBN 0–85365–175–2. ISSN 0071–5662.

This work is continued by *British librarianship and information science, 1971–1975* and *British librarianship and information work 1976–1980*. For further information see entry **110**.

110 British librarianship and information work 1976–1980. Ed. by H. A. Whatley. London: Library Assn., 1982. 2v. LC 83–643529. ISBN 0–85365–763–7 (v.1). ISBN 0–85365–835–0 (v.2). ISSN 0071–5662.

This is the most recent in a quinquennially published series reviewing the major achievements, events, trends, and developments in the British library world. This and earlier volumes, covering the years 1966–1970 and 1971–1975, are successors to *Five year's work in librarianship* (entry **111**). The publication has now expanded to two volumes. Volume 1 is concerned with general libraries and the library profession. Volume 2 deals with special libraries, library materials, and library processes. Each volume is comprised of a number of essays, written by separate contributors. Each essay is accompanied by bibliographical references identifying the most significant materials on the topic. Although not written in quite the same fashion as the review articles appearing in *Annual review of information science and technology* (entry **114**), the articles are nevertheless a useful guide to literature in the field.

111 Five years' work in librarianship, 1951/55–1961/65. London: Library Assn., 1958–1968. Every 5 years. LC 58–2169.

These essays provide accounts of the previous five years' work in various aspects of librarianship (e.g., classification and library cooperation). Although the emphasis is on British library activities, separate units cover library work in Europe, the United States, and

Commonwealth countries. Each article is supported by a brief but carefully selected bibliography of publications on the topic covered. A subject index is provided, but no separate listing of all bibliographic citations is included.

112 Year's work in librarianship, 1928–1950. London: Library Assn., 1929–1954. Annual. LC 30–18367 rev. ISSN 0084–4144.

These essays examine major trends and achievements in various fields of librarianship during the previous year. Each essay is augmented by bibliographic citations to key periodicals and monographs that provide more coverage of the topic. Although emphasis is on librarianship within the United Kingdom, secondary coverage of European and American library service is provided.

United States

113 Advances in librarianship. New York: Academic Pr., 1970– . Annual. LC 79–88675.

Six to eight lengthy review articles are included in each volume. Written in essay style, each article discusses recent or older, but still relevant, literature on a given topic. Each essay is followed by a list of all citations covered in the text. In recent years, the articles are preceded by a table of contents of subtopics covered. Each volume has a separate subject index; a general subject index covering the first ten volumes was published in 1980. Recent articles have focused on such topics as reference service, library users, networking, and music librarianship.

114 Annual review of information science and technology. White Plains, NY: Knowledge Industry, 1966– . Annual. LC 66–25096. ISSN 0066–4200.

Each annual volume carries approximately nine to ten articles dealing with major subfields of information science or information technology. During the first few years, selected topics were repeated frequently; a wider range of topics has been covered recently. Each bibliographic essay provides coverage of significant contributions to the literature subsequent to the previous essay on the same topic. A list of references cited in the text follows each essay. Recent essay titles include "Information Analysis Centers," "Artificial Intelligence Applications in Information Technology," "Computers in Publishing," and "Computer Assisted Legal Research." Volume 15 (1980) carries a key-word-in-context (KWIC) index to the first fifteen volumes of the annual review.

ONLINE DATA BASES

Data bases that focus on library and information science or provide unique access to materials in the field are arranged alphabetically by title without regard to geographic coverage, place of publication, or location of data base.

115 ERIC (Educational Resources Information Center). Washington, DC: National Inst. of Education; Bethesda, MD.: ERIC Processing and Reference Facility, 1966– . Updated monthly. Available through Lockheed's DIALOG, System Development Corporation's ORBIT, and Bibliographic Retrieval Service's BRS.

The library and information science component of this data base is derived from items indexed by the ERIC-IR Clearinghouse, located at Syracuse University. It includes citations from *Resources in education* (entry **55**) as well as library and information science journal articles indexed in *Current index to journals in education* (entry **46**). Several hundred of these entries are added each year; total entries in the data base approaches 450,000. References include journal articles, technical reports submitted by U.S. government contractors, conference proceedings, government publications, and other miscellaneous information formats. Although entries on library and information science topics constitute a limited percentage of the total number of entries in this data base, the total number of entries on these topics is substantial enough to qualify it as one of the largest online files of material in this field.

116 Indeks IOD. Oslo: Norsk Senter for Informatikk.
This data base is now named *Nordisk BDI-indeks.* For further information see entry **119**.

117 INFODATA. Frankfurt/Main: Informationzentrum, Gesellschaft für Information und Dokumentation, 1977– . Updated quarterly. Available through EURONET and DATEX-P.
This data base includes citations and abstracts to serials, monographs, technical reports, and government publications on various facets of librarianship, documentation, and information science. Emphasis is on topics concerned with information retrieval systems. Entries are in the original language (sixty percent are in English); abstracts are in English, French and German. At present, the data base contains more than 16,500 bibliographic records, and approximately 3,000 new entries are added each year.

118 LISA (Library and information science abstracts). London: Learned Information, 1969– . Updated 6 times per year. Available through Lockheed's DIALOG and System Development Corporation's ORBIT.
This is the online version of *Library and information science abstracts* (entry **38**). The data base has the same scope as the paper copy abstracting service. More than 48,000 entries are available online, and approximately 6,000 new entries are added each year. Coverage extends to all facets of librarianship and information science as well as to other aspects of the information industry. Related areas, including archives, publishing, the book trade, and education, are also included, to a lesser degree. The items entered into the data base have been acquired as part of the library science collection of the British Library or by the library of Aslib. Coverage is international and more than 300 journals are currently examined for inclusion. Conference papers, government documents, monographs, and theses or dissertations are also included. Entries are arranged by the Classification Research Group scheme and appear in the original language, with an English translation. A user handbook, *LISA online user manual* (entry **1088**), is available; it describes online use and provides a list of primary subject headings used.

119 Nordisk BDI-indeks. Oslo: Norsk Senter for Informatikk, 1979– . Updated 2 times per year. Available through SCANNET.
Scandanavian-language literature in library and information science is indexed here. More than half of the entries are from the journal literature, but government publications, proceedings, conference papers, and report literature are also cited. Approximately twenty

percent of the items listed are in English. The data base currently has about 5,500 entries, and 1,500 new entries are added per year. This data base was formerly known as *Indeks IOD* (entry **116**).

120 NTIS (National Technical Information Service). Springfield, VA: NTIS, 1964– .
  Updated 26 times per year. Available through Lockheed's DIALOG and System
  Development Corporation's ORBIT.
The contents of this online version of *Government reports, announcements and index* consists of technical reports and other documents submitted to the National Technical Information Service for distribution by approximately 250 U.S. government agencies, and other publications originating with state or local governments or private organizations. At present the total number of items in the data base exceeds 860,000. Library and information science titles are only a small percentage of this total, but their number is large enough to make this one of the major files of these materials. Key items dealing with library and information science are identified in the weekly publication *Library and information sciences: weekly government abstracts* (entry **51**).

DISSERTATIONS AND THESES

Sources that provide a list of American and Canadian theses and doctoral dissertations in library and information science, and closely related disciplines, are arranged alphabetically by title without regard to geographic coverage or place of publication.

121 Dissertations in library science, 1951–1966. Ann Arbor, MI: University Microfilms, n.d.
This work is superseded by *Doctoral dissertations in library science: titles accepted by accredited library schools, 1930–1972, Doctoral dissertations in library science: titles accepted by accredited library schools, 1930–1975*, and *Library science: a dissertation bibliography*. For further information see entry **125**.

**122 Doctoral dissertations in library science: titles accepted by accredited library
  schools, 1930–1975.** By Charles H. Davis. Ann Arbor, MI: University Microfilms,
  1976. 27p.
This work is superseded by *Library science: a dissertation bibliography*. For further information see entry **125**.

**123 Doctoral dissertations in library science: titles accepted by accredited library
  schools, 1930–1972.** By David H. Eyman. Ann Arbor, MI: University Microfilms,
  1973. 17p.
This work is superseded by *Doctoral dissertations in library science: titles accepted by accredited library schools, 1930–1975* and *Library science: a dissertation bibliography*. For further information see entry **125**.

124 **FLA theses: abstracts of all theses accepted for the fellowship of the Library Association from 1964.** By L. J. Taylor. London: Reference Division, British Library, 1979. 90p. LC 80–507982. ISBN 0–904654–20–6.

In the United Kingdom, from 1964, the thesis has been required to gain fellowship into the Library Association. This work abstracts the 274 theses accepted by the Library Association from 1964 to October 1978. Not all of the theses deal with librarianship or library topics. The theses are arranged under broad headings, such as "Information Retrieval," "Library History," and "User and Reading Studies." Subject and author indexes provide further access to the numbered abstracts.

125 **Library science: a dissertation bibliography.** By Charles H. Davis. Ann Arbor, MI: University Microfilms, 1980. 30p.

This is the fourth in a series of bibliographies produced by University Microfilms. Dissertations cited were completed at the twenty-six universities in the United States and Canada that participate in the listing of new dissertation topics accepted in the "Research Record" column of the *Journal of education for librarianship*. A total of 915 titles are listed here. Main entry citations, arranged alphabetically by author, include author, title, field in which the degree was conferred, degree (i.e., Ph.D., D.L.S., etc.), university granting the degree, and number of pages. Also cited is the abstract of the dissertation in *Dissertation abstracts international* between June 1915 and June 1980. Completing the entry is a publication number to be used when ordering the dissertation from University Microfilms International. Access to the main entry is augmented by a subject index and an index, by institution, of degrees and recipients. This work supersedes three earlier bibliographies: *Doctoral dissertations in library science: titles accepted by accredited library schools, 1930–1975* (entry **122**), *Doctoral dissertations in library science: titles accepted by accredited library schools, 1930–1972* (entry **123**), and *Dissertations in library science, 1951–1966* (entry **121**). Each of the titles is cumulative, but arrangement and entry information differs for the first two published.

126 **Library science dissertations, 1973–1981: an annotated bibliography.** By Gail A. Schlachter and Dennis Thomison. Littleton, CO: Libraries Unlimited, 1983. 414p. LC 82-17172. ISBN 0–87287–299–8.

This work and the compilers' earlier bibliography (covering 1925–1972) constitute the most extensive list of dissertations in this field. The main body of the 1983 work is a chronologically arranged, annotated bibliography of more than 1,000 dissertations from librarianship, information science, and closely related fields, such as education and communication (where librarianship is the topic of the dissertation). The annotations, as far as possible, identify the purpose, procedure, and findings of each dissertation in a parallel fashion. For those dissertations available from University Microfilms, the order number from *Dissertation abstracts international* is included. Access to the main entries is facilitated by thorough author and subject indexes, and by the work's chronological arrangement. The bibliography is augmented by a special section titled "A Statistical Profile of Library Science Dissertations," which provides analyses of such matters as the completion date, the sponsoring school, the degree received, the methodology employed, and the sex of the author. For descriptions of dissertations completed before 1973, see *Library science dissertations, 1925–1972* (entry **127**).

127 Library science dissertations, 1925–1972: an annotated bibliography. By Gail A. Schlachter and Dennis Thomison. Littleton, CO: Libraries Unlimited, 1974. 293p. LC 73–90497. ISBN 0–87287–074–X.
This work is continued by *Library science dissertations, 1973–1981: an annotated bibliography.* For further information see entry **126**.

128 Library science dissertations: 1925–1960: an annotated bibliography of doctoral studies. By Nathan M. Cohen, Barbara Dennison and Jessie C. Boehlert. Washington, DC: Office of Education, U.S. Dept. of Health, Education and Welfare, 1963. New York: Gordon Pr. Reprint, 1980. 120p. (The library science series) LC 72–8773. ISBN 0–8490–3167–2.
The earliest annotated bibliography of dissertations in librarianship, this work was an outgrowth of a project of the 1959 Research Committee of AALS. Dissertations are arranged chronologically under eight broad topics, such as resources, reader services, and methods of research and evaluation. A total of 224 dissertations are identified. Each entry includes the author's name, the title, the degree title, and the date of the dissertation, followed by the annotation. The scope includes all library science dissertations completed in schools accredited by the American Library Association and some additional dissertations completed in other university departments, particularly history and education. Access is provided by author and subject indexes. Six pages of analysis follow the final bibliographic entry. Although this listing essentially has been superseded by Schlachter and Thomison (entry **126**), it retains value because the abstracts in the two works sometimes emphasize different aspects of the dissertations.

129 Master's theses in library science, 1970–1974. By Shirley Magnotti. Troy, NY: Whitson, 1976. 198p. LC 75–8232. ISBN 0–87875–100–9.
This work supplements and continues *Master's theses in library science, 1960–1969.* For further information see entry **130**.

130 Master's theses in library science, 1960–1969. By Shirley Magnotti. Troy, NY: Whitson, 1975. 366p. LC 75–8232. ISBN 0–87875–074–6.
This is the most complete list of theses in library and information science currently available. The compiler has identified and listed approximately 2,500 titles, produced during the 1960's. The list is arranged by author and includes a subject index. Theses cited are those reported from thirty-one library schools accredited by the American Library Association. Those schools represented are identified in an appendix to the work. A 1976 supplement, *Master's theses in library science, 1970–1974* (entry **129**), adds another 700 theses, most completed during the early 1970's and some completed earlier, but received too late for inclusion in the main volume.

2.

Terminology

INTRODUCTION

As in other professions and subject disciplines, professionals in the library and information fields require sources that clarify the meaning and use of terminology and nomenclature. Described in this chapter are over eighty vocabularies and glossaries; lists of acronyms, abbreviations, and initialisms; thesauri; and foreign-language handbooks. Emphasis is on recently issued sources (since the mid–1960s) of use to English-language readers. Several classics and foreign-language dictionaries are also described if they serve as unique or landmark works.

Vocabularies and Glossaries: In its most elemental form, a vocabulary is simply a list of words and/or word phrases. In practice, most monolingual vocabularies in the library and information field also include definitions and are therefore glossaries, i.e., sources providing a specialized vocabulary accompanied by brief definitions related to the field. Library-related vocabularies and glossaries exist in monolingual, bilingual, and multilingual form and are the most common of all the specialized terminology sources issued in the field. Bilingual vocabularies usually contain two separate lists of equivalent terms, with the definition often provided in both languages. Multilingual sources frequently give the definition in the base language only, followed by a list of equivalent terms. The "main entry" is generally accessed by alphabetical lists of terms for each of the other languages. While the most common type of organizational structure for vocabularies and glossaries is alphabetical (either word-by-word or letter-by-letter), several library-related sources employ a classified structure, the most common of which is the Universal Decimal Classification system (UDC). In classified sources, terms are grouped under the appropriate UDC number and listed alphabetically within each grouping. Typically, the technical glossaries covering library and information services do not include features found in multipurpose dictionaries or specialized word books—etymology, pronunciation, or syllabication. Therefore, while glossaries do extend the vocabulary of multipurpose dictionaries into the specialized literature of the field, they do so with limited results.

This chapter focuses on sixty-five library-related vocabularies and glossaries, twenty-six of which are multilingual (providing access in three or more languages), twenty-three are bilingual, and sixteen are monolingual. Except for five sources, all of the dictionaries described here provide English-language access.

Acronyms, Initialisms and Abbreviations: The widespread use of acronyms, initialisms, and abbreviations for associations, companies, government agencies, equipment, and methods in the library field has created a need for sources that identify these terms. Many of the abbreviations used are international in application, but most reflect usage within a specific country. A substantial number of acronyms and initialisms apply to more than one entity, some to as many as six or seven. Because names of organizations, associations, and other entities constantly change, so do their acronyms and initialisms. Consequently, both retrospective and current dictionaries defining these abbreviations are important.

A number of general glossaries also list acronyms, abbreviations, and initialisms, but none is as comprehensive as the major sources covering only these shortened designations. This chapter includes seven publications that specialize in acronyms, initialisms, and/or abbreviations in librarianship and related areas. Although published in six different countries, each title is multinational in scope, and only one does not feature English-language terms.

Thesauri: By showing the relationships between and among terms within a field, controlled vocabulary sources serve two major purposes: they structure the terminology for an indexing system, and they aid in the retrieval of indexed literature. Access to published thesauri or subject heading lists is important for individuals involved in subject searches. This chapter describes six thesauri of subject descriptors covering the library and information fields in general. Controlled vocabulary lists restricted to specific subjects have been omitted. The majority of titles were developed for use in a manual or automated document retrieval system. All are English-language based and recently produced.

Foreign-Language Handbooks: Librarians, in their capacity as catalogers, bibliographers, and acquisitions or reference librarians, frequently must use languages other than English, but often they lack a working knowledge of these languages. To assist them, handbooks have been prepared to cover terms and concepts related to bibliolinguistics—the vocabulary and linguistic information found in bibliographic citations of foreign languages. The five foreign-language handbooks described in this chapter are limited to one language, but one of the citations provides bibliographic information for thirty-seven languages. These cited handbooks emphasize languages most likely to be encountered by librarians in their jobs—Russian and the European languages.

MULTILINGUAL VOCABULARIES AND GLOSSARIES

Vocabularies and glossaries providing access in three or more languages are arranged alphabetically by title under the language of the main entry. Works with main entries in English are listed first. Foreign language sections follow in alphabetical order by the English name of the language.

English Language

131 Bibliotheeksterminologie: engels, frans, duits, nederlands. By Unesco. The Hague: Centraal Vereniging voor Openbare Bibliotheken, 1967. 294p. LC 68–96305.
A classified list of approximately 2,800 library terms, this follows the same basic pattern as the 1962 edition of *Vocabularium bibliothecarii* (entry **143**). The main entry is in English, followed by a brief definition in English and equivalent terms in French, German, and Dutch. Access to main entries from the other languages is through separate indexes.

132 Complete dictionary of library terms: technical terms used in libraries, bibliographies and by printing and binding trades in english, german, french, chinese and japanese languages. Ed. by Fujio Mamiya. Rev. ed. Tokyo: Japan Library Bureau, 1951. 615p.
In this revised and enlarged edition, library terms from each of the five languages are listed alphabetically in a single alphabet followed by equivalent terms in English and Japanese, with an occasional listing of terms in other languages. Terms from Japanese and Chinese are transliterated into the Roman alphabet. No definitions are provided.

133 Dictionary of library science, information, and documentation: in six languages: english/american, french, spanish, italian, dutch, and german. Comp. by W. E. Clason. Arabic supplement by Shawky Salem. Amsterdam: Elsevier Scientific Publishing, 1976. 708p. LC 76–40344. ISBN 0–444–41475–5.
This glossary includes 5,439 terms, with equivalents for six European languages plus a supplement listing Arabic terms. Emphasis is on technical terms in library and information science; coverage of such related areas as publishing and bibliography is limited. Arrangement is by numbered, alphabetical English/American terms. Each entry includes the English term, a brief definition in English, the five equivalent terms, and the entry number. Cross-references guide the reader to variant English and American spellings and alternate terms. Access to the main entry from the other languages is provided by alphabetical lists of terms for each language.

134 Dort dilde kütüphaneclik terimleri sozlugu. Vocabularium bibliothecarii. By A. Thompson. Turkish terms by Leman Senalp. Ankara: Türk Tarih Kurumu Basımevi, 1959. 379p. LC 60–33751.
This glossary of library terms is based on *Vocabularium bibliothecarii* (entry **143**), with the addition of Turkish equivalents to the English, French, German, Spanish, and Russian terms.

135 **English-chinese-japanese lexicon of bibliographical, cataloguing and library terms.** By Harold A. Mattice. New York: New York Public Library, 1944. 38p.

More than 600 English terms are listed alphabetically, with parallel columns showing the Chinese and Japanese symbols for each term. In some cases symbols appear for only one language because the term has no application in the other. No access from Chinese or Japanese is provided.

136 **Glossary of documentation terms/Glossaire de termes relatifs à la documentation/Glossar der dokumentationbegriften.** London: British Standards Inst., 1976. 81p.

The more than 1,300 terms in documentation and librarianship are arranged alphabetically with brief definitions. Equivalent terms are in English, French, and German. In a separate section, terms are grouped by broad subjects to show their relationship to one another.

137 **A Könyvtáros hatnyelvu szótára: angol, francia, német, spanyol, orosz, magyar.** By Anthony Thompson. Hungarian terms by Zoltan Pipics. Budapest: Akad. Kiadó, 1972. 676p.

This version of *Vocabularium bibliothecarii* is based on the 1962 edition and follows the same classified arrangement. However, it also includes equivalent terms in Hungarian as well as English, French, German, Spanish, and Russian. The Hungarian terms are shown in the right-hand column of a divided page. For further information see entry **143**.

138 **The librarian's practical dictionary in 22 languages/Dictionarium bibliothecarii practicum: ad usum internationalem in XXII linguis/Worterbuch des bibliotekars: in 22 sprachen.** Ed. by Zoltan Pipics. 7th ed. Munich: Verlag Dokumentation, 1977. 385p. LC 78–378421. ISBN 3–7940–4110–0.

Equivalent terms in twenty-two languages are provided for 377 commonly used library terms. The first section lists terms in tabular form, arranged by the English term. The second section consists of word lists for each language, which serve as indexes to the first section. The work was designed especially for catalogers and others needing assistance with foreign-language documentation. Four languages, Greek, Bulgarian, Russian, and Serbian, appear in both the Cyrillic and Romanized forms. Synonyms are displayed with cross-references. The twenty-two languages are English, French, German, Russian, Spanish, Bulgarian, Croatian, Czech, Danish, Dutch, Finnish, Greek, Hungarian, Italian, Latin, Norwegian, Polish, Portugese, Romanian, Serbian, Slovak, and Swedish.

139 **Technical terms used in bibliographies and by the book and printing trades.** By Axel Moth. Boston: Longwood Press Reprint, 1977. 263p. LC 77–6172. ISBN 0–89341–153–1.

This work provides a list of terms in English with equivalents in Danish, Dutch, French, German, Italian, Latin, Spanish, and Swedish. Originally published in 1917, this work is intended as a supplement to Walter's *Abbreviations and technical terms* (entry **196**). It tends to emphasize terms related to the book trade.

140 **Terminology of documentation/Terminologie de la documentation/Terminologie der dokumentation/Terminologija v oblasti documentacii/Terminologiá de la**

documentación. By Gernot Wersig and Ulrich Neveling. Paris: Unesco, 1976. 274p. LC 76–355220. ISBN 92–3–001232–7.

Commissioned by Unesco and prepared by the German Society for Documentation, this work is a classified multilingual vocabulary and glossary. Various aspects of documentation and information science, such as linguistic problems, communication theory, documentary languages, and systems analysis and design, are covered. The arrangement is by broad classes, designated by UDC numbers, and then alphabetically within classes. English is the language of the 1,200 entry words and definitions. Each entry includes the English term, a brief definition, and equivalent terms in French, German, Russian, and Spanish, in that order. Cross-references create a syndetic structure through the use of these terms and symbols: broader term (BT), narrower term (NT), and related term (RT). Cross-references are to terms found in the definitions and to terms related to the definitions. Also provided are an alphabetical index for each language and an index of UDC numbers.

141 Vocabularium bibliothecarii. By Anthony Thompson. Slovak terms by Mikulas Micatek. Martin, Czechoslovakia: Matica Slovenska, 1970. 686p.

An edition of *Vocabularium bibliothecarii*, based on the 1962 edition, with terms in English, French, German, Spanish, Russian, and with terms in Slovak added. For further information see entry **143**.

142 Vocabularium bibliothecarii: english/anglais: french/français: german/alemand. Begun by Henri Lemaitre. Rev. and enl. by Anthony Thompson. Paris: Unesco, 1953. 296p. (Unesco bibliographical handbooks) LC 54–310.

This work is superseded by the second edition, *Vocabularium bibliothecarii: english, french, german, spanish, russian*. For further information see entry **143**.

143 Vocabularium bibliothecarii: english, french, german, spanish, russian. By Anthony Thompson. Russian terms by E. I. Shamurin; Spanish terms by Domingo Buonocore. 2d ed. Paris: Unesco, 1962. 627p.

Initiated as a Unesco project to foster uniform use of library terminology, this is a landmark work that has served as a model for several other multilingual and bilingual vocabularies and glossaries. The 2,800 terms were selected to reflect balanced coverage of the subdivisions of the field. Arrangement is by UDC numbers. English is the language of the main entry, and equivalent terms in the five other languages follow. Access to the main entries is through separate indexes for each other language. Only words having two or more meanings and those which have no equivalent in one or more of the languages are defined. The first edition was published in 1953 (entry **142**), followed by a supplement in 1958.

144 Vocabularium bibliothecarii: english, french, german, spanish, russian, with arabic translation Ed. by M. A. Hussein, et al. Cairo: National Commission for Unesco, 1965. 692p.

This is a photo offset reproduction of the 1962 edition by Anthony Thompson (entry **143**), which includes Arabic translation of the terms. The list is arranged alphabetically by the English term. Arabic equivalents are provided in a separate column. Separate indexes for each language provide access to the main entries.

145 Vocabularium bibliothecarii nordicum: engelsk, dansk, norsk, svensk, finsk. Ed.
by Torben Nielsen. Copenhagen: Bibliotekscentralen, 1968. 278p. LC 77–422414.
Based on the 1962 edition of *Vocabularium bibliothecarii* by Anthony Thompson (entry
143), this work, published by the Nordic Union of Research Librarians, identifies approximately 2,400 terms. The vocabulary is listed alphabetically by the English term, and
equivalent terms for the other languages follow. Definitions are not provided. Arrangement
of the main entries is by UDC number. Access to the main entry from other languages is
provided by separate alphabetical lists for each language.

Foreign Languages

CZECH

**146 Slovnik knihovnickych terminu v šesti jazycich: česky, ruský, polský, nemecký,
anglický, francouzský.** By Miroslav Nadvornik. Prague: Statni Pedagogicke
Nakladatelstvi, 1958. 632p. LC 59–30054.
This work consists of five separate bilingual lists of library terms: Russian-Czech; Polish-
Czech; German-Czech; English-Czech; and French-Czech. Each list consists of approximately 3,000 terms. These are augmented by a Czech-Russian-Polish-German-English-
French list of terms that covers nearly 300 pages.

147 Terminologický slovnik: informacni prameny. By Eva Hlavata, et al. Prague:
UVTEI, 1979. 331p. LC 80–476857.
Each of the 634 Czech terms in informatics and information science is accompanied by a
brief definition and equivalent terms in Russian, English, German, and French. The
arrangement is alphabetical, with access from an alphabetical list of terms for each
language.

ESTONIAN

148 Information science and processing vocabulary: estonian, english, german, russian/Eesti, inglise, saksa, vene infosonastik. By Ustus Agur, et al. Tallinn: Valgus,
1977. 278p. LC 78–350598.
This dictionary of Estonian terms in information science and librarianship provides equivalent terms in English, German, and Russian. Separate indexes offer access to the Estonian
entries from each of the other languages.

GERMAN

149 Terminologie der information und dokumentation. Ed. by Ulrich Neveling and
Gernot Wersig for the Deutsche Gesellschaft für Dokumentation. Munich: Verlag
Dokumentation, 1975. 307p. LC 76–455533. ISBN 3–7940–3625–5.
Definitions are given here for approximately 1,000 terms in information science and
documentation, with emphasis on analysis and indexing, storage and retrieval, evaluation,
document description, and documentary languages. Each main entry is in German and
includes a brief definition, followed by equivalent terms in English and French as well as
synonyms and cross-references to related terms. Main entries are arranged in classified

order using a conceptual index unique to this work. There is an alphabetical permuted term index for each of the three languages. The glossary was compiled by the Komitee Terminologie und Sprachfragen (KTS) der Deutschen Gesellschaft für Dokumentation (DGD).

HEBREW

150 Dictionary of library terms. Jerusalem: Acad. of the Hebrew Language, 1976. 174p.
This list of 1,116 library terms in non-Romanized Hebrew, with English, French, and German equivalents, is divided into twenty-one broad topic categories. Separate English, French, and German indexes provide access to the main entries. Definitions are not given for commonly used terms in librarianship and information science. The dictionary was prepared by the Academy of the Hebrew Language, which is responsible for standardizing the terminology of modern Hebrew for specialized and technical fields.

ITALIAN

151 Dizionàrio tècnico de biblioteconomía italiano, spagnolo, inglese. By Beatriz Massa de Gil. Mexico City: Editorial Trillas, 1971. 242p. LC 75–537451.
Library terms are listed in Italian with equivalent terms in Spanish and English. Brief definitions are provided. Access to the main entries is by means of alphabetical lists of Spanish and English terms.

JAPANESE

152 Dictionary of librarianship and bibliographical terms. By Chozaburo Uemura. Tokyo: Yurindo, 1967. 726p. LC 70–803112.
More than 3,800 terms from librarianship and bibliography are listed in Japanese (represented by Chinese characters) and followed by English, French, German, and Russian equivalents. Definitions are in Japanese.

POLISH

153 Podreczny slownik bibliotekarza. By Helena Wieckowska and Hanna Pliszczynska. Warsaw: Państwowe Wydawn. Naukowe, 1955. 309p. LC 55–39069.
Approximately 3,000 Polish library terms are listed and defined (in Polish). Each main entry also includes equivalent terms for English, French, German, and Russian. Access to the main entries from each of the other languages is by means of separate glossaries listing Polish equivalents.

154 Slownik terminologiczny informacji naukowej. Comp. by Krystyna Tittenbrun, et al. Warsaw: Inst. Informacji Naukowej, Technicznej i Ekonomicznej, 1979. 237p. LC 79–385566.
In addition to terms in information science, this dictionary covers librarianship, bibliography, linguistics, computer science, and related fields. There are 1,660 main entries plus about 540 cross-references. Main entries and brief definitions are in Polish. Equivalent terms in English, French, German, and Russian follow. Arrangement is alphabetical by Polish spelling. Separate indexes provide access to the main entries from each of the other

languages. One special feature is a lengthy bibliography of sources from the several languages used to compile the vocabulary.

RUSSIAN

155   Dictionary of informatics terms/Terminologicheskiĭ slovar, po informatike.
Moscow: Mezhdunarodnyi Tsentr Nauchnoĭ i Tekhnicheskoĭ Informatsii, 1975. 752p.
This is a multilingual dictionary of 2,235 informatics and information science terms, with main entries and definitions in Russian. Equivalent terms are provided for Bulgarian, Hungarian, Spanish, Macedonian, German, Polish, Romanian, Serbo-Croatian, Slovak, Slovenian, Czech, English, and French. Definitions are brief with equivalent terms found in the right hand column, labeled by language. Arrangement is alphabetical by Russian term. Each term is assigned a number that signifies its subject relationship to other terms. There is an index to the main entry for each language named above. The coverage includes terms from the fields of librarianship, documentation, and information science. The introduction is published in each of the languages represented in the dictionary. In addition, there is an international bibliography (205 entries) of glossaries of library and information terms.

SWEDISH

156   Bibliotekstermer: sẅenska, engelska, frankska, tyska. 2d ed. Lund: Utokade
Uppl, 1965. 70p. LC 65–68875.
Library and bibliographical terms in Swedish are listed with equivalents in English, French, and German. Arrangement is by broad topicu the 409 terms are presented in four parallel columns. Access is through separate indexes for each language.

BILINGUAL VOCABULARIES AND GLOSSARIES

The bilingual vocabularies and glossaries cited in this section are arranged alphabetically by title under the non-English language without regard to which language appears first in the publication.

Afrikaans

**157   Biblioteekkundige vakterme: proewe van'n vertalende woordelys, engels-
afrikaans.** Comp. by P. C. Coetzee. Pretoria: Staatsbiblioteek, 1961. 2v. LC
77–206978.
This includes approximately 3,500 library terms in English followed by the Afrikaans equivalent. Volume 1 covers letters A-L and volume 2 covers M-Z. This work served as a basis for the *Dictionary of library terms/Biblioteekwoordboek*. For further information see entry **158**.

158 Dictionary of library terms/Biblioteekwoordboek. Comp. by the Vaktalburo of the South African Academy of Science and Art. Johannesburg: Voortrekkerpers, 1971. 149p. LC 72–438710.

Definitions are not included in this bilingual technical vocabulary. Terms are arranged in two separate sections: Afrikaans-English and English-Afrikaans. The vocabulary was developed by a committee of the South African Academy of Science and Art, in cooperation with the South African Library Association. Insofar as possible, authentic Afrikaans terms were used. In some cases, however, equivalent terms did not exist in Afrikaans, and it was necessary to invent equivalents based on translation of English terms. In other cases, because of the inconsistent use of terms in English, the Afrikaans version was rendered as a literal translation of the English.

Arabic

159 Dictionary of library terms: english-arabic. By Mohamed Amin El-Benhawy. Cairo: Dar A-Fikr Al-Arabi, 1970. 129p. LC 72–961866.

Approximately 2,300 English terms in librarianship and the book trade are listed here, followed by the Arabic equivalent, written in Arabic script. Arabic terms are not transliterated. The arrangement is alphabetical by English words. The compiler's name is shown above as it appears on the title page. However, the Library of Congress has transliterated the author's name as al-Banhawi, Muhammad Amin, and it is entered in the *National union catalog* in that form.

Chinese

160 Glossary of library terms. By Cheng Wang. Taichung, Taiwan: Wen Chung, 1969. 128p. LC 73–839473.

This is a list of roughly 1,400 Chinese terms in librarianship, with English equivalents. Entries are in Chinese characters and are numbered. An alphabetical list of English terms provides access to the entries.

French

161 Dictionnaire d'informatique français/angalis. By Michel Ginguay. Paris: Masson, 1981. 188p. ISBN 2–225–69333–1.

More than 8,000 information-related terms are listed alphabetically in this French-English dictionary. The focus is on informatics, documentation, information science, and related disciplines. Definitions vary in length and some are quite extensive. Also included are lists of English and French abbreviations and a list of symbols used in such areas as programming.

162 Vocabulaire technique de la bibliothéconomie et de la bibliographie: suivi d'un lexique anglais-français. By Paulle Rolland-Thomas, et al. Montreal: Assn. Canadienne de Bibliothécaires de langue Française, 1969. 187p. LC 72–458879.

Approximately 1,600 French library terms are defined (in French). An English-language index provides access to the main entries. Multiple definitions are included for some terms.

German

163 Library terms: englisch-deutsch und deutsch-englisch. By Otti Gross. Hamburg: Eberhard Stichnote, 1952. 163p.

The approximately 3,000 equivalent terms are arranged into alphabetical lists in each language. Also included are lists of English and German abbreviations and symbols commonly used in librarianship.

Greek

164 Vivliothekonomikon lexicon. By Georgios M. Kakoures. Athens: Kollegion Athanon, 1974. 89p. LC 75–566829.

Library terms in Greek are listed with English-language equivalents. Access to the main entries is provided by an index in English.

Indonesian

165 Istilah perpustakaan & i. e. dan dokumentasi: inggeris-indonesia. Djakarta: Pusat Dokumentasi Ilmiah Nasional, 1970. 39p. LC 77–941426.

This is a list of Indonesian library terms with English equivalents. Access to the terms is by means of an English-language index.

Italian

166 Nomenclatura bibliografica e biblioteconomica: inglese-italiano, italiano-inglese. By Battistina Gambigliani-Zoccoli. Rome: Edizioni Ricerche, 1964. 143p. LC 72–204765.

This bilingual vocabulary has two separate lists of equivalent terms: English-Italian and Italian-English.

Japanese

167 Japanese dictionary of terms. Comp. by Nihon Keiei Kyokai and Jōhō Kanri Kenkyu Iinkai. Tokyo: Nihon Keiei Shuppankai, 1974. 583p. LC 74–804165.

This dictionary of library and information science terms is characterized by definitions of almost encyclopedic length. Some are accompanied by illustrations or textual excerpts. The approximately 700 terms and the definitions are in Japanese printed in Chinese characters. Each entry also includes an English equivalent; access is available through an alphabetical English index of terms.

168 Japanese scientific terms: library science/Gakujutsu yogoshu toshokangakuhen. Comp. by Ministry of Education, Japan. Tokyo: Dai-nippon Tosho, 1958. 307p. LC J 60–77.

This glossary has two lists of approximately 5,000 equivalent terms. The first is transliterated Japanese terms, arranged alphabetically. Two parallel columns follow: one lists Japanese terms represented by Chinese characters, and the other gives English equivalents. The second list is English terms, again with two parallel columns: Japanese terms in Chinese characters and transliterated Japanese equivalents. This work is entered in the *National union catalog* with the main entry "Japan-Mombusho."

Korean

169 Dictionary of library terms: with explanations. Ed. by the Commission for Technology. Seoul: Korean Library Assn., 1962. 282p.
This work consists of two lists of approximately 2,300 terms: Korean-English and English-Korean. Definitions are not provided. Because of the date of publication, current information science terminology will not be found here.

Malay

170 Istilah perpustakaan: inggeris-malaysia-inggeris. Kuala Lumpur: Dewan Bahasa dan Pustaka, Kementerian Pelajaran Malaysia, 1978. 421p. LC 79–102563.
Terms are arranged into two separate, alphabetical lists: English-Malay and Malay-English. No definitions are included for the approximately 4,000 librarianship and information science terms.

Russian

171 English-russian bookman's glossary/Anglo-russkii slovar' knigovedcheskikh terminov. By T. P. Elizarenkova. Moscow: Sovetskaia Rossiia, 1962. 510p. LC 63–36755.
This work is a list of English terms with Russian equivalents and Russian definitions in cyrillic. The terms are oriented toward various aspects of the book world, including librarianship, but also covering bookbinding, literature, and a wide range of other topics. A related work, *Russian-english bookman's dictionary/Russko-angliiskii slovar' knigovedcheskikh terminov* (entry **174**), lists Russian terms alphabetically in cyrillic with English equivalents, providing the same wide range of subject terminology. Over 9,300 terms are listed in the second work. Some entries have definitions, but this is not consistent.

172 English-russian dictionary of library and bibliographical terms/Anglo-russkii biblio-techno-bibliograficheskii slovar'. Comp. by Mikhail Khachaturovich Saringulian. Ed. by P. H. Kananov and V. V. Popov. Moscow: All-Union Book Chamber, 1958. 286p. LC 59–36330.
This is a list of approximately 15,000 English library terms followed by Russian equivalents and definitions in Cyrillic. The vocabulary ranges well beyond technical terms and covers some words related to publishing and book production. Several illustrations supplement the text. Because this work was published in 1958, it does not include the current terminology in informatics, information science, and documentation.

173 Essential problems in terminology for informatics and documentation: some methodological recommendations on dictionary development: new terms in informatics. By the Committee on Terminology of Information and Documentation, FID. Moscow: All-Union Inst. of Scientific and Technical Information, 1980. 111p. LC 81–163301. ISSN 0203–6444.

Approximately 1,000 English terms in informatics, information science, and documentation are listed with Russian equivalents. Each term is concisely defined in English. Entries
are numbered, and access to the main entries is available through a Russian list of terms.
This list represents current terminological usage in both languages.

**174   Russian-english bookman's dictionary/Russko-angliiskii slovar' knigoved-
cheskikh terminov.** Moscow: Sovetskaia Entsiklopediia, 1969. 264p. LC
72–447223.

This work is the companion to *English-russian bookman's glossary/Anglo-russkii slovar'
knigovedcheskikh terminov.* For further information see entry **171**.

175   Slovar' terminov po informatike na russkom i angliiskom iazykakh. By G. S.
Zhdanova and Aleksandr Ivanovich Mikhailov. Moscow: Vsesoiuznyi Inst. Nauchnoi
i Tekhnicheskoi Informatsii, 1971. 359p. This glossary lists and defines Russian
information science and informatics terms in cyrillic, with equivalent terms in English. Index access to main entries is provided by a list of English terms.

Serbo-Croatian

**176   Rječnik bibliotekarskih stručnih izraza: vocabularium bibliothecarii: englesko-
hrvatskosrpski: english-croatian/serbian.** By Anthony Thompson. Serbo-Croatian
terms by Dana Cucković and Sime Jurić. Zagreb: Skolshka Knjiga, 1965. 185p. LC
66–91142.

Following the same arrangement as the multilingual *Vocabularium bibliothecarii* (entry
143), this bilingual vocabulary is classified, with terms assigned Universal Decimal Classification numbers. The terms are arranged in two parallel columns: the English vocabulary is
on the left and the Serbo-Croatian on the right. Additionally, an alphabetical index for each
language refers the user to the appropriate UDC number. Terms are not defined.

Sinhalese

**177   Glossary of technical terms-documentation: english-sinhala/Pabhasika sabda
malava, pralekhana vidyava: ingrisi-simhala.** By Jayasiri Lankage. Kolamba: As.
Godage, 1979. 47p. LC 81–901610.

This work lists approximately 850 English terms in librarianship and documentation with
their Sinhalese equivalents. No definitions are included. Terms in Sinhalese terms are not
Romanized. Pages are mimeographed rather than printed, and the quality of the reproduction of Sinhalese characters is poor. Consequently, those unacquainted with Sinhalese
characters will find the work virtually illegible.

Slovak

**178   Anglicko-slovenský, Slovensko-anglický slovnik z knihovnictva a informacnej
vedy.** By Jozef Hajdusek. Enl. and rev. ed. Martin, Czechoslovakia: Matica Slovenska, 1981. 426p. LC 82–132804.

Equivalent terms are found in two lists: English-Slovak and Slovak-English. The 7,500
terms are drawn from information science and informatics as well as library science and

bibliography. However, definitions are not included. An additional feature is a list of English abbreviations.

Spanish

179 Technical dictionary of librarianship, english-spanish/Diccionario técnico de biblioteconomía, español-inglés. By Beatriz Massa de Gil, Ray Trautman and Peter Goy. 4th ed. Mexico City: Editorial Trillas, 1973. 387p.

More than 3,000 terms are listed in this bilingual glossary, which consists of two parts: Spanish-English and English-Spanish. In each, the terms are arranged in word-by-word alphabetical order. Each entry in both sections is defined briefly and followed by the equivalent term in the other language. Multiple definitions are listed in order of common use. However, only definitions pertaining to library science or related areas are included. Publishing, bookselling, illustration, and copyright are among the related fields from which terms or definitions are taken.

MONOLINGUAL VOCABULARIES AND GLOSSARIES

Monolingual vocabularies and glossaries for several languages are arranged alphabetically by title under the language in which they are published. Works in the English language are listed first. Foreign language sections follow in alphabetical order by the English name of the language.

English Language

180 A.L.A. glossary of library terms, with a selection of terms in related fields. By Elizabeth H. Thompson. Chicago: American Library Assn., 1943. 159p. LC 43–51260.

Although now out of date, for years this work, prepared under the direction of the Committee on Library Terminology of the American Library Association, was the standard glossary of American terminology and practice. The preface states that it "includes terms used in American libraries, except those purely, or largely, of local significance." Some terms from related fields are listed, but with few exceptions, foreign terms are excluded. More than 2,800 terms are defined. Numerous see references draw attention to synonyms. Special features in the appendices include a table of book sizes, a table of type sizes, and a select list of abbreviations. A new edition of this work, titled the *ALA glossary of library and information science* (entry **181**), was published by ALA in 1983.

181 The ALA glossary of library and information science. Ed. by Heartsill Young. Chicago: American Library Assn., 1983. 245p. LC 82–18512 ISBN 0–8389–0371–1.

Definitions are provided in this glossary for terms from library and information science, as well as from the related fields of printing and publishing, computer science, micrographics, and archives administration. This work updates and expands the 1943 *A.L.A. glossary of library terms, with a selection of terms in related fields* (entry **180**). Added terms reflect the growing assimilation of electronic data processing and information science vocabulary into the language of the library field. Numerous cross references enable the user to move to synonymous or related terms when necessary.

182   Bookman's glossary. Ed. by Jean Peters. 6th ed. New York: Bowker, to be published in 1983. LC 83–2775. ISBN 0–8352–0732–3.
First published in 1924 in an issue of *Publisher's weekly,* this work now has about 1,800 entries. It is a glossary of terms and persons involved with book production (including computerized typesetting), printing, and publishing. Contemporary and historical terms, as well as biographical entries, are provided concise and well-written definitions/explanations. Featured in this new edition are terms that deal with electronic publishing.

183   Compilation of terms in information sciences technology. By Florence Casey. Springfield, VA: NTIS, 1970. 240p. NTIS, PB 193 346. LC 77–612498.
Prepared through funding from the National Science Foundation (contract no. NSF C605), this glossary covers approximately 3,700 terms in librarianship, information science, documentation, and information technology. Although more than a decade old, this is one of the best English-language glossaries available for the specialized terminology of information science. The definitions are concise, well written, and informative.

184   Documentary lexicon for scientific information. By Natacha Gardin and Francis Levy. Marseilles: Groupe d'Etude sur l'Information Scientifique, 1969. 80p. NUC 74–43377.
Terms that apply to concepts and processes of information storage and retrieval are defined and classified in this work. It was created by the Groupe d'Etude sur l'Information Scientifique through a contract with the Délégation Général à la Recherche Scientifique et Technique (the French advisory board to the prime minister) and had as its purpose "to build up an inventory about research and development in the field of non-numerical data processing." The result is a lexicon of 6,000 information storage and retrieval terms organized according to major topics. Terms and definitions are in English. Terms are drawn not only from information storage and retrieval but also from linguistics, mechanical translation, and equipment used in information processing.

185   Glaister's glossary of the book. By Geoffrey Glaister. 2d rev. ed. Berkeley: Univ. of California Pr., 1979. 551p. LC 76–47975. ISBN 0–520–03364–7.
Substantially revised and rewritten from the earlier edition (published in 1960), this work defines approximately 4,000 terms from the fields of papermaking, printing, bookbinding, and publishing. Many of the entries are biographical, and some are illustrated. Although a number of definitions are of encyclopedic length, most are brief. Terms are arranged alphabetically. Emphasis tends to be on British terms and usage. Appendices provide type specimens, Latin place names for early imprints, and proof correction symbols.

186   Glossary of documentation terms. By H. A. Stolk. Washington, DC: Science Assoc., 1969. 40p. LC 78–473362.
This work was prepared under the auspices of the Technical Information Panel of AGARD,

an agency of NATO. Approximately 1,800 terms in documentation and information science are briefly defined. Indexing, abstracting, bibliographic description, and machine information retrieval are emphasized; terms associated with the operation of libraries or information centers are excluded.

187 Glossary of library science technical terms. By P. N. Gour. Patna, Bihar, India: Library Science Publications, 1980. 264p. LC 81–908978.
Designed as a resource for library science students in India, this glossary covers approximately 3,000 terms in the various areas of librarianship, with emphasis on usage in India.

188 The librarian's glossary of terms used in librarianship, documentation and the book crafts, and reference book. By Leonard Montague Harrod. 4th rev. ed. Boulder, CO: Westview, 1977. 903p. LC 76–52489. ISBN 0–89158–727–6.
The most extensive English-language glossary of terms in the field, this work has nearly 7,000 entries, of which 690 are new in this edition and nearly 800 others are expanded from the previous edition. There is also more complete coverage of American terms and practice than in the previous editions. Definitions range in length from one sentence to half a page. See references are used liberally. Acronyms are found in a separate list, but the full names they represent are included in the main vocabulary. Earlier editions were published in 1938, 1959, and 1971 (publisher varies).

189 Tutorial glossary of documentation terms. Comp. by Renee C. Evans. Santa Monica, CA: American Documentation Inst., 1966. 78p.
The work was prepared for distribution at the 29th Annual Meeting (October 3-7, 1960) of the American Documentation Institute, the predecessor organization to the American Society for Information Science. The approximately 6,000 terms emphasize information retrieval, computational linguistics, abstracting, indexing, and information technology. Terms from various related disciplines are included as well. Some acronyms are given. Arrangement is alphabetical, with cross-references.

Foreign Languages

CZECH

190 Terminologický slovnik: Knihovnický a bibliografický. By Hana Vodickova. Prague: Statni Pedagogicke Nakladatelstvi, 1965. 119p. LC 66–40988.
Approximately 2,600 Czech library terms are briefly defined (in Czech). Terms drawn from other languages are included and identified by the country of origin.

RUSSIAN

191 Terminologiia informatiki. By Arkadii Ivanovich Chernyi and Aleksandr Ivanovich Mikhailov. Moscow: Vsesoiuznyi Inst. Nauchnoi i Tekhnicheskoi Informatsii, 1976. 122p. LC 78–408764.
This work lists and defines informatics and information science terms in Russian. Terms adapted from other languages, as well as those originating in Russian, are included.

SLOVENE

192 Slovenska knihovnicka terminologia: Vykladovy slovnik. By Stephan Hanakovic, et al. Martin, Czechoslovakia: Matica Slovenska, 1965. 164p.

Approximately 2,500 library science terms are listed and briefly defined in Slovene. Terms taken from other languages are identified, along with their language of origin.

SPANISH

193 Diccionario de bibliotecología: términos relativos a la bibliología, bibliografía, biblifilia, biblioteconomía, archivología, documentología, tipografía y materias afines. By Domingo Buonocore. 2d ed. Buenos Aires: Ediciones Marymar, 1976. 452p. LC 77–551343.

Approximately 3,000 Spanish terms covering librarianship, documentation, information science, bibliography, book publishing, printing, and archives are defined (in Spanish). Some entries are of encyclopedic length; several are biographies. This edition has about 1,000 more terms than the first edition, titled *Vocabulario bibliográfico*.

194 Diccionario sobre ciencias de la información. Comp. by Arley Agudelo Clavijo and William Hernández O. Turrialba, Costa Rica: Asociacion Interamericana de Bibliotecarios y Documentalistas Agricolas, 1976. 72p. (Boletin técnico, no. 15) ISSN 0074–0756.

This bilingual glossary of information science terms in English and Spanish is arranged in two parts. The first section lists terms in Spanish, followed by the English equivalent and a definition in Spanish. The second section is limited to Spanish equivalents of English terms, without definitions.

TURKISH

195 Kitaplikblim terimleri sozlugu. By Berin U. Urdadog. Ankara: Turk Dil Kurumu, 1974. 111p. LC 79–971266.

Turkish library terms are defined in Turkish.

ACRONYMS, INITIALISMS AND ABBREVIATIONS

Publications that specialize in acronyms, initialisms, and/or abbreviations in librarianship, information science, documentation, or informatics are arranged alphabetically by title without regard for language or place of publication.

196 Abbreviations and technical terms used in book catalogues and in bibliographies. By Frank Keller Walter. Boston: Boston Book, 1915. 167p. LC 18–10870.

These several hundred abbreviations found in bibliographic citations in dealers' catalogs and other bibliographies are drawn from the following languages: English, French, German, Danish, Norwegian, Dutch, Italian, Latin, Spanish, and Swedish. Each abbreviation is fully defined. This work is supplemented by Axel Moth's *Technical terms used in bibliographies* (entry **139**).

197 Acronyms and abbreviations in library and information work. By A.C. Montgomery. 2d ed. London: Library Assn., 1982. 132p. ISBN 0–85365–904–4.
More than 5,000 acronyms and abbreviations from the fields of library and information science are identified and defined in this work. Also covered are acronyms in archival and museum administration, the commercial book trade, education, translation, management, computer science, and micrographics. The acronyms and abbreviations included represent organizations, associations, projects, indexes, journals, and professional services. Although only terms encountered in English-language librarianship are addressed, the emphasis is clearly British, both in scope and description. An earlier edition was published under the same title in 1975.

198 Dictionary of abbreviations in informatics/Rečnik na sŭkrashteniiata po informatika. By M. M. Balakhovskiĭ, et al. Moscow: Mezhdunarodny Tsentr Nauchnoi i Tekhnicheskoĭ Informatsii, 1976. 405p.
More than 10,000 abbreviations dealing with information theory and practice are listed in this work, published by the International Centre of Scientific and Technical Information. Terms come from such various fields as librarianship, bibliology, information systems, bibliographic description, publishing, and microreproduction. Included are abbreviations in the following languages: Bulgarian, Hungarian, Spanish, German, Polish, Romanian, Russian, Slovak, Czech, English, French, and Latin. The publication is divided into two parts: abbreviations from Bulgarian and Russian, using the Cyrillic alphabet; and abbreviations from the remaining languages, using the Roman alphabet. Acronyms are arranged alphabetically without regard to such marks as hyphens and fraction strokes. The abbreviations are identified by language, then by the full name they represent, followed by a Russian translation. Extensions or explanations are sometimes provided.

199 A Dictionary of acronyms in library and information science. Comp. by R. Tayyeb and K. Chandna. Ottawa: Canadian Library Assn., 1979. 146p. LC 80–104671. ISBN 0–88802–129–1.
Approximately 2,900 library and information science acronyms and abbreviations are listed here. Although coverage is international, emphasis is on acronyms from the United States, Canada, and the United Kingdom. The place of origin is identified when it is not evident from the full name. Included are acronyms for organizations, institutions, government agencies, publications, and processes. In some cases, only an acronym derived from the English translation of an agency name is given. However, most are acronyms for the name in the original language.

200 An international dictionary of acronyms in library and information science and related fields/Miedzynarodowy slownik akronimów z zakresu informacji naukowej, bibliotekoznawstwa i dziedzin pokrewnych. By Henry Sawoniak. Wroclaw: Zaklad Narodowy Imienia Ossolinskich, 1976. 244p. LC 77–363599.
This is an extensive international list of acronyms from library and information science as well as such related fields as publishing, printing, and archives. Included are acronyms for

organizations, library and information systems, methods and problems, equipment, classification systems, and methods of EDP. All of the acronyms taken together (including the various designations for the same entity) total 12,744. More than half of the acronyms are in English, and nearly eighty percent are from English, Russian, French, and German, with the frequency from each language in that order. Most are of recent origin, although some older acronyms are included. Entries provide the full name that the acronym represents and, when applicable, the country of origin. Former names and acronyms, country of origin, and the dates during which the former acronym was valid are also given. Many entries have multiple listings.

201 International directory of acronyms in library, information and computer sciences. By Pauline M. Vaillancourt. New York: Bowker, 1980. 518p. LC 80–18352. ISBN 0–8352–1152–5.

More than 5,500 United States, foreign, and international acronyms and initialisms are identified here. Of these, roughly 2,000 are international or foreign in origin. Only acronyms occurring in two or more instances in the literature of the field are included. The acronyms are arranged in letter-by-letter alphabetical order. Each entry has three parts: 1) the acronym or initialism, 2) the full name spelled out, 3) a definition or explanation, when the identity or purpose is not implicit in the name. Explanations include such information as the address of the organization identified by the acronym and alternate, former, and succeeding acronyms. The acronyms cover nine categories: associations, societies and organizations; commonly used terms from the field; meetings, conferences, or workshops of a continuing nature; publications; libraries and information centers; information-related government agencies; commercial firms; consortia, networks, and systems; and research projects and services. Access is enhanced by an extensive index of key words and phrases extracted from the full names which the acronyms signify. This index occupies half the book.

202 Osteuropäische bibliographische abkürzungen. By Franz Gorner. 3d ed. Munich: Verlag Dokumentation, 1975. 301p. LC 75–508857. ISBN 3–7940–3196–2.

This is the third edition of a list of library and bibliographic abbreviations from east and southeastern Europe and the western Soviet Union. Non-Roman alphabets are transliterated. The terms are in Slavic languages, with a preface in German and English. Approximately 3,500 abbreviations are included. Terms from all languages covered are in one alphabetical listing. Following each abbreviation is the meaning in the original language and in German.

THESAURI

The publications in this section are thesauri of subject descriptors in librarianship and/or information science. Most were developed for use in a manual or automated document retrieval system. Subject descriptors that cover the terminology of librarianship, documentation, or information science can be found in thesauri from various subject fields, but only works that emphasize the terminology of these areas or cover closely related fields are included here. Entries are arranged alphabetically by title without regard for language or place of publication.

203 Automated informatics documentation system: a thesaurus for informatics.
Rome: Intergovernmental Bureau for Informatics, 1980. 167, 75p.
While this thesaurus of terms from informatics (which also includes librarianship and documentation) was prepared for the retrieval of terms from the texts of materials created by the Intergovernmental Bureau for Informatics, the application is broader and extends to other texts that deal with informatics, documentation, information science, and librarianship. Designed with an open structure, the vocabulary in this work can be augmented without restructuring the entire vocabulary.

204 Automated informatics documentation system trilingual dictionary. Rome: Intergovernmental Bureau for Informatics, 1980. 216p.
This work lists more than 2,100 terms currently in use in the operation and management of bibliographical data base systems. It applies particularly to terminology used at the Intergovernmental Bureau for Informatics. It is intended to provide assistance in retrieving texts found in the Automated Informatics Documentation System (AIDS), but can be used for identifying informatics terms that apply to other systems as well. Terms are listed in English (the main entry), Spanish, and French, in three parallel columns, with equivalent terms side by side. Where synonyms are appropriate, they are listed below the main entry.

205 Compressed term index language for library and information science. Comp. by Alan Gilchrist and Kathleen Gaster. London: Aslib, 1973. 123p. LC 74–186049. ISBN 0–85142–043–5.
This alphabetically arranged thesaurus of key words was developed as a result of two separate research projects concerned with the construction of thesauri. The thesaurus lists basic key words in librarianship and information science and identifies broader, narrower, and related terms, as well as exhibiting other syndetic features. Geographical key words, subject fields and identifiers (terms that do not fit into the descriptor vocabulary) are listed separately. An alphabetical index refers the user to each term found in the thesaurus. The intent of the project which led to this work was to demonstrate that effective information retrieval could be achieved with a limited number of terms. Consequently, highly specialized terms are generally not included. Good balance is maintained between the various facets of library and information science.

206 Terminology: Unesco: IBE education thesaurus. Paris: Unesco, 1978. 348p. LC 78–388857. ISBN 92–3–101531–5.
The subtitle identifies this as *A faceted list of terms for indexing and retrieving documents and data in the field of education with French and Spanish equivalent*. It is produced by Unesco's International Bureau of Education. Terms are listed alphabetically in English, with French and Spanish equivalents provided. Cross-references, by means of the commonly used terms and symbols, relate terms to one another. In addition to the alphabetical array (list of terms), a faceted array (terms grouped by a facet held in common) and a rotated list of descriptors are also included. Although most of the terms are not explicitly library- or information science-related, many have application to this field. This work is similar to the *Thesaurus of ERIC descriptors* (entry **207**), but provides greater international emphasis.

207 Thesaurus of ERIC descriptors. Rev. ed. Phoenix: Oryx, 1980. 419p. LC 80–52477. ISBN 0–912700–53–X.

This thesaurus is the controlled vocabulary for the Educational Resources Information Center (ERIC) data base, sponsored by the National Institute of Education, U. S. Department of Education. The more than 8,000 terms pertain to various educational topics and public issues. Library and information science terminology is integrated into the entire vocabulary. It is impossible to determine what percentage of the terms are applicable to library and information science since, in the ERIC data base, terms not unique to this field are assigned to documents in the field. The vocabulary is designed for use with the paper copy indexes, *Resources in education* (entry **55**) and *Current index to journals in education* (entry **46**), and the machine retrievable *ERIC* data base (entry **115**). Arrangement is alphabetical, with standard cross-reference symbols creating the syndetic structure. Many terms also have scope notes that define or explain their use within the context of this controlled vocabulary. Additional features include a rotated descriptor display that lists in alphabetical order all words found in one-, two-, or three-word descriptors.

208   Thesaurus of information science terminology. By Claire K. Schultz. Rev. and exp. ed. Metuchen, NJ: Scarecrow, 1978. 288p. LC 78–16878. ISBN 0–8180–1156–1.
This alphabetical list of terms in information science, library science, and related areas is structured hierarchically, in five broad categories: environment, input, processing, output, and feedback. Every term fits into one of these categories. The following concepts and symbols create a syndetic structure: USE; refer from (X); partial refer from (PX); broader term (BT); narrower term (NT); and related term (RT). This thesaurus was designed for use with the author's personal collection of documents and tends to give preference to general rather than specific terms. A consequence is a large number of USE references, which refer the user to approved general terms. Special features include a separate hierarchical listing of terms and an extensive index to multi-word terms.

FOREIGN-LANGUAGE HANDBOOKS

Publications that assist librarians with the bibliolinguistics (the vocabulary and linguistic information found in bibliographic citations) of languages other than English are arranged alphabetically by title under the languages or language covered.

European Languages

209   Manual of european languages for librarians. Ed. by C. G. Allen. New York: Bowker, 1975. 803p. LC 73–6062. ISBN 0–85935–028–2.
The purpose of this publication is to provide basic language instruction for librarians who work with foreign-language materials. It is intended for catalogers, collection development and acquisition librarians, and bibliographers. The publication consists of separate sections which provide information about each of thirty-seven European languages. The languages are grouped into the following broad families: Germanic; Latin and the Romance; Celtic; Greek and Albanian; Slavonic; Baltic; Finno-Ugrian; and other. Each section concentrates on information likely to be required by librarians: title, volumes and parts, corporate authors, etc. The work's organization makes an index unnecessary.

French

210 **French language: a manual for english-speaking librarians/Le français: manuel des bibliothécaires de la langue anglaise.** By Mod Mekkawi. Arlington, VA: Mod Mekkawi, 1980. 90p. LC 80–142044.

This basic introduction to French, especially as applied to librarianship and bibliography, covers grammar, style, vocabulary, and bibliolinguistic terms in French, with English equivalents. A separate section identifies selected French reference sources.

German

211 **German for librarians.** By G. W. Turner. Rev. and ed. by A. J. A. Vieregg and J. W. Blackwood. Palmerston North, New Zealand: Massey Univ., 1972. 137p. (Massey University library series, no. 5) LC 73–152603.

This guide to German grammar and bibliolinguistics is intended to assist librarians in ordering and cataloging German-language materials. The work identifies elements typically found in bibliographic entries.

Russian

212 **Reading the russian language: a guide for librarians & other professions.** By Rosalind Kent. New York: M. Dekker, 1974. 229p. LC 74–81799. ISBN 0–8347–6263–3.

A basic Russian grammar, this work is designed to enable librarians and other professionals to read Russian or, as stated in the introduction, "to teach Russian to librarians who have never tried to learn the language or who have tried and given up." Examples illustrate the types of language usages that might be encountered by librarians trying to catalog Russian-language materials. The publication is an outgrowth of a course at the University of Pittsburgh GSLIS.

213 **Russian for librarians.** By G. P. M. Walker. Hamden, CT: Shoe String, 1973. 126p. LC 72–13440. ISBN 0–208–01199–4.

This handbook provides a basic introduction to aspects of the Russian language that are of particular use to librarians: the Cyrillic alphabet, transliteration, punctuation, and grammar. One chapter deals with major Russian reference works, with emphasis on bibliography (including indexing and abstracting services); another deals with acquisition of Russian publications. Brief general information about other east European languages is included. The final section is a classified bilingual vocabulary of terms commonly used in librarianship and the book trade.

3.

Encyclopedias, Yearbooks, Handbooks and Manuals

INTRODUCTION

Practitioners, educators, and students all require readily available factual information as well as systematic interpretations and reviews of activities and developments in their respective fields. These requirements are typically met by encyclopedias, yearbooks, and handbooks or manuals. Each of these publications has certain general qualities that distinguish the types, one from another. However, in some publications, these generic qualities overlap. For example, directories and yearbooks are often combined. Moreover, distinctions are sometimes unclear because publishers or authors assign titles to publications that do not accurately reflect their generic qualities. In the paragraphs below, each type of reference source is described, and observations are made about the way each meets the special needs of library and information services.

Encyclopedias: Most general encyclopedias, at least those currently published in English, include a substantial number of articles about libraries, librarianship, and related topics. However useful, this coverage is rarely sufficiently specialized to meet the needs of librarians, library educators, or students. Thus, several encyclopedias have been published that deal exclusively with library and information science and/or the book world. Explanations in these subject-specialized sources are quite technical and detailed. Furthermore, these library-related sources, usually arranged alphabetically, represent the structure of the field more accurately through cross-references and lengthy articles on broad topics than do the general sources.

It is possible to generalize only to a limited degree about the nature of the eleven library-related encyclopedias covered in this chapter. Each was intended for a different function, and the overlap among them is not as substantial as one might expect. The encyclopedias are published in five languages, the majority issued in English or German. Those with more recent publication dates integrate information science concepts and terminology with those of librarianship, whereas the older encyclopedias place more emphasis on the book world and bibliographic aspects associated with libraries and librarianship. Some of the sources survey library services prevalent in various countries throughout the world. Others emphasize explanations of technical terms and thus have much in common with glossaries. However, encyclopedias provide more depth of coverage and, in some cases, include lists of other references to be consulted. Several of the cited encyclopedias contain biographical entries, while others do not. Many of the encyclopedias have signed articles; a few do not.

Yearbooks: The purpose of a yearbook, whether general or subject specialized, is to provide an annual summary of significant events in the subject areas covered. Yearbooks frequently include statistics, a chronology of events, biographical information, and narrative descriptions of ongoing activities. Library and information science yearbooks attempt to identify new developments within the various subfields and major library-related organizations. They also provide data on library service and the book trade. For example, the *Bowker annual* (entry no. 239) provides a compilation of facts and is similar in format to a general almanac.

Fifteen general library-related yearbooks are described in this chapter. Only those sources that include at least some English text are covered. Several of the citations are no longer being published. However, since yearbooks chronicle events of a specified period and subject area, they retain their value as a record of developments within in the field and are, therefore, included here. Other types of annual publications that do not fit the generic definition of a yearbook (annual directories, annual membership lists, annual reports) are treated elsewhere in the guide.

Handbooks and Manuals: Handbooks and manuals are designed to bring together frequently needed factual or documentary information. They provide "how-to-do-it" instructions. In some respects, these works are similar to encyclopedias. However, the coverage is usually less comprehensive. While it was our intent to exclude from this guide publications intended specifically as textbooks for basic library science courses, in practice we frequently found it difficult to distinguish between a textbook and a manual or handbook. We discovered that a number of publications function interchangeably. In the end, we selected those titles which, in our view, could be used successfully as reference manuals to provide practical guidance to librarians or library educators, whether or not they had been prepared as textbooks. Only six general handbooks or manuals cover the library and information fields, and these are oriented toward library service within particular countries. The remainder of the handbooks in the field are subject specialized or present specific types of information, as in a library chronology. Those handbooks are covered in appropriate subject sections in Chapter 7.

ENCYCLOPEDIAS

Encyclopedias are arranged alphabetically by title under the language of publication. English-language works are listed first. Foreign-language sections follow in alphabetical order by the English name of the language.

English Language

214 **ALA world encyclopedia of library and information services.** Ed. by Robert Wedgeworth. Chicago: American Library Assn., 1980. 601p. LC 80–10912. ISBN 0–8389–0305–3.

The intent of this work, as stated by the editor, is to serve as a means by which library and information services can "inform and educate its students, its practitioners, and the public about the interests and activities of the field"; it "seeks to explain fundamental ideas, record historical events and activities, and portray those personalities, living and dead, who have shaped the field." The encyclopedia consists of 452 articles of varying length, ranging from less than a column to several pages. The articles deal with such broad topics as library education and indexing and abstracting; cover library and information services in specified geographical areas and time periods; or are biographical. More than 160 articles treat libraries and librarianship in various countries; many are devoted to individual nations. Biographical coverage extends to prominent contemporary as well as historical figures. The numerous illustrations include photographs of subjects or biographees. Articles are signed; most have cross-references and a list of further readings. The cross-references and alphabetical arrangement make the encyclopedia self-indexing. However, a topical guide at the front of the work, which outlines the contents under broad topic headings, is useful for those interested in pursuing broad topics.

215 **Australian librarian's manual.** Comp. by David J. Jones. Sydney: Library Assn. of Australia, 1982– . 3v. v.1, **Documents,** 1982. ISBN 0–86804–009–6.

Eventually, this work will consist of three volumes containing documents relating to librarianship in Australia. In the first volume, which was published in 1982, policy statements, standards of service for various types of libraries, extracts of Library Association of Australia submissions, and other documents or parts of documents concerned with Australian librarianship are included.

216 **Encyclopaedia of librarianship.** Ed. by Thomas Landau. 3d rev. ed. New York: Hafner Publishing, 1966. 484p. LC 66–3776.

Although information on some topics is now dated, the majority of the entries are still useful. Least dated are the entries concerned with physical aspects of the book or the history of libraries. The work predates the development of information science terminology. Most entries are brief, but they vary from one sentence to two or three pages. Emphasis is definitely on library service in the United Kingdom. Biographical articles are included, primarily for persons involved in the printing, binding, or publishing of books. This edition was preceded by two earlier editions (1958, 1961), each of which is less extensive than the third.

217 Encyclopedia of library and information science. Ed. by Allen Kent, Harold Lancour and Jay Daily. New York: M. Dekker, 1968– . 33v. LC 68–31232.

This work is the most comprehensive library and information science encyclopedia in any language. The anticipated total number of volumes is thirty-five; thirty-three have been published to date. When completed, the work will include at least ten times as many words as the next largest English-language encyclopedia, the ALA *world encyclopedia of library and information services* (entry **110**). The editors have included articles ranging from less than a column to almost monographic length. The depth and scope of the articles vary considerably. Some articles deal with topics not addressed elsewhere and represent significant contributions to the literature. Most articles attempt a synthesis, and some have lengthy bibliographies. Some early articles are now out of date. However, updated data often appear under a related subject term occurring later in the alphabetical sequence. Among the many subjects covered are library architecture, laws of scattering, *Sears list of subject headings*, library and information services in various countries, and the history of each library education program accredited by the American Library Association. The individual volumes are not indexed, but a general index is planned on completion of the work.

Foreign Languages

GERMAN

218 Handbuch der bibliothekswissenschaft. By Fritz Milkau and Georg Leyh. Wiesbaden: Harrassowitz, 1950–1965. 4v. in 5. LC A 52–1997.

Lengthy, signed articles in German are found in this encyclopedia, which covers librarianship, history of libraries, history of the book, and book publishing. It is similar in format and style to general European encyclopedias. Emphasis is on Germany and Europe. Many of the articles are accompanied by lengthy bibliographies. Coverage is divided into the three volumes, with the first volume covering the history of the book and writing, the second volume concerned with librarianship, and the third volume covering the history of libraries. A separate subject index appears in the fourth volume. This is generally considered to be the major work of scholarship in this field.

219 Handbuch der büchereiwesens. Ed. by Johannes Langfeldt. Wiesbaden: Harrassowitz, 1976. ISBN 3–447–01732–5.

This encyclopedic work on the public library in Germany and German-speaking countries covers the history and present conditions of library services in the Federal Republic of Germany, the German Democratic Republic, Austria, and Switzerland. Articles are lengthy and are contributed by various authors.

220 Lexikon des bibliothekswesens. Ed. by Horst Kunze and Gotthard Ruckl. Leipzig: VEB Bibliographisches Inst.; Munich: Verlag Dokumentation, 1974–1975. 2v. LC 75–527321.

The more than 3,000 articles in this German-language encyclopedia range from biographical sketches to descriptions of library and information service in various countries. The contributors are identified by initials at the end of each article. Emphasis is on librarianship, with some coverage of topics concerned with bibliography and the physical book. Both historical and contemporary coverage is provided. Articles range in length from less than a column to several pages. Most include bibliographical references, and some have lengthy citations lists. One valuable feature is a glossary of terms in five languages (German, Russian, English, French, and Spanish). The encyclopedia was first published in 1969, under the same title but with fewer entries.

POLISH

221 Encyklopedia wiedzy o ksiaze. By Aleksander Birkenmajer, Bronislaw Kocowski, and Jan Trzynadlowski. Wroclaw: Zaklad Norodowy Imienia Ossolinskich, 1971. 2,874 cols. LC 72–227017.

An extensive, heavily illustrated Polish-language encyclopedia of the book world, this work tends to emphasize literature, publishing, bibliography, and biographical information about prominent authors, rather than librarianship or information science. However, it does include articles on libraries and tends to complement *Encyklopedia wspólczesnego bibliotekarstwa polskiego* (entry **220**).

222 Encyklopedia wspólczesnego bibliotekarstwa polskiego. By Karol Glombiowski, Boleslaw Swiderski and Helena Wieckowska. Wroclaw: Zaklad Narodowy Imienia Ossolinskich, 1976. 337p. LC 76–528067.

Subjects covered in this encyclopedia include librarianship, bibliography, information science, and informatics. Some of the articles are biographical, but most deal with library service, library practice, bibliographical practice, and technical topics. Emphasis is on library practice and individuals in Eastern Europe, particularly Poland. Articles are initialed and vary in length from one column to two pages. A number of illustrations are included. Many articles have bibliographic references to additional reading matter. The work is cross-referenced, and access is augmented by a topical index of terms.

RUSSIAN

223 Slovar' bibliotechnykh terminov. Comp. by Ogan Stephanovich Chubar'ian, I. M. Suslova and L. N. Ulanova. Moscow: Kniga, 1976. 222p. LC 77–503344.

This work combines the characteristics of a glossary and encyclopedia in that it provides comprehensive definitions and explanations of library and information science and bibliographic terms. Articles range in length from less than half a column to two or three columns. Bibliographic citations are incorporated into the articles. Terms and articles appear in Russian, with no access from other languages.

SERBO-CROATIAN

224 Enciklopedijski leksikon bibliotekarstva: priucnik. By Kosta Grubacić. Sarajevo: Zavod za Izdavanje Udzbenika, 1964. 336p. LC 65–73308.

Although this is largely a glossary of terms, its lengthier entries qualify it as a short article encyclopedia. The articles cover various aspects of the book world, with emphasis on libraries, librarianship, and documentation in Eastern Europe. Introductory notes appear in English, Russian, German, and French. A bibliography of sources used is found at the end of the work. Terms and articles are in Serbo-Croatian, without access from other languages.

YEARBOOKS

Yearbooks are listed in alphabetical order by title under country of publication. Countries are arranged in alphabetical order by country name without regard to continental location.

Netherlands

225 Library progress: an international review of developments in the field of libraries. Amsterdam: J. L. P. M. Krol, 1968?–1973?. Annual. LC 68–59140. ISSN 0024–2497.

This work carries articles about library service on a national and international basis for various countries of the world. Emphasis is on European, especially Western European, library activities. Articles appear in Dutch, English, French, German, or Spanish.

Norway

226 Library and research yearbook/Bibliotek og forskning aarbok. Oslo: Norske Forskningbibliotekarers Forening and the Norsk Bibliotekarlag, 1954–1974. Annual. LC 55–32676. ISSN 0405–993X.

This yearbook reports on library activities and library research in Scandanavian countries. The articles are in Norwegian, but summaries appear in English. Published from 1952 to 1954 under the title *Norsk aarbok for bibliotek og forskning* (entry **227**), it ceased publication in 1974.

227 Norsk aarbok for bibliotek og forskning. Oslo: Norske Forskningbibliotekarers Forening and the Norsk Bibliotekarlag, 1952–1954. Annual.

This work is continued by *Library and research yearbook/Bibliotek og forskning aarbok*. For further information see entry **226**.

Republic of Ireland

228 The libraries, museums and art galleries yearbook. Cambridge and London: James Clarke, 1897– . Irreg. ISSN 0075–899X. ISBN 0–227–7835–4.

This work provides detailed directory information for more than 3,000 libraries and museums in the United Kingdom and the Republic of Ireland. For further information see entry **232**.

United Kingdom

229 British librarianship and information science, 1971–1975. Ed. by H. A. Whatley. London: Library Assn., 1977. 379p. NUC 80–229549. ISBN 0–85365–099–3.

This work is listed with Review Publications under the current title, *British librarianship and information work*. For further information see entry **110**.

230   British librarianship and information science, 1966–1970. Ed. by H. A. Whatley. London: Library Assn.; Detroit: Gale Distr., 1972. 712p. Every 5 years. LC 73–157654. ISBN 0–85365–175–2.

This work is currently titled, *British librarianship and information work.* For further information see entry **110.**

231   Five year's work in librarianship, 1951/55–1961/65. London: Library Assn., 1958–1968. Every 5 years. LC 58–2169.

This title contains essay accounts of the previous five years' work in various aspects of librarianship. For further information see entry **111.**

232   The libraries, museums and art galleries yearbook. Cambridge and London: James Clarke, 1897– . Irreg. ISSN 0075–899X. ISBN 0–227–7835–4.

This work provides detailed directory information for more than 3,000 libraries and museums in the United Kingdom and the Republic of Ireland. The first section lists public libraries in the United Kingdom. Academic and special libraries in the United Kingdom are listed in the second section and all types of libraries in the Republic of Ireland in the third. Section four covers museums in the United Kingdom. Library entries are arranged alphabetically by name of the town in which they are located. The entries contain name, address, telephone number, name of the chief librarian, governing body, branches, hours of opening, cooperative arrangements to which they belong, equipment and facilities, holdings, size of staff, and finances. A combined index provides access to subjects, names of institutions, and names of special collections.

233   Progress in library science, 1965–1967. Ed. by Robert L. Collison. Washington, DC: Butterworths, 1966–1968. Annual. LC 66–2926.

Only three volumes of this work were published. The objective, as stated in the foreword, was "to offer a readable account by experts of items of current interest to librarians." Each volume provides articles on various facets of library service. For example, the first volume includes articles on Latin American libraries, public libraries, and the Dewey Decimal Classification system. Subsequent volumes cover training for librarianship, book publishing, and book production. The intent was to cover a variety of selected subjects over a period of several years and then repeat coverage of those subjects. The work's format resembles that of review articles except that bibliographic coverage is not extensive. One special feature is a chronology of major events in library service within the United Kingdom during the previous year. A subject index provides access.

234   Year's work in librarianship, 1928–1950. London: Library Assn., 1929–1954. 17v. LC 30–18367.

This title contains essays that examine major trends and achievements in librarianship during the previous year. For further information see entry **112.**

United States

235   The ALA yearbook. Chicago: American Library Assn., 1976– . Annual. LC 76–647548. ISSN 0364–1597.

Initiated during the centennial year of the American Library Association, this yearbook carries approximately 140–150 articles per year. Many are lengthy feature articles covering such broad topics as book publishing, library buildings, personnel and employment, and social responsibilities. Shorter articles deal with activities of state and other national library associations, units of ALA, prominent contemporary librarians, and types of library service. Emphasis is on library developments and library association activities in the United States, but coverage of other countries is included also. The *Yearbook* is heavily illustrated and self-indexed through the numerous cross-references found in the wide outside margins. A useful list of acronyms that appear in the text is included at the work's end. The first volume of the *Yearbook* preceded the *ALA world encyclopedia of library and information services* (entry **214**). When the *Encyclopedia* was published, it followed the physical and conceptual format of the *Yearbook*. Volumes of the *Yearbook* published subsequent to the *Encyclopedia* refer back to relevant articles in the *Encyclopedia*.

236   American library and book trade annual. New York: Bowker, 1959–1960. Annual. LC 80–1379. ISSN 0271–7441.
This title is continued as *The Bowker annual of library and book trade information*. For further information see entry **239**.

237   American library annual. New York: Bowker, 1956–1958. Annual. LC 55–12434.
This title is continued as *American library and book trade annual* and *The Bowker annual of library and book trade information*. For further information see entry **239**.

238   American library annual, 1911/12–1917/18. New York: Bowker, 1912–1918. 7v. LC 12–13594 rev.
This is an early attempt to provide a compendium of information about libraries and book publishing, with emphasis on the United States and Canada. It includes articles about library schools, book publishing, library organizations, periodical publishing, and major bibliographies published during the year. Biographies of prominent librarians are also provided. Early volumes included directories of libraries, publishers, and leading booksellers as well. The first volumes of the *Bowker annual* (entry **239**) used the same title and were intended to follow a similar pattern.

239   The Bowker annual of library and book trade information. By the Council of National Library and Information Associations. New York: Bowker, 1961– . Annual. LC 55–12434. ISSN 0068–0540.
This work is a compendium of information about library and book publishing activities during the previous year. Each volume comprises numerous signed articles. Although the content has increased substantially since the early volumes, several categories of information can be traced through much of the period during which this has been published. The current volume is divided into seven broad sections (each subdivided): 1) reports from the field; 2) legislation, funding, and grants; 3) library education, placement, and salaries; 4) research and statistics; 5) international reports and statistics; 6) reference information; and 7) directory of organizations. Many of the articles provide summaries of the previous year's activities and trends. Most also provide statistical information, either in tabular form or incorporated into the text. Some of the information is published elsewhere, but other sources often provide less convenient access. Moreover, some information provided here is not readily available elsewhere. For example, a current directory of state, provincial, and regional library associations, with current officers, appears in each annual volume. The

publication has a subject/title/name-author index. The title of this work has varied: from 1956 to 1958, it was known as *American library annual* (entry **237**); during 1959–1960, it was titled *American library and book trade annual* (entry **236**); and since 1961, it has been known by the present title.

HANDBOOKS AND MANUALS

Handbooks and manuals are arranged alphabetically by title without regard to language or place of publication.

240 The basics of librarianship. By Colin Harrison and Rosemary Oates. London: Library Assn., 1981. 220p. LC 81–125279. ISBN 0–85365–523–5.
This is a concise guide to the basic functions of librarianship, such as classification and cataloging, conservation and care of materials, information sources and services, and library procedures and routines. Library practice in the United Kingdom is emphasized. Intended as a manual for practicing librarians, this work includes practical suggestions, sample forms of various types, and illustrations, charts, and, when appropriate, computer printouts. Librarians in smaller installations who are responsible for a variety of functions will find this guide of particular value.

241 British librarianship today. Ed. by W. L. Saunders. London: Library Assn., 1976. 378p. LC 77–361648. ISBN 0–85365–498–0.
Each chapter is an essay by a different author on some aspect of British librarianship. Chapters deal with library associations, the British Library, types of libraries, the expected impact of computerization on libraries, and other topics. Access is through the general topic of the article or through a general index.

242 Canadian library handbook/Guide des bibliothèques canadiennes, 1979–1980. Ed. by James Quantrell. Toronto: Micromedia, 1980. 256p. LC 79–31603. ISBN 0–88892–600–2.
Although much of this work is a directory of libraries, additional included information broadens its scope. Reviews of the year's activities in research, children's literature, association activities, and publishing are provided in essay form. Selected statistics on Canadian public and academic libraries and citations to recent literature are also provided. The directory identifies libraries by location, name, and subject area(s) covered. A calendar of Canadian library events for the year is also included. The text of the handbook is in English and French. Access is by topic or through the general index.

243 A librarian's handbook. Comp. by L. J. Taylor. London: Library Assn., 1976–1980. 2v. LC 77–362108. ISBN 0–85365–079–9 (v.1). ISBN 0–85365–651–7 (v.2).
These two volumes constitute a compendium of information about library service and librarianship in the United Kingdom. Although some information can be found elsewhere, no source provides a more convenient package. The index to volume 2 provides access to both volumes. Volume 1 provides coverage of significant documents and other information useful to the practicing librarian up to the mid-1970's. It also includes a number of bibliographies on a wide range of library-related topics. Volume 2 covers more current

source material, some of which is difficult to find elsewhere. Presented are the texts of government or association policy statements, library standards, regulations pertaining to libraries, statistics, information about library education, and much additional practical information. A valuable feature in both volumes is a set of directories to libraries, equipment suppliers, book vendors, local cooperative schemes, publishers that specialize in books on librarianship, and numerous others. The directories are largely limited in their coverage to the United Kingdom.

244 Library manual: for library authorities, librarians and honorary library workers. By S. R. Ranganathan. 2d ed. Bombay: Asia Publishing House, 1966. 415p.
A classic work, this introduction to librarianship provides a general statement of the theoretical and practical philosophy of S. R. Ranganathan. The first section includes a statement of Ranganathan's five laws of library science, together with other related matters. Subsequent sections deal with such topics as reference service, circulation work, classification, and cataloging. The manual represents an intermingling of the philosophy of the author with practical recommendations and instructions on basic aspects of library practice. Access is available through an index. An added feature is an English-Sanscrit glossary of library terms.

245 Manual of library economy. Ed. by R. Northwood Lock. 7th ed. Hamden, CT: Shoe String, 1977. 447p. LC 77–5034. ISBN 0–208–01538–8.
British public library practice is emphasized in this manual. The twenty-one chapters deal with the functions of library service, such as reference, lending, nonbook materials, as well as other, more general topics, such as library cooperation, professional literature, and the compilation and use of statistics for management purposes. The text is augmented by numerous photographs, forms, and line drawings. Chapters are written by eighteen different authors, and they provide practical, common sense observations and recommendations about current library practice.

4.

Biographical and Membership Directories

INTRODUCTION

Professionals often need to locate facts about other people in their field. Although this information may be gathered through informal, person-to-person communication, much biographical information is available only in published sources. Any publication that supplies data on an individual can be considered a biographical source. Even a card catalog entry which identifies an author's birth and death dates is, to a limited extent, a biographical tool. Publications that identify individuals and provide their institutional affiliations are, of course, more substantial biographical sources.

Information about some library and information professionals can be found in general biographical directories, such as *Who's who in America* or regional "who's who" publications. Also helpful are the biographical notes appearing in journal articles or other publications. Some journals, such as *Government publications review* (entry no. 899), request that authors provide a biographical paragraph to accompany their published article. In other journals, a brief note indicating the author's current position and institutional affiliation accompanies the article. *Library literature* (entry no. 52) and other indexes can also be used to identify articles that may carry biographical information. A less efficient and less predictable source of basic biographical data is the news notes section of such publications as *Library journal*, which announce job changes, retirements, deaths, and similar facts. Names of individuals mentioned here generally are not indexed in *Library literature*, but if the researcher knows the approximate date of the event, the news notes section can be scanned sequentially.

In-depth biographical data on information professionals may also be found in basic library reference works. The *ALA world encyclopedia of library and information services* (entry no. 214) and the *ALA yearbook* (entry no. 235) include a large number of biographical entries. The *Yearbook* is particularly valuable because each new volume contains biographical information about persons who might not have been covered previously. Books and articles on selected librarians can be found by consulting *The dictionary catalog of the Library of the School of Library Service, Columbia University* (entry no. 69), under the name of the individual, or by checking such standard general biographical sources as *Biography index*.

The most useful biographical sources in any profession are those that concentrate on the professionals in that particular field. In librarianship, however, the scope and quality of biographical sources covering the field vary considerably. Therefore, individuals seeking biographical information on librarians or library educators must often use considerable ingenuity. The major biographical or membership directories alone are not sufficient to identify all or even the majority of librarians or other information professionals. For example, while the new biographical directory published by the American Library Association, *Who's who in library and information services* (entry no. 280), includes 12,000 library and information service professionals in the United States and Canada, the membership of the ALA alone now exceeds 37,000. Furthermore, there are many professionals who are neither members of ALA nor other national associations, but belong to local associations only, or to none at all. Therefore, because none of the major biographical directories is truly comprehensive, a variety of sources must be used to locate information about persons in library and information science. The most useful of these are "who's who" directories and membership directories.

Who's Who Directories: In general, one of the most commonly published types of biographical sources is the "who's who" directory. But in the library and information fields, "who's who" biographical sources are available for only a few countries. Some of these sources are published separately; others are issued as supplements to directories of libraries. In most cases, they provide only a minimum of information about each individual.

Described in this chapter are twenty-five biographical directories. The scope is international, although most of the items included are for English-speaking countries. While the emphasis is on current publications, directories issued as many as twenty years ago are cited when more recent biographical sources are unavailable. These older directories should not be discounted or overlooked; they have value for both retrospective information and information about individuals not covered in current sources.

Membership Directories: Although the membership directories of most organizations contain only a minimum of information about individual members, they are a very important source of relatively current information, particularly on present position, institutional affiliation, work or home address, and, in some cases, telephone number. Some membership directories also code the individual's professional interests, usually determined by membership in sections or divisions of the organization.

Two factors influence the comprehensiveness of membership directories. First, membership is voluntary. Second, a library and information service professional may belong to several, one, or none of the multitude of national, regional, state, and local associations. Consequently, the researcher will probably have to consult several membership directories to locate information about an individual.

Included in this chapter are twelve membership directories issued by major library or information science associations, particularly those located in English-speaking countries. Only general library associations (those consisting of persons from a variety of specialized areas) are listed here. Membership directories for subject-specialized associations or those directed toward a specific constituency are cited in Chapter 7. Membership directories for local, state/provincial, and regional associations have been omitted entirely; there are too many to list and information about them can be obtained directly from the associations.

It is unreasonable to expect any library to acquire all directories of all library associations on a regular and systematic basis, but knowledge of the existence of various associations can help librarians collect the most valuable directories. Several sources are useful for identifying library and information science associations. For information on national associations throughout the world, the *International guide to library, archival, and information science associations* (entry no. 736) is invaluable. To identify state and provincial, regional, and national associations in the United States and Canada, consult the most recent volume of *The Bowker annual* (entry no. 239); while it does not specify the directories, it does provide a current address for each association's executive office and the names of current officers. For a list of current local, regional, and national library associations in the United Kingdom, *A librarian's handbook* (entry no. 243), by L. J. Taylor, is the best source. This, too, provides addresses from which directories can be obtained.

AFRICA AND THE MIDDLE EAST

African and Middle Eastern biographical sources are listed alphabetically by title within country of coverage.

India

246 **Directory of booksellers, publishers, libraries and librarians in India (who's who).** Ed. by Raj K. Khosla. 2d ed. New Delhi: Premier, 1973. 300p. LC 73–9000620.

The first section provides brief information about major state, public, and special libraries in India (see entry **303**). The second section offers biographical entries for approximately 800 prominent Indian librarians. Each entry indicates professional affiliation, education, and previous positions held. Some entries are accompanied by photographs. An earlier edition was published in 1968.

247 **Directory of libraries and who's who in library profession in Delhi.** Ed. by N. K. Goil, et al. Delhi: Delhi Library Assn., 1964. 91p. LC 65–1646.

The biographical portion lists and identifies 580 librarians in the Delhi area at the time of publication. Entries include affiliation and address, education, and date of birth. A separate list of 105 libraries in the Delhi area includes size, types of resources, type of classification system used, and type of catalog (see entry **304**).

248 **Men of library science and libraries in India.** Ed. by Raj K. Khosla and M. K. Gaur. New Delhi: Premier, 1967. 74p. LC 75–646305. ISSN 0377–1342.

The biographical section of this work lists and identifies about 400 librarians. Each entry includes professional affiliation, education, and previous positions held. Some entries are accompanied by photographs. A separate section provides a classified list of libraries, including academic, state, and public libraries (see entry **308**). Each entry describes the library briefly and provides address and rules for library use. Access to the directory of libraries is by type, subdivided by state.

Nigeria

249 **Nominal list of practising librarians in Nigeria, 1975.** Lagos: National Library of Nigeria, 1976. 24p. LC 79–303967. ISBN 978–128–008–5.

This work includes 330 librarians, up from 289 in 1975, the first year of publication. Names are listed alphabetically, and each entry specifies institutional affiliation, qualifications, and nationality. Also included is a list of Nigerian libraries.

Pakistan

250 **Who's who in librarianship in Pakistan.** Comp. by Ghaniul Akram Sabzwari and M. Wasil Usmani. Karachi: Library Promotion Bureau, 1969. 273p. LC 70–930618.

Entered here are biographies of 564 Pakistani librarians, and foreign librarians serving in Pakistan in the late 1960's. A "who was who" section lists librarians then deceased. The entries give affiliation, education, previous career information, and date of birth. There is also a list of libraries, arranged geographically.

ASIA

Asian biographical sources with continental coverage are listed first, alphabetically by title. Sources with national coverage are arranged alphabetically by title under the country name.

251 **Directory of librarians in southeast Asia.** Ed. by Marina G. Dayrit. Quezon City: Univ. of the Philippines Library, 1980. 140p. LC 80–145597.

Nearly 1,000 librarians working in southeast Asia are listed in this directory that was published by the University of the Philippines Library for the Congress of Southeast Asia Librarians. The countries covered include Indonesia, Malaysia, Singapore, Thailand, and the Philippines. The directory is written in English. Names are arranged alphabetically, by the Romanized version. Entries specify name, position or title, business address and telephone number, nationality, languages spoken, date and place of birth, sex and marital status, education, training/seminars/conferences attended, career positions, consultantships and memberships in advisory committees, membership in associations, awards or honors, publications, professional interests, and residence address and telephone number.

Malaysia

252 Panduan pustakawan, 1973. Kuala Lumpur: Perpustakaan Negara Malaysia, 1973. 37p. LC 73–942712.
This alphabetical list of Malaysian librarians includes some who were out of the country at the time of publication. Entries supply address and telephone number as well as institutional affiliation.

AUSTRALIA AND THE SOUTH PACIFIC

Australian and South Pacific biographical sources are listed alphabetically by title within country of coverage.

Australia

253 Biographical directory of australian librarians: formerly Who's who in australian libraries. Ed. by Geza A. Kosa. 2d ed. Melbourne: Burwood State College, 1979. 215p. LC 80–485047. ISBN 0–909184–08–9.
More than 1,500 librarians who live in Australia are included in this work. Although not all who are qualified are listed, most prominent librarians are represented. Entries include name and address, current and previous employment, and other professional activities. This work supersedes *Who's who in australian libraries,* (entry **255**). A third edition is schedule to be published during 1983.

254 Library Association of Australia: handbook. Sydney: Library Assn. of Australia, 1943– . Annual.
Beginning with the 1982 volume, the individual and institutional members of the association are listed alphabetically. The entries in the directory section include the name, position, institutional affiliation, and address of each member. Elsewhere in the handbook, there is information about the association, including the bylaws and names of officers.

255 Who's who in australian libraries. Comp. and ed. by Geza A. Kosa and Doreen M. Goodman. Sydney: Library Assn. of Australia, 1968. 181p. LC 75–398852.
The approximately 950 biographical articles in this listing of Australian library personnel include address, current and previous employment, and other professional activities. There is also a directory of members of the Library Association of Australia and a directory of Australian libraries. This work is updated by the *Biographical directory of australian librarians* (entry **253**).

New Zealand

256 Who's who in New Zealand libraries, 1980. Comp. by Al Olsson and Alan D. Richardson. 8th ed. Wellington: New Zealand Library Assn., 1981. 35p. LC 58–17222. ISBN 0–908560–06–0.
The first edition of this work appeared in 1951, and subsequent editions have appeared

71

periodically. The current edition has approximately 1,050 entries, about 500 of which are new since the previous edition (1975). The compilers tried to make the work as complete as possible. When information was not supplied by individuals, it was obtained from public records. Included are persons engaged in library work in New Zealand (or on temporary leave of absence) who hold professional qualifications from New Zealand or elsewhere. Although the entries are brief, they include name, present position and date of appointment, place and year of birth, degrees and dates awarded, previous positions held, positions in the New Zealand Library Association, publications, home address, and other information. A separate list identifies all persons included by the name of the library where they are employed.

EUROPE

European biographical sources are listed alphabetically by title within country of coverage.

Finland

257 Suomen kirjastonhoitajat, 1973/Finlands bibliotekarier, 1973. Comp. by Juuso Salokoski and Teena Teinila. Helsinki: Suomen Kirjastoseura, 1974. 216p. LC 75–593093. ISBN 951–9025–16–2.

Biographical information on Finnish librarians is given here in brief, "telegraphic" entries. The arrangement is alphabetical. An earlier edition, which contained 900 entries, was published in 1968.

German Democratic Republic

258 Jahrbuch der bibliotheken, archive und informationstellen der Deutschen Demokratischen Republik. Leipzig: VEB Bibliographisches Inst., 1959– . Biennial. LC 63–28931.

Although the major purpose of this work is to provide information about approximately 2,000 libraries in the German Democratic Republic, each volume includes brief biographical information about the directors of the libraries identified. The first issue was published by the Deutsche Staatsbiblothek (Berlin); the current publisher took over in 1961. For further information see entry **359**.

Germany, Federal Republic of

259 Jahrbuch der deutschen bibliotheken: herausgegeben vom verein deutscher bibliothekare. Wiesbaden: Harrassowitz, 1902– . Biennial. LC 2–17084.

This is a directory of libraries in the Federal Republic of Germany and West Berlin. The latest edition lists 689 libraries. Librarians are identified in the entries, and a separate section provides biographical information about each. For further information see entry **363**.

Italy

260   Aggiunte al "dizionàrio biografico dei bibliotecari e bibliofili italiani" di Carlo Frati. By Marino Parenti. Florence: Sansoni Antiquariato, 1952–1960. 3v.
This work is a continuation of the biographical directory by Carlo Frati (entry **261**). The two include biographies of Italian librarians and others associated with books, through publishing or book collecting. The coverage is retrospective. The length of the entries varies, but some are quite long and accompanied by extensive bibliographies. Arrangement is alphabetical, with a geographical index to libraries identified in the text provided. There is also an author index to all items cited in the bibliographies. The three-volume supplement adds entries not found in Frati's earlier work.

261   Dizionario bio-bibliografico dei bibliotecari e bibliofili italiani dal sec. XIV al XIX. By Carlo Frati. Florence: Olschki, 1933. 705p. LC 33–37953.
This work is continued by *Aggiunte al "dizionario biografico dei bibliotecari e bibliofili italiani" di Carlo Frati*. For further information see entry **260**.

Norway

262   Norsk bibliotekarmatrikkel. By Tore Hernes. Oslo: Biblioteksentralen, 1969. 166p. LC 73–481070.
These brief biographical sketches of Norwegien librarians are arranged alphabetically. Persons who attended the Bibliotekskole from 1940 to 1969 are also included.

United Kingdom

263   Aslib membership list, 1964– . London: Aslib, 1964– . Annual.
Currently, Aslib's membership exceeds 24,000, making it one of the largest library associations in the world. A high percentage of the special librarians in the United Kingdom are among the members identified by position held, institutional affiliation, and address. This publication supersedes the *Aslib yearbook* (entry **264**), which in turn superseded *Members and associate members* (entry **266**), published when the organization was known as the Association of Special Libraries and Information Bureaux. The association became known as Aslib in 1948.

264   Aslib yearbook. London: Aslib, 1948–1963. Annual.
This work is superseded by *Aslib membership list*. For further information see entry **263**.

265   Library Association: yearbook. London: Library Assn., 1891– . LC 01–15606. ISSN 0075–9006.
The *Yearbook* is a combination directory and handbook. It includes the names of all members, with position, institutional affiliation, address, and professional interests. Home and overseas affiliated institutional members are also listed. In addition, basic information about the association is presented in the handbook section. The royal charter and the bylaws are printed, together with the names of officers of the association, group and section officers, and other miscellaneous information.

266 Members and associate members. London: Assn. of Special Libraries and Information Bureaux, 1926–1947. Annual.
This work is superseded by *Aslib yearbook* and *Aslib membership list, 1964– .* For further information see entry **263**.

267 Who's who in librarianship and information science. Ed. by Thomas Landau. 2d ed. London: Abelard-Schuman, 1972. 311p. LC 70–184398. ISBN 0–200–71871–1.
Biographical sketches for approximately 2,000 British librarians are included here. Each entry provides the person's name, home address, position and place of employment, year and place of birth, all schools attended, previous professional experience, association memberships, publications, and special interests. Because no preface is included, there is no way to establish the criteria for inclusion. An appendix identifies persons by special interest or competency. The first edition of this work, published in 1954 and titled *Who's who in librarianship*, had approximately 3,000 entries.

NORTH AND SOUTH AMERICA

American biographical sources are listed alphabetically by title under country of coverage within three main divisions: Canada, Latin America, and United States.

Canada

268 CLA directory, 1978–1979. Ottawa: Canadian Library Assn.; New York: K. G. Saur, distr., 1979. 115p. ISBN 0–88802–128–3.
Personal, associate, institutional, and life members of the Canadian Library Association are listed here, along with their addresses and institutional affiliations. Information about the association, such as the organizational structure, position statements, constitution and bylaws, and names of officers, makes this a handbook for the association as well as a membership directory. This work was formerly known as the *CLA list of members* (entry **269**) and later as the *CLA organization handbook and membership list* (entry **270**).

269 CLA list of members. Ottawa: Canadian Library Assn., 19??–1978. Irreg.
This title is superseded by *CLA directory, 1978–1979.* For further information see entry **268**.

270 CLA organization handbook and membership list. Ottawa: Canadian Library Assn., 19??–1978. Irreg.
This title is superseded by *CLA directory, 1978–1979.* For further information see entry **268**.

Latin America

BRAZIL

271 **Quem é quem na biblioteconomia e documentaçao no Brasil.** Rio de Janeiro: Inst.
Brasileiro de Bibliografia e Documentação, 1971. 544p. LC 72–502390.
A total of 1,386 Brazilian librarians and documentalists are included in this work. Listings
are arranged state by state, and then alphabetically by name within each state. There is also
alphabetical access by personal name. Entries include education, experience, and institutional affiliation.

WEST INDIES

272 **West indian library and archival personnel: a directory of individuals engaged in
library service, archival activities and related areas in the West Indies.** Comp. by
Robert V. Vaughn. 2d ed. Christiansted, St. Croix: 1972. 90p. LC 18–7164.
Coverage of library and archival personnel extends to all islands in the Caribbean and
includes the Bahamas, Bermuda, Guyana, and Surinam. Approximately 1,200 persons are
listed. Entries are arranged geographically and then by political subdivision. Each entry
includes the full name, institutional affiliation, and address of the institution. A useful
feature is a map showing the location of geographical and political subdivisions.

United States

273 **ALA handbook of organization and membership directory.** Chicago: American
Library Assn., 1980– . Annual. LC 73–617320. ISSN 0084–6406.
This work is the product of a merger of the *ALA handbook of organization* with the *ALA
membership directory*, each of which was published separately until 1980. The *Handbook* is
still published separately, but the *Membership directory* is available only in this combination
format. The 1982–1983 volume lists nearly 38,000 persons. It is arranged alphabetically,
and each entry includes position, affiliation, and mailing address. In addition, extensive
information is provided about the association, including the names of elected and appointed
officers, ALA divisions and round tables, members of committees, the headquarter's staff,
the constitution and bylaws, and all current policies. Numerous other miscellaneous items
are also included in the handbook section.

274 **ALA membership directory, 1949–1979.** Chicago: American Library Assn.,
1950–1979. Annual. LC 50–3095.
Beginning with the 1980 volume, the *Directory* was merged with the *ALA handbook of
organization* to form the *ALA handbook of organization and membership directory* (entry
273). Entries are arranged alphabetically and include the individual's position, affiliation,
and mailing address. When the *Directory* was first published, ALA's membership was less
than 20,000, and when it merged with the *Handbook,* membership had exceeded 35,000.

275 **ASIS handbook and directory.** Washington, DC: ASIS, 1971– . Annual. LC
79–5696. ISSN 0066–0124.
The membership directory is reproduced from the ASIS Member Records System and is
current to late March of the year covered. The 1982 directory lists 3,800 regular and retired

members, 472 student members, and more than 100 institutional members. The entries are alphabetical by last name and include position, affiliation, address, telephone number, and chapter and special interest codes. Lists of chapter and special interest group memberships are also available. Information about ASIS—such as the constitution and bylaws, chapter and special interest group officers, and officers of the association—augments the directory. The organization was originally established in 1937 as the American Documentation Institute. During the years it was known by that name, its directory was titled, successively, *A.D.I. membership list, The A.D.I. directory,* and *A.D.I. handbook and directory.* In 1968, the association changed its name and the title of its directory.

276 Biographical directory of librarians in the United States and Canada. Ed. by Lee Ash. 5th ed. Chicago: American Library Assn., 1970. 1,250p. LC 79–118854. ISBN 0–8389–0084–4.
Approximately 20,000 librarians, information scientists, archivists, and other individuals involved in some type of information service activity are identified in this work. Although this is updated by *Who's who in library and information services* (entry **280**), there are several thousand individuals listed here who are not found in the later publication. Also, for those persons included in the later or earlier editions, added information can be found here. The abbreviated, "telegraphic" entries list name, place and date of birth, name of spouse, education, languages read or spoken with facility, positions held (in progressive order), professional activities, principal associations in which the individual has held positions of responsibility, honors and awards, publications, and other information. This publication is the fifth edition of a work formerly titled *Who's who in library service* (entry **281**), which began in 1933.

277 Dictionary of american library biography. Ed. by Bohdan S. Wynar. Littleton, CO: Libraries Unlimited, 1978. 596p. LC 77–28791. ISBN 0–87287–180–0.
Patterned after the major national biographies, this publication provides biographical articles for 301 individuals who, in the judgment of the editorial board, have made a significant contribution to librarianship in the United States. The articles vary in length, from about 1,000 words to 6,000 words or more. One major criterion for inclusion was that the individual must have been deceased prior to June 30, 1976. Coverage extends backward to colonial times. An advisory board consisting of fourteen prominent contemporary librarians with a strong knowledge of library history selected those included. Articles were contributed by 217 authors. Most entries provide information about family background and personal interests, as well as the expected educational and career data. Also, bibliographic references identify other biographical sources and primary resource materials. All articles are signed, and access to the alphabetical listing is augmented by a detailed name index. Although there are a number of separate scholarly biographies of prominent librarians and others who made contributions to librarianship in the United States, this is the only major scholarly compilation on American librarians.

278 Librarians of Congress, 1802–1974. Washington, DC: Library of Congress, 1977. 273p. LC 77–608073. ISBN 030–001–00080–0.
These lengthy biographical articles on the eleven persons who held the position of Librarian of Congress prior to the appointment of Daniel J. Boorstin, the incumbent, deal not only with

the details of the person's professional and personal life, but also indicate how the library itself developed under each administration.

279 The librarian's phone book, 1981– . Ed. by Jaques Cattell Press. New York: Bowker, 1980– . Annual. LC 81–640061. ISSN 0195–332X.

Phone numbers for more than 55,000 individuals are listed here. Included are library directors, library branch and department heads, heads of library consortia, heads of library education programs, and others. Each entry provides the individual's name, institutional affiliation, an identifiable branch or department listing, the city and state, and the telephone number. The listing is based in large part on the information found in *The american library directory* (entry **425**).

280 Who's who in library and information services. Ed. by Joel M. Lee. Chicago: American Library Assn., 1982. 559p. LC 81–20450. ISBN 0–8389–0351–7.

This is the sixth edition of the major biographical directory of librarians and other information professionals in the United States and Canada. The earlier editions have appeared under the sponsorship of various organizations, under different titles, and at irregular intervals since the first edition was published in 1933. The current work includes biographical sketches for 12,000 individuals. Eligible for inclusion were all librarians, information scientists, archivists, and library educators with professional credentials who are employed (or recently retired) in the United States and Canada. Also eligible were professionals employed abroad for United States or Canadian military, diplomatic, professional, or other agencies. Information was obtained from respondents and, when prominent persons failed to respond, from other public sources. Specific requests not to be included were honored. A substantial amount of information is available in each entry, although some of it is coded in order to reduce the space required. Entries include preferred form of name, birth date, employment history, education, library/information-related organization memberships, other memberships, honors and awards, principal publications, and principal areas of professional activities. The last category is coded, requiring the user to refer to numbered categories at the bottom of each page for type of institution, functions/activities, or special subjects/services. The previous edition appeared under the title *Biographical directory of librarians in the United States and Canada* (entry **276**), and earlier editions under the title *Who's who in library service* (entry **281**).

281 Who's who in library service: a biographical directory of professional librarians in the United States and Canada. Ed. by Lee Ash, B. A. Uhlendorf, and Martha J. Sullivan. 4th ed. Hamden, CT: Shoe String, 1966. 776p. LC 66–24910.

Biographical entries for more than 20,000 librarians and other information professionals appear in this work. It is similar to *A Biographical directory of librarians in the United States and Canada* (entry **276**), which is considered the fifth edition of the work. The first edition appeared in 1933 with 5,764 entries. Subsequent editions were published in 1943 (8,869 entries) and 1955 (11,000 plus entries). The earlier editions continue to have value for retrospective biographical searching.

282 Who's who in special libraries, 1980/81– . New York: Special Libraries Assn., 1980– . Annual. LC 82–644142. ISSN 0278–842X.

The directory lists individuals alphabetically, geographically (by SLA chapter membership), and by membership in the association's professional interest divisions. The more than 11,000 names included in the 1982–1983 volume represent the association's membership at that time. Each entry includes name, position, affiliation (for most members), home or work address, and in many instances telephone number. Also included here are SLA bylaws, officers of the association, chapter officers, division officers, and a list of all division bulletins, with information about the coverage, editor, frequency, etc. Other miscellaneous information about the association is also provided. This directory was first published in 1937 and then irregularly until 1970 (1948, 1951, 1956, 1962, and 1969–1970). The directory was then incorporated as a separate issue of *Special libraries,* until 1980, when it was again published separately.

5.

Directories of Libraries and Archives

INTRODUCTION

Within the library field, there is an ongoing need for comprehensive and up-to-date listings of libraries, archives, information centers, and other information agencies. Despite the hundreds of library-related directories that are currently in print, however, various regions of the world are served unequally by these publications. For some areas in the United States, directory coverage is excellent; for others, it is not. This situation also applies to other nations of the world. Not all libraries or archives in a country (not even the major ones) are necessarily listed in a directory.

Most directories are compiled from information received from the listed libraries. This means that the compilations are seldom comprehensive; invariably, some libraries fail to respond. The nature of the information included in a directory corresponds to the purposes intended by the compiler. Some directories have been prepared to facilitate contact among libraries or archives. These directories tend to be limited to institutional name, address, telephone number, and other locational data. Other directories have been compiled to report basic information about the nature of the holdings and the services offered. Among the categories of additional information found in these directories are library hours; name and address of the director (and sometimes other staff members); services available (e.g., photocopying, online searching); public access policies; special collections; subject strengths; and library network affiliations. A small number of directories, however, describe the resources, holdings, and facilities available in some depth and detail (including such information as the availability of parking and public transportation near the library or archives).

Although most directories are issued serially (because up-to-date data on information agencies is vital), not all titles are updated systematically. Some important directories have never been revised. Although it is true that directory information becomes dated quickly, older directories still retain value for researchers. Often, older directories contain detailed information about library holdings. While not current, the information does provide some insight into the nature of the collection. Furthermore, there may be no other place to uncover the scope of libraries or collections that over the years have ceased to exist. Finally, no single directory is comprehensive. It is necessary for researchers to use a variety of sources, both current and outdated, to identify all relevant agencies. For these reasons, we have chosen to cover both contemporary and retrospective library-related directories in this chapter of the guide.

Ongoing bibliographic coverage of all library-related directories would be impractical and impossible. So, too, would be the comprehensive acquisition of these directories. However, bibliographic coverage of selected major directories is desirable as a means of further increasing their utility to librarians and archivists. Therefore, this chapter lists and describes 262 international, continental, national, regional, state, and local directories of libraries and other information agencies. The emphasis is on current listings; retrospective sources are included only if more recent or comprehensive publications covering the same area are not available. Only general directories are covered here, i.e., those surveying all types of libraries—public, academic, school, and/or special. Special purpose directories—those focusing on cooperative ventures, special collections, or other specialized areas—are treated in appropriate subject sections in Chapter 7.

There are few important library-related directories that provide international coverage. Of the 262 sources included in this chapter, less than six percent of them fall into this category. Directories that identify libraries within a single country or countries within a single region are more commonly available. This guide describes 146 of these more geographically-restricted directories. These publications typically cover national, college and university, public, state and provincial, and various types of special libraries. (School libraries are usually excluded.) Directories have also been compiled for major and minor political subdivisions (regions, states, provinces, departments) and for local areas (cities, counties, etc.). This guide features directories surveying library and other information agencies in six Australian provinces or territories, seven Canadian provinces, forty-nine states (only Mississippi is without a separately published library listing), and two U.S. possessions.

INTERNATIONAL

International directories are listed alphabetically by title without regard to countries of coverage or publication.

283   The international directory of manuscripts collections, libraries, private collections, repositories and archives/Répertoire des bibliothèques, collections, dépòts de manuscrits et archives dans le monde. Paris: Berger-Levrault, 1978– . v.1– . v.1, pt.1, **Europe: The manuscript collections.** Ed. by G. E. Weil. 1978. 301p. LC 79–309603. ISBN 2–7013–0231–5.

This is intended to be a comprehensive guide to manuscript collections in libraries and other types of institutions throughout the world. Volume 1, part 1, the only part currently available, provides coverage of Europe; volume 2 will provide coverage of the rest of the world. Volume 1 provides data for 3,209 European institutions that have manuscript holdings. Manuscripts include "hand-written works, books, documents, bundles of papers or deeds." Each volume is to be divided into three parts. Part 1 lists the locations of manuscript collections. Arrangement is alphabetical by name of the city or town in the language of the country. An exception is the use of the English translation of place names not in the Roman alphabet. Within city or town sections, institutions are arranged alphabetically by name. This part is accompanied by an alphabetical index of institutions, an index of private collections, and an alphabetical index of all the cities or towns. Part 2, yet to be published, will list the manuscripts held by the collections according to the languages they contain. It will also list collections by type of resource, such as incunabula, epigraphical collections, numismatic collections, and print collections. Part 3 will list titles of catalogs and other bibliographical sources that identify and describe the holdings of manuscript and archive collections. When complete, this will be the most extensive directory of manuscript collections ever produced. However, the description provided for each is brief. The various sections of the publication must be used together to obtain maximum information about any particular manuscript collection.

284 International library directory: a world directory of libraries, 1969–70. By A. P. Wales. 3d ed. London: A. P. Wales Organization, 1968. 1,222p. LC 63–23734.
Approximately 40,000 libraries in more than 150 nations are listed in this directory. Arrangement is by country, state or province, city or town, and alphabetically within each locale. Entries contain the name and address of the library, name of the library director, numerical data on the holdings, subject areas covered, and type of library. Subject areas (forty) and type of library are indicated by means of symbols. Library names and subjects are not indexed. Although dated, this work is helpful when used in conjunction with more current and more detailed directories for individual countries.

285 Internationales bibliotheks-handbuch: world guide to libraries. 2d ed. Munich: Verlag Dokumentation, 1968. 2v. LC 72–627058.
This work is superseded by *World guide to libraries.* For further information see entry **288**.

286 Internationales bibliotheksadressbuch: world guide to libraries. Comp. by Klaus Gerhard Saur. Munich: Verlag Dokumentation, 1966. 2v. LC 67–4109.
This work is superseded by *World guide to libraries.* For further information see entry **288**.

287 Major libraries of the world: a selective guide. By Colin Steele. New York: Bowker, 1976. 479p. LC 77–369002. ISBN 0–85935–012–6.
Although highly selective in coverage, this work provides considerable detail for each of the 300 libraries, from seventy-nine countries, covered. Each entry includes name, address, and telephone number, a brief history of the library, identification of special collections, hours of opening, access by public transportation, services offered, type of catalogs and classification used, requirements for admission, and reprographic services available. Arrangement is alphabetical by country and city. The text is augmented by numerous black-and-white photographs of library facilities and publications. Most of the information is current to 1974 or 1975. This is the only international directory that provides such detailed coverage for individual libraries. But because of the limited number of libraries covered, many users will probably still find it necessary to consult national directories.

288 World guide to libraries. Ed. by Helen Lengenfelder. 6th ed. Munich: K. G. Saur, 1983. 1,181p. ISBN 0–89664–043–4. ISSN 0000–0221.

The most comprehensive international directory of libraries, this work lists 42,700 libraries in 167 countries. All old entries have been updated. National libraries, college and university libraries, public libraries with at least 30,000 titles, general research libraries, and special libraries with at least 3,000 titles are included. Size limitations are waived for some newly established Third World countries. The guide consists of two sections: the directory and a detailed subject index which provides 120,000 subject references. The directory is arranged by country, then by type of library, e.g., national libraries; university, college, and professional school libraries; corporate and business libraries. Each entry contains the name, address, telephone and telex numbers of the library, name of the director, departmental libraries, special collections, affiliation with national library associations, some statistical information about each library, and interlibrary loan status. Title varies slightly for earlier editions (entries **285, 286,** and **289**).

289 World guide to libraries/Internationales bibliotheks-handbuch. 4th ed. Munich: Verlag Dokumentation, 1974. 2v. ISBN 3–7940–1788–9.

This work is superseded by *World guide to libraries.* For further information see entry **288.**

290 World guide to technical information and documentation services/Guide mondial des centres de documentation et d'information technique. 2d ed., rev. and enl. Paris: Unesco, 1975. 515p. LC–325752. ISBN 92–3–001228–9.

Listed and described in this 1975 directory are international and national centers for the documentation of scientific and technical information. A total of ninety-three countries are represented. While much of the information is now out of date, the directory can still be used to indicate the existence and types of responsibilities held by the centers. Entries are arranged by the English spelling of the name of the country, and then by the name of the institution within that country. The information provided includes name, address, telephone number, names of key personnel, size of staff, size of holdings, bibliographic publications produced by the centers, policies regarding the copying of materials, methods of payment, and languages in which the centers will correspond.

291 The world of learning. London: Europa, 1947– . 2v. Annual. LC 47–30172.

This well-established directory of cultural and educational institutions throughout the world includes brief information about leading libraries in most countries. The arrangement is alphabetical by country and then by type of institution. Within the section for each country is a subheading for libraries and archives. For larger countries, libraries not listed in that section are sometimes noted under the name of the institution of which they are a part. For example, most college and university libraries in the United States are given under the name of the institution. Entries are brief, usually listing the city of location, date of establishment, any affiliations with other institutions, subject strengths, holdings, and the name of the library director. For some countries, a separate archives section is provided. Access to separately listed libraries is available under the general heading "Library" in the index. This directory is especially valuable for identifying libraries where no current national directory is available. However, when compared to extensive national directories, the number of libraries listed here is very limited. For example, fewer than fifty special libraries are listed for the United States.

AFRICA AND THE MIDDLE EAST

African and Middle Eastern directories with continental coverage are listed first, alphabetically by title. Directories with national coverage are arranged alphabetically by title under the country name.

292   The african book world & press. Ed. by Hans Zell. 2d ed. Munich: K. G. Saur, 1980. 224p. LC 76–56994. ISBN 0–8103–0990–4.

Libraries, booksellers, publishers, newspapers, literary associations, and various related activities are listed for the nations of Africa. Arrangement is alphabetical by country, and then by topic within each country section. Information is in both English and French. Although libraries are only one type of institution included, a number of important academic, public, government, and special libraries are identified for each country. Entries include the name, address, and telephone number of the library, library director, name of the acquisitions and serials librarians of the larger libraries, professional staff size, collection size, acquisitions budget, subject strengths and special collections, and any publications issued by the library. Similar data are provided for publishers and related organizations. A useful feature is a list of principal dealers in African books in the United States and Europe. Also included is a directory of government and major commercial printers in Africa.

293   A book world directory of the arab countries, Turkey and Iran. Comp. by Anthony Rudkin and Irene Butcher. Detroit: Gale, 1981. 143p. LC 81–171146. ISBN 0–8103–1185–2.

This directory provides information on eighteen Arab countries of North Africa and the Middle East, plus Turkey and Iran. Approximately 1,400 numbered entries identify such book world-related institutions and organizations as libraries, publishers, booksellers, newspapers, and periodicals. The entries for libraries are brief, but include name, address, type of library, and subject strengths. Libraries are indexed by subject areas covered, booksellers by subject area and nature of business, and publishers by subjects of specialization.

294   Directory of archives, libraries and schools of librarianship in Africa/Répertoire des archives, bibliothèques et écoles de bibliothéconomie d'Afrique. By E. W. Dadzie and J. T. Strickland. Paris: Unesco, 1965. 112p. LC 65–5420.

This work is superseded by *Directory of documentation, libraries and archives services in Africa/Répertoire des services de documentation, de bibliothèque et d'archives d'Afrique.* For further information see entry **295**.

295   Directory of documentation, libraries and archives services in Africa/Répertoire des services de documentation, de bibliothèque et d'archives d'Afrique. By Dominique Zidouemba. 2d ed. Rev. and enl. by Eric de Grolier. Paris: Unesco, 1977. 311p. LC 78–363372. ISBN 92–3–001479–6.

Arranged by country, this directory covers national libraries, archives, national documentation centers, college and university libraries, public libraries, special libraries, library education or training programs, and library associations for each nation listed. All countries in Africa are included except South Africa, Namibia, and some of the smaller territories.

Information was compiled through May 1975. The information for each country is either in English or French, depending on the European language predominantly used in the country. Data contained in each entry vary, depending on the type of institution. Entries for libraries or archives include a brief historical statement, the name and address of the institution, hours of opening, services, number of seats available, percentage of the collection in various languages, classification scheme used, publications, and, where applicable, number of branches or departments. For library education or training programs, a brief statement of the degree offerings, admission requirements, program of study, and faculty members is provided. The directory is indexed in English and French. The second edition was revised and enlarged to add North African countries. South Africa, which was included in the first edition, *Directory of archives, libraries and schools of librarianship in Africa* (entry **294**), is dropped from the second edition.

296 Directory of southern african libraries/Gids van biblioteke in Suider-Afrika. Comp. and ed. by M. M. Boshoff. 3d ed. Pretoria: State Library, 1976. 301p. LC 77–362748. ISBN 0–7989–0036–9.

This work covers 865 libraries in South Africa and ninety-one libraries in Botswana, Lesotho, Malawi, South West Africa (Namibia), Swaziland, and Zambia. Zimbabwe (Rhodesia) is not included, although it was covered in the previous edition. All types of libraries, except school libraries and depots of provincial library services, are listed, although for some, no information was supplied to the compiler. Arrangement is by country and, for South Africa, by type of library, then alphabetically by library name. Entries give the name and address, hours of opening, services, classification system used, holdings, a brief history, and budget data. Fields of specialization and special collections are also indicated. The work is indexed by institutional name, subject, and geographical area. The previous edition was titled *Handbook of southern african libraries* (entry **297**).

297 Handbook of southern african libraries/Handboek van biblioteke in Suider Afrika. Pretoria: State Library, 1970. 939p. LC 75–14937.

This work is superseded by the *Directory of southern african libraries/Gids van biblioteke in Suider-Afrika.* For further information see entry **296**.

Botswana

298 Directory of libraries in Botswana. Comp. by B. L. B. Mushonga. Gaborone: Documentation Unit, National Inst. for Research in Development and African Studies, 1977. 55p. LC 78–307980.

Brief information is given on fifty-three government, private, and school libraries in Botswana. Entries contain name, address, telephone number, characterization of the library, size of collection, subject areas covered, loan period, and hours open. Some of the libraries described are very small and probably not listed elsewhere.

Ethiopia

299 Directory of ethiopian libraries. Comp. and ed. by Geraldine Odester Amos, et al. Addis Ababa: Ethiopian Library Assn., 1968. 76p. LC 70–980981.

This alphabetical list covers ninety-four Ethiopian college and university, public, special, and school libraries. Entries are brief, but contain location by city and province, the name of the governing body, size of staff, number of volumes, subjects covered, classification system used, and whether or not photocopying equipment is available. Although out of date, the directory can be used to augment more current listings.

300 Directory of special libraries in Ethiopia. Addis Ababa: Special Library Committee, Ethiopian Library Assn., 1976. 15p. LC 78–980825.
A total of forty-one entries are included here. In typed copy, each entry lists the name, address, telephone number, size and composition of the collection, classification system used, availability of public catalog, publications, and name of the librarian. Librarians are also listed separately.

Ghana

301 Directory of libraries in Ghana. Comp. by Andre Nitecki. Legon: Dept. of Library and Archival Studies, Univ. of Ghana, 1974. 62p. (University of Ghana, Department of Library and Archival Studies, Occasional papers, no. 1) LC 79–312700.
Of the 130 libraries identified here, fifty-two are listed in the main directory, twenty-two are noted at the work's end, and fifty-six branches are cited with the main libraries. Various types of libraries are covered. Arrangement is alphabetical by name of library. Entries include address, hours of opening, area of specialization, staff size, size of collection, clientele, and seating accommodations.

302 Directory of special and research libraries in Ghana. Comp. by L. Agyei-Gyane. Accra: CSIR Central Reference and Research Library, 1977. 81p. LC 80–120212.
This alphabetical list of sixty-six special libraries provides name and address, librarian's name, staff size, hours of opening, public access, scope of the collection, special collections, stock (by type of material), services, and publications issued by the library. A subject index is included.

India

303 Directory of booksellers, publishers, libraries and librarians in India (who's who). Ed. by Raj K. Khosla. 2d ed. New Delhi: Premier, 1973. 300p. LC 73–900620.
This directory updates the 1968 edition and includes information about state, public, and special libraries in India. Entries are brief and provide little more than the name and address of the library and an indication of type. A second section contains biographical information on 800 librarians in India (see entry **246**).

304 Directory of libraries and who's who in library profession in Delhi. Ed. by N. K. Goil, et al. Delhi: Delhi Library Assn., 1964. 91p. LC 65–1646.
This classified list of 105 academic, state, and public libraries in India provides the name and address and a brief description of the library, including size, types of resources, classification system used, type of catalog, and rules for use. Although the information about individual libraries is now out of date, the directory can still be used to identify and locate major libraries. However, coverage is not comprehensive. A biographical section lists and identifies over 500 librarians in the Delhi area (see entry **247**).

305 Directory of libraries in Delhi. By Kumar Surendar. New Delhi: Sterling Publishers, 1973. 63p. LC 73–902263.

A total of 332 libraries of various types in the Delhi area are listed in this 1973 directory. Entries are arranged alphabetically and specify library name, date of establishment, address, number of volumes held, name of librarian, and size of staff. There is a subject index.

306 Indian library directory. 3d ed. Delhi: Indian Library Assn., 1951. 117p. LC 52–8140.

Although this work is badly out of date, it provides extensive coverage of 363 Indian libraries with collections of more than 5,000 titles. Entries, grouped by location and type of library, describe collection size, personnel, subject specializations, and expenditures. Library schools are also identified, and one chapter provides biographical data on 125 notable librarians. Previous editions were published in 1938 and 1944.

307 Libraries in Delhi: a comprehensive list. Ed. by S. K. Bhatia. Delhi: D. K. Publications, 1979. 48p. LC 79–906170.

Approximately 600 libraries of various types in the Delhi area are listed in this directory. Included are international and foreign organizations or agencies as well as municipal, college and university, business, medical, and government libraries. The only information contained in each entry is name and address.

308 Men of library science and libraries in India. Ed. by Raj K. Khosla and M. K. Gaur. New Delhi: Premier, 1967. 74p. LC 75–646305. ISSN 0377–1342.

The directory portion of this work lists 540 major libraries throughout India. Arrangement is geographical, with additional access by subject coverage. Entries are brief and include name and address and name of the librarian. The biographical section of this work lists and identifies about 400 persons (see entry **248**).

309 Research facilities in Delhi. By W. Robert Holmes and S. Raj Gopal. 2d ed. Delhi: Kwalitz Booksellers and Publishers, 1969. 124p. LC 79–908049.

Listed here are 114 major academic, public, special, and research libraries in the Delhi area. Information provided includes type and size of collection, hours of opening, staff size, and publications. A subject index is included. The first edition was issued in 1967.

Iran

310 A book world directory of the arab countries, Turkey and Iran. Comp. by Anthony Rudkin and Irene Butcher. Detroit: Gale, 1981. 143p. LC 81–171146. ISBN 0–8103–1185–2.

This directory provides information on eighteen Arab countries of North Africa and the Middle East, plus Turkey and Iran. For further information see entry **293**.

Israel

311 Directory of special libraries in Israel. 5th ed. Tel Aviv: COSTI, 1980. 132p. ISBN 965–228–000–3. ISSN 0070–637X.

Directory information is presented in Hebrew and English for 320 special libraries throughout Israel, in such fields as agriculture, medicine, and public affairs. Included are libraries in colleges and universities, technical institutes, professional organizations, businesses, and other types of special libraries. Entries contain the name, address, and telephone number of the library, the director's name, numerical data on the holdings, and an indication of collection strengths.

312   A guide to Jerusalem libraries. By Mathilde A. Tagger. Jerusalem: Inst. for Israel
 Studies, 1982. 123p.
Approximately 250 public, academic, special, church and monastic, and religious libraries in Jerusalem are described in this directory. Entries are written in English and supply name, address, and telephone number. Indexing is by library name, language (for those libraries specializing in foreign literature), subject, and libraries with nonbook collections.

Kenya

313   Directory of libraries in Kenya. Comp. and ed. by J. R. Njuguna. Nairobi: Gazelle,
 1977. 102p. LC 77–981076.
A total of ninety-six libraries of all types are covered in this directory. Arrangement is alphabetical by the name of the library. Each entry contains name and address, subject strengths, special collections, classification system used, type of catalog, and name of the person in charge. Libraries listed range from the largest in the country to some that are very small. The directory is indexed by subject and personal names.

Pakistan

314   Libraries in Pakistan: a comprehensive list. Karachi: Library Promotion Bureau,
 1970. 54p. LC 79–932570.
About 1,500 libraries are listed in this directory. School, public, academic, and special libraries are covered, but information is very limited. For most, only the name appears; for a few, the address is also included. Published prior to the breaking away of East Pakistan into Bangladesh, this directory is broadly divided into East and West Pakistan sections.

315   Libraries in Pakistan: a guide. Karachi: National Book Centre, 1968. 36p. LC SA
 68–11959.
This simple list offers no information about individual libraries. Public and academic libraries are divided into two categories, East Pakistan and West Pakistan. Special libraries are grouped into twenty-four subject categories.

**316   Pakistan library directory: a classified list of libraries in Pakistan with personnel
 and statistical data, a list of major publishers and book-sellers, a bibliography of
 Pakistan librarianship, and an area index.** Ed. by A. B. M. Shamsuddoulah.
 Dacca: Great Eastern Books, 1970. 156p. LC 71–931634.
This work covers 751 academic, public, and special libraries. Arrangement is alphabetical by name of library. In addition to the name and address of the library, each entry includes a brief statement about the collection and the librarian's name. The directory is indexed by geographical location. Also included is a list of publishers and booksellers in Pakistan.

Turkey

317 **A book world directory of the arab countries, Turkey and Iran.** Comp. by Anthony Rudkin and Irene Butcher. Detroit: Gale, 1981. 143p. LC 81–171146. ISBN 0–8103–1185–2.

This directory provides information on eighteen Arab countries of North Africa and the Middle East, plus Turkey and Iran. For further information see entry **293**.

Zimbabwe

318 **Directory of rhodesian libraries.** Comp. and ed. by Digby Hartridge and Toba Robarts. 2d ed. Salisbury: National Archives of Rhodesia, 1975. 24p. LC 78–301444. ISBN 0–7974–0062–1.

A total of 237 libraries are listed in this directory. Arranged geographically by city or town and indexed by subject, entries cover public, academic, and special libraries. The information provided includes name and address, hours of opening, subject strengths and special collections, numerical data on holdings, and policies regarding public access.

ASIA

Asian directories are arranged alphabetically by title within country or region of publication.

China, People's Republic of

319 **Directory of chinese libraries.** Ed. by Wu Renyong, Wang Enguang, and Xia Wanruo. Beijing: China Academic Pr.; Detroit: Gale, distr., 1982. 428p. (World books reference guide, v.3).

This directory provides bilingual (English and Chinese) coverage of more than 3,000 libraries in the People's Republic of China. It describes many libraries about which little or no information has previously been available in the West. Included are major libraries that have foreign-language holdings; public libraries; college and university libraries; special libraries and libraries of government agencies and major academies. Emphasis is on libraries of the Academia Sinica (Chinese Academy of Sciences), the Academies of Social Sciences, Agricultural Sciences, Medical Sciences, Forestry, and the Beijing Astronomical Observatory. The directory is arranged in four parts. The first lists and describes in detail 658 libraries with holdings in Chinese and foreign languages. The second part provides names and addresses of 2,887 Chinese libraries. Entries that appear in the first part are noted. The third part is an index of library names by the English equivalent. Citations are to the numbered entries. The fourth part, an appendix, includes an additional seventy-three libraries. Parts 1 and 2 are subdivided by type of library, with public libraries listed first, followed by academic and special libraries, and then libraries of higher education establishments. The detailed entries in Part 1 include name and address, date founded, telephone and cable numbers, numerical data on holdings, scope and features of the collection, number of seats available, services, exchange policies, publications available for exchange, name of the librarian, staff size, and publications produced by the library. A separate list at the end of the volume identifies all libraries with holdings of more than 500,000 volumes, ranked by size.

Hong Kong

320 Library services in Hong Kong, a new directory. Comp. by Kan Lai-bing. Hong Kong: Hong Kong Library Assn., 1975. 228p. LC 76–370140.

A total of 317 libraries in Hong Kong are listed alphabetically by name. All types of libraries are included: forty-five government department and British Armed Forces libraries; 119 school libraries, twenty-one postsecondary institutions, thirty-six special libraries, seven club/society libraries, one private library, and eighty-eight general libraries. Entries provide name and address, a description of the library, hours of opening, facilities for borrowing or consulting, copying facilities, book stock, annual expenditures, classification system used, type of catalog, seating capacity, and publications issued by the library. An index lists libraries of all types that are open to the public. An earlier edition (1968) listed about 200 libraries.

Indonesia

321 Directory of special libraries in Indonesia. Comp. by H. Kusbandarrumsansi. 5th ed. Djakarta: Indonesian National Scientific Documentation Center, Indonesian Inst. of Science, 1978. LC 77–940567. ISSN 0376–8600.

This work, first issued in 1966 and updated four times since then, is arranged geographically. It covers approximately 145 libraries. Entries contain name and address of library, name of person in charge, number of books and other materials, budget, subject areas covered, and service policies. Names and addresses are in Indonesian and English; other information is in English. The work is not indexed, but a table of contents lists the libraries.

Japan

322 Directory of information sources in Japan, 1980. Ed. by Japan Special Libraries Association. Tokyo: Nichigai Assoc., 1979. 300p. LC 81–451960.

This work identifies 1,468 public, academic, prefecture, and special libraries and other types of information services throughout Japan. The volume, in English, is based on a directory published in 1978 in Japanese, which identified more libraries (2,019), including many small public libraries not found here. Each entry provides the name of the library in Japanese (in both Chinese characters and Romanized form), the address, telephone number, number of staff members, budget, collection size, scope of the collection, public access, and name of the director of the library. Text is in Japanese and English. Entries for information services other than libraries indicate the nature of the institution, its information resources, holdings, public access, and services. An index of libraries by name in English and in Japanese and a subject index provide access to the entries.

323 Directory of special libraries, Japan. Tokyo: Japan Special Libraries Assn., 1982. n.p.

More than 1,500 special libraries in Japan are listed here. The directory is in English and based on an earlier work in Japanese. Entries are by the Romanized Japanese name of the parent institution. Entries provide name and address, telephone number, holdings, subject content, and public access policies.

324 Libraries in Japan. Ed. by International Exchange Committee, Japan Libraries Association, New ed. Tokyo: Japan Library Assn., 1980. 48p. LC 82–466119.

This is a highly selective English-language directory of libraries in Japan, intended for use by foreign visitors. Only twenty-six libraries are listed, but these are the most important academic, prefecture, special, and national government libraries. Entries include a picture of the library, a map showing the library's location, address and telephone number, a list of special collections, services offered, hours of opening, and whether or not the library loans materials. In addition, there is a narrative for each library that briefly traces its history and development. Although limited in coverage, this publication would be useful as a means of identifying major libraries in Japan.

Malaysia

325 Directory of libraries in Malaysia/Panduan perpustakaan di Malaysia. By Chng Kim See and Ahmad Bakeri bin Abu Bakar. Kuala Lumpur: Perpustakaan Negara Malaysia, 1978. 324p. LC 79–940201.

In this directory, 177 academic, special, public, and national libraries in Malaysia are covered. Entries are in Maylay and English and specify the name and address of the library, hours of opening, number of staff, size of collection, types of services offered, type of catalogs available, type of classification system used, and publications issued by the library. Indexing is by name of library and by special collections' subjects.

Philippines

326 Directory of libraries in the Philippines. Comp. by Marina G. Dayrit and others. Quezon City: Univ. of the Philippines Library, 1973. 131p. LC 75–311895.

Data on 498 libraries are supplied in this directory. Arrangement is in three broad divisions, by type of library: academic, special, and public and government. Entries list name, address, and telephone number, date established, librarian's name, number of staff members, hours of opening, collection size, and any publications produced by the library. Earlier editions were published in 1957, 1961, and 1968.

Singapore

327 Directory of libraries in Singapore. Comp. by Lena Wen Lim, Yoke-Lan Wicks, and Jenny Neo. 2d ed. Singapore: Library Assn. of Singapore, 1975. 166p. LC 76–941130.

This directory contains information on 132 libraries: public libraries, academic libraries, libraries in government agencies and religious organizations, and libraries of diplomatic missions. Each entry lists the name and address of the library, the name of the director, subject strengths, classification system used, staff size, and publications issued by the library.

Thailand

328 A directory of libraries and library training programmes in Thailand. 3d ed.
Bangkok: Unesco Regional Office for Education in Asia, 1974. 150p. LC 81–928575.
The current volume, arranged alphabetically by name of library, includes approximately 100 libraries of various types in Thailand. Entries supply name and address of the library, public access policies, subject strengths, numerical data on the size and nature of the collections, staff size, classification system used, equipment available, and publications issued by the library.

329 Directory of scientific libraries in Thailand. By S. Yanyong. Bangkok: Applied
Scientific Research, 1973. 52p.
This work lists fifty-two publicly accessible libraries with holdings in science and technology. Arrangement is alphabetical by name of library or parent organization. Entries are brief, but include name and address, staff size, subjects covered in the collections, special collections, and type of classification system used.

AUSTRALIA AND THE SOUTH PACIFIC

Australian and South Pacific directories with national coverage are arranged alphabetically by title under the country name. Directories with state coverage are listed alphabetically by title under the state name following the national directories for that country.

Australia

330 Australian and New Zealand library resources. By Robert B. Downs. London:
Mansell, 1979. 164p. ISBN 0–7201–0913–2.
This guide covers the subject holdings and collections of academic and research, state, government, and other special libraries, but does not include public libraries. Arrangement is by subject heading, such as "Transportation," "Whaling," and "Medieval Manuscripts." Libraries in both countries are grouped together rather than listed separately. Appended to the guide is a bibliography of 565 publications that reflect library holdings. Libraries are also listed by country and, for Australia, by state. Entries are indexed by subject and collection name. This guide can be used to augment other directories for both countries.

331 Bookmark 1983: an annual diary and directory. Ed. by Michael Dugan and J. S.
Hamilton. Melbourne: Australian Library Promotion Council, 1974– . Annual. ISSN 0310–0391.
This compendium of current and up-to-date information about the book world in Australia is aimed at readers, writers, librarians, publishers, and booksellers. It provides directory information about library associations, publishers, booksellers, and libraries. Also included are lists of publications related to the book world; courses in library education and programs for writers, editors, and those in the book trade; and literary events. In addition, miscellaneous information about the book world is supplied, including copyright, preparation

of manuscripts for publication, legal deposits of published matter, and symbols for correcting proofs.

332 Directory of australian academic libraries. 2d ed. Melbourne: Footscray Inst. of Technology, 1981. 139p. LC 79–646513. ISSN 0155–1027.
The directory covers 470 university, college, and other postsecondary school libraries in Australia and also includes the National Library and the state libraries. Arrangement is alphabetical. Entries specify name and address, hours of operation, size of collection, nature and scope of the collection, interlibrary loan policies, name of the chief librarian, and any special features of the library. There is an index to special collections by topic and also a guide to publications and an index to personnel.

333 Directory of special libraries in Australia. Comp. and ed. by Gabrielle Watt, Heather Howard and Jean Geue. 5th ed. Surry Hills, N.S.W.: Special Libraries Section, Library Assn. of Australia, 1982. 425p. ISBN 0–909915–93–8.
In this listing of more than 900 special libraries throughout Australia, entries supply name, address, and telephone number of the library, holdings, subject strengths, policies regarding public access, services available, and name of director. Arrangement is by political jurisdiction; indexing is by library name and subject areas covered in the library. The directory is now in machine readable form and it is planned to be updated frequently.

AUSTRALIAN CAPITAL TERRITORY

334 Canberra special libraries guide. Canberra: Dept. of Primary Industry Library, 1982. 50p.
Also included in this directory of special libraries in Canberra are some large general libraries with special collections. Arranged alphabetically by name of library, entries contain address, telephone number, subject specialization, and hours of opening.

335 Directory of A.C.T. libraries. Canberra: A.C.T. Branch, Library Assn. of Australia, 1977. 82p. ISBN 0–909915–47–4.
In this directory, 124 libraries in the Australian Capital Territory are entered by name of library or parent institution. School libraries are listed in a separate section, following the other entries. Information provided for each library includes address, telephone number, areas of subject strength, service, and hours of opening other than Monday through Friday. The entries are indexed by name and subject.

NEW SOUTH WALES

336 Libraries of Sydney. Ed. by Alan L. Bundy. Melbourne: Footscray Inst. of Technology, 1979. 90p. ISBN 0–9596942–6–9.
Approximately 400 public, special, and academic libraries located in Sydney are covered in this directory. Entries are brief and contain name, address, telephone number, nature of collection, size of collection, interlibrary lending policy, and hours of opening. Arrangement is alphabetical by name of library; indexing of public libraries is by suburb.

337 **New South Wales government department libraries: a directory.** 4th ed. Sydney: Government Depts. Unit, State Library of N.S.W., 1982. 62p. LC 83–640099.
This directory identifies and provides information about the services available from the State Library and from departmental libraries within state government. It includes not only those staffed by the State Library, but also those involved in the State Library's Departmental Network. In addition, those libraries not within the jurisdiction of the State Library are included, marked by an asterisk. Arrangement is alphabetical. Entries supply name, address, telephone number, subject areas, and services available.

338 **Public libraries in New South Wales, 1981.** Sydney: Public Libraries Division, State Library of N.S.W., 1981. 30p.
Brief information about all public libraries in New South Wales is provided in this directory. The work is divided by type of library, with metropolitan libraries listed first, followed by county libraries. Libraries in the Sydney metropolitan area are arranged by suburb. Other public libraries, in the rural areas, are listed by town. Entries specify name, address, and telephone number of the library.

NORTHERN TERRITORY

339 **List of libraries and resource centres in the Northern Territory.** Darwin: Northern Territory Branch, Library Assn. of Australia, 1980. n.p.
A total of eighty-one libraries in the Northern Territory are described in this directory. All types are covered, except school libraries. Entries supply name, address, and telephone number of the library. Indexing is by subject and geographical area.

QUEENSLAND

340 **Directory of state and public library services in Queensland.** Brisbane: Library Board of Queensland, 1978– . Annual. ISSN 0314–9307.
This directory identifies the locations and describes the services of the State Library of Queensland, lists the addresses of departmental libraries in state government staffed by the Library Board of Queensland, and covers public libraries in Queensland, listing the regional library headquarters and local authority libraries separately. Directory information is brief, giving name, address, and telephone number. There is also a separate list of School of Arts libraries.

VICTORIA

341 **Directory of public library services in Victoria.** Melbourne: Public Libraries Division, Library Council of Victoria, 1976– . Annual. ISSN 0313–5829.
This directory supersedes the *Register of public library services and list of public libraries in metropolitan Melbourne* (entry **343**). Described here are the services of the Public Libraries Division and the State Library of Victoria; the cooperative services and metropolitan public library services in Melbourne; the names, addresses, and telephone numbers of public library services outside of the metropolitan area; and public libraries within the Melbourne telephone district.

342 Libraries of Melbourne. Ed. by A. L. Bundy. 2d ed. Melbourne: Footscray Inst. of Technology, 1980. 114p. LC 81–201712.
This directory covers all types of libraries in the Melbourne area, except primary and secondary school libraries. In all, approximately 400 libraries are described. Arrangement is by type of library, within these three sections: business, industrial, government, professional and hospital libraries; university, college of advanced education, technical college, theological college, and specialist college libraries; and public reference and lending libraries. Entries are brief, specifying name, address, telephone number, and information about the collection. There is an index of public libraries by suburb.

343 Register of public library services and list of public libraries in metropolitan Melbourne. Melbourne: Public Libraries Division, Library Council of Victoria, 19??–1975. Irreg.
This title is superseded by *Directory of public library services in Victoria.* For further information see entry **341**.

WESTERN AUSTRALIA

344 Guide to library services in Western Australia. Perth: Western Australian Group, Special Libraries Section, Library Assn. of Australia, 1980. 89p. ISSN 0705–1220.
Brief directory information is provided for 167 academic, public, and special libraries in Western Australia. Identified are name, address, telephone number, name of librarian, and subjects covered. Entries are indexed by name and subjects. Two maps show locations of libraries in Central Perth and Metropolitan Perth. A lengthy introduction describes the types of libraries in Western Australia.

Fiji

345 Fiji library directory. Comp. by Jocelyn Waqa. 4th ed. Suva: Fiji Library Assn., 1981. 112p. LC 74–647036.
Brief information on 162 public, school, and special libraries in the Fiji Islands is provided here. Entries, arranged alphabetically by name of library, list name and address, collection characteristics, budget, and name of librarian.

New Zealand

346 Australian and New Zealand library resources. By Robert B. Downs. London: Mansell, 1979. 164p. LC 80–343414. ISBN 0–7201–0913–2.
This guide covers the subject holdings and collections of academic, research, state, government, and other special libraries. A full description is provided under entry number **330**.

347 Directory of special libraries in New Zealand. Ed. by Paul Szentirmay. 3d ed. Wellington: New Zealand Library Assn., 1974. 163p. LC 75–320950.
This directory includes special libraries, special collections, and a few information centers in New Zealand. Of the 260 entries, 210 are special libraries, eleven are public or national libraries, and three are information centers. Arrangement is by the name of the parent

organization. Entries include name and address of library, date founded, library symbol, telephone number, name of librarian, size of staff, hours of opening, services, number of books and other materials held, classification system used, types of catalogs, any special indexes created by the library, publications, and subject strengths and special collections. The work is indexed by name and special collections, personnel, location, type of organization, degree and course subjects taught at universities, and subjects.

EUROPE

European directories with continental coverage are listed first, alphabetically by title. Directories with national coverage are arranged alphabetically by title under the country name. Directories with state or regional coverage are listed alphabetically by title under the state or regional name, following the national directories for that country.

348 Subject collections in european libraries. Comp. by Richard C. Lewanski. 2d ed. New York: Bowker, 1978. 495p. LC 77–72343. ISBN 0–85935–011–8.
Listed here are approximately 12,000 subject collections in libraries in continental Europe, the British Isles, and the European island nations of Cyprus, Greenland, Iceland, and Malta. The directory is arranged by Dewey number. Entries contain the name and location of the library, name of the director, date the library was founded, subject strengths and special collections, and an indication of current holdings.

Austria

349 Handbuch österreichischer bibliotheken. Vienna: Österreichische National-bibliothek, 1963–1971. 3v. LC 72–357833.
This directory of more than 1,900 libraries in Austria is arranged by Länder and then by city or town. Libraries in larger cities are further subdivided by type. Entries include name and address, size and characteristics of holdings, staff size, subject strengths and special collections, and services. The directory is published in three volumes: Volume 1, *Bibliotheksverzeichnis* (1971, 394p.), is the directory of libraries; Volume 2, *Statistik und personalverzeichnis* (1972, 193p.), provides statistical information and biographical data; Volume 3, *Rechtsvorschriften und erlasse zum österreichischen bibliothekswesen* (1963, 202p.), covers Austrian library law and regulations. In addition to statistical information, volume 2 includes biographical information about librarians identified in volume 1. The first edition was published in 1953 and titled *Verzeichnis österreichischer bibliotheken* (entry **350**). Revision of individual volumes is somewhat irregular.

350 Verzeichnis österreichischer bibliotheken. Vienna: Österreichische National-bibliothek, 1953. 191p. LC 54–34669.
This work is superseded by *Handbuch österreichischer bibliotheken.* For further information see entry **349**.

Belgium

351 Bibliotheekgids van Belgie/Guide des bibliothèques de Belgique. By G. Beirens. Brussels: Archives et Bibliothèques de Belgique, 1974–1975. 9v. LC 75–528635. This extensive directory of libraries in Belgium, arranged by province and then alphabetically by name, covers academic, public, special, government, and research libraries. Among other information, the entries provide name and address, subject holdings, services, and name of library director. Volumes 2, 4, 6, and 8 carry only the French title.

352 Inventaire des centres belges de recherche disposant d'une bibliothèque ou d'un service de documentation/Inventaris van belgische onderzoekscentra die over een bibliotheek of documentatiedienst beschikken. Ed. by Janine Verougstraete. 3d ed. Brussels: Bibliothèque Royale Albert, 1979. 430p. LC 79–122952. This directory provides brief information in French and/or Flemish on more than 950 research libraries, information centers, and other institutions providing documentation services. Entries contain name and address of the institution, name of the director, areas of specialization, and services offered. Subject access is provided by a detailed index. Two earlier editions were published, in 1967 and in 1971.

Denmark

353 Biblioteksvejviser. Copenhagen: Bibliotekscentralen, 1981. 157p. ISBN 87–87244–04–7. This major directory of libraries in Denmark covers academic, public, and special libraries; library names are given in English and Danish. An English-language index of library names provides access to specific libraries. The directory also lists associations, foundations, and library periodicals.

Finland

354 Guide to research libraries and information services in Finland. Ed. by Matti Liinamaa and Marjatta Heikkila. 6th ed. Helsinki: Finnish Research Library Assn., 1981. 175p. ISBN 951–95382–1–6. This directory provides information on approximately 400 major research and special libraries in Finland. Entries briefly describe subject content of collections, services, public access, and holdings. The work is indexed by library name and location. There is also an index of library names in English.

France

355 Libraries and archives in France: a handbook. By Erwin K. Welsch. Rev. ed. New York: Council for European Studies, Columbia Univ., 1979. 146p. LC 79–114022. This is a practical guide to the use of libraries and archives in France. Introductory material provides helpful background information. Arrangement is in three parts: the first covers libraries in Paris; the second covers archives in Paris; and the third identifies and describes libraries and archives elsewhere in France. Entries contain the address, hours of opening, data on holdings, procedure for obtaining a user's card, photocopying facilities and rules, library catalogs, and other publications. In many instances, the information is presented in narrative form and represents firsthand experience. The work is not indexed. The previous edition was published under the same title in 1973.

356 Libraries in Paris: a student's guide. By L. M. Newman. Scorton, England: Conder Research, 1971. 175p.

Practical information is given here for the English-speaking student who has no previous experience with French library collections. Much of the publication is devoted to characterizing the major types of libraries in France, what they offer, and the conditions of use. An appendix provides a directory of libraries and documentation centers, but information about each is limited. The chapters describing types of libraries can be used to supplement the directory.

357 Répertoire des bibliothèques et organismes de documentation. Paris: Bibliothèque Nationale, 1971. 733p. LC 76–501813. ISBN 2–7177–1119–8. **Supplement.** 1973. 265p.

This major directory of libraries and documentation centers in France is divided into two sections: the first covers organizations in and around Paris; the second covers those located elsewhere in France. The main volume has 3,210 entries, and the supplement an additional 957. Entries provide basic information, including name, address, telephone number, hours of opening, use policies, subject resources, and publications. An earlier edition was issued in 1963 under a slightly different title.

German Democratic Republic

358 Bibliotheken und informationsstellen im Bezirk Leipzig. By Bezirksgruppe Leipzig, Bibliotheksverband der DDR. Berlin: Bibliotheksverband der DDR, 1979. 164p. LC 81–102366.

Information is given on 389 libraries in the Leipzig area. Most are academic, public, special, and government libraries. Arranged by library name, each entry includes address, telephone number, and other pertinent information about library facilities and services. Much of this information is conveyed through coded graphic symbols. Subject strengths are listed for each library, and the directory is indexed by subject and by the name of the library. Entries and index subject references are in German.

359 Jahrbuch der bibliotheken, archive und informationstellen der Deutschen Demokratischen Republik, 1959– . Leipzig: VEB Bibliographisches Inst., 1961– . Biennial. LC 63–289316. ISSN 0075–2215.

This major national directory of libraries, archives, and information centers for the German Democratic Republic was formerly published in Berlin by the Deutsche Staatsbibliothek. Approximately 1,900 academic, public, and special libraries are listed. Entries include the name, address, telephone and telex numbers, numerical data on the size of the collection, subject areas of emphasis, special collections, name of the director, and publications issued by the library. The work is indexed by subject and by names of librarians. The personal name index also provides brief biographical information (see entry **258** for information on the biographical content).

360 Libraries and archives in Germany. By Erwin K. Welsch. Pittsburgh: Council for European Studies, 1975. 275p. LC 76–361075.

This work contains materials about libraries in the Federal Republic and the German Democratic Republic. For further information see entry **365**.

Germany, Federal Republic of

361 Deutsches bibliotheksadressbuch: verzeichnis von bibliotheken in der Bundesrepublik Deutschland einschliesslich Berlin (West). 2d ed. Berlin: Deutscher Bibliotheksverband, 1976. 498p. LC 75–570951. ISBN 3–87068–326–6.

This directory provides names and addresses, and limited additional information, for more than 13,400 libraries in the German Federal Republic. Libraries with fewer than 1,000 volumes are omitted. The directory is arranged alphabetically by city; all types of libraries are listed together under location. Entries include name and address, an identification number, telephone and telex numbers, type of library, a code indicating the size of the holdings, and the sponsoring agency. The work is indexed by identification number and by library name.

362 Handbuch der öffentlichen bibliotheken. Berlin: Deutsches Bibliotheksinstitut, 1952– . Biennial.

This geographically arranged directory of public libraries in the Federal Republic provides brief information about each, including name and address, the director's name, and services offered. This work was published from 1926 to 1940 under the title *Jahrbuch der deutschen volksbuechereien* (entry **364**).

363 Jahrbuch der deutschen bibliotheken: herausgegeben vom verein deutscher bibliothekare. Wiesbaden: Harrassowitz, 1902– . Biennial. LC 2–17084.

The most recent edition of this directory lists 689 libraries—582 scientific libraries and 107 others. Arrangement is alphabetical by location. Each entry provides address and telephone number, number of volumes, facilities for photocopying, and collection size. The name of the director is also included, and a separate section provides biographical data on persons listed (entry **259**). This directory was formerly published in Leipzig.

364 Jahrbuch der deutschen volksbuechereien: herausgegeben vom verband deutscher volksbibliothekare. Leipzig: Harrassowitz, 1926–1940. Biennial. LC 32–20777.

This work was superseded by *Handbuch der öffentlichen bibliotheken* in 1952. For further information see entry **362**.

365 Libraries and archives in Germany. By Erwin K. Welsch. Pittsburgh: Council for European Studies, 1975. 275p. LC 76–361075.

Intended for use as a practical guide for the scholar or student, this work contains a great deal of useful material about libraries in the Federal Republic and the German Democratic Republic (entry **360**). The directory section is preceded by background information about the types of library in Germany and the conditions of access to them. The arrangement of the directory is geographical by city or town. Entries give the name of the library and the director, subject areas collected, hours of opening, use restrictions, copying facilities, and a list of publications. Much of this is presented in narrative form, with observations and comments specific to each library, often based on firsthand knowledge. A separate section provides the same type of information for archives.

366 Special collections in german libraries: Federal Republic of Germany incl. Berlin (West)/Spezialbestände in deutschen bibliotheken: Bundesrepublik Deutschland einschl. Berlin (West). Commissioned by the Deutsche Forschungsgemeinschaft. Ed. by Walther Gebhardt. Berlin: Walter de Gruyter, 1977. 739p. LC 77–22288. ISBN 3–11–005839–1.
Coverage of West German subject collections in this work exceeds that of any other directory. Special collections of 877 libraries are identified and described. Arrangement is alphabetical by location. In addition to name, address, and telephone number, each entry indicates the subject strengths of the collection. Subject access is provided by a key word index. Key words are categorized separately to facilitate access through the index.

367 Verzeichnis deutscher informations- und dokumentationsstellen. By Institut Dokumentationswesen Frankfurt (Main). Wiesbaden: L. Reichert Verlag, 1974– . Irreg. LC 76–641544.
Approximately 500 special libraries in the Federal Republic and West Berlin are listed in this work. Arranged by Dewey classification number, the entries include name and address of the library, name of the library director, numerical data on the holdings, facilities, and conditions of public access. Cross-references from names of libraries to main entries are numerous. The work is indexed by subject, geographical location, and personal name.

Hungary

368 Hungarian library directory. Ed. by Lili Farago. Budapest: OSzK Könyvtár-tudományi es Módszertani Központ, 1965. 2v. LC 66–40147.
This work is sponsored by the National Board for Librarianship and Documentation, and published by the Centre of Library Science and Methodology. The first volume provides extensive coverage of 1,980 libraries of various types in Hungary. Arrangement is by category, including national libraries, libraries in networks, and libraries outside of networks. Entries provide name and address, subject coverage, holdings, services, and public access. The text of the directory is in Hungarian, but a table of contents and an introductory, explanatory essay are provided in English. The second volume contains alphabetical indexes to the names of libraries in Hungarian, Russian, and English. There is also a list of libraries by subject specialization.

369 Libraries in Hungary. By Jeno Kiss. Budapest: National Szechenyi Library Centre for Library Science and Methodology, 1972. 58p. LC 74–152533.
Although not a directory in the strictest sense, this work still provides useful descriptive information, in narrative form, about the largest or most important libraries in Hungary. The history of each the library, collection strengths, and general information about use of its collections are provided.

Italy

370 Annuario delle biblioteche italiane. Comp. by Direzione Generale delle Accademie
e Biblioteche Italiane. 3d ed. Rome: Palombi, 1969. 3v. LC 51–30361.
One of the most extensive lists of Italian libraries, this directory covers public, academic,
government, and special libraries throughout Italy. Arrangement is alphabetical by location.
Each volume covers a part of the alphabet. Entries supply name and address, size of
holdings, public access, a brief history of the library, and a list of publications. The work is
not indexed. The first edition was published in four volumes (1949–1954).

371 Guida delle biblioteche italiane. Prov. ed. Rome: Ente Nazionale per le Biblioteche
Popolari e Scholastiche, 1969. 622p. LC 71–563487.
This extensive list covers more than 21,000 libraries, including overseas libraries sponsored
by the Italian government or by the private sector. Entries are arranged by province, then by
city or town. Information about each library is basically limited to name and address. The
work is indexed by name of library, location, and subject.

**372 Guida delle biblioteche scientifiche e tecniche e dei centri di documentazione
italiana.** Ed. by R. P. Pavesi and M. Salimei. Rome: Consiglio Nazionale delle
Ricerche, 1965. 610p. LC 68–130514.
Scientific and technical libraries and other institutions involved in scientific and technical
documentation are covered here. The 1,600 entries provide brief information on subject
emphasis and services. This directory is published under the sponsorship of Associazione
Italiana Biblioteche.

373 Guide to italian libraries and archives. Comp. by Rudolf J. Lewanski. Ed. by
Richard C. Lewanski. New York: Council for European Studies, 1979. 101p. LC
79–114337.
This directory provides varying levels of information about libraries and archives in Italy.
For the major libraries and archives, entries contain a substantial amount of data, including
the full name, address, telephone number, date established, holdings by type of item, scope
and subject profile, list of special collections, unique items, catalogs, hours of opening,
periods of time when closed, and availability of facilities for photocopying and microfilming. Following this detailed section, brief information is given for subject collections: name,
address, and holdings. Other sections in the directory list the names and addresses of minor
state archives, local administration archives, notaries public archives, and private archives.
A separate list of library-related services is provided, along with a list of archives and
libraries in other Italian-speaking countries, countries with Italian-speaking minorities, and
countries with past ties to Italy. A bibliography of national, regional, and local guides to the
collections identifies sources of additional information about the resources of the libraries
and archives.

Netherlands

374 Jaarboek openbare bibliotheken. The Hague: Nederlands Biblioteek en Lektuur
Centrum (NBLC), 1979. 247p. LC 78–646780.

Included in this directory are 570 public libraries in the Netherlands. Arranged by name of city, entries include name and address of the library and name of the director. There is also an alphabetical list of persons and some brief statistical information.

Norway

375 Norske vitenskapelige og faglige biblioteker: en handbok. Ed. by Liebena Vokac. 3d ed. Oslo: Riksbibliotektjenesten, i Kommisjon hos Biblioteksentralen, 1979. 255p. LC 81–110038. ISBN 82–7195–021–5.

This directory includes approximately 300 libraries of various types in Norway, including public, special, college and university, and national. Entries contain the name and address, collection strengths and special collections, services, public access, and name of library director. The work is indexed by geographical location. Previous editions appeared in 1963 and 1975.

Poland

376 Guide to polish libraries and archives. Comp. by Richard C. Lewanski. Boulder, CO: East European Quarterly; New York: Columbia Univ. Pr., distr., 1974. 209p. (East european monographs, no. 6) LC 73–91484. ISBN 0–231–03896–8.

This is the only English-language directory of Polish libraries and archives. Arrangement is by city or town, and then alphabetically by name of library. Each entry provides an extensive description of the library and includes a paragraph on the history of the library, scope and subject profile, numerical data on the holdings, the content of special collections, readers' services (including hours of opening), and a bibliography of published catalogs or other works that reflect the holdings of the institution. A subject index to institutions, named collections, and subject areas covered completes this work.

377 Informator o bibliotekach i ósrodkach informacji naukowej w Polsce. By I. Klimowiczowa and E. Suchodolska. Warsaw: Biblioteka Narodowa, 1973. 557p. LC 75–561938.

More than 880 libraries of various types are listed in this directory. Included are college and university libraries, medical libraries, libraries in museums, archives, and public libraries. Entries are in Polish and include information about the nature of collection, holdings, name of library director, any subject strengths or special collections, and services. The work is indexed by name of library, location, and subject.

Romania

378 Ghidul bibliotecilor din România. By Valeriu Moldoveanu, Gheorghe Popescu and Mircea Tomescu. Bucharest: Editura Enciclopedica Română, 1970. 475p. LC 72–21781.

More than 1,000 Romanian libraries of various types are listed here. Entries and descriptions are in Romanian. Arrangement is geographical, by city or town where the library is located. Entries include the name and address, name of the library director, subject areas covered, and services.

Spain

379 Directorio de bibliotecas de Catalunya. Prep. by the Vocalia de Cultura de l'Associació de Bibliotecaries de Barcelona. Barcelona: Associació de Bibliotecaries, 1979. v.p. LC 81–121629.

This is a loose-leaf directory of libraries in Barcelona and in other areas of Catalonia. Basic directory information in Spanish is provided for each of the libraries.

380 Nueva guía de las bibliotecas de Madrid. Comp. by Isabel Morales Vallespín. Madrid: ANABAD, 1979. 321p. ISBN 84–600–1378–2.

Public, college and university, special, and school libraries in Madrid are identified in this directory. Arrangement is by type of library, and libraries are numbered within each category. Entries contain name, address, and telephone number of the library, hours of opening, public access, a brief history, a description of the collection, number of seats, type of catalog(s), and public services offered. Each entry also provides a bibliography of publications issued by the library.

Sweden

381 Information and documentation in Sweden. Comp. by Ewa Erikson. Stockholm: Information Section, National Swedish Board for Technical Developments, 1977. 87p. LC 78–300116.

Agencies responsible for the production and dissemination of information services in Sweden are identified and described here. The organizations included cover a broad spectrum of subject areas, from agriculture, to patents, to paint research. The following information is provided in each entry: agency name, address, telephone number, subjects covered, types of services (e.g., literature surveys, publication of bibliographies), and level of reference service offered. Entries and text are in English, but the Swedish name of the institution is always given. Included in the appendix are the addresses of research libraries, associations of manufacturers, and county agricultural boards in Sweden. A subject index completes the work.

Switzerland

382 Archive, bibliotheken und dokumentationsstellen der Schweiz/Archives, bibliothèques et centres de documentation en Suisse/Archivi, biblioteche e centri di documentazione in Svizzera. 4th ed. Bern: Schweizerische Vereinigung für Dokumentation, 1976. 805p. LC 78–363804.

This directory offers information on approximately 450 libraries, archives, and centers for documentation in Switzerland that are open to the public, either for loans, reference purposes, or photocopying. Among the types of institutions covered are university libraries, libraries in research institutions, government agencies, museums, professional associations, cultural organizations, and commercial firms. Arrangement is geographical, by the city or town in which the library is located. Information provided for each library includes name and address, telephone and telex numbers, telegraphic address, collection strengths, services, loan policies, hours of opening, copying facilities, other equipment available, and numerical data on the holdings. An index by library name, in German, French, and Italian, is provided.

U.S.S.R.

383 **Archives and manuscript repositories in the USSR, Estonia, Latvia, Lithuania, and Belorussia.** By Patricia Kennedy Grimsted. Princeton: Princeton Univ. Pr., 1981. 929p. LC 79–15427.

This work is a combination bibliographic guide and directory to the archival and manuscript holdings of institutions in the U.S.S.R. It is the second in a series of works projected ultimately to cover all such institutions in the U.S.S.R. This volume includes an extensive bibliography of reference aids, catalogs, institutional directories, surveys of sources, and other works that are of value to the user in identifying the archival and manuscript holdings of institutions. In addition, there is a description of the holdings of individual archives and manuscript collections. Appendices deal with the use of materials in Soviet institutions, including working conditions, duplication and microfilming, and public access to records. Indexing is by author-title and by subject, the latter covering directory entries.

384 **Archives and manuscript repositories in the USSR: Moscow and Leningrad.** By P. K. Grimsted. Princeton: Princeton Univ. Pr., 1972. 436p. LC 73–166345. ISBN 0–691–05149–6.

This is the first volume in a series on archives and manuscripts in the U.S.S.R. produced by Patricia Grimsted. The arrangement is essentially the same as the second volume in the series, described in entry **383**. However, the coverage focuses on archives and manuscript collections in Moscow and Leningrad only. This volume has been supplemented by a work entitled: *Supplement 1: bibliographical addenda* (Zug: International Documentation Company, 1976).

385 **Biblioteki SSSR.** By Biblioteka SSSR im. V. I. Lenina. Moscow: Kniga, 1973–74. 2v. v. 1, **Biblioteki Soiuznykh Respublik.** 1973. 367p. v.2, **Biblioteki RSFSR.** 1974. 429p.

This directory covers various types of libraries, divided geographically and published in two volumes. The first volume, arranged by state and then by type of library, covers approximately 1,750 state, regional, academic, and educational libraries. The second volume, also arranged geographically and then by type of library, covers an additional 1,927 libraries. The entries are indexed by library names and by library location. Entries and text are in Russian.

United Kingdom

386 **Aslib directory.** Ed. by Ellen M. Codlin. 4th ed. London: Aslib, 1977–80. 2v. LC 79–370666. v.1, **Information sources in science, technology and commerce.** 1977. 634p. ISBN 0–85142–104–0. v.2, **Information sources in the social sciences, medicine and the humanities.** 1980. 871p. ISBN 0–85142–130–X.

This is the most extensive directory of information sources (6,500 entries) in the United Kingdom and Republic of Ireland. Coverage is not limited to libraries but extends to all types of organizations making information available, including commercial and scientific organizations, learned societies, government agencies, professional groups, art galleries, banks, museums, congresses, councils, and others. Organizations are included whether they make information available without cost or charge for the information. The volumes are arranged alphabetically by name of organization, with numerous cross-references. Entries are numbered and include name of parent organization, address, telephone and telex number, nature of the organization, contact person, subject coverage, and special collections. The format of the two volumes is essentially the same. A subject index in each volume provides detailed access. Earlier editions of this directory were published in 1928, 1957, and 1970.

387 Libraries in the United Kingdom and the Republic of Ireland. 9th ed. London: Library Assn., 1981. 174p. LC 81–160870. ISBN 0–85365–741–6.

This directory covers public libraries (central libraries and branches); libraries in colleges, universities, and polytechnic schools; selected special and government libraries; and library education programs. The entries are brief, supplying only the name, address, telephone and telex numbers, and name of the chief librarian and assistant librarian. A library index is provided. Until 1969, the directory was published under the title *Address list of public library authorities in the United Kingdom and the Republic of Ireland*; since 1971, the editions have been published with the current title.

388 Research libraries and collections in the United Kingdom: a selective inventory and guide. Comp. by Stephen Roberts, Alan Cooper, and Lesley Gilder. Hamden, CT: Scarecrow, 1978. 278p. LC 78–11560. ISBN 0–208–01667–8.

This highly selective guide provides basic directory information about major research collections in the United Kingdom. The "Inventory," the main portion of the work, is arranged by type of library; categories include national, specialist, and public libraries; university and polytechnic libraries in England and Wales; and Scottish central institutions. Entries for each library provide name, address, telephone number, name of librarian, nature of the collection, policies regarding public access, classification system used, special facilities, current publications, and a bibliography. Indexing is by name (person, library, and collection), subject, and geographic location.

389 The United States: a guide to library holdings in the U.K. Comp. by Peter Snow. Westport, CT: Meckler, 1982. 717p. ISBN 0–930466–45–4.

This is a guide to libraries in the United Kingdom with extensive collections on the United States. More than 350 libraries are covered. The types of materials represented in the collections include books and other printed materials (except periodical holdings), microform holdings, and audiovisual materials. Entries describe each library's facilities, hours of opening, availability of copying services, and holdings on subjects, individuals, or time periods. An appendix lists more than 1,800 microform sets or multivolume publications, designated by symbols to indicate their location.

ENGLAND

390 Directory of London public libraries. Ed. by Lawrence H. Cudby. 7th ed. London: Assn. of London Chief Librarians, 1982. 167p. LC 68–419320. ISBN 0–902814–05–2.

In this directory of public library services in London, arrangement is alphabetical by name of the library service. Entries contain the name of the library service, address, telephone number, a map reference to the location, date of establishment, services offered, cooperative arrangements, hours of opening, extension services, and a list of publications.

391   **Oxford libraries outside the Bodleian: a guide.** By Paul Morgan. Oxford: Bodleian Library, 1980. 264p. LC 80–504593. ISBN 0–900177–73–X.
The remarkable collections of Oxford University are identified and described in this volume. Included are descriptions of more than 200 libraries outside of the Bodleian library. Both printed and manuscript collections found in the departmental collections and individual colleges at Oxford are covered. In addition, a list of 100 other collections are identified in the appendix but are not described in the main body of the text.

NORTHERN IRELAND

392   **Directory of Northern Ireland libraries.** Ed. by W. R. H. Carson and A. Morrow. 2d ed. London: Northern Ireland Branch, Library Assn., 1977. 53p. LC 78–313531. ISBN 0–906066–00–X.
Listed in this directory are forty-six public, academic, and special libraries, plus branches of public libraries or units of university libraries. Entries include name, address, telephone number, hours of opening, subject specialization, special collections, size of collection, type of classification used, staff size, and lending policies. Index access to special collections is provided by subject.

SCOTLAND

393   **Library resources in Scotland.** By James A. Tait and H.F.C. Tait. 4th ed. Glasgow: Scottish Library Assn., 1981. 149p. ISBN 0–900649–19–4.
A total of 404 entries are included in the latest edition of this directory. Arrangement is by name of the library. Excluded are school libraries, private libraries, and libraries operated for profit. Entries contain name, address, telephone number, librarian's name, size of staff, numerical data on book and periodical holdings, policies regarding admission, and type of classification and catalog used. Indexing is by location, type of library, subject, and name. Previous editions were published in 1968, 1973, and 1976.

WALES

394   **Library resources in Wales/Adnoddau llyfrgelloedd Cymru.** Ed. by M. June Maggs and L. Jones. 2d ed. London: Reference, Special and Information Section, Western Group, Library Assn., 1976. 51p. LC 77–364224. ISBN 0–85365–458–1.
Approximately 200 libraries are listed in this directory, which updates the 1967 edition. Arrangement is alphabetical and entries specify name, address, telephone and telex numbers, size of staff, size of collection, type of catalog and classification schemes used, services, and subject strengths. Location and subject indexes are provided.

Yugoslavia

395   **A guide to yugoslav libraries and archives.** Comp. by Slobodan Jovanovic and Matko Rojnic. Ed. by Paul L. Horecky and Elizabeth Beyerley. Trans. by Elizabeth Beyerley. Columbus: American Assn. for the Advancement of Slavic Studies, 1975. 113p. (The Joint Committee on Eastern Europe publication series, no. 2) LC 76–370246.
This work is divided into seven sections, the first six corresponding to the six constituent

republics of Yugoslavia and the seventh covering autonomous provinces. Libraries and archives are then listed by town or city. Various types of libraries are included. Entries provide basic information about the collection and the services of the institution. A useful feature is a glossary of library terms in Turkish, Arabic and Slavic.

NORTH AND SOUTH AMERICA

All entries are arranged within three main divisions: Canada, Latin America, and United States. Directories with national coverage are arranged alphabetically by title under the country name. Directories with regional coverage are listed next under the specified region. Directories with state coverage are listed alphabetically by title under the state or province name following the national and regional directories for that country.

Canada

396 American library directory. Ed. by Jaques Cattell Press. New York: Bowker, 1923– . Annual. LC 23–3581. ISSN 0065–910X.
Canadian libraries are included in this directory. For a further description of the work see entry **425**.

397 Canadian library handbook/Guide des bibliothèques canadiennes, 1979–1980. Ed. by James Quantrell. Toronto: Micromedia, 1980. 256p. LC 79–31603. ISBN 0–88892–600–2.
In addition to providing an overview of library practice and research in Canada, this source also contains an extensive directory of more than 3,000 Canadian libraries. For further information see entry **242**.

398 Directory of canadian records and manuscript repositories. Ottawa: Bonanza Press for the Assn. of Canadian Archivists, 1977. 115p. LC 78–307606.
This work identifies and describes 300 public archives of Canada, including municipal, church, and museum archives. Arrangement is alphabetical by province or territory, and then by name of archive. Each entry specifies the name and address of the institution, name of the archivist or curator, hours of opening, nature of the collection, and subject areas covered. The information is indexed by name of archive.

399 Directory of special libraries and information centers. Ed. by Lois Lenroot-Ernt. 7th ed. Detroit: Gale, 1983. 2v. v.1, **Special libraries and information centers in the United States and Canada.** 1,425p. LC 79–16966. ISBN 0–8103–0258–6. v.2, **Geographic and personnel indexes.** 715p. LC 79–16788. ISBN 0–8103–0259–4.
Canadian libraries are included in this directory. For a further description of the work see entry **427**.

400 Research collections in canadian libraries. Ottawa: Information Canada, National Library of Canada, 1972– . Irreg. LC 74–159990. ISSN 0316–0319.

This major survey of library collections in Canada was conducted and published over a period of several years. The result is a two-part work issued in six separate volumes. The first volume, *Universities*, contains information about the subject collections of universities offering graduate studies in the humanities and the social sciences. The subject strengths of these collections are identified. Also provided is comparative statistical information about collection size in various subject areas. Entries are arranged by geographical categories: Prarie provinces; Atlantic provinces; British Columbia; Ontario; Quebec; and Canada. Volume 2, *Special studies. Part 1: Theatre resources in canadian collections* (1973. 113p.), describes the holdings of 151 libraries or special collections and includes an index by name of collection. *Part 2: Federal government libraries* (1974. 231p.), provides brief information about the collections of libraries operated by the federal government. The focus is on the subject areas covered by the holdings, rather than the individual libraries. However, lists of libraries by subject area are provided. *Part 3: Law library resources in Canada* (1975. 321p.), identifies Canadian law libraries and presents information about the subject coverage of each. Libraries are categorized by type of law library. *Part 4: Slavic and east european resources in canadian academic and research libraries* (1976. 595p.), covers the holdings of individual libraries. Extensive descriptions are included, as are an index by name of library and a bibliography. *Part 5: Collections of official publications* (1976. 888p) is similar to a union catalog of government publications in Canadian libraries. Major series of official publications are listed, with the symbols of libraries holding the series shown below. Information about the holdings of individual libraries and data derived from the survey that resulted in this work are also provided. Since 1980, two new volumes have been issued, one dealing with music resources (1980. 103p.) and the other identifying dance resources (1982. 136p.).

401   Subject collections: a guide to special book collections and subject emphases as reported by university, college, public, and special libraries and museums in the United States and Canada. Comp. by Lee Ash. 5th ed. New York: Bowker, 1978. 1,184p. LC 78–26399. ISBN 0–8352–0924–5.
Canadian libraries are included in this work. For further information see entry **430**.

402   Symbols of canadian libraries. 9th ed. Ottawa: National Library of Canada/Bibliothèque Nationale du Canada, 1981. 151p.
Identified in this directory are the library symbols assigned to Canadian libraries by the National Library of Canada. The symbols are arranged in alphabetical order, letter by letter. Symbols assigned since the latest edition are listed in *National Library technical news*, a monthly published by the National Library of Canada. The 10th edition of this work is scheduled for publication in late–1983.

ALBERTA

403   Alberta library directory. Edmonton: Cultural Development Division, Library Services Branch, 1972– . Annual. LC 76–361442. ISSN 0710–3123.
This annual directory of libraries in Alberta covers 1,200 public, academic, and special libraries. Arrangement is by type of library. Entries identify name, address, telephone number, name of library director, subject strengths, special collections, hours of opening, population served, number of books and periodicals, borrowing policies, and method of classification. Indexing is by locality and by name of library.

BRITISH COLUMBIA

404   Focus: a directory of library services in British Columbia. Victoria: British
    Columbia Library Assn., Douglas College, and the Greater Victoria Library Federa-
    tion, 1980. 89p.
Public, academic, and special libraries throughout the province are described in this
directory. Entries, arranged by location, contain name, address, telephone and telex
numbers, name of librarian, number of hours open, holdings, documents depository status,
photocopy service, special collections, and policy regarding public access. The information
is indexed by type of library and names of librarians. This information is updated annually
by an untitled, mimeographed library directory of municipal, public, college, and institute
libraries, published by the British Columbia Library Services Branch, the provincial library.
Included in this annual update are the name and address of the library, the name of the chief
librarian, and the library's telephone number.

MANITOBA

405   Directory of libraries in Manitoba. Winnipeg: Public Libraries Services Branch,
    Dept. of Cultural Affairs and Historical Resources, 1973– . Biennial. LC
    75–642968. ISSN 0317–8536.
Public, college, university, special, hospital, and government libraries throughout the
province are covered in this directory. The 171 numbered entries in the latest edition are
arranged by type and then by name of library. The following information is provided: name,
address, telephone number, librarian's name, size of collection, availability of interlibrary
loan service, subject specialties, languages in which the materials are available, policy
regarding availability of materials, and year founded. The entries are indexed by geographical area, name of library, and language in which materials are available.

NOVA SCOTIA

406   Directory of Nova Scotia libraries. Halifax: Reference Services Division, Nova
    Scotia Provincial Library, 19??– . Irreg. ISSN 0714–3699.
Information about all types of libraries in Nova Scotia, except school libraries, is presented
alphabetically by name of library. Entries specify name of library, street address, telephone
number, name of chief librarian, and the library's national symbol for interlibrary loan.
There is no index.

ONTARIO

407   A directory of Ontario public libraries. 2d ed. Toronto: Ontario Ministry of
    Citizenship and Culture, 1982. 119p. LC 80–501270. ISBN 0–7743–7106–4.
Listed in the main body of the directory are all public libraries in Ontario, including branch
libraries. Entries specify legal name of the library board, federal documents depository
status, size range of the population served, street address, postal region, telephone number,
name of the regional library system to which it belongs, and name of the library board's chief
executive. A separate listing, arranged by postal regions, refers back to the main entry. The
first edition was published in 1979.

408 **Directory of special libraries in the Toronto area.** 8th ed. Toronto: Toronto Chapter, Special Libraries Assn., 1979. 94p. LC 80–511924. ISBN 0–9690105–1–6.

In this directory, 247 special libraries in the metropolitan Toronto area are arranged by name of library or parent institution. Entries contain name, address, hours of opening, special collections, services offered, interlibrary loan, and whether or not open to visitors. Also included are cross-references from alternate forms of the name or institution and a subject index.

QUEBEC

409 **Répertoire des bibliothèques publiques Quebec.** Grande Vallée: Service des Bibliothèques Publiques, Quebec Ministère des Affaires Culturelles, 1982– . Annual. ISBN 2–550–02654–3.

In this directory of public libraries in Quebec, entries are arranged alphabetically by name of city or town and provide name, address, and telephone number of the library. Statistical information about the libraries is also included (entry **548**).

SASKATCHEWAN

410 **Directory of Saskatchewan libraries.** 4th ed. Regina: Bibliographic Services Division, Provincial Library, 1981. 77p. LC 78–315359. ISSN 0228–7617.

Public, regional, school, college, university, and special libraries in Saskatchewan are covered in this directory. Arrangement is alphabetical by city of location. Entries indentify type of library, location, name, address, telephone and telex numbers, name of person in charge, collection size, subject specialties, languages of the materials held, specialized services offered, and publications issued. Public library entries also specify the number of branches.

Latin America

ARGENTINA

411 **Guía de las bibliotecas universitarias argentinas.** Prep. by the Centro de Documentación Bibliotecológica, Universidad Nacional del Sur. 3d ed. Buenos Aires: Casa Pardo, 1976. 207p. LC 77–568272.

Entries for each of the 189 college and university libraries in Argentina listed here specify name and address of library, size of collection, nature of collection, type of classification system used, special collections or specialized subject strengths, key personnel, and any publications issued by the library. There is a separate table of statistics showing the number of volumes and number of periodical titles in each library.

BOLIVIA

412 **Directorio de bibliotecas y centros de documentación de Bolivia.** Prep. by the Centro Nacional de Documentación Científica y Tecnológica. La Paz: Univ. Boliviana and Univ. Mayor de San Andrés, 1978. 109p.

In this 1978 directory of more than 100 academic, special, and municipal libraries and archives in Bolivia, arranged by province, the following information is provided for each: address, whether or not open to the public, subject coverage, telephone number, hours open, type of organization sponsoring the library, date created, and size of library. The first edition of this work was published in 1973 under the title *Guía de bibliotecas, centros y servicios documentarios de Bolivia*.

BRAZIL

413 Guía das bibliotecas brasileiras. 2d ed. Rio de Janeiro: Secretária de Planejamento da Presidência da República, Fundação Inst. Brasileiro de Geografia e Estatística; (IBGE); Inst. Nacional de Livro, 1979. 1,018p. LC 80–646415.

This is the major national directory of libraries in Brazil. Numbered entries provide name and address, number of volumes, equipment available, classification system used, specialized subject areas, and staff size for 488 Brazilian libraries. Arranged geographically by location, the entries are indexed by type of library, subdivided by state.

414 Guía das bibliotecas do estado de São Paulo. São Paulo: Divisão de Bibliotecas, Departamento de Artes e Ciências Humanas, São Paulo (estado), 1978. 397p. LC 79–645196.

In this directory of 1,061 public, school, college and university, and special libraries in São Paulo state, arrangement is by type of library and then by city. Entries contain the name, address, telephone number, name of director, size of collection, system of classification used, type of cataloging system, and types of catalogs available to the user.

CHILE

415 Guía de bibliotecas especializadas y centros de documentación de Chile. 3d ed. Santiago: Comisión Nacional de Investigación Científica y Tecnologica, Dirección de Información y Documentación, Centro Nacional de Información y Documentación (CONICYT/CENID), 1979. 169p. LC 82–232697.

Included in this list of 397 special libraries and documentation centers in Chile are special collections in university libraries as well as those in government and the private sector. Arrangement is geographical by region and then alphabetical. Information is brief: institution name and address, telephone, staff, subject areas covered, and numerical data on holdings. Indexing is by subject area, institution name, and city of location. The previous two editions were published in 1970 and 1976.

416 A select guide to chilean libraries and archives. By Peter J. Sehlinger. Bloomington: Latin American Studies Program, Indiana Univ., 1979. 35p. (Latin american studies working papers, v.9) LC 80–108172.

Information in English about the characteristics and use of the principal libraries and archives of Chile is presented in narrative form in this guide. A total of twenty-two institutions are covered. Intended to be of use to foreign scholars, the text provides information about the procedures required to obtain access to the institutions as well as about collection characteristics. Entries also indicate the location of the library. The volume groups libraries and archives in Santiago and then libraries and archives outside of Santiago by location. Although selective, the guide covers the libraries and archives most likely to be of interest to foreign users, particularly serious researchers.

COLOMBIA

417   Directorio colombiano de bibliotecas y centros de información y documentación. Comp. and ed. by Octavio G. Rojas and Aníbal Salazar Alonso. Bogotá: COLCIENCIAS, Division de Documentación, 1973. 187p. LC 80–144458.

Approximately 150 libraries and documentation centers in Colombia are listed in this 1973 directory. Entries contain the name, address, and telephone number of the institution, hours of opening, holdings, system of classification used, nature of the library (private or public), services offered, and a list of publications issued by the library.

418   Directorio colombiano de unidades de información. Bogotá: COLCIENCIAS, Ministerio de Educatión Nacional, Fondo Colombiano de Investigaciones Científicas y Proyectos Especiales "Francisco José de Caldas," 1976. 182p. LC 78–641315.

A total of 317 Colombian libraries and other information agencies are listed in this 1976 directory. Arrangement is by place, and entries contain name, address, type of institution (library, archives, documentation center, etc.), specialties, collection size, services offered, hours open, publications, and name of director. The directory is indexed by initials or acronym of the library, geographic location, name of institution, subject, and personal name.

MEXICO

419   Directorio de bibliotecas de la república Mexicana. Comp. by Cecilia Culebra y Vives. 6th ed. Mexico City: Dirección General de Publicaciones y Bibliotecas, Secretaría de Educación Pública, 1979. 2v. ISBN 968–804–074–6.

This national directory of libraries in Mexico includes public, academic, and some special libraries. Arrangement is by state and then city, with a special section for the Federal District. Libraries are arranged by type under their location. A total of 1,572 numbered entries appear, with an addendum of 227 more libraries; an annex lists libraries with 500 or more volumes. Entries include name, address, and telephone number of the library, name of the library director, date founded, number of volumes, hours of opening, access policies, and an indication of special collections held. An index by name of parent institution, an index by name of library director (or other staff members if included), a geographical index, an index by postal zone, and a subject index provide access to the entries.

420   Directorio de fuentes y recursos para la información documental. Mexico City: Consejo Nacional de Ciencia y Tecnología, 1978. 361p. ISBN 968–823–000–6.

In this directory of academic and special libraries in Mexico, which includes individual branches and departmental collections in college and university libraries, a total of 287 entries are covered, one to a page. Entries indicate the name, address, and telephone number of library, name of director, type of library, subject areas of the collection, hours of opening, number of volumes, number of periodical titles, requirements for use of the library, system of classification, publications, and whether or not the library is a participant in the union catalog of periodicals in Mexican libraries (*Catálogo colectivo de publicaciones periódicas existentes en bibliotecas de la República Mexicana*, 2d ed.). The directory is indexed by subject, name of director or chief librarian, and name of participating institution.

PERU

421 Guía de bibliotecas del sistema nacional de la Universadad Peruana, 1974. Lima:
Consejo Nacional de la Univ. Peruana, Dirección de Evaluación de Universidades,
Oficina de Evaluación, 1975. 97p. (Informaciones bibliotecológicas, no. 1).
A total of ninety-one academic libraries in Peru are listed in this 1975 directory. Brief entries
specify name, address, telephone number, subject matter coverage, date library was
founded, hours of opening, classification system used, type of catalog used, and name of the
director.

URUGUAY

422 Bibliotecas del Uruguay. Ed. and comp. by Maria Teresa Goicoechea de Linares,
Cristine O. de Pérez Olave and Lilián Fernández Citera. Montevideo: La Biblioteca,
Palacio Legislativo, 1978. 252p. LC 79–102436.
Arranged by geographical location, and then alphabetically by the name of library, this
directory covers the major municipal, university, government, and special libraries in
Uruguay. A set of maps for each department (province) shows the location of the libraries in
that political subdivision. A substantial number of the libraries listed are in Montevideo.
Brief entries describe the location, collection strengths, services, and facilities. Some
entries provide additional background information about the library.

423 Directorio de servicios de información y documentación en el Uruguay. Montevideo: Biblioteca Nacional, Centro Nacional de Documentación Científica, Tecnica
y Económica, 1980. 128p. ISBN 84–8290–006–4.
A total of 199 documentation and information centers in Uruguay are described here.
Entries contain name of parent institution, telegraphic and postal addresses, telephone
number, hours of opening, date established, collection size, subject strengths, type of
cataloging and classification system, types of services available, policies regarding use of
services, equipment available, and publications issued by the library. Indexing is by
geographic location (by department), subject, and name of parent institution.

VENEZUELA

424 Directorio de bibliotecas venezolanas. Comp. by Olivia Martín. Caracas: Univ.
Central de Venezuela, Dirección de Bibliotecas, Información, Documentación y
Publicaciones, Dept. de Orientación, Información y Documentación, 1973. 999p. LC
76–474325.
In this lengthy 1973 directory, 185 special, university, public, and school libraries in
Venezuela are described. Entries contain name and address, date founded, number of
volumes, hours of opening, number of volumes, number of periodicals, and availability to
the public.

United States

425 American library directory. Ed. by Jaques Cattell Press. New York: Bowker,
1923– . LC 23–3581. ISSN 0065–910X.
More than 32,000 libraries in the United States and Canada are listed in the 1982 edition of

this work. It is, thus, the most comprehensive national directory of libraries published. The arrangement is by state and province, and then by city or town. Within each city or town section, libraries are arranged alphabetically. Coverage includes all types of public, academic, and special libraries, but does not include school libraries. Entries vary in length and complexity, depending on the library. Entries typically include name, address, and telephone number; date founded; library director and other key staff, including department and branch heads; the most recent expenditure figures; numerical data on the holdings, by type of material; special collections; departmental libraries; branches; public access policies; publications; and occasionally other information. One useful feature is the population and telephone area code for each city, printed by the name of the city. In addition to the main body of the directory, there are several useful lists: 1) networks, consortia, and other cooperative library organizations; 2) library schools and training courses; 3) library systems; 4) libraries for the blind and physically handicapped; 5) libraries serving the deaf and hearing impaired; 6) state and provincial public library agencies; 7) state school library agencies; 8) national and model interlibrary loan codes; 10) U.S. Armed Forces libraries overseas; and 11) International Communication Agency centers. A detailed index provides name access to all libraries listed. From the publication of the first edition in 1908 until 1978, the *American library directory* was published biennially. Since 1978, it has been published on an annual basis. Further updating is available through *American library directory updating service* which is published bimonthly. Although this directory is the most comprehensive available for libraries in the United States and Canada, a number of libraries still are not included for one reason or another. Consequently, the user will find it worthwhile to consult local or state directories of public, academic, or special libraries. In addition, the exclusion of school libraries means that directories published by state school library agencies must be consulted when this information is required.

426 Directory of archives and manuscript repositories in the United States. Washington, DC: National Historical Publications and Records Commission, 1978. 905p. LC 78–23870.

Approximately 3,250 archival and manuscript repositories are identified in this work. An attempt was made to include all those that maintain records deemed of historical importance; more than 500 that did not respond to the publisher's inquiries are included. Various types of institutions are covered, such as college libraries and archives, public libraries, religious archives, and historical societies. Arranged by location, the entries specify name and address of the repository, holdings, acquisition policies, hours of service, availability of a guide to the collection, and user fees, if required. The directory is indexed by type of repository, subject, and personal names.

427 Directory of special libraries and information centers. Ed. by Lois Lenroot-Ernt. 7th ed. Detroit: Gale, 1983. 2v. v.1, **Special libraries and information centers in the United States and Canada.** 1,425p. LC 79–16966. ISBN 0–8103–0258–6. v.2, **Geographic and personnel indexes.** 715p. LC 79–16788. ISBN 0–8103–0259–4.

More than 16,000 special libraries and information centers in the United States and Canada are described in volume 1 of this directory. It includes a substantial number not listed in the *American library directory* (entry **425**). Among the libraries found here are departments of academic or public libraries, business and medical libraries, historical archives, technical information centers, and many other types of information institutions. Entries are arranged alphabetically by the name of the parent institution. There are cross-references from the names of libraries and a detailed subject index. Entry length varies, depending on the information sent to the editors. However, a full entry includes name of organization, name of the library or information center, a principal subject key word, mailing address, telephone number, head of the library or information center, founding date, number of staff members, subjects covered, special collections, holdings, number of subscriptions, services, automated library operations, computerized information services, membership in networks or consortia, publications, catalogs published, and special indexes. A useful feature is the listing of any former or alternate names, a report of any mergers, and the location address if it is significantly different from the mailing address. Several appendices provide additional lists of libraries or information centers: 1) networks and consortia; 2) libraries for the blind and physically handicapped; 3) patent depository libraries; 4) federal information centers; and 5) federal job information centers. Volume 2 consists of geographic and personnel indexes. Libraries are listed by name of state and then name of city. All persons identified in the directory are listed alphabetically with the name of the organization with which they are affiliated. An updating service entitled *New special libraries* (entry **428**) is published periodically. The format of this service is essentially the same as the main directory.

428   New special libraries: a periodic supplement. Ed. by Lois Lenroot-Ernt. Detroit: Gale, 1982– . Irreg. LC 81–158640. ISSN 0193–4287.

This work provides a periodic supplement to the first volume of the seventh edition *Directory of special libraries and information centers* (entry **427**). It follows the same format as the *Directory* and is augmented by cumulative indexes similar to those provided in the second volume.

429   Special libraries directory: institutions where SLA members are employed. New York: Special Libraries Assn., 1977. 163p. LC 77–152511. ISBN 0–87111–238–8.

This directory is a reversal of the membership directory of the Special Libraries Association, *Who's who in special libraries* (entry **282**). Compiled from the membership records of SLA as of December 31, 1976, this work lists 5,869 libraries or other institutions in which members of the association were employed. The vast majority of the institutions are in the United States and Canada, although some other countries are also represented. The information provided for each library is minimal, and this list is not as extensive as that provided in the *Directory of special libraries and information centers* (entry **427**).

430   Subject collections: a guide to special book collections and subject emphases as reported by university, college, public, and special libraries and museums in the United States and Canada. Comp. by Lee Ash. 5th ed. New York: Bowker, 1978. 1,184p. LC 78–26399. ISBN 0–8352–0924–5.

This is the most comprehensive guide to subject holdings of libraries in the United States and Canada. Revised and enlarged, the current edition of this work covers the holdings of more than 15,000 libraries as well as collections in more than 1,000 museums. Pertinent information about subject collections is found under Library of Congress subject headings, and then alphabetically by state under each subject heading. Each entry contains the name and address of the library, the number of volumes in the collection, holdings of non-book materials, such as pictures and maps, and photocopying policies. The first edition of this work was published in 1958. Subsequent editions have been enlarged substantially, and this is now the standard source of information on subject holdings in U.S. and Canadian libraries.

However, some small libraries, historical societies, and other institutions that have subject collections are not represented here. Consequently, regional and state subject collection guides should also be consulted.

NORTHWESTERN STATES

431 Resources of pacific northwest libraries: a survey of facilities for study and research. By John Van Male. Seattle: Pacific Northwest Library Assn., 1943. 404p. LC 43–14518.

Although outdated, in part, this work can be used to augment the more current *Subject collections* (entry **430**). The resources of 108 libraries in the Pacific Northwest (Washington, Oregon, Idaho, Montana, and British Columbia) are listed. Brief information about collection strengths is arranged by topic. An index provides access by subject, names of collection, and names of institution.

SOUTHEASTERN STATES

432 Roads to research: distinguished library collections of the southeast. Athens: Univ. of Georgia Pr., 1968. 116p. LC 68–54088.

Brief entries describe important subject collections in southeastern college and university libraries. The entries identify the subject specialties and areas of emphasis of each collection. Although now somewhat dated, this work is still useful in connection with other directories of subject holdings; it is not as comprehensive as Downs (entry **487**) or Howell (entry **433**).

433 Special collections in libraries of the southeast. Ed. by J. B. Howell, Southeastern Library Association. Jackson, MI: Howick House, 1978. 423p. LC 78–113852.

Subject collections in ten southeastern states (Alabama, Florida, Georgia, Kentucky, Mississippi, North Carolina, South Carolina, Tennessee, Virginia, and West Virginia) are identified and described in this publication. A total of 2,022 subject collections are listed, without regard to size or depth. The list is more comprehensive than that for the Southeast found in Ash's *Subject collections* (entry **430**), but the descriptions in Ash tend to be longer. This directory is arranged geographically, by state and then by city. Access is provided by a detailed subject index, which identifies all collections with significant holdings on a particular subject.

SOUTHWESTERN STATES

434 Guide to humanities resources in the southwest. Ed. by Sandra Warne, Southwestern Library Association. New York: Neal-Schuman; Santa Barbara: ABC-Clio, distr., 1978. 237p. LC 78–55030. ISBN 0–918212–04–9.

A total of 420 humanities collections in six southwestern states are identified and described in this publication. As the work was funded in part by the National Endowment for the Humanities, the endowment's definition of humanities is used as a criterion for inclusion. Language, linguistics, literature, history, philosophy, archaeology, ethics, history, and several other topics are covered. Entries provide brief information about the nature of each collection. The major humanities holdings in the Southwest are in large academic or public libraries and these are all listed. In addition, there are listings of numerous county or local historical societies with very limited holdings. Many of these are not found in Ash's *Subject collections* (entry **430**), the standard directory for this type of information. In addition to collections, 340 humanities scholars are listed, by state, then alphabetically. Index access is provided by names of collections, subjects, and scholars' names, in a single alphabet.

INDIVIDUAL STATES

Alabama

435 Alabama public libraries. Montgomery: Alabama Public Library Service, 1961–1976. Annual.
This title was merged with *Statistics of public libraries in Alabama* to form *Annual report: Alabama public library service, 1977– .* For directory information see entry **436**. For statistics information see entry **599**.

436 Annual report: Alabama public library service, 1977– . Montgomery: Alabama Public Library Service, 1977– . Annual. LC 78–645259.
A directory of public libraries in Alabama is incorporated into this annual report. It is arranged alphabetically by city. Each entry includes the name of the library, county, mailing address, telephone, name of the library director, chairperson of the board, name of the regional system to which the library belongs, and hours of opening. A separate section provides this information for regional libraries. Access by library name is available through a name index. The *Annual report* also includes public library statistics for the preceding year (see entry **599**). This work was formed by the union of *Alabama public libraries* (entry **435**) and *Statistics of public libraries in Alabama* (entry **600**).

Alaska

437 Alaska libraries and library personnel directory. Juneau: Office of Public Information and Publications, Alaska Dept. of Education, 19??– . Annual. LC 72–620212. ISSN 0146–1036.
This source provides directory information on public libraries in Alaska. Each entry specifies name, address, and telephone number of the library along with the position, affiliation, and address of the librarians working there.

438 Directory of special libraries in Alaska. Ed. by Alan Edward Schorr. New York: Special Libraries Assn., 1975. 67p. LC 75–29043. ISBN 0–87111–239–6.
Listed here are sixty-four special libraries, several of which are not found in other directories. Each entry includes the library name, address, telephone and telex numbers, a contact person, hours of opening, services, major subject areas covered, and bibliographic information on any published list of holdings. Arrangement is alphabetical by the name of the library or parent organization. Index access is by names of persons, city of location, and subject.

Arizona

439   Arizona public libraries statistical report and directory, 1942/1944– . Phoenix: Dept. of Library, Archives and Public Records, Arizona State Library, 1942/1944– . Annual.

Although this is primarily a statistical report (see entry **601**), brief directory information for public and academic libraries is included. The directory provides coverage of all public libraries and libraries in state and private colleges and universities and community colleges. The information contained in each entry is the address, and, for public libraries, the names of any branches, the name of the president of the library board, and the population served by the library. Special and school libraries are not included.

Arkansas

440   Biennial report, 1937–1977. Little Rock: Arkansas Library Commission, 1939–1979. Biennial.

This publication was discontinued after the twentieth report. The directory section is partially superseded by *Public libraries of Arkansas by library development district* (entry **441**). For statistics information see entry **602**.

441   Public libraries of Arkansas by library development district. Little Rock: Arkansas State Library, 1980– . Annual.

This directory includes only headquarter libraries for city, county, or regional systems. Each entry specifies the name of the library, address, territory served, name of the librarian, telephone number, and population of the area served. This directory succeeds that which formerly appeared in the *Biennial report* of the Arkansas Library Commission (entry **440**). The *20th biennial report* was the last volume published before that agency ceased to exist and the Arkansas State Library came into being, on July 1, 1979. The State Library plans in the near future to begin publication of a more extensive directory that will include all local public libraries, headquarter libraries, and statistical data. The current directory does not include academic, special, or school libraries.

California

442   California library statistics and directory. Sacramento: California State Library, 1976– . Annual. LC 77–643048. ISSN 0148–4583.

The directory's coverage extends to public, academic, special, state government, and county law libraries throughout California. Library systems and networks as well as reference centers are listed separately. Arrangement is geographical, by city in which the library is located. Entries cover name and address of the library, name of the director, subject emphasis of the collections, holdings, population served, hours of opening, name of cooperative system to which the library belongs, financial information, and other statistical data (see entry **603**). This title was formerly published as the winter issue of *News notes of California libraries.*

443   Directory of special libraries in southern California. 5th ed. Canoga Park: Southern California Chapter, Special Libraries Assn., 1980. 120p.

More than 300 special libraries in the Southern California area are listed in this directory.

Entries contain organization name, name of the library within the organization, mailing address, telephone number, staff size, collection size, nature of the subjects covered, services offered, and names of key library personnel. The directory also lists the 625 members of the Southern California Chapter of SLA and indicates their SLA divisional affiliation. The previous edition was published in 1972.

Colorado

444   Directory of Colorado libraries. Denver: Office of Library Services, Colorado Dept. of Education, 1970– . Annual. LC 74–646552. ISSN 0094–8403.

This directory covers public, academic, special, and school libraries. Public and academic coverage is complete, special library coverage is extensive, and coverage of school libraries is limited to the thirteen Boards of Cooperative Service, which provide services to school districts in the state. Entries include the name, address, and telephone number of each library, and, for public libraries, the names of professional staff in the main library and the branches. Public library board members are listed with addresses and telephone numbers. Academic libraries are listed by institution, with address and personnel information. Special libraries are listed by company name, and each entry indicates if public access is permitted, whether or not telephone reference service is provided, and whether or not the library will provide interlibrary loan. A separate section indicates location, director, membership, and names of members of the governing boards for the regional library system. The directory also includes statistical information for public libraries (see entry **605**).

445   Specialized library resources of Colorado. Comp. and ed. by Barb MacDonald. 3d rev. ed. Denver: Colorado Chapter, Special Libraries Assn., 1974. 107p. LC 72–241148. ISSN 0146–7301.

Approximately 200 specialized subject collections in Colorado are identified in this directory. Each entry includes the name and address of the library, name of librarian, year of establishment, hours of opening, description of the subject content of the collection, and a list of services. Publications, where applicable, are listed. Index access is by names of staff members, name of library, and subject.

Connecticut

446   Directory of Connecticut libraries and media centers, 1980– . Bayside, NY: Library Directory Assoc., 1980– . Annual. LC 81–640093. ISSN 0275–2131.

More than 800 public, academic, special, and school libraries are identified and described in this directory. The entries are arranged by geographical area, corresponding to the six Cooperating Library Service Units in Connecticut. Within each area, libraries are listed by type, and then alphabetically by name. Entries include name, address, telephone number, town of location, hours of opening, holiday closings, interlibrary loan period, availability of meeting rooms, nature of special collections, online services, and personnel. The directory also provides information about the various library- and media-related associations in the state, including address, telephone number, and officers' names. The first volume of this directory was published in 1980, and prior to that there was no library directory providing this level of coverage for Connecticut.

447   Directory of subject strengths in Connecticut libraries. Ed. by Patt Snyder, Connecticut Valley Chapter of Special Libraries Association and the Connecticut Library Association. 2d ed. Hartford: Connecticut State Library, 1973. 118p. LC 74–195005.
Libraries in Connecticut with specialized subject holdings are listed, along with a descriptive note about the subject content of each collection. Of particular value is the description of the subject collections at Yale University. A map is included that shows the locations of the libraries listed. Index access is by collection name, library, and subject. The previous edition was published in 1968.

Delaware

448   A directory of Delaware libraries. Wilmington: College and Research Libraries Division, Delaware Library Assn., 1974– . Irreg. LC 82–644052. ISSN 0730–5222.
Coverage of all types of libraries is provided in this directory. Entries include the name of the organization, library name, address, telephone number, date founded, hours of opening, key staff members and their titles, and number of items held by type of material. Also noted, where applicable, are subject strengths and special collections, access to computer data bases, automated routines, photocopying charges, interlibrary loan protocols, name(s) of networks with which the library is affiliated, and borrowing privileges extended to users. Extensive cross-referencing exists, by common name of library, network, special collections, subjects, and individuals. To date, three directories have been published, in 1974, 1978 and 1982.

District of Columbia

449   Guide to special book collections in the Library of Congress. Washington, DC: Library of Congress, 1968. 66p.
This work is superseded by *Special collections in the Library of Congress: a selective guide*. For further information see entry **451**.

450   Library and reference facilities in the area of the District of Columbia. Comp. by Margaret Jennings. 11th ed. White Plains, NY: Knowledge Industry, 1983. 288p. LC 44–41159. ISBN 0–86729–021–8.
Compiled for the American Society for Information Science with the Joint Venture, this extensive directory of library holdings and other reference facilities in the Washington, D.C. area has over 400 numbered entries. It is particularly useful because of the rich information resources available in the environs. Each entry includes the name of the library, building and mailing address, telephone number, name of the person in charge, hours of opening, regulations for use, interlibrary loan policies, data base services, and a characterization of the resources. The amount of information for each institution varies, depending on its size and complexity, but for some libraries, information is extensive. The characterizations of resources are especially useful for determining the relevance of a collection to specific information requirements. Entries are listed alphabetically by name of institution, with numerous cross-references from library or collection names. Names of key personnel listed, subjects, and names of special collections are indexed. An additional useful feature is an appendix identifying libraries that have disbanded, moved from the area, or requested omission. This directory was first published in 1943 by the Library of Congress Legislative

Reference Service, and was published by LC until 1971 (eighth edition) when it was published by the Joint Venture. The 9th edition was also published by LC; the 10th edition was the first which involved the American Society for Information Science and Knowledge Industry Publications.

451 Special collections in the Library of Congress: a selective guide. Comp. by Annette Melville. Washington, DC: Library of Congress, 1980. 464p. LC 79–607780. ISBN 0–8444–0297–4.

The special collections of the world's largest library are described in a series of essays arranged alphabetically by name of the collection. The 269 collections were selected on the basis of rarity and possible interest to scholars and researchers. Each entry includes information about the history, content, scope, and subject strengths of the collection. In addition, there is information about the method used to organize the collection. Listed are such varied collections as Chinese manuscripts from the Ming dynasty, photographs of Mathew Brady, as well as numerous prints, drawings, maps and charts, musical instruments, letters and diaries, and others. The essays are supplemented by sixty-one illustrations. Access is provided by a detailed subject/name index. An appendix identifies special collections held by the various divisions of the library. This work supersedes and expands an earlier, out-of-print publication entitled *Guide to special book collections in the Library of Congress* (entry **449**).

Florida

452 Directory of special libraries and collections in Florida. Comp. and ed. by M. Judy Luther. Boynton Beach: Florida Chapter, Special Libraries Assn., 1982. 347p. LC 17–784. ISBN 0–87111–300–6.

This directory identifies and describes the holdings of more than 500 collections and special libraries in Florida. Arrangement is by city. Information about each library includes the name, address, and telephone number, as well as the name of the librarian, collection size, collection specialties, and use policies. Index access is by location, name of institution, type of institution, subject content of collection, and name of key personnel. Separate lists identify libraries that did not supply data and that are no longer operational in Florida.

453 Florida library directory and public library statistics. Tallahassee: Division of Library Services, Florida Dept. of State, 1951–1952. Annual.

This work is currently titled *1982 Florida library directory with statistics for 1952–* . For directory information see entry **454**. For statistics information see entry **610**.

454 Florida library directory with statistics for 1952– . Tallahassee: Division of Library Services, Florida Dept. of State, 1953– . Annual. ISSN 0430–7763.

All types of libraries and library associations are covered in this directory. Libraries are divided by type and listed by name of library or by name of sponsoring institution. For school library/media centers, listed by county, only names of key personnel are provided. Coverage is uneven in this section. Entries in other sections vary slightly, depending on type of library, but generally include the name, address, and telephone number of the library and the name of the person in charge. Public library entries include the name of the regional system with which the library is affiliated. Entries for academic libraries list names of persons in charge of departments. Special library entries indicate the size of the library's holdings by type of materials, services available to the public, and the subject emphasis of the collections. The directory is indexed by names of personnel listed. A separate section is included for statistics of public, academic, and institutional libraries (see entry **610** for further information on this section). This work was originally titled *Florida library directory and public library statistics* (entry **453**).

Georgia

455 Georgia public library statistics. Atlanta: Division of Public Library Services, Georgia Dept. of Education, 1960– . Annual

Although not a formal directory, public library directory information is available in this annual statistical report. The names of the libraries and the library systems are identified by location. For description of statistics information see entry **612**.

Hawaii

456   A directory of libraries and information sources in Hawaii and the Pacific Islands. Comp. by Arlene Leong Luster. Ed. by Y. Bartko and Marjorie Smith. 6th ed. Honolulu: Hawaii Library Assn., 1981. 125p.

This directory of libraries of various types in the state of Hawaii and other Pacific Islands is arranged geographically, then alphabetically by name of the library or parent institution. Entries include the name and address, librarian's name, service policies, and subject holdings of the libraries. Some libraries not found in national directories are covered here.

457   A directory of special libraries in Hawaii. By Marc A. Levin and Kathryn L. Creely. Honolulu: Special Libraries Assn./Hawaii, 1979. 15p. LC 80–621981.

Prepared for distribution to attendees at the 70th Annual Conference of the Special Libraries Association in Honolulu, this directory identifies all special libraries in Hawaii as of early 1979. Libraries are listed alphabetically by name of the organization. Entries include address and telephone number, holdings, subject specialties, services, and public access. Subject specialized departments of academic and other special libraries are included. The work is not indexed.

Idaho

458   Directory of Idaho libraries. Boise: Idaho State Library, 19??– . 3 per year.

This brief directory of libraries in Idaho is available from the Idaho State Library on request. Each issue is updated and current as of the time of publication. The name of the library, name of the library director, address, and telephone number are provided.

Illinois

459   "Directory of public libraries." Appears annually in **Illinois libraries.** Springfield: Illinois State Library, 1919– . 10 per year. LC 29–23175. ISSN 0019–2104.

The November issue of *Illinois libraries* includes statistics for public libraries for the previous year (see entry **615**) and a directory of all public libraries in the state. The directory is arranged by the city or town in which the library is located, and each entry contains the name, address, and telephone number of the library, the name of the librarian, the name and address of the board president, and the name of the system to which the library belongs. A separate list indicates public libraries by county, and yet another provides a list of libraries by system. The entries are indexed by name of librarian, library name, and area served.

460 Guide to Illinois library resources. Ed. by Robert B. Downs. Chicago: American Library Assn., 1974. 565p. LC 74–7074. ISBN 0–8389–0171–9.

This guide is published in cooperation with the Illinois State Library Association. Collections of academic, public, and special libraries are identified and described. Coverage is unrestricted as far as subject fields or types of materials are concerned. The work is divided into three major divisions. The first is arranged by subject and describes collections with holdings on the subjects identified; the second describes collections that deal with notable individuals—their papers, manuscripts, or other materials; the third cites 458 publications that list or describe the holdings of Illinois resource collections. Each entry in the first two divisions identifies the library and describes principal subject holdings by size (number of items, when known), by type of materials, and, in some cases, with specific titles. Entry length depends on the size and complexity of the collection. The third division (bibliography of publications) has one-sentence annotations. The guide is indexed in a single alphabet by subject, name of collection or institution, and name of individuals who are objects of special collections. This is one of the most detailed guides to the subject holdings of libraries in any state.

461 Illinois libraries and information centers. Ed. by Ellen Palmer. Chicago: Illinois Regional Library Council, 1981. 579p. LC 82–621212. ISBN 0–91760–14–8.

Detailed information for approximately 1,500 Illinois libraries is reported in this directory. Coverage extends to academic, public, special, and school libraries along with library consortia and associations. Each entry contains the institution and library name, mailing address, telephone number, background information, cooperative affiliations, numerical data about the holdings, areas of subject strength, special collections, services, and names of key staff members. For each subject area identified, most libraries have indicated whether theirs is a 1) general collection; 2) substantial collection; 3) research collection; or 4) comprehensive research collection. Definitions of these categories are provided in the section on use of the directory. Entries are arranged alphabetically, and additional access to each entry is provided by a geographic index, a subject index, an index by name of library or information center, and an index to librarians and information specialists whose names appear in the directory. This directory is an expansion of an earlier work titled *Libraries and information centers in the Chicago metropolitan area* (entry **462**). The second edition (revised and enlarged) had about 300 entries and was limited to just the Chicago metropolitan area. The first edition was published in 1973.

462 Libraries and information centers in the Chicago metropolitan area. Ed. by Joel M. Lee. 2d ed. Chicago: Illinois Regional Library Council, 1976. 592p. LC 76–8351. ISBN 0–917060–01–6.

This work is superseded by *Illinois libraries and information centers.* For further information see entry **461**.

India na

Indiana

463 Directory of library resources in central Indiana. Ed. by Susan A. Cady. Indianapolis: Central Indiana Area Library Services Authority, 1975. 221p. LC 75–33200.
Designed to assist libraries in resource sharing, this directory provides entries for every library and school in central Indiana (covering Boone, Hamilton, Hancock, Hendricks, Johnson, Marion, Morgan, and Shelby counties). More than 100 libraries are listed and described. Annual updates are provided with loose-leaf pages. Entries include the library name, address, telephone number, a brief description of each library, an indication of areas of subject strength and special collections, and numerical data on the holdings. Additional valuable information includes hours of opening, parking facilities, and photocopying facilities. The directory is indexed by library name, location, and subject. No general directory of libraries is published by the state, but the Indiana State Library produces a list of public libraries on an irregular basis. A similar directory has been published for another section of the state: *Directory of library resources in northwest Indiana* (entry **464**).

464 Directory of library resources in northwest Indiana. Valparasio: Northwest Indiana Area Library Services Authority, 1976. 94 leaves.
Published for another part of the state, this directory is similar to the *Directory of library resources in central Indiana* in scope, content and format. For further information see entry **463**.

Iowa

465 Iowa library directory, 1980– . Des Moines: Office of Library Development, State Library of Iowa, 1979– . Annual. LC 80–622364.
All types of libraries except school libraries are included in this directory. Public, academic, institutional, health science, state agency libraries, and special libraries that fall into one of these categories are listed. Entries contain name of place, county, regional system, population served, name of librarian, name, address, and telephone number of the library, hours open, interlibrary loan code number, and a population size code. The directory was formerly included with *Iowa public library statistics* (entry **617**); later it was published separately and titled *Iowa public library directory* (entry **467**). Beginning with the 1982 volume, it is published in two parts, the first covering public libraries and the second all other types of libraries. It is punched to fit into a loose-leaf binder.

466 Number not used.

467 Iowa public library directory. Des Moines: Office of Library Development, State Library of Iowa, 19??–1978. Annual.
This work is currently titled *Iowa library directory.* For further information see entry **465**.

Kansas

468 Kansas public library directory. Topeka: Kansas State Library, 1967– . Annual.
Arranged alphabetically by town, this directory provides the name, address, and telephone number of the library, the county in which it is located, the type of public library (city,

county, etc.), and the name of the library system to which it belongs. The directory information is duplicated in the annual titled *Kansas public library statistics* (entry **618**).

Kentucky

469   Sources: the Kentucky library directory and calendar. Frankfort, KY: Dept. of Library and Archives, 19??– . Annual.
In the most recent edition of this annual directory of public, academic, and special libraries in the state of Kentucky, brief entries specify county and town of location, library name and address, telephone number, and name of librarian. Public libraries are listed under the regional library system to which they belong and then by county. Entries for special libraries are arranged by town and identify name, address, and telephone number of the library. Entries for academic libraries contain name and address of library, telephone number, and name of librarian.

Louisiana

470   Public libraries in Louisiana: statistics of use: salary and staff study, 1953– . Baton Rouge: Louisiana State Library, 1954– . Annual.
This publication is primarily concerned with public library statistics. But, since individual libraries are listed by location, it also can be used as a directory. For a more complete description of this publication, see entry **621**. There is no general current directory of Louisiana libraries. The Louisiana State Library issues a list of parish, special, and institutional libraries on an annual basis, but this is intended primarily for internal use.

471   Resources in Louisiana libraries: public, academic, special and in media centers. By Sue Hefley. Baton Rouge: Louisiana State Library, 1971. 160p. LC 72–610144.
The subject strengths of Louisiana libraries are identified in this directory, arranged by region and then by library. Academic, public, and special libraries and media centers are covered. Entries contain subject strengths, subject emphasis, special collections, and numerical data on holdings by type of material, as well as the name of the library. Special sections identify federal, state, and foreign or international depository libraries in the state, archives and manuscript collections, and library retention policies. This work has not been updated, but it still is useful for identifying subject strengths.

Maine

472   Libraries of Maine: directory and statistics. Augusta: Maine State Library, 1971– . Annual. LC 73–646640. ISSN 0992–833X.
The directory lists public libraries in Maine, arranged alphabetically by county. Each entry provides the name, address, and telephone number of the library, the name of the director, and hours of opening. This information is published in the same volume, but in a separate section from the annual statistical compilation (see entry **623**). This work was formerly titled *Public libraries of Maine* (entry **473**).

473   Public libraries of Maine. Augusta: Maine State Library, 19??–1970. Annual. LC 75–646343.

This title is continued by *Libraries of Maine: directory and statistics.* For directory information see entry **472**. For statistics information see entry **623**.

Maryland

474 Directory of public libraries. Baltimore: Division of Library Development and
Services, 19??– . Annual.
This directory lists public libraries only. Entries contain library name, address, telephone
number, name of the library directory or administrator, estimated population served, and a
coded indication of the number of branches and bookmobiles in service.

475 Directory of subject collections in Maryland libraries. By Baltimore Chapter,
Special Libraries Assn. and Division of Library Development and Services, Maryland
State Dept. of Education. Parkton, MD: Baltimore Chapter, Special Libraries Assn.,
1979. 168p. LC 80–120328.
Maryland libraries considered to have subject strengths are identified. Special libraries,
academic libraries, and a limited number of public library collections are listed. Information
provided includes areas of subject strength, special collections, numerical data about
holdings, services, address, telephone number, and contact person.

476 Guide to specialized subject collections in Maryland libraries. Ed. and comp. by
Richard Parsons. 2d ed. Baltimore: Baltimore Chapter, Special Libraries Assn., 1974.
342p. LC 77–379053.
This revised and enlarged edition provides coverage of subject collections and subject
strengths of public, academic, and special libraries throughout Maryland. Specific characteristics of the specialized collections, with numerical data indicating size and types of
materials, are given. Indexing is by subject area, name of individuals represented in the
collections, and collection name.

Massachusetts

477 Directory of special libraries in Boston & vicinity. Ed. by Catharine Schoellkopf.
8th ed. Cambridge, MA: Boston Chapter, Special Libraries Assn., 1978. 200p. LC
78–20399.
Listed here are special libraries in New England, including Massachusetts, Vermont,
Maine, New Hampshire, and Rhode Island. The arrangement is alphabetical first by state,
then by name of library or organization. Entries contain the organization name, address,
telephone number, name of the chief librarian, hours open, availability of interlibrary loan
service and microform readers, and public access. Also included are a brief description of
the library and a brief indication of subject specialties. Numerical data on the size of the
collection by type of item, staff size, and availability of online data bases for reference
service complete the entry. The work is indexed by geographic area, subject, and names of
librarians.

478 Free public libraries in Massachusetts. Boston: Massachusetts Board of Library
Commissioners, 19??– . Annual.

This is a mimeographed directory, produced primarily for internal use, but available free on request. It includes the names and telephone numbers of public libraries in the state.

Michigan

479 Michigan library directory. Lansing: Michigan State Library, 1978– . Annual. LC 78–646734.

This directory of public and cooperative libraries in Michigan is arranged by city of location. If name of library is different than city of location, it is included in a separate alphabetical listing preceding the main body of the directory. Entries contain name, address, telephone number, name of the library cooperative to which it belongs, and hours of opening. Separate directories of public library trustees and public library friends groups are also published by the State Library. The *Directory* was titled *Michigan library directory and statistics* from 1967–1976 (entry **480**).

480 Michigan library directory and statistics. Lansing: Michigan State Library, 1967–1976. Annual. LC 74–649625. ISSN 0076–8081.

This title is continued by two titles, *Michigan library directory* (entry **479**) and *Michigan library statistics* (entry **629**).

Minnesota

481 The Hill directory of library and information resources in the Twin Cities area. Ed. by Marilyn Mauritz and Diane Brown. New rev. ed. St. Paul: James J. Hill Reference Library, 1978. 191p. LC 78–103795.

This privately published directory of approximately 400 libraries and information centers in the St. Paul-Minneapolis area is intended to inform potential users of available resources, services, and public access policies. Included are public, academic, and special libraries, information centers, and other information resources, including historical and art museums. This work updates *Library and information resources in the Twin Cities area* (entry **482**), which was published in 1972.

482 Library and information resources in the Twin Cities area. Ed. by Marilyn Mauritz. St. Paul: James J. Hill Reference Library, 1972. 403p. LC 72–487173.

This work is superseded by the revised edition, *The Hill directory of library and information resources in the Twin Cities area.* For further information see entry **481**.

483 "Minnesota public library statistics." Appears annually in **Minnesota libraries.** St. Paul: Office of Public Libraries and Interlibrary Cooperation, Minnesota Dept. of Education, 1904– . Quarterly. LC 10–33240. ISSN 0026–5551.

Statistical information about public libraries in Minnesota appears in the Spring issue of *Minnesota libraries* (see entry **629**). A directory of public libraries in the state serves as an index to the statistical portion of the issue. The directory includes the name of the library, name of the system, address and telephone number, and name of the librarian. Arrangement is alphabetical by library name, with the names of branch libraries included in the alphabetical listing.

Missouri

484 Directory of libraries in the St. Louis area. St. Louis: Higher Education Council of
St. Louis, 19??– . Biennial.

The most recently issued biennial edition includes approximately 200 libraries of various
types in the metropolitan St. Louis area. The arrangement is alphabetical by name of the
library or parent institution. Entries cover the name, address, telephone number of the
library, hours of opening, names of the director and key personnel, areas of subject
emphasis, special collections, numerical data on the size of the collection, public access
policies, and subject strengths. The directory is indexed by subject and by personal names.

485 Directory of Missouri libraries: public, special, college and university, 1971– .
Jefferson City: Missouri State Library, 1972– . Annual. LC 73–645566. ISSN
0092–4067.

Directory information and statistics are integrated into each entry in this publication. The
arrangement is alphabetical by name of the city or town in which each library is located.
Libraries of each of the three types covered are listed under the name of the city or town.
Each entry includes the name, address, telephone number, date founded, and hours of
opening. Most entries also supply statistics (for details see entry **632**). Entries for larger
libraries list branches and/or departments, with addresses and telephone numbers. All
entries also contain the name of the librarian in charge. A separate section provides an
overview of library service in each county of Missouri; noted are names of libraries, library
systems, tax levy, operating income, volumes available, and state aid available in each
county. Index access to the main part of the directory is provided by library name. This work
was issued as *Directory of Missouri libraries: statistics*, from 1966 to 1971 (entry **486**).

486 Directory of Missouri libraries: statistics. Jefferson City: Missouri State Library,
1966–1971. Annual. LC 73–645566. ISSN 0092–4067.

This work is continued by *Directory of Missouri libraries: public, special, college and
university*. For further directory information see entry **485**. For further statistics information
see entry **632**.

487 Resources of Missouri libraries. Ed. by Robert B. Downs. Jefferson City: Missouri
State Library, 1966. 190p. LC 67–63286.

Although now somewhat dated, this publication can still be used to augment Ash's *Subject
collections* (entry **430**) to determine the subject strengths of Missouri libraries. It includes
approximately 125 public, academic, special, and state-supported libraries, and is arranged
by subject. Under each subject heading is the name of the library, with brief information
about its holdings in that subject area. This is sometimes accompanied by numerical data
indicating the strength of the holdings. The work is indexed by subject, name of library, and
name of collection.

Montana

488 Montana library directory, with statistics of Montana public libraries. Helena:
Montana State Library, 1972– . Annual. LC 74–646588. ISSN 0094–873X.

127

The directory portion of this publication is separate from the compilation of statistics. Arranged by type of library and then location, the directory provides brief information for each public, academic, special, institutional, and school library. Entries include name of the library, mailing address, telephone number, name of the library director, hours of opening, and the county in which the library is located. For information about the statistical compilation, see entry **634**.

Nebraska

489 Nebraska library directory. Lincoln: Nebraska Library Commission, 1982– . Biennial.

Formerly published on an irregular basis, this is now issued every two years. Arrangement is by city or town, with a listing of all libraries located in each municipality. Entries include the name of the library or institution, address and telephone number, name of the director, name of the board chairperson for public libraries, and an indication of whether or not the library is a state documents depository or a participant in the state union catalog or other cooperative ventures.

490 Special, unique, or comprehensive collections located in Nebraska libraries: summary with index. By the Nebraska Library Commission and the Nebraska Library Association, Advisory Committee to the Nebraska Library Commission on Special Collections in Libraries in Nebraska. Lincoln: Nebraska Library Commission, 1973. 77p. LC 74–622481.

The intent of this directory is to provide information to libraries in the state to facilitate resource sharing. The holdings of the major libraries that are a part of the state's fifteen regional library systems are characterized. Although this directory consists largely of the holdings of public libraries, some academic libraries that serve as backups for the regional library system are included. The entries describe the collection and indicate special reference or bibliographic materials as well.

Nevada

491 Nevada library directory and statistics. Carson City: Library Development Division, Nevada State Library, 1976– . Annual. LC 77–644335.

This work provides directory information for all types of libraries in the state. It also includes library consortia, library association officers, and friends organizations. Arrangement is by type of library and then geographically by city or town in which the library is located. Entries contain the name of the library, address, telephone number, library director's name, hours of operation, and names of personnel. The directory was titled *Statistics with directory of Nevada libraries and library personnel* from 1974 to 1975 (entry **492**). For information on the statistics compilation see entry **636**.

492 Statistics with directory of Nevada libraries and library personnel. Carson City: Nevada State Library. 1974–1975. Annual. LC 74–644965. ISSN 0094–2596.

This title is continued by *Nevada library directory and statistics.* For directory information see entry **491**. For statistics information see entry **636**.

New Hampshire

493 Directory of New Hampshire libraries, 1972– . Concord: New Hampshire State
Library, 1972– . Annual.

Primary coverage is for public libraries, but the directory also lists college libraries, libraries
of state institutions, library cooperatives, and state document depositories. Special and
school libraries are not listed. Arrangement is by type of library. Public libraries are
arranged by location, and the entries include name, address, telephone number, population
served, name of librarian, names of the chairpersons and other members of the board, and
hours of opening. Similar information is presented for other types of libraries.

New Jersey

494 New Jersey area library directory. Trenton: Division of the State Library, Archives
and History, 1976–1979. Annual. LC 76–642916.

This title is continued by the *Public/area library guide*. For further information see
entry **496**.

495 New Jersey public library directory. Trenton: Library Development Bureau, New
Jersey State Library, 1977–1979. Annual. LC 79–642493.

This title is continued by the *Public/area library guide*. For further information see
entry **496**.

496 Public/area library guide. Trenton: Library Development Bureau, New Jersey State
Library, 1980– . Annual. ISSN 0362–2967.

This is a directory of public and area (regional) libraries. Information about public libraries
is arranged alphabetically by municipality. Each entry specifies the name, address, telephone number, county in which it is located, library director's name, address, telephone
number, and name of the board president. Entries also include the five regional film centers,
names of county libraries with branches, and separate information for area libraries. Entries
for area libraries provide additional information: the number of staff members, hours of
opening, population served, municipalities served, services available, and film centers. The
directory also includes alphabetical lists of library directors and area librarians. This
directory was formerly published as two directories, one which listed public libraries (entry
495) and the other area libraries (entry **494**).

497 Special libraries in New Jersey: a directory. Ed. by Annette Corth. Kenilworth:
New Jersey Chapter, Special Libraries Assn., 1978. 58p. LC 78–112061.

Special libraries, including special collections from academic (but not public) libraries are
listed here. Arrangement is alphabetical by county and then by parent organization. Each of
the 336 entries contains the name, address, and telephone number of the library, and then
brief information on subjects covered and the nature of the library. Index access is by subject
and organization name.

New Mexico

498 New Mexico library directory, 1975/76– . Santa Fe: New Mexico State Library, 1976– . Irreg.
Directory information is provided for public, academic, special, institutional, and school libraries in the state. Arrangement is by city. Entries are brief and include name, address, and telephone number of the library, with departments or branches included for larger libraries. Characteristics of the library are not provided. The latest volume was published in 1981.

New York

499 Directory of college and university libraries in New York state: with statistical data. Albany: Library Development, Cultural Education Center, Univ. of the State of New York, 1965– . Annual. LC 66–7962. ISSN 0070–5276.
All academic libraries accredited for one or more diploma offerings by the State Board of Regents are listed in this directory. The latest edition lists 266 libraries. Arrangement is alphabetical by name of the institution, with cross-references from alternative names. Institutions that have ceased to exist since the previous edition are also identified, but no other information about these is given. Each entry supplies the address, telephone numbers, name of library director, president of the institution, and statistical information, including holdings, periodicals received, expenditures, size of professional staff, and interlibrary loans. The names of the reference and interlibrary loan librarians are also specified. An appendix with several statistical tables is provided at the end (see entry **641**). There is also an alphabetical directory of head librarians. Publication began in 1965, but the directory was not published in 1966. The fourteenth directory was published in 1981.

500 The directory of library systems in New York state. Albany: Division of Library Development, State Univ. of New York, 1976– . Annual.
Information about the headquarters and all members of each library system affiliated with the New York State 3R Councils is found in this directory. Arranged by 3R region, the following is provided for each system within the region: address, year of establishment, president of the board of trustees, counties included in the system, and member libraries. For county libraries that are members, the name, address, and telephone number are given. A valuable additional feature is a set of maps showing the coverage of the systems. This publication was formed by the union of *Directory of New York state public library systems* (entry **501**) and the *Directory of reference and research resources systems in New York state* (entry **502**).

501 Directory of New York state public library systems. Albany: Division of Library Development, State Univ. of New York, 1964–1975. Annual. ISSN 0070–5950.
This title was merged with *Directory of reference and research resources systems in New York State* to form *The directory of library systems in New York state.* For further information see entry **500**.

502 Directory of reference and research resources systems in New York state. Albany: Division of Library Development, State Univ. of New York, 1967–1975. Annual.

This title was merged with *Directory of New York state public library systems* to form *The directory of library systems in New York state*. For further information see entry **500**.

503 **Guide to the reference collections of the New York Public Library.** By Karl Brown. New York: New York Public Library, 1941. 416p.

This work is superseded by *Guide to the research collections of the New York Public Library.* For further information see entry **504**.

504 **Guide to the research collections of the New York Public Library.** Comp. by Sam P. Williams. Chicago: American Library Assn., 1975. 336p. LC 75–15878. ISBN 0–8389–0125–5.

The major special collections of the New York Public Library are identified and characterized in this guide. It is arranged by four major categories: 1) general materials, 2) humanities, 3) social sciences, and 4) pure and applied sciences. These are divided into sixty-four narrower subject classes, which are in turn subdivided when warranted. The entry for each subject class includes a statement of the scope of any collections in the library falling into that subject class, an indication of collection development policy, a history of the collection, and, in some cases, numerical data which indicate the size of the collection. Detailed descriptions of the collections follow. Collection strength is indicated by the terms *representative, selective, comprehensive,* and *exhaustive*. An appendix identifies published catalogs of the collections, and another provides a locator guide to NYPL buildings. The work is indexed by subject and collection name. The information is current to the end of 1969 and is supplemented by information appearing in the *Bulletin of the NYPL*. This guide supersedes an earlier publication by Karl Brown titled *Guide to the reference collections of the New York Public Library* (entry **503**).

505 **Library resources in New York City: a selection for students.** Ed. by Cornelia Marwell. 2d ed. New York: School of Library Service, Columbia Univ., 1979. 270p.

A total of 233 libraries in Manhatten and the other boroughs are listed in this directory. The following information is included in each entry: name of library, affiliation, date founded, address and telephone number, director or person in charge, hours of opening, policies and regulations regarding use, types of services available, type of classification system used, type of catalog, and characterization of library's resources (including any special collections). In addition to data about the libraries, there are lists of more than sixty bookstores located in Manhatten, of additional information sources about libraries in the greater New York area, and of libraries by category. Also provided is a subject index to the resources of the libraries listed. The first edition of this work was published in 1971.

506 **METRO directory of members, 1970/71– .** New York: METRO, 1970– . Biennial. LC 77–644203. ISSN 0362–8744.

This directory lists libraries that participate in the New York Metropolitan Reference and Research Library Agency (METRO), one of the nine regional multi-type library systems in New York State. Because METRO is involved in both cooperative acquisitions and cooperative reference service, the directory is useful for libraries and library users in the metropolitan area. Information contained in each entry includes name, address, telephone number of the library, names of key staff members, policies regarding use of the library, types of services available (such as photocopying), subject strengths, names of special collections, and types of computer services available. An index to subject strengths and to special collections completes each issue.

507 Special libraries directory of greater New York. New York: New York Chapter, Special Libraries Assn., 1928– . Irreg. LC 54–1093. ISSN 0093–9587.

A total of 1,080 libraries in the metropolitan New York City area are listed in the latest (1980) directory, including some libraries in Connecticut and New Jersey. Of these, sixty are new from the previous edition. Special collections in academic and public libraries are included. Entries are arranged by broad topic categories and then alphabetically by name of library. Each entry contains the name, address, telephone number, date founded, name of library director, hours of opening, volume count, subject areas covered, special collections, and public access. The work is indexed by name of library or organization, by subject, and by librarian's name.

North Carolina

508 North Carolina libraries, 1931–1937. Raleigh: Division of the State Library, North Carolina Dept. of Cultural Resources, 1932–1938. Annual.

This title has varied since 1938. It is currently published under two titles, *Statistics and directory of North Carolina public libraries* and *Statistics of North Carolina university and college libraries*. For directory information see entry **510**. For statistics information see entry **644** and entry **645**.

509 Resources of North Carolina libraries. Ed. by Robert B. Downs. Raleigh: Governor's Commission on Library Resources, 1965. 236p. LC 65–64746.

The subject strengths and subject collections of academic, public, and special libraries in North Carolina are identified and described in this work. Arrangement is by subject. Each collection is described in terms of its specific characteristics, size and strengths, and, in some cases, specific titles. The work is indexed by name of library and name of collection. A revised edition was issued in microcard by the University of Rochester Press for the Association of College and Research Libraries in 1970.

510 Statistics and directory of North Carolina public libraries, July 1–June 30. Raleigh: Division of the State Library, North Carolina Dept. of Cultural Resources, 1939– . Annual. LC 78–647664. ISSN 0164–0844.

This directory covers only public libraries. It is arranged alphabetically by county and cross-referenced to regions. Each entry identifies the name, address, telephone number of the library, and librarian's name. A separate list of regional libraries identifies all of the branches as well as the central libraries within the region. It also includes statistical information about public libraries within the state. The title varies. It was first published as *North Carolina libraries 1932–1938* (entry **508**). For more information on the statistical compilation, see entry **644**.

North Dakota

511 Directory of North Dakota libraries. Bismarck: North Dakota State Library, 19??– . Annual.

Public, academic, and special libraries in North Dakota are listed by city or town of location, with all types of libraries in the same community listed together. Entries contain name, address, and telephone number of library and names, titles and telephone numbers of library staff members. Coverage is complete for public and academic libraries.

Ohio

512 Directory of Ohio libraries, 1935– . Columbus: State Library of Ohio, 1935– . Annual. LC 82–644621. ISSN 0734–0389.

Listings for public, academic, special, and institutional libraries as well as school library/media centers are included. Arrangement is by type of library. Public libraries are listed by name of the city where the main library is located. Other types of libraries are entered by name of the library, parent institution, or company. Entries identify name, address, telephone number, director, board president for public libraries, names of branches or departments, and names of persons in charge of branches or departments. A separate section provides listings for all library- and media-related associations in the state. There is also a section on regional systems and library consortia. The work is not indexed. It was titled *Ohio directory of libraries* from 1972 to 1979 (entry **514**), and earlier, *Directory of Ohio libraries: with statistics for 19––*. For information about statistical data presented see entry **647**.

513 Directory of special libraries. Akron: Cleveland Chapter, Special Libraries Assn., 19??– . Annual. LC 75–642556. ISSN 0098–065X.

Also included in this annual membership directory of the Cleveland Chapter of SLA is a listing of special libraries in the Cleveland area. Entries include the name, address, telephone number of the library, library director, hours of opening, staff size, public access, subject areas covered, interlibrary loan policies, collection size, special collections, network memberships, and types of equipment available.

514 Ohio directory of libraries. Columbus: State Library of Ohio, 1972–1979. Annual. LC 79–644836. ISSN 0196–3872.

This work continues *Directory of Ohio libraries: with statistics for 19––*, and it is currently published under the title, *Directory of Ohio libraries*. For directory information see entry **512**. For statistics information see entry **647**.

Oklahoma

515 Annual report and directory of libraries in Oklahoma. Oklahoma City: Oklahoma Dept. of Libraries, 1955–1981. Annual. LC 81–643509. ISSN 0066–4065.

This title is continued by *Annual report and directory of Oklahoma libraries*. For directory information see entry **516**. For statistics information see entry **650**.

516 Annual report and directory of Oklahoma libraries. Oklahoma City: Oklahoma Dept. of Libraries, 1982– . Annual. ISSN 0066–4065.

This publication includes statistical information for public, academic, institutional, school, and special libraries (see entry **650**); directory information for public and institutional libraries; and brief biographic information for individual librarians from various types of libraries. The directory information for public libraries is arranged by city, with name, address, telephone number, name of librarian and assistant librarian, names of selected other staff members, and a list of all members of the library board, with the chairperson designated. The directory of institutional libraries includes the institution's name and address, division of state government in which it is placed administratively, and name of the librarian. Directory information for the other types of libraries can be obtained by examining the statistical portion of the work which lists libraries by name. This title continues *Annual report and directory of libraries in Oklahoma* (entry **515**).

Oregon

517 Directory and statistics of Oregon libraries. Salem: Oregon State Library, 1977– . Annual. LC 78–645032. ISSN 0162–0290.
This annual provides directory coverage and statistics for public, academic, special, and institutional libraries in Oregon. Entries include name, address, telephone number, library director, a list of the trustees for public libraries, and an indication of U.S. document depositories. This work continues the *Directory of Oregon libraries* (entry **518**). For information on the statistical coverage of this work, see entry **651**.

518 Directory of Oregon libraries. Salem: Oregon State Library, 1950–1976. Annual.
This title is continued by *Directory and statistics of Oregon libraries.* For directory information see entry **517**. For statistics information see entry **651**.

519 Directory of special libraries in Oregon and southwest Washington. Comp. by Mary Devlin, Julie Kawabata and Donna Shaver. Salem: Oregon Chapter, Special Libraries Assn., 1978. 68p. LC 78–107133.
Special libraries and subject collections in academic and public libraries are listed in this directory. Entries are arranged by name of library or parent organization, with brief information about each. Included in each entry is the name, address, telephone number, name of the library director, subject strengths and special collections, information on public access, and special services.

Pennsylvania

520 Directory of libraries and information sources in the Philadelphia area: eastern Pennsylvania, southern New Jersey and Delaware. Ed. by Anna MacPenrose and Darla Wagner. 16th ed. Philadelphia: Philadelphia Chapter, Special Libraries Assn., 1983. 118p.
A total of 810 special, academic, and public libraries and information centers in the greater Philadelphia metropolitan area are listed here. The geographical spread takes in Philadelphia, eastern Pennsylvania, southern New Jersey, and Delaware. Arrangement is alphabetical by name of library or sponsoring institution. Each entry includes name, address, telephone number, director's name and names of other key staff members, hours of opening, numerical data on the holdings, subject strengths and special collections, public access policies, copying facilities, microform facilities, and names of networks or consortia with which the library is affiliated. The directory is indexed by subject, collection name, personnel, and network or consortium name.

521 Directory of Pennsylvania academic and research libraries. Harrisburg: Bureau of
Library Development, State Library of Pennsylvania, Pennsylvania Dept. of Education, 1971–1973. 2v. LC 72–620202.
This work is superseded by *Directory of Pennsylvania library resources: a guide to the
resources and services of academic, special and large public libraries.* For further information see entry **522**.

**522 Directory of Pennsylvania library resources: a guide to the resources and services
of academic, special and large public libraries.** Harrisburg: Bureau of Library
Development, State Library of Pennsylvania, Pennsylvania Dept. of Education,
1973– . Annual. LC 79–3200. ISSN 0193–8436.
This statewide directory lists nearly 500 libraries, arranged alphabetically by the name of
the parent institution. Covered are academic, special, and the larger public libraries of the
state. Each entry provides name, address, telephone number, library director and other key
staff members, size of staff, hours of opening, number of items by type of material, annual
budget, and subject specialization and special collections. The work is indexed by subject
area and type of institution. Earlier, this was published as *Directory of Pennsylvania
academic and research libraries* (entry **521**).

523 Directory of special libraries in Pittsburgh and vicinity. 9th ed. Pittsburgh: Pittsburgh Chapter, Special Libraries Assn., 1977. 135p.
Approximately 130 special libraries in the greater Pittsburgh area are covered in this
directory. Entries specify name, address, telephone number, name of chief library officer,
staff size, year established, public access policies, interlibrary loan policies, subject specializations, special collections, and numerical data on the holdings. Index access is by subject
and personal name. The work is produced in loose-leaf form for additions and revisions. A
new edition is now in progress.

524 Pennsylvania public libraries directory. Harrisburg: Pennsylvania State Library,
1962– . Annual. LC 63–7065.
All public libraries in the state are covered here. Arrangement is by city, and entries supply
city where located, county, name of district to which the library belongs, proper name of the
library, address, telephone number, name of the librarian, name, address, and telephone
number of the board president, the same information for the president of the friends group,
and the name, location, telephone number, and head librarian of branches. The work is
indexed by library district, county, and proper name of the library. There is no personal
name index.

Puerto Rico

525 Directorio de bibliotecas de Puerto Rico. By Daisy Alamo de Torres. Rio Piedras:
Puerto Rico Asociación Estudiantes Graduados de Bibliotecología, Univ. de Puerto
Rico, 1979. 100p. LC 80–128849.
Covered in this directory are academic, school (including public, private, and military),
special (private and government), and public libraries. Also included are libraries in penal
institutions. Entries specify name, address, telephone number, person in charge, comments
on holdings, number of microforms, and hours open.

Rhode Island

526   Directory of Rhode Island public libraries. Providence: Rhode Island Dept. of State Library Services, 19??– . Annual.

Brief information, for all types of libraries, is organized into five sections, representing the state's five interrelated library systems. Within each section, libraries are listed by location. Entries include library name, address, telephone number, name of librarian, name of board chairperson, and hours of opening. There is an alphabetical index by name of library. This directory is updated by supplements twice a year.

South Carolina

527   Research materials in South Carolina: a guide. Comp. and ed. by John Hammond Moore, South Carolina State Library Board, and South Carolina Library Association. Columbia: Univ. of South Carolina Pr., 1967. 346p. LC 67–25916.

Specialized subject collections and other information resources are identified and briefly described in this guide, which includes newspaper files, manuscript and archival collections, periodical holdings, and other resources of value for scholarly research (in the original or in microform). Because this publication is now dated, its primary value is for locating subject collections not identified in Ash (entry **430**) or Howell (entry **433**).

South Dakota

528   Statistics of South Dakota libraries. Pierre: South Dakota State Library, 1975– . Annual. LC 78–642415.

A brief directory of public libraries in the state is included in this annual statistical report. Arranged by location, it supplies the name and address of the library. See entry **657** for description of statistical information provided.

Tennessee

529   Directory of regional and public libraries of Tennessee. Nashville: Development and Extension Services Section, Tennessee State Library and Archives, Office of the Secretary of State, 19??– . Annual.

This directory only lists public libraries. Arrangement is alphabetical by regional library systems, then by county, and finally by individual library. Entries are brief, containing the name, address, telephone number of the library, and librarian's name.

Texas

530   Central Texas library resources directory: a guide to libraries and information agencies, 1981. Comp. by Beth Fuller. Austin: Texas Public Library, Central Texas Library System, 1981. 382p.

This directory covers 1,383 libraries in central Texas. It includes libraries of various types and is arranged by county, then by library name. Entries are numbered and contain name, address, telephone number of the library, type of library, number of staff, hours open, patron access, collection strengths, and loan and interlibrary loan policies. Index access is alphabetical by name of library or parent institution, by subject, and by type of library.

531   Directory of special libraries and information centers in Texas. Austin: Development Division, Texas State Library and Texas Chapter, Special Libraries Assn., 1981– . Irreg. LC 78–625489. ISSN 0082–3163 .

Directory coverage of 414 libraries and information centers in Texas is provided in the 1982 edition of this work. Arrangement is alphabetical by corporate or institutional name. Entries are numbered and include name, address, telephone, telex and TWX numbers, year established, dates of the last complete fiscal year, numerical data on holdings, publications, types of services, use policies, automated equipment, number of employees, expenditures, floor space, affiliations, name of head librarian, and former names by which the library was known. The work is indexed by subject, institutional name, and personal name. Prior to publication of the ninth edition in 1981, the *Directory* was titled, *Texas special libraries directory* (entry **535**).

532   Resources of Texas libraries. By Edward G. Holley and Donald D. Hendricks. Austin: Field Service Division, Texas State Library, 1968. 352p. LC 68–65335.

Resources and holdings of eighty-four libraries in Texas are covered. Arranged by type of library, this work describes the special collections and subject strengths of each library. There is also comparative information about collections on similar subjects. The types of libraries covered are public libraries, private and public universities, law, medical, and other special libraries, and junior college libraries. There is an alphabetical subject/name index to topics related to subject strengths. Also, maps show the locations of the libraries. Although this work is now several years old, it can be used in conjunction with Ash's *Subject collections* (entry **430**).

533   Texas academic library statistics. Austin, TX: Texas Council of State University Librarians and Library Development Division, Texas State Library, 1972– . Annual. LC 78–642170. ISSN 0276–458X.

Directory information is provided for approximately 100 academic libraries in Texas: name, address, and telephone number of the library, and the name and title of the chief administrative officer. For further information see entry **659**.

534   Texas public library statistics for 1974– . Austin: Library Development Division, Texas State Library, 1975– . Annual. LC 75–646379. ISSN 0082–3120.

In addition to statistical data (see entry **660**), this work provides directory information about public libraries and regional resource centers. Specifically, included here are the state library, resource centers and regional system coordinators, regional historical resource depositories, state document depositories, and all public libraries and their branches. Public libraries are arranged alphabetically by name of city or town. Entries include name and address, name of librarian, name of regional system to which the library belongs, name and address of board chairperson, and name and address of president of the friends group. Cross-references relate the directory to the detailed statistical section. This work was originally titled *Texas public library statistics*.

535   Texas special libraries directory. Austin: Field Services Division, Texas State Library, 1967–1980. Irreg. LC 78–625489.

This work is continued under the title, *Directory of special libraries and information centers in Texas.* For further information see entry **531**.

Utah

536   Utah public libraries. Annual report. Salt Lake City: Utah State Library, Division of
Economic and Community Development, 1959– . Annual. ISSN 0566–4276.
A directory of public libraries is combined with a statistical report (see entry **661**) in this
publication. The directory provides the name, address, telephone number, and name of the
director of each public library in the state. In addition, there is a directory of public library
trustees.

Vermont

**537   Biennial report of the Vermont Department of Libraries: including Vermont
library directory: statistics of local libraries.** Montpelier: Vermont Dept. of Libraries, 1976– . Biennial. LC 76–647865. ISSN 0364–7382.
Directory information for all libraries in the state is here arranged by town or city. All types
of libraries are listed. Entries contain name, address, telephone number of the library,
librarian's home telephone, hours of opening, Vermont Union Catalog symbol assigned to
the library, regional library system to which it belongs, and for public libraries, the name
and home telephone number of the board chairperson. Statistical information is also
included (see entry **662**). Until the 1979 volume, the directory was published separately
under the title, *Vermont library directory* (entry **538**).

538   Vermont library directory. Montpelier: Vermont Dept. of Libraries, 1968–1977.
Biennial. ISSN 0364–7382.
This title was merged with *Statistics of local libraries* in 1979 to form *Biennial report of the
Vermont Department of Libraries.* For directory information see entry **537**. For statistics
information see entry **662**.

Virginia

539   Statistics of Virginia public libraries and institutional libraries, 1975/76– . Richmond: Library Development Branch, Virginia State Library, 1976– . Annual. LC
82–641407. ISSN 0731–8464.
Although the title suggests a more limited scope, this publication includes a directory listing
academic and special libraries as well as public and institutional libraries. Directory
information for each type of library is provided in a separate section. Public library
information is arranged alphabetically by name of the library and includes name and
address, a list of the branches, and the name of the head librarian of each unit. Academic and
special library listings also specify collection size, computer services, lending restrictions,
and, for academic libraries, the number of students served. Statistics are limited to public
libraries (see entry **664**). This title continues *Statistics of Virginia public libraries.*

Washington

540   Directory of libraries in Washington state. Olympia: Washington State Library,
1978– . Annual.
Directory information covering public and academic libraries in Washington is included in
this annual directory. Entries provide name, address, and telephone number, as well as

information about the holdings. This title supplements the directory information contained in *Annual statistical bulletin,* (see entry **665**).

West Virginia

541 WVLC statistical report. Charleston: West Virginia Library Commission, 1971– . Annual.
Although primarily a statistical compilation (see entry **667**), this work also provides a directory of public, academic, and special libraries in the state. Only brief information is included. Entries contain the name, address, and telephone number of the library and the name of the head librarian.

Wisconsin

542 Wisconsin library service record, 1972– . Madison: Division for Library Services, Dept. of Public Instruction, 1974– . Annual. LC 76–640787. ISSN 0361–2848.
Detailed directory information is provided for academic, special, and public libraries. Academic libraries are listed by name of institution and include address, telephone, name of director, and year established. Entries for special libraries add to that information the subjects covered and the number of periodical titles and volumes. Public libraries are arranged by county and community. The information presented indicates name of the cooperative service system to which it belongs, name and telephone number of library director, number of staff, and number of hours open. This publication also contains statistics for individual public libraries in Wisconsin (see entry **668**).

Wyoming

543 Wyoming libraries directory. Cheyenne: Wyoming State Library, 1979– . Annual. LC 83–643625.
This directory covers public, academic, and institutional libraries in Wyoming. Entries for public libraries supply the name, address, telephone number, name of library director, hours of opening, and name and address of branches. Entries for academic and institutional libraries are similar. Special libraries are listed from time to time, the last occasion being the 1980–1981 directory. Also included is a list of trustees of county public libraries, which provides names and addresses. In the past, statistical information was incorporated in the directory, but this has not been done for several years. This title supersedes the *Wyoming public libraries directory* (entry **544**).

544 Wyoming public libraries directory. Cheyenne: Wyoming State Library, 1975/76–1978/79. Annual.
This title is superseded by *Wyoming libraries directory.* For further information see entry **543**.

6.

Sources of Library Statistics

INTRODUCTION

The availability of library statistics has long been recognized as essential for effective library management. Furthermore, statistical data are necessary components of much of the current research dealing with library services. The case for the value of library statistics was perhaps best stated by John Carson Rather and Nathan M. Cohen more than two decades ago when they observed in the introduction to their landmark bibliography of American library statistical publications,

> Statistics are a respected aid to enlightened library administration. By recording the operation of a library in quantitative terms, they make possible its evaluation and provide the means of describing it concisely for the benefit of a governing authority. Used alone or compared with data from other libraries, statistics provide a factual basis for budget preparation.
>
> More than a tool of management, statistics are the indispensable raw material for any sound research to determine trends in the growth and development of libraries. Apart from their utilitarian aspect, statistics have great cultural value in defining the role of libraries in our society (*Statistics on libraries: an annotated bibliography of recurring surveys*. Washington, DC: U.S. Office of Education, 1961, p.1).

The process of obtaining statistical data is often complex and frustrating. While there are several reasons for this, two are particularly important. First is fragmentation; there is tremendous diversity in the organizations that compile and publish library statistics. The number and variety of statistical publications frequently make the task of identifying an appropriate source a formidable one. Second is inconsistency; there is a general lack of adherence to accepted guidelines in compiling and reporting library statistics. This results in variations that compromise the usefulness of the available data.

The major problem associated with the use of any statistical reporting series is that over time the data categories change, either as a result of new methods for the compilation of the data or the addition or deletion of new data categories. The lack of standardization in data compilation undertaken by different organizations further compounds the problem. Despite the lack of standardization, there are some common types of library statistics that appear consistently in ongoing reporting services. Among these are population served, number of book and serial titles, the previous year's expenditures, and the previous year's income. Frequently, some of these categories are further subdivided, e.g., expenditures by category or sources of income by category.

This chapter describes over 120 publications providing library-related data for the major English-speaking areas of the world: Australia and New Zealand, Canada, the United Kingdom, and the United States. No attempt has been made in this edition of the *Guide* to describe statistical sources covering libraries in other areas. Similarly, research reports that generate statistics as an incidental part of their findings and individual monographs that include but do not focus on data have been omitted. The emphasis is on serially-issued statistics or data found in reference works published during the last decade. Statistics published in journal articles or in sections of a serial are identified only if the data provided are unavailable in separately-published reference works. Since many of the statistical sources in this chapter also function as directories, cross listings are supplied where needed. Only library-related sources providing general quantitative data are treated here; for statistics on specific subjects, see the appropriate sections in Chapter 7.

AUSTRALIA AND NEW ZEALAND

545 "Library statistics." Appears annually in **Australian academic and research libraries.** Bundoora: Univ. and College Libraries Section, Library Assn. of Australia, 1970– . Quarterly. LC 71–16626. ISSN 0004–8623.

Statistics for university libraries in Australia and New Zealand, as well as Australian colleges of advanced education, are provided annually in the library statistics supplement to this journal. Statistics are reported toward the end of the year following the year covered by the data. The tables for university libraries include both Australian and New Zealand universities. Institutions are identified individually by initials. The data reported cover staff, including numbers of staff members qualified at different levels; number of persons serving in various capacities in the library (e.g., reader's services, technical services); number of items loaned from the central library, branches, and the reserve collection; number of interlibrary loan transactions; seating; hours open; number of monograph and serial volumes; current unique serial titles; number of volumes held; number of unique serial titles held; sources of funds for materials; expenditures for materials, binding, and various other items; number of academic staff; number of full-time and part-time students seeking higher degrees and other degrees; and total number of students. Basically, the same categories of information are reported for the colleges of advanced education.

CANADA

Canadian library statistical reports are arranged alphabetically by title within four main divisions: Public Libraries, School Libraries, College and University

Libraries, and Provincial Statistical Sources. Provincial reports are listed alphabetically under the province name.

Public Libraries

546 **Culture statistics: public libraries in Canada/Statistiques de la culture: bibliothèques publiques au Canada, 1975– .** Ottawa: Statistics Canada, 1978– . Annual. LC 80–30384. ISSN 0704–884X.

Public library data collected by the provincial library agencies are compiled by Statistics Canada and reported in English and French by this annual survey. Regional library systems, metropolitan libraries, and individual public libraries are covered. Information provided includes population served based on census data, holdings, number of items circulated, income by category, and expenditures by category. This work was formerly published under the titles, *Public libraries in Canada* (entry **547**) and *Survey of libraries: part I, public libraries* (entry **550**).

547 **Public libraries in Canada, 1970–1974.** Ottawa: Statistics Canada, 1973–1977. Annual. LC 74–645254.

This title is continued by *Culture statistics: public libraries in Canada/Statistiques de la culture: bibliothèques publiques au Canada.* For further information see entry **546**.

548 **Répertoire des bibliothèques publiques Quebec.** Grande Vallée: Service des Bibliothèques Publiques, Quebec Ministère des Affaires Culturelles, 1982– . Annual. ISBN 2–550–02654–3.

Statistical data are provided for the public libraries listed in this directory. For directory information see entry **409**.

549 **Statistics of public libraries in the United States and Canada serving 100,000 population or more.** Comp. by Rick J. Ashton. Fort Wayne, IN: Allen County Public Library, 1981. 9 leaves. LC 81–211358.

Statistical information about public libraries is arranged alphabetically by name of city. For further information see entry **575**.

550 **Survey of libraries: part I, public libraries, 1958–1968.** Ottawa: Dominian Bureau of Statistics, 1960–1970. Annual. ISSN 0527–6292.

This title was continued in 1970 by *Public libraries in Canada*, and it is currently titled, *Culture statistics: public libraries in Canada/Statistiques de la culture: bibliothèques publiques au Canada.* Statistical data from 1931 to 1950 were reported for public libraries under the title, *Survey of libraries.* For further information see entry **546**.

School Libraries

551 **Culture statistics: centralized school libraries in Canada/Statistiques de la culture: bibliothèques scolaires au Canada, 1974/75– .** Ottawa: Statistics Canada, 1977– . Annual. LC 78–641841. ISSN 0708–7888.

This is an annual compilation of data on centralized school libraries throughout Canada as reported by school systems and submitted to Statistics Canada, the central agency for the compilation of statistics in Canada. Information is provided on number of volumes, number of students served, expenditures, and circulation. The text of the report is in English and French.

College and University Libraries

552 Culture statistics: university and college libraries in Canada/Statistiques de la culture: bibliothèques des universités et des collèges du Canada, 1972/1973– . Ottawa: Statistics Canada, 1978– . Annual. LC 80–39017. ISSN 0707–7610.

Reported in this annual compilation are library data for various types of postsecondary public and private institutions throughout Canada. Among the data presented are student enrollment, holdings, circulation, income, expenditures by categories, and interlibrary loan transactions. The text appears in English and French, in parallel columns. This work was formerly published under the titles, *University and college libraries in Canada* (entry **554**) and *Survey of libraries: part II, academic libraries* (entry **553**).

553 Survey of libraries: part II, academic libraries, 1958–1968. Ottawa: Dominian Bureau of Statistics, 1960–1970. Annual. ISSN 0527–6292.

This title was continued in 1970 by *University and college libraries in Canada,* and it is currently titled, *Culture statistics: university and college libraries in Canada/Statistiques de la culture; bibliothèques des universités et des collèges du Canada.* Statistical data from 1931 to 1950 were reported for college and university libraries under the title, *Survey of libraries.* For further information see entry **552**.

554 University and college libraries in Canada, 1970–1972. Ottawa: Statistics Canada, 1973–1976. LC 74–641774. ISSN 0318–7179.

This title is continued by *Culture statistics: university and college libraries in Canada/ Statistiques de la culture: bibliothèques des universités et des collèges du Canada.* For further information see entry **552**.

Provincial Statistics Sources

ALBERTA

555 Alberta public library statistics, 1960– . Edmonton: Library Services, Alberta Dept. of Culture, 1976– . Annual. LC 78–82543.

Issued from 1960–1970 by the Alberta Department of Provincial Secretary and from 1970–1975 by the Alberta Department of Culture, Youth and Recreation, this annual includes statistics for regional individual municipal libraries. Data reported include population, book stock by volumes, circulation, total income and income by source, total expenditures and expenditures by category, and per capita expenditures.

BRITISH COLUMBIA

556 Public libraries statistics, 1966– . Victoria: Library Services Branch, British

Columbia Ministry of Recreation and Conservation, 1966– . Annual. LC 75–80785. ISSN 0084–8034.

The data presented for public libraries in British Columbia in this annual compilation include population served, volumes held, volumes added, total and per capita circulation, income by source, expenditures by source, staff size, number of service points, and provincial expenditures for library construction or direct service.

MANITOBA

557 Manitoba public library statistics, 1976– . Winnipeg: Public Library Services Branch, Manitoba Dept. of Cultural Affairs and Historical Resources, 1976– . Annual. LC 79–80187.

This annual report supplies the following data for public libraries in Manitoba: population, income and expenditures, holdings, and circulation transactions.

NEWFOUNDLAND

558 Annual report. St. John's: Newfoundland Public Library Services, 193?– . Annual. LC 57–27883. ISSN 0317–1523.

Public library statistics are incorporated into the annual report of the Newfoundland Public Library Services agency. The data reported include number of service points, bookstock, circulation, number of registered borrowers, and hours open weekly.

NOVA SCOTIA

559 Nova Scotia regional public libraries statistics, 1977– . Halifax: Nova Scotia Provincial Library, 1978– . Annual. LC 79–81831. ISSN 0708–5087.

The following data are reported for public libraries in Nova Scotia by region: income and expenditures, circulation data for branches and bookmobiles, holdings, interlibrary loan transactions, hours open per week, and bookmobile hours per week.

ONTARIO

560 Public library statistics. Toronto: Library Development Commission, Ontario Ministry of Citizenship and Culture, 19??– . Annual.

The data reported for the province as a whole and for individual library systems in Ontario cover physical facilities, holdings, transactions, personnel, hours open, sources and amounts of revenue, and expenditures. Information on audiovisual services and capital operations is provided separately.

PRINCE EDWARD ISLAND

561 Annual report, 1976–1977. Charlottetown: Division of Libraries, Prince Edward Island Dept. of Education, 1976–77. v.p.

The Division of Libraries serves as the regional library and collects data on public library activity within the province. Covered in the report are income, expenditures, holdings, and circulation transactions.

QUEBEC

562 "Statistiques des bibliothèques publiques du Quebec." Appears annually in **Biblio-contact: bulletin du service des bibliothèques publiques du Quebec.** Montreal: Quebec Ministère des Affaires Culturelles, 19??– . Annual.

Included in this annual report are summary statistics for public libraries in Quebec province. Data reported cover population served, number of employees, number of books and journals, average number of hours open, revenue by type, and expenses by category.

SASKATCHEWAN

563 Annual report: Saskatchewan Provincial Library. Regina: Saskatchewan Provincial Library, 1953– . Annual. LC 75–082415.

Brief data are reported for the regional and municipal libraries in Saskatchewan. Covered in the statistics are population served, interlibrary loan transactions, holdings, circulation of all materials, revenue from various sources, and expenditures by category.

UNITED KINGDOM

Library statistical reports for the United Kingdom are arranged alphabetically by title within three divisions: General, Public Libraries, and University and College Libraries.

General

564 Census of staff in librarianship and information work in the United Kingdom: 1972– . London: Dept. of Education and Science, 1975– . Every 5 years. LC 76–375970.

This national census of individuals employed in all types of libraries and information units in the United Kingdom covers 1972 and 1976. There is a three-year time lag in the publication of the statistics. Data are presented on qualifications of staff, type of library or information unit, geographical location, age, sex, whether part-time or full-time, turnover (resignations, job changes, etc.), and other areas. This series constitutes the most comprehensive compilation of information on the staff members of libraries and information units in the United Kingdom.

Public Libraries

565 County buroughs and London library statistics, 1958–1960. Westminster: Inst. of Municipal Treasurers and Accountants, 1959–1961. Annual.

This title is continued by *Public library statistics* and *Public library statistics: actuals, 1972/73.* For further information see entry **567**.

566 "Public library staff establishment and grading census." Appears in the **Library Association record.** London: Library Assn., 1899– . Biennial. LC 6–1204. ISSN 0024–2195.

This census of public library staff in the United Kingdom appears, in odd years, in the November issue of the *Library Association record*. Data reported include management structure, designation of post, qualification required, salary or grade, name of department heads and above, qualifications, turnover (number left for posts in non-public libraries, retired, or left for other kinds of employment), part-time positions, and additional remuneration.

567 Public library statistics: actuals, 1972/73– . London: Statistical Information Service, Chartered Inst. of Public Finance and Accountancy, and Society of County Treasurers, 1975– . Annual. LC 74–648283. ISSN 0309–6629.

This work is the primary source of current public library statistics for the United Kingdom. Although the data are collected by a private organization, they are used by the Secretary of State to meet requirements for gathering statistics under the Public Libraries and Museums Act of 1964. Published in the early part of the calendar year following the end of the fiscal year covered, the data generally cover population served, rateable value, area served, service points, collection size, serials received, additions of book and non-book materials, expenditures by category, income, capital expenditures, staff by category, number of items loaned, number of photocopies and microtexts supplied, interlibrary loans, and services to institutions. This work is a continuation of *Public library statistics, 1961/1962–1971/1972* (entry **569**), which continues *County buroughs and London library statistics* (entry **565**).

568 Public library statistics: estimates, 1974/75– . London: Statistical Information Service, Chartered Inst. of Public Finance and Accountancy, and Society of County Treasurers, 1974– . Annual. LC 82–646754. ISSN 0307–0522.

Early statistical information, prior to the publication of final data, is reproduced in this annual. The report is intended to include all public library authorities in England and Wales and it follows the same format as *Public library statistics: actuals, 1972/73–* (entry **567**). Data cover population, rateable value, area, staff size, number of service points, total number of books, expenditures, income capital payments, and number of books on loan.

569 Public library statistics, 1961/62–1971/72. London: Inst. of Municipal Treasurers and Accountants, and Society of County Treasurers, 1963–1974. Annual. LC 65–56045.

This title is continued by *Public library statistics: actuals, 1972/1973–* . For further information see entry **567**.

College and University Libraries

570 Libraries in major establishments of education. London: Dept. of Education and Science, 1974– . Annual.

Statistical information on colleges and universities, colleges of technology, colleges of further education, and polytechnics in the United Kingdom is provided by institution. Data are included on library accomodations, holdings, audiovisual facilities, expenditures by categories, staff by categories, number of staff and students served, and interlibrary loans.

UNITED STATES

Entries are arranged alphabetically by title within four main divisions: Public Libraries, School Libraries, College and University Libraries, and State Statistical Sources. State reports are listed alphabetically under the state name.

Public Libraries

571 1962 statistics of public libraries serving populations of less than 35,000. Urbana: Graduate School of Library Science, Univ. of Illinois, 1966. 237p. NUC 68–27672.
Statistics for small public libraries in fiscal year 1962 are reported in this publication in three categories: libraries serving populations from 0–9,999; libraries serving populations from 10,000–24,999; and libraries serving populations from 25,000–34,999. An attempt was made to include all libraries in the size ranges noted above. Data reported cover population, collection size, income, expenditures, and staff size.

572 The report of the Commissioner of Education, 1870–1895. Washington, DC: U.S. Office of Education, 1870–1896. Annual.
The public and school library statistics reported in this document were sometimes reprinted separately. After 1900, library statistics were published as separate government reports. For further information see *Statistics of public, society and school libraries 1929* (entry **583**) for public library information and entry **590** for school library statistics information.

573 Statistics of county and regional libraries serving populations of 50,000 or more, 1944–1959. Washington, DC: U.S. Office of Education, 1945–1959. Annual.
The first several volumes of this title were published irregularly. Data for the 1960 fiscal year were absorbed by *Statistics of public library systems serving populations of 100,000 or more* (entry **581**) and *Statistics of public library systems in cities with populations of 50,000 to 99,999* (entry **580**).

574 Statistics of county and regional library systems serving populations of 35,000 to 49,999. Washington, DC: U.S. Office of Education, 1944–1959. Annual.
Separate data were published for county and regional public library systems and for municipal public libraries serving populations in these size ranges until the FY 1960. However, essentially the same data were reported, including population, staff size in FTE, beginning professional salaries, total number added, total circulation, circulation of juvenile and adult books, operating expenditures by category, and per capita information for several categories. This title was absorbed by *Statistics of public library systems serving populations of 35,000 to 49,999* in 1960. For further information see entry **582**.

575 Statistics of public libraries in the United States and Canada serving 100,000 population or more. Comp. by Rick J. Ashton. Fort Wayne, IN: Allen County Public Library, 1981. 9 leaves. LC 81–211358.
Statistical information about public libraries serving 100,000 population or more is arranged alphabetically by name of city. In the latest published survey, a total of 316 public libraries are included, representing about sixty-three percent of the potential. Included in the

report are data for each library on size of population served, total budget, per capita expenditures, appropriation for materials and for total salaries, salary of director, tenure of director, salary of assistant director, tenure of assistant director, and current salary for beginning professionals.

576 Statistics of public libraries, 1978 (LIBGIS III). Washington, DC: National Center for Education Statistics, 1980. 142p.

This work is the most recent in a long series of national reports of public library statistics, compiled by various agencies of the federal government. This title and the 1976 edition, *Statistics for public libraries, 1974: (LIBGIS I),* are the public library component of a library statistics project known as Library General Information Survey (LIBGIS), initiated by the Learning Resources Branch of the National Center for Education Statistics. These volumes include data on public libraries serving populations of various sizes and consolidate several previously published series that reported data on public libraries serving various population sizes. The public library statistical reports are now compiled and published every four years, with about a two-year time lag between the time period covered and the date of publication. Data contained in the series include: income and expenditures, circulation, and library holdings. Other publications identified in this section contain public library statistics for communities of various population sizes and for various time periods. This title continues the coverage of public library statistics reported for 1965 and 1968 in *Statistics of public libraries serving communities with at least 25,000 inhabitants (entry **578**)* and for 1962 in *Statistics of public libraries, 1962: part 1, selected statistics of public libraries serving populations of 35,000 and above: institutional data (entry **577**).*

577 Statistics of public libraries, 1962: part 1, selected statistics of public libraries serving populations of 35,000 and above: institutional data. Washington, DC: U.S. Office of Education, 1965. 2v.

This work was formed by the union of *Statistics of public library systems serving populations of 35,000 to 49,999* (entry **582**), *Statistics of public library systems in cities with populations of 50,000 to 99,999* (entry **580**) and *Statistics of public library systems serving 100,000 or more* (entry **581**). It is continued by *Statistics of public libraries serving communities with at least 25,000 inhabitants: 1965–1968* (entry **578**) and superseded by *Statistics of public libraries, 1978 (LIBGIS III)* (entry **576**).

578 Statistics of public libraries serving communities with at least 25,000 inhabitants: 1965–1968. Washington, DC: U.S. Office of Education, 1968–1970. 2v.

This work continues *Statistics of public libraries, 1962: part 1, selected statistics of public libraries serving populations of 35,000 and above: institutional data* (entry **577**). It is superseded by *Statistics of public libraries, 1978 (LIBGIS III)*. For further information see entry **576**.

579 Number not used.

580 Statistics of public library systems in cities with populations of 50,000 to 99,999: fiscal year 1944–1960. Washington, DC: U.S. Office of Education, 1945–1961. Annual.

Covered in this compilation are all cities in the population size range indicated for 1944 to

1960. As new library systems met the eligibility requirement by size, they were added. Data reported include population, staff size, total number of volumes, number of volumes added, circulation by adult or juvenile, total circulation, expenditures by category, and per capita data for some of the data elements. In addition to data for individual libraries, there are also comparative summary tables. Volumes were not published for 1946–1949, 1951 and 1954. A variant title of this work is *Statistics of public library systems serving populations of 50,000 to 99,999*. In 1960, *Statistics of county and regional libraries serving populations of 50,000 or more* (entry **573**) was absorbed in part by this title. This work is continued by *Statistics of public libraries, 1962: part 1, selected statistics of public libraries serving populations of 35,000 and above: institutional data*; (entry **577**) and by *Statistics of public libraries serving communities with at least 25,000 inhabitants: 1965–1968* (entry **578**). It is superseded by *Statistics of public libraries, 1978 (LIBGIS III)* (entry **576**).

581 Statistics of public library systems serving populations of 100,000 or more, 1944–1960. Washington, DC: U.S. Office of Education, 1945–1961. Annual.
Statistical summaries of all library systems in the United States serving populations of 100,000 or more during the inclusive years of the coverage are provided here. New library systems were added as they met the minimum population criteria. Also, over the period of time covered by the reports, additional data items were added in response to suggestions from library administrators, governing boards, and others. Data reported include population, revenue from local sources and various outside sources, per capita revenue, expenditures by category, total circulation, per capita circulation, number of books, number of periodicals, and number of staff members. In addition to data for individual libraries, there are also comparative tables. Although not all data categories are represented throughout the history of the series, those which are provide comparable data for the reporting libraries. A variant title of this work is *Statistics of public libraries in cities with population of 100,000 or more*. In 1960, *Statistics of county and regional libraries serving populations of 50,000 or more* (entry **573**) was absorbed in part by this title. This work is continued by *Statistics of public libraries, 1962: part 1, selected statistics of public libraries serving populations of 35,000 and above: institutional data* (entry **577**) and by *Statistics of public libraries serving communities with at least 25,000 inhabitants: 1965–1968* (entry **578**). It is superseded by *Statistics of public libraries, 1978 (LIBGIS III)* (entry **576**).

582 Statistics of public library systems serving populations of 35,000 to 49,999, 1944–1960. Washington, DC: U.S. Office of Education, 1945–1961. Annual.
This work reports data for individual libraries in the size categories noted in the title. Libraries were added as they met population eligibility requirements. Data are provided on population, staff size in FTE, beginning salary for new library school graduates, total number of volumes at end of year, total number added, total circulation, circulation for adult and juvenile books, revenue by source, operating expenditures by category, and per capita information for several categories. With the FY 1960 report, county and regional libraries were combined with municipal public libraries. A variant title of this work is *Statistics of public library systems in cities with populations of 35,000 to 49,999*. In 1960, *Statistics of county and regional library systems serving populations of 35,000 to 49,999* (entry **574**) was absorbed by this title. This work is continued by *Statistics of public libraries, 1962: part 1, selected statistics of public libraries serving populations of 35,000 and above: institutional data* (entry **577**) and by *Statistics of public libraries serving communities with at least*

25,000 inhabitants: 1965–1968 (entry **578**). It is superseded by *Statistics of public libraries, 1978 (LIBGIS III)* (entry **576**).

583 **Statistics of public, society and school libraries, 1929.** Washington, DC: U.S. Office of Education, 1931. 365p.
Although the extent of statistical detail varies over the years, in some instances these early volumes provide extensive data on the acquisitions, holdings, revenues, expenditures, and circulation of libraries. Inclusion is extended to libraries with 1,000 volumes or more until 1908, when the criteria was increased to 5,000 volumes or more. Reference is made in each volume to other earlier reports which provide public library statistics. Other volumes in this series cover the years 1923, 1913, 1908, 1903, and 1900. Titles vary from volume to volume. Prior to 1900, public library statistics were reported in *The report of the Commissioner of Education* (entry **572**). For information about school library statistics included in this report see entry **590**.

584 **Statistics of southern public libraries.** Memphis, TN: Memphis Public Library, 19??– . Annual.
Brief statistical information on major public libraries in southern states is reported annually in this publication. Included are public libraries with annual budget of $500,000 or more. Libraries are listed in descending order, by total budget. The following information is provided: population reported in the latest census, budget, total circulation, total expenditures for salaries, total expenditures for library materials, and salary figures for beginning clerks, beginning subprofessionals, beginning professionals, top of the scale for department heads, assistant librarians, and the library director. Although the information is brief, it is more current than data available on these libraries in other sources.

School Libraries

585 **Public school library statistics, 1962–63.** Washington, DC: U.S. Office of Education, 1964. 21p. LC 78–281658. OE–15020.
This work is the second in a set of brief surveys providing basic data on public school libraries. The first survey was published in 1960, under the same title, and covers the years 1958–1959. They are not part of the more comprehensive surveys published under the title, *Statistics of public school libraries* (entry **589**). The data were derived from a sample of elementary and secondary schools with enrollments over 150 students. Only information on centralized library service is reported. Data categories include school enrollment, holdings, and amount of formal library education held by persons serving as librarians.

586 **The report of the Commissioner of Education, 1870–1895.** Washington, DC: U.S. Office of Education, 1870–1896.
The public and school library statistics reported in this document were sometimes reprinted separately. After 1900, library statistics were published as separate government reports. For further information see *Statistics of public, society and school libraries, 1929* (entry **583** for public libraries information; entry **590** for school libraries information).

587 **Statistics of public school libraries/media centers, fall 1978 (LIBGIS IV).** Washington, DC: Learning Resources Branch, National Center for Education Statistics, 1980.

This is the second statistical report on public school library and media centers compiled as a part of the LIBGIS project. This report is arranged by school enrollment, grade level, and geographic location. It includes data on collection size, size of staff, expenditures, receipts, loans, and facilities. Its format is similar to that of the first report (entry **588**).

588 Statistics of public school libraries/media centers, fall 1974 (LIBGIS I). Washington, DC: Learning Resources Branch, National Center for Education Statistics, 1977. University of Illinois, Graduate School of Library Science Reprint, 1978. 59p. NCES 77–203.

The data reported in this document were collected as part of the LIBGIS (Library General Information Survey) project of the National Center for Education Statistics. Included are statistics on size of collections, staffing, expenditures, receipts, loan transactions, and physical facilities. These data are arranged by enrollment size of school, grade level, and geographic location.

589 Statistics of public school libraries, 1960–61. Washington, DC: Library Services Branch, U.S. Office of Education, 1964. **Part I: basic tables.** 90p. OE–15049. **Part II: analysis and interpretation.** 13p. OE–15056.

This work is a continuation of *Statistics of public school libraries,* a series of periodic and detailed general surveys of public school libraries in the United States. Earlier reports (covering the years 1934–35, 1941–42, 1947–48, and 1953–54) were originally issued as chapters of the *Biennial survey of education in the United States* and later published as separates. Data are reported for regions of the United States and by enrollment size categories for schools. Tables specify number and membership of schools with centralized libraries; total library expenditures and per pupil library expenditures; number of volumes added to centralized libraries during 1960–61; total number of volumes and volumes per pupil in schools with centralized libraries; and number of schools served by school librarians. Also included are data on circulation of materials by types of materials; times of service; number of school libraries with various components of school library quarters; number of school librarians by extent of professional education; salary categories; months of employment annually; ratio of school librarians to pupils; other adult personnel and number of students working in the library; and percent of total instructional budget of public school districts allotted to school libraries. Two other brief surveys providing basic data were issued in 1960 and 1964 under the title *Public school library statistics* (entry **585**). They are not a part of this series.

590 Statistics of public, society and school libraries, 1929. Washington, DC: U.S. Office of Education, 1931. 365p.

School library statistics are included here with those of public and society libraries. Inclusion is limited and does not cover all school libraries, but only those which meet certain size criteria: 1,000 volumes prior to 1908; 5,00 volumes in 1908 and following years. Data reported include number of titles acquired, holdings, revenues, expenditures, and circulation figures. Other volumes in this series cover the years 1923, 1913, 1908, 1903, and 1900. Prior to 1900, school library statistics were reported in *The report of the Commissioner of*

Education (entry **572**). For information about public library statistics included in this report see entry **583**.

College and University Libraries

591 Academic library statistics, 1963–1973. Washington, DC: Assn. of Research Libraries, 1964–1974. Annual. ISSN 0571–6519.
This title is continued by *ARL statistics.* For further information see entry **592**.

592 ACRL university library statistics. Chicago: Assn. of College and Research Libraries, 1978/79– . Triennial.
Fiscal year statistics from Ph.D. granting institutions that are not members of the Association of Research Libraries (ARL) are reported in this survey. Data are reported in the same format as *ARL statistics* (entry **592**) and include collection size, interlibrary loan, expenditures, microform holdings by type of microform, and enrollment statistics by category. The current issue (1981/82; ISBN 0–8389–6596–2) covers ninety-two institutions in the United States and Canada. Similar statistics are collected on a regional basis by other agencies. Data for 138 academic institutions in the Pacific Northwest are reported in *Library statistics of colleges and universities in the pacific northwest 1980–81,* comp. by James D. Lockwood for the Academic Division of PNLA in cooperation with the Interinstitutional Library Council of the Oregon State System of Higher Education (Corvallis, OR: Pacific Northwest Library Association, 1982). Regional data for midwest academic libraries are presented in *Library data: Associated Colleges of the Midwest and library data: Great Lakes College Association,* comp. by Dennis Ribbens (Appleton, WI: Great Lakes College Library Assn., 19??– . Annual); this report covers twenty-five small, private liberal arts colleges located in the Midwest. Data for colleges and universities in the South have been reported in *Statistics of southern college and university libraries* (Baton Rouge: Louisiana State Univ. Library, 1960– . Annual); this series provides statistical information on fifty colleges and universities in southern states from the Atlantic coast to Texas and from Maryland to Florida.

593 ARL statistics, 1974– . Washington, DC: Assn. of Research Libraries, 1975– . Annual. LC 77–647280. ISSN 0147–2135.
Fiscal year statistics from institutions that are members of the Association of Research Libraries are reported in this annual. Data reported include collection size; interlibrary loan; expenditures; microform holdings by type of microform; and enrollment statistics by category. In addition, there are rank order lists for fourteen variables: volumes; volumes added; microform holdings; current serials; professional staff; non-professional staff; total staff; materials expenditures; materials and binding expenditures; salaries and wages; total operating expenditures; total items loaned; total items borrowed; and current serials expenditures. This work continues *Academic library statistics* (entry **591**).

594 College and university library statistics, 1919/20 to 1943/44. Princeton, NJ: Princeton Univ. Library, 1947. n.p.
Compiled and distributed by Princeton University Library, these statistics of forty college and university libraries cover 1919/20 through 1943/44. The Princeton compilation is actually an improvement over the original annual statistical report because in it differences

in methods of reporting data, omissions, and other problems are resolved. The data are reported by individual library for the years during which each institution participated in the project. Data categories include size of book stock, volumes added, total expenditures, total appropriations, staff size, and total expenditures for salaries.

595 Library statistics of colleges and universities, 1959/60– : part 1, institutional data. Washington, DC: Learning Resources Branch, National Center for Education Statistics, 1961– . Annual.

Included here are statistics for most colleges and universities in the United States. Data are presented for individual institutions and are consolidated in the *Analytic report* (entry **596**). The data vary over the life of the series, but basically include type of control and type of institution; number of volumes and titles held at end of the year; government documents held at end of year; microforms held at end of year; volumes and titles added during the year; current periodical subscriptions; library operating expenditures for salaries and wages, by category; operating expenditures for materials, by category; FTE enrollment for the fall term; operating expenditures per FTE student, faculty members, and as a percent of the general expenditures; volumes and titles per FTE student; and FTE students per FTE staff. Beginning with the volume for 1975, this report became a part of the LIBGIS (Library General Information Survey) program.

596 Library statistics of colleges and universities, 1959/60– : part 2, analytic report. Washington, DC: Learning Resources Branch, National Center for Education Statistics, 1962– . Annual.

The data reported in this series are derived from the same source as that in *Part 1, institutional data* (entry **595**). This volume differs in that it contains aggregate data for the United States as a whole and for libraries of different size categories and control types. The report consists of summary tables broken down by such categories as public institutions, public four-year institutions with graduate programs, public two-year institutions, etc. Data reported in the summary tables include library staff and operating expenditures; number of nonprinted resources; number of libraries and physical facilities; number of resource materials and interlibrary loans; number of vacant positions, regular staff, filled positions, and contributed services staff; and number of administrative units, service points and other learning resource centers.

597 Library statistics of colleges and universities, 1939–1956. Washington, DC: U.S. Office of Education, 1940–1957. Every five years.

Statistics of college and university libraries in the United States are reported for 1939–1940, 1946–1947, 1951–1952 and 1956–1957. Data categories included total number of volumes added, total at end of the year, student enrollment (undergraduate and graduate), faculty size, circulation, operating expenditures by category, capital outlay, and number of staff by category. This work was formerly titled, *Statistics of libraries in institutions of higher education* (entry **598**).

598 Statistics of libraries in institutions of higher education, 1939–1956. Washington, DC: U.S. Office of Education, 1940–1957. Every 5 years.

This title is continued by *Library statistics of colleges and universities.* For further information see entry **597**.

State Statistics Sources

ALABAMA

599 Annual report: Alabama public library service. Montgomery: Alabama Public Library Service, 1977– . Annual.

Fiscal year statistics for Alabama public libraries are reported in this annual. For the purpose of the report, the fiscal year is defined as October 1 through September 30. Statistics are presented in three tables. The first, arranged alphabetically by county of location, identifies the region, population served, number of hours open per week, numerical data on resources, circulation data, funding from various sources, and expenditures for various purposes. The second table gives statistics for multicounty regional library headquarters, with the same type of data reported. The third table provides totals for multiunit libraries, listed alphabetically by name of library. The *Annual report* also includes a directory of public libraries (see entry **436**). This work was formed by the union of *Alabama public libraries* (entry **435**) and *Statistics of public libraries in Alabama* (entry **600**).

600 Statistics of public libraries in Alabama. Montgomery: Alabama Public Library Service, 1961–1976. Annual.

This title was merged with *Alabama public libraries* to form *Annual report: Alabama public library service*. For directory information see entry **436**. For statistics information see entry **599**.

ARIZONA

601 Arizona public libraries statistical report and directory, 1942/1944– . Phoenix: Dept. of Library, Archives and Public Records, Arizona State Library, 1944– . Annual.

Fiscal year statistical information for all public libraries in Arizona is presented in this annual. The data are arranged by location and include hours open, collection size, volumes added, circulation, sources and amounts of funding, expenditures by category, and bookmobile services. Access to public libraries is provided by county through a separate list at the end. In addition to statistical information, this publication also provides directory coverage for public and academic libraries (see entry **439**).

ARKANSAS

602 Biennial report, 1937–1977. Little Rock: Arkansas Library Commission, 1939–1979. Biennial. LC 39–28687.

When the Arkansas State Library was created, on July 1, 1979, this publication was discontinued. The final issue was the *20th biennial report*. When published, the reports contained data for Arkansas public libraries on funding from local, state, and federal sources; collection size; circulation; and expenditures. In addition, the biennial issues included a directory of public, academic, and special libraries. The State Library intends to produce a new publication that will include library statistics and a directory of public libraries. The directory section has already been partially superseded by *Public libraries of Arkansas by library development district* (entry **441**).

CALIFORNIA

603 California library statistics and directory. Sacramento: California State Library, 1976– . Annual. LC 77–643048. ISSN 0148–4583.

This very detailed statistical report on public, academic, and institutional libraries in California was formerly published as the winter issue of *News notes of California libraries*. It includes data for individual libraries on collections, receipts and expenditures, staff, and various types of services. Also included is information on working conditions, compensation and fringe benefits, building size and capacity, and holdings and use by type of materials. The most detailed statistical information is reported for public libraries. Less detailed reports are provided for academic and institutional libraries. This publication also includes a directory of California libraries (see entry **442**).

COLORADO

604 Biennial report. Denver: Colorado State Library, 19??–1969. Biennial.

Statistical information formerly reported in this title is now included in the *Directory of Colorado libraries*. For further information see entry **605**.

605 Directory of Colorado libraries. Denver: Office of Library Services, Colorado Dept. of Education, 1970– . Annual. LC 74–646552. ISSN 0094–8403.

Since 1970, statistical information for public libraries in Colorado have been reported in this annual directory. The statistics are divided into three sections, covering services and collections; expenditures; and income. Included in the first section are data on size of population served, number of hours open, staff size, circulation, number of borrowers, interlibrary loan transactions, number of volumes, number of titles, and number of films. The second section reports salaries, expenditures for books, periodicals, audiovisual materials, supplies, binding, equipment, physical plant, capital outlays, and totals. The third section indicates income from local, state, federal, and other sources, and gives totals as well as local mill levies. Also included in this publication is directory information (see entry **440**). Prior to 1970, statistical information on public libraries in Colorado was included in the *Biennial report* (entry **604**) of the Colorado State Library.

CONNECTICUT

606 Annual report. Hartford: Connecticut State Library, 19??– . Annual.

This report provides statistical information on the services and operations of the Connecticut State Library. Statistics for other public libraries in the state are reported in *Statistics of public libraries* (entry **607**).

607 Statistics of public libraries, 1974– . Hartford: Connecticut State Library, 1975– . Annual.

Statistics of public libraries, arranged by town, are presented in this annual report. Data provided for individual libraries include population of the town, number of volumes, volumes per capita, total circulation, income from various sources, and operating expenditures by category (e.g., books, binding, salaries, etc.). Statistical information on the services and operations of the Connecticut State Library is published in the library's *Annual report* (entry **606**).

DELAWARE

608 Annual report, 1962– . Dover, DE: Division of Libraries, Dept. of Community
    Affairs and Economic Development, 1963– . Annual. LC 64–63419. ISSN
    0416–8755.
Data on individual public libraries in Delaware are presented in this annual. The data are
arranged by county and cover population of the service area, expenditures, income from
various sources, collection size, circulation, number of hours open, and number of programs sponsored. Prior to 1962, statistical information on public libraries was included in
the *Biennial report* of the Delaware State Library Commission.

FLORIDA

609 Florida library directory and public library statistics. Tallahassee: Division of
    Library Services, Florida Dept. of State, 1951–1952. Annual. LC 52–62285. ISSN
    0430–7763.
This work is currently titled *Florida library directory with statistics for 1952– .* For
directory information see entry **454**. For statistics information see entry **610**.

610 Florida library directory with statistics for 1952– . Tallahassee: Division of
    Library Services, Florida Dept. of State, 1953– . Annual. ISSN 0430–7763.
The following statistics for public libraries in Florida are reported in this annual: population
served, bookmobile operation, number of hours open, collection size, number of personnel,
circulation, physical facilities, amount of funding by source, and expenditures by category.
Less detailed data are available for academic and institutional libraries in the state. In
addition to statistical information, this publication also contains a directory of public,
academic, and institutional libraries in Florida (see entry **454**). In 1951 and 1952, this work
was titled *Florida library directory and public library statistics* (entry **453**).

GEORGIA

611 Annual report. Atlanta: Georgia Dept. of Education, 1897– . Annual.
Public library statistical data were included in this report prior to the publication of *Georgia
public library statistics.* For further information see entry **612**.

612 Georgia public library statistics. Atlanta: Division of Public Library Services,
    Georgia Dept. of Education, 1960– . Annual.
Statistical information for regional and large county public library systems in Georgia is
presented in this annual. Included are data on facilities, staff, collection size, audiovisual
materials, equipment, registered borrowers, library sponsored programs, funding by
source, expenditures by category, and total book circulation. Also reported are statistics for
state agency services and for expenditures by institution libraries under the Library Services
and Construction Act. Prior to the publication of this work, public library statistics were
included in the *Annual report* (entry **611**) of the Georgia Department of Education.
Directory information is also included in *Georgia public library statistics.* For a description
of the contents, see entry **455**.

HAWAII

613 Office of Library Services: annual report, 1962– . Honolulu: Office of Library
Services, Dept. of Education, 1963– . Annual. LC 64–63864. ISSN 0073–103X.
Statistical data are included in the *Annual report* for the state library system for Hawaii. The
information provided is brief, covering population served, revenues, expenditures, number
of items reserved, number of items circulated, items processed, items cataloged, items
withdrawn, and items transcribed into Braille or sound. The data presented for each fiscal
year are compared to earlier periods.

IDAHO

614 "Statistics for Idaho public libraries." Appears annually in **The Idaho librarian.**
Boise: Idaho Library Assn., 1945– . Quarterly. LC 58–19346. ISSN 0019–1213.
The April issue of *The Idaho librarian* includes public library statistics for the previous
fiscal year (which ends in September). Data, reported by region and then by library, include
income by category, expenditures, population, borrowers added, total borrowers, books
added, total books, circulation, per capita circulation, per capita local tax income, and hours
open.

ILLINOIS

615 "Statistics of library service." Appears annually in **Illinois libraries.** Springfield:
Illinois State Library, 1919– . 10 per year. LC 29–23175. ISSN 0019–2104.
The November issue of *Illinois libraries* contains detailed statistics for public libraries in the
state. Information is presented alphabetically by location of the library. Data reported
include population served, non-resident fee, hours open per week, total transactions, total
staff (FTE), book stock, non-book titles, periodical titles, equalized assessed valuation, tax
rate, receipts, and expenditures by category. The November issue also includes a directory
of all public libraries in the state (see entry **459**).

INDIANA

616 Statistics of Indiana libraries. Indianapolis: Indiana State Library, 1946– . Annual.
LC 60–63233. ISSN 0081–5152.
Statistical information on Indiana public libraries is presented in this annual, with data
arranged in tabular form by size of population served by the library. Statistics are provided
on population served, tax rate, income, expenditures, holdings, circulations, and staff
positions.

IOWA

617 Iowa public library statistics. Des Moines: State Library of Iowa, 1973– . Annual.
LC 81–643203.
Only public library statistics are included in this annual. Summary data for Iowa public
libraries are presented first. Following this, sections are arranged in categories by size of
population served, then alphabetically by name of library. The data presented include

financial information (income and expenditures); materials; holdings and circulation; staff; number of hours open; salary ranges; and ratios and percentages. In 1973, this title was issued as *Public library information:* in 1975 as *Iowa library information.* All other years, the annual was published as *Iowa public library statistics.* Early volumes included a directory, but several years ago the State Library began to publish the directory separately (see entry **465**).

KANSAS

618 Kansas public library statistics, 1950/51– . Topeka: Kansas State Library, 1951– . Annual.
This detailed statistical report covers all public libraries in Kansas for the year indicated in the title. Information is presented by broad categories and then by the seven regional library systems, with individual libraries listed from largest to smallest. Data focus on amount and sources of financial support; expenditures, by category; resources, including hours open, number of volumes owned, volumes per capita, periodical subscriptions, and records; circulation; and personnel. Similar date are reported for regional systems. The directory information included here can also be found in the *Kansas public library directory* (entry **468**).

KENTUCKY

619 Statistical report of Kentucky public libraries. Frankfort, KY: Dept. for Libraries and Archives, 1977– . Annual.
Substantial statistical information on public library service in Kentucky is presented in this annual, aggregated by region, county, congressional district, and the state as a whole. Some of the data categories included are population, tax rate in cents per $100, recurring income, state aid, local income, income per capita, total expenditures, expenditures by category, number of branches, number of employees, square feet in the library's main building, circulation, total number of programs, salary of director, and number of registered borrowers.

LOUISIANA

620 Biennial report. Baton Rouge: Louisiana State Library, 19??– . Biennial.
Statistical data on public libraries are provided by this title and by *Public libraries in Louisiana: statistics of use: salary and staff study* (entry **621**).

621 Public libraries in Louisiana: statistics of use: salary and staff study, 1953– . Baton Rouge: Louisiana State Library, 1954– . Annual. ISSN 0456-7056.
Statistics on the resources and use of public libraries in Louisiana are presented in this annual. A statistical profile of all public libraries in the state reports additions to library resources, volume of library use, operating receipts by source, operating expenditures by purpose, capital outlay by source, personnel, and data for library systems within the state. Statistical information on public libraries is also included in the *Biennial report* (entry **620**) of the Louisiana State Library. Arrangement of entries makes it possible to use *Public libraries in Louisiana* also as a directory (see entry **470**).

MAINE

622 Biennial report. Augusta: Maine State Library, 19??– . Biennial.
Public library statistics are reported in this publication as well as in *Libraries of Maine: directory and statistics*. For further information see entry **623**.

623 Libraries of Maine: directory and statistics. Augusta: Maine State Library, 1971– . Annual. LC 73–646640.
This work includes directory and statistical information on public libraries in Maine. For information about the directory section, see entry **472**. The statistical information is arranged by size of the community and includes population of the community; number of hours open; circulation; collection size; municipal appropriations; total expenditures; expenditures for books; and per capita expenditures. This title continues *Public libraries of Maine* (entry **624**). Public library statistics are also reported in the *Biennial report* (entry **622**) of the State Library.

624 Public libraries of Maine. Augusta: Maine State Library, 1965–1970. Annual.
This title is continued by *Libraries of Maine: directory and statistics*. For directory information see entry **472**. For statistics information see entry **623**.

MARYLAND

625 Annual report, 1972/73– . Baltimore: Division of Library Development and Services, Maryland State Dept. of Education, 1973– . Annual. LC 76–624238. ISSN 0147–5703.
Statistical information for public libraries in Maryland is provided in this annual. The statistics section of the report is arranged by county and includes data on collection size, circulation, expenditures, and receipts by source. Only data that are required by the legal responsibilities of the Department of Education are reported.

MASSACHUSETTS

626 Data for Massachusetts, FY 1974– : comparative public library report. Boston: Planning and Evaluation Unit, Massachusetts Board of Library Commissioners, 1975– . Annual. LC 79–625399.
Extensive statistical data for public libraries in Massachusetts are published annually in this title and its supplement, *Data for Massachusetts, FY 1974– : public library personnel report* (entry **627**). The *Comparative public library report* includes summary data for the state and then for individual municipalities, grouped by population size in seven categories. Data contained here cover various income and expenditure categories shown on a per capita basis, holdings per capita, and circulation per capita. The supplemental title reports personnel data, again in summary form and also for individual libraries. Included are salary data, education levels, and fringe benefits. Some of these data were formerly contained in the *Annual report* of the unit.

627 Data for Massachusetts, FY 1974– : public library personnel report. Boston: Planning and Evaluation Unit, Massachusetts Board of Library Commissioners, 1975– . Annual. LC 79–623423.

This title supplements *Data for Massachusetts, FY 1974– : comparative public library report*. For further information see entry **626**.

MICHIGAN

628 Michigan library directory and statistics. Lansing: Michigan State Library, 1967–1976. Annual. LC 74–649625. ISSN 0076–8081.
This title is continued by two separate publications, *Michigan library directory* (see entry **479**) and *Michigan library statistics* (see entry **629**).

629 Michigan library statistics. Lansing: Michigan State Library, 1977– . Annual. LC 74–649625. ISSN 0076–8081.
Statistical information about public libraries in Michigan is reported annually for five different categories: income, operating expenses, resources, resources and services, and audiovisual resources. Within each of these categories, individual libraries are divided into six groups, according to population served. The data reported are detailed. For income, funds received from all sources are listed. Expenditures are broken down by salaries and wages; books, periodicals, and newspapers; audiovisual materials; other expenses; total expenditures; percent of salaries to total expenditures; and expenditures per capita. Similar detail is reported for the other categories. Summary statistics are presented for each category for the population groupings. Data are also reported for public library cooperatives. In addition, there are statistical profiles (accompanied by maps) of each of the cooperatives within the state. This publication continues the statistical portion of *Michigan library directory and statistics* (entry **628**).

MINNESOTA

630 "Minnesota public library statistics." Appears annually in **Minnesota libraries.** St. Paul: Office of Public Libraries and Interlibrary Cooperation, Minnesota Dept. of Education, 1940– . Quarterly. LC 10–33240rev. ISSN 0026–5551.
Presented here is statistical information for public libraries in regional library systems and for unaffiliated public libraries. Data reported include population, bookmobiles, staff, hours open per week, total materials owned, and circulation. For the systems only, receipts and expenditures are reported, as are expenditures per capita. For unaffiliated libraries, the full range of data are reported. For a description of the directory information contained in this title see entry **483**.

MISSISSIPPI

631 Statistics of public libraries. Jackson: Mississippi Library Commission, 19??– . Annual.
This source reports data on Mississippi public libraries for the fiscal year. Information is presented alphabetically by regional, county, and major city library systems. Statistics include population served, number of personnel, hours open to the public, number of service units, items owned (total and per capita), circulation (total and per capita), operating income by source, and expenditures by category.

MISSOURI

632 Directory of Missouri libraries: public, special, college and university, 1971– . Jefferson City: Missouri State Library, 1972– . Annual. LC 73–645566. ISSN 0092–4067.

This publication is primarily a directory, but statistical information is also included. Entries are arranged alphabetically by name of the city or town where the libraries are located, and then directory information for the public, academic, and special libraries in that location is presented. This is followed by statistics on expenditures, holdings, and circulation for most libraries. The data are complete for public libraries but not available for some of the academic and special libraries. For more information on the directory section, see entry **485**. This title continues *Directory of Missouri libraries: statistics* (entry **633**).

633 Directory of Missouri libraries: statistics. Jefferson City: Missouri State Library, 1966–1971. Annual.

This title is continued by *Directory of Missouri libraries: public, special, college and university.* For further directory information see entry **485**. For further statistics information see entry **632**.

MONTANA

634 Montana library directory, with statistics of Montana public libraries. Helena: Montana State Library, 1972– . Annual. LC 74–646588. ISSN 0094–873X.

In this annual report, statistics are separated from the directory section (for information about the directory, see entry **488**). The statistics section includes data on the collections of individual public libraries, circulation figures, hours of service, number of staff, population served, and financial support.

NEBRASKA

635 Biennial report of Nebraska libraries. Lincoln: Nebraska Library Commission, 19??– . Biennial. LC 75–646701. ISSN 0099–0299.

The statistics for public libraries in Nebraska provided in this biennial include, for each library, population, receipts and expenditures, collection size, and circulation. This title continues *Nebraska Library Commission: biennial report*, which continues *Nebraska Library Commission: annual report.*

NEVADA

636 Nevada library directory and statistics. Carson City: Library Development Division, Nevada State Library, 1976– . Annual. LC 77–644335.

In addition to directory information (see entry **491**), this publication includes statistics on Nevada libraries. Data are reported for various types of libraries and for the state as a whole. Included are data on personnel, receipts and expenditures, circulation, and library services. This work was formerly titled, *Statistics with directory of Nevada libraries and library personnel* (entry **637**).

637 Statistics with directory of Nevada libraries and library personnel. Carson City: Nevada State Library, 1974–1975. Annual. LC 74–644965. ISSN 0094–2596.

This title is continued by *Nevada library directory and statistics.* For directory information see entry **491**. For statistics information see entry **636**.

NEW HAMPSHIRE

638 New Hampshire library statistics. Concord: New Hampshire State Library, 1947– . Annual.

Statistics for public libraries in New Hampshire are reported on a calendar year basis in this annual. The data summarize receipts and expenditures, number of volumes, circulation registration, hours open, and registered borrowers.

NEW JERSEY

639 New Jersey public libraries statistics. Trenton: Library Development Bureau, New Jersey State Library, 1970– . Annual. LC 73–647717. ISSN 0093–1098.

This annual presents statistical information for public libraries, arranged by county. Included are data on population, receipts by source, expenditures by categories, size of staff, size of collection, circulation, and number of hours of service.

NEW MEXICO

640 Annual report. Santa Fe: New Mexico State Library, 1959/60– . Annual. LC 60–64019.

Included here is statistical information for the State Library and for public libraries in the state. The data reported for public libraries cover population, number of registered borrowers, number of hours library is open, annual circulation, total number of volumes, volumes per capita, income by source, and expenditures by categories.

NEW YORK

641 The directory of college and university libraries in New York state: with statistical data. Albany: Division of Library Development, Cultural Education Center, Univ. of the State of New York, 1965– . Annual. LC 66–7962. ISSN 0070–5276.

Statistical information covering college and university libraries in New York state is reported in this annual. Arrangement is by size of collection. Data reported include number of volumes, number of periodicals currently received, interlibrary loan provided and received, annual expenditures for library materials, and annual total expenditures. Also presented are data on FTE professional and non-professional staff members at each institution. Summary tables indicate aggregate data for institutions by highest earned-degree granted, by size, and by type of institution. This source also provides directory information on colleges and universities in the state (see entry **499**).

642 Public and association libraries statistics: 1965– . Albany: Division of Library Development, Cultural Education Center, State Univ. of New York, 1965– . LC 76–64673. ISSN 0077–9326.

Provided here is detailed statistical information on public libraries in New York state. Data are reported for systems and for individual library units. Statistical categories include book stock by type, other print and non-print sources by type, additions to the collection, number of items borrowed on interlibrary loan, circulation, receipts by source, and disbursements by categories.

NORTH CAROLINA

643   North Carolina libraries, 1931–1937. Raleigh: Division of the State Library, North Carolina Dept. of Cultural Resources, 1932–1938. Annual. LC 34–27619.
The title of this publication has varied since 1938. It is currently published under two titles, *Statistics and directory of North Carolina public libraries* and *Statistics of North Carolina university and college libraries.* For directory information see entry **510**. For statistics information see entry **644** and entry **645**.

644   Statistics and directory of North Carolina public libraries. Raleigh: Division of the State Library, North Carolina Dept. of Cultural Resources, 1939– . Annual. LC 78–647664. ISSN 0164–0844.
This title varies; it was originally issued as *North Carolina libraries* (entry **643**). It provides statistical information on public libraries in North Carolina for the fiscal year. Data are reported in six tables: receipts and expenditures; sources of local receipts; public library collections, including totals, adult and juvenile volumes, volumes and titles added and withdrawn, and non-book materials by type; use, including circulation by category, reference questions, and interlibrary loan; use of non-book materials by type; and such miscellaneous categories as personnel and vehicles operated. This annual also includes directory information (see entry **510**).

645   Statistics of North Carolina university and college libraries. Raleigh: Division of the State Library, North Carolina Dept. of Cultural Resources, 1939– . Annual.
The title of this publication varies; it was originally issued as *North Carolina libraries* (entry **643**). Statistical information about North Carolina college and university libraries is reported here. Institutions are listed alphabetically, and for each institution data are provided on staff size, enrollment of the institution, number of books at the end of the year, number of microtext titles at the end of the year, number of other formats at the end of the year, number of serial titles, and expenditures by categories.

NORTH DAKOTA

646   "North Dakota library statistics." Appears annually in **North Dakota library notes: an occasional publication of the State Library Commission.** Bismarck: North Dakota State Library Commission, 1970– . LC 78–17168. ISSN 0024–2446.
Statistics for all libraries in North Dakota, except school libraries, are presented annually in *North Dakota library notes.* Data include income and expenditure, collection size (reported by type of library), staff size, square footage, circulation, and number of reference questions.

OHIO

647   Directory of Ohio libraries, 1935– . Columbus: State Library of Ohio, 1935– .
Annual. LC 82–644621. ISSN 0734–0389.

This title continues *Ohio directory of libraries* (entry **648**), which continues *Directory of Ohio libraries: with statistics for 19––*. Statistical information for academic, special, and institutional libraries is presented here. Data are reported by type of library, with public libraries further arranged by name of city where the main library is located. Other types of libraries are arranged by name of library, parent institution, or company. Statistical information includes collection size, income from tax sources, total income, expenditures, circulation, and personnel data. This work also includes directory information (see entry **512**).

648   Ohio directory of libraries. Columbus: State Library of Ohio, 1972– . LC 79–644836. ISSN 0196–3872.

This work continues *Directory of Ohio libraries: with statistics for 19––*, and it is currently published under the title, *Directory of Ohio libraries, 1980–* . For directory information see entry **512**. For statistics information see entry **647**.

OKLAHOMA

649   Annual report and directory of libraries in Oklahoma, 1954–1980. Oklahoma City: Oklahoma Dept. of Libraries, 1955–1981. Annual. LC 81–643509. ISSN 0066–4065.

This title is continued by *Annual report and directory of Oklahoma libraries.* For directory information see entry **516**. For statistics information see entry **650**.

650   Annual report and directory of Oklahoma libraries, 1981– . Oklahoma City: Oklahoma Dept. of Libraries, 1982– . Annual. ISSN 0066–4065.

Detailed statistics for public, academic, institutional, school, and special libraries are presented in this annual publication. Public library statistics are arranged by system and then by community size. Data cover population, income from various sources, per capita support, expenditures, collection size, and services and programs. Academic library statistics include expenditures by category, collection size, and staff size. Institutional libraries (human services institutions and juvenile and adult correctional institutions) are described in terms of income, expenditures, collection and staff size, and services and programs. Similar data are reported for school and special libraries. In addition to statistical information, this source also contains directory information on Oklahoma libraries (see entry **516**). This title continues *Annual report and directory of libraries in Oklahoma* (entry **649**).

OREGON

651   Directory and statistics of Oregon libraries. Salem: Oregon State Library, 1977– . Annual. LC 78–645032. ISSN 0162–0290.

This title continues *Directory of Oregon libraries* (entry **652**). It provides statistical information for public, academic, and institutional libraries in Oregon for the fiscal year. Data reported for public libraries include size of collection, circulation, volumes added, receipts, expenditures, staff size, facilities, and, service outlets. For academic and institutional libraries, the reported data are less detailed and include collection size, circulation, interlibrary loan, staff size, and expenditures. This publication also provides directory information for libraries in Oregon (see entry **517**).

652 Directory of Oregon libraries. Salem: Oregon State Library, 1950–1976. Annual. This title is continued by *Directory and statistics of Oregon libraries.* For directory information see entry **517**. For statistics information see entry **651**.

PENNSYLVANIA

653 Pennsylvania public library statistics. Harrisburg: State Library of Pennsylvania, 1958– . Annual. LC 60–9149. ISSN 0553–562X.
Detailed statistical information on public libraries in Pennsylvania is presented in several tables in this annual. Data, reported alphabetically by county, cover resources, services, income, and expenditures. Also, the same data are reported for branch libraries and for bookmobiles. A separate table provides rankings of libraries, from highest to lowest, for population served, collection size, and circulation size. Also included are a statistical summary for the state and data on State Library activities.

RHODE ISLAND

654 Table showing comparable statistics as reported for service of public libraries of Rhode Island. Providence: Rhode Island Dept. of State Library Services, 19??– . Annual.
Organized by library system in Rhode Island, the data cover local appropriations, income from other sources, per capita support, circulation, number of hours open, size of book stock, total audiovisual resources, and interlibrary loan requests.

SOUTH CAROLINA

655 Annual report. Columbia: South Carolina State Library, 1970– . Annual. LC 78–648699.
State library and county public library fiscal year statistics for South Carolina are presented in this annual. Data, reported by county, summarize income, operating expenditures by category, size of bookstock, circulation, interlibrary loan, and reference transactions. Statistics are also available for regional, college, and university libraries; these cover operating expenditures, library collections (total, added, and withdrawn), and enrollment.

SOUTH DAKOTA

656 Statistics for South Dakota public libraries. Pierre: South Dakota State Library, 19??–1974. Annual. LC 75–645940.
This title is expanded and superseded by *Statistics of South Dakota libraries.* For further information see entry **657**.

657 Statistics of South Dakota libraries. Pierre: South Dakota State Library, 1975– . Annual. LC 81–64500. ISSN 0099–0655.

This annual provides statistics for public, academic, and special libraries in South Dakota. The data describe collection size, income and expenditures, and population served. In addition, there is a summary of library statistics by size and type of library. Directory information on South Dakota libraries is also included (see entry **528**). This title supersedes *Statistics for South Dakota public libraries* (entry **656**).

TENNESSEE

658 Tennessee public library statistics: July 1–June 30. Nashville: Public Libraries Section, Tennessee State Library and Archives, 1972/73– . Annual. LC 76–646559. ISSN 0363–7158.

Presented annually are statistics on metropolitan libraries, regional centers, and local libraries in Tennessee. Included first is a statewide summary of data and then a breakdown for metropolitan and city libraries, regional library centers, and local libraries. Statistics are also included for the Tennessee Regional Library for the Blind and Physically Handicapped. Data reported include income, expenditures, expenditures by percentages, film library cooperative expenditures, bookstock, circulation figures, non-book holdings, non-book circulation, books withdrawn, books lost and paid, vehicle operation, and reference statistics. Not all of these categories are reported for each of the levels of library service, but each is reported for one or more levels.

TEXAS

659 Texas academic library statistics. Austin: Texas Council of State University Librarian and Library Development Division, Texas State Library, 1972– . Annual. LC 78–642170. ISSN 0276–458X.

In this directory, statistical information is provided on approximately 100 private and public college and university libraries in Texas. Included are libraries in two year, four year, and graduate programs. The entries are grouped by type and level of parent institutions. The following statistical data are presented: size of library holdings, size of staff, budget, and expenditures by category. Directory information is also offered (see entry **533**).

660 Texas public library statistics for 1974– . Austin: Library Development Division, Texas State Library, 1975– . Annual. LC 75–646379. ISSN 0082–3120.

This annual provides a statistical profile for public libraries, academic libraries, and the Texas State Library. Data reported include population served, income, expenditures, holdings, circulation, and number of library staff. In addition, summary data are grouped by region, by size of population, and by amount of expenditures. This publication also presents directory information for public, academic, and institution libraries in Texas (see entry **534**). This work continues *Texas public library statistics*.

UTAH

661 Utah public libraries: annual report, 1959– . Salt Lake City: Utah State Library, Division of Economic and Community Development, 1959– . Annual. LC 67–57352. ISSN 0566–4276.

In this annual, statistics for Utah public libraries are arranged by county and then by city or town. Data reported include income and expenditures, collection size, staff size, services, and per capita expenditures. Data are also summarized for the state in pie charts; these include population figures, valuation, and service potential. In addition, directory information for public libraries in Utah is provided (see entry **536**).

VERMONT

662 Biennial report of the Vermont Department of Libraries: including Vermont library directory: statistics of local libraries. Montpelier: Vermont Dept. of Libraries, 1976– . Biennial. LC 76–647805. ISSN 0364–7382.
In this biennial, statistics for public libraries are presented in one table and statistics for academic, special, institutional, and state agency libraries are presented in another. Public library statistics are arranged alphabetically by town and cover income, expenditures, volumes held, volumes added, circulation, hours open, per capita tax support, number of registered borrowers, and population of the town. Data for the other libraries are less detailed but include number of volumes, other holdings, and number of circulations during the year. Directory information is also provided (see entry **537**). Until the 1979 volume, statistical information was published separately under the title, *Statistics of local libraries* (entry **663**).

663 Statistics of local libraries. Montpelier: Vermont Dept. of Libraries, 1968–1977. Biennial.
This title was merged with *Vermont library directory* in 1979 to form *Biennial report of the Vermont Department of Libraries.* For directory information see entry **537**. For statistics information see entry **662**.

VIRGINIA

664 Statistics of Virginia public libraries and institutional libraries, 1975/76– . Richmond: Library Development Branch, Virginia State Library, 1976– . Annual. LC 82–641407. ISSN 0731–8464.
Statistical information is reported by regional and county libraries and then by city and town. Included are tables for income, expenditures, circulation, collection size, and miscellaneous categories. The sources of local library income are also reported. This work provides directory information for academic and institutional libraries, but does not include statistical information for them (see entry **539**). The title continues *Statistics of Virginia public libraries.*

WASHINGTON

665 Annual statistical bulletin: Washington State Library. Olympia: Washington State Library, 1977– . Annual. LC 78–643506. ISSN 0097–9945.
This source provides detailed statistics for public libraries in Washington. Data are reported for individual libraries grouped into categories by size of population served. Covered are population served, operating expenditures, expenditures per capita, capital outlay, total expenditures, expenditures for materials by type of materials, assessed valuation, tax revenues, millage equivalent, revenue from other sources, total income, non-print holdings and circulation by type of material, and salary ranges for individual libraries. It was

formerly published under the title, *Library news bulletin: annual statistical issue* (entry **666**).

666   **Library news bulletin: annual statistical issue.** Olympia: Washington State Library, 1974–1977. Annual. LC 75–642700. ISSN 0097–9945.

This title is continued by *Annual statistical bulletin: Washington State Library* (entry **665**).

WEST VIRGINIA

667   **WVLC statistical report.** Charleston: West Virginia Library Commission, 1971– . Annual. LC 74–645697. ISSN 0094–6486.

Statistics on public, academic, and special libraries in West Virginia are provided in this annual. It is arranged by type and then by name of library. Public libraries are grouped by regional library or service center. Data reported cover population served, volumes added, total number of volumes, percent of juvenile volumes, number of non-print items, number of books, number of periodicals, number of recordings, number of staff, and hours open per week. A separate table indicates income by source and expenditures by category. Statistics on the use of the Library Commission film service are also presented. In addition, this work contains directory information for public, academic, and special libraries in the state (see entry **541**).

WISCONSIN

668   **Wisconsin library service record, 1972– .** Madison: Division for Library Services, Dept. of Public Instruction, 1974– . Annual. LC 76–640787. ISSN 0361–2848.

Statistical information for individual public libraries in Wisconsin is arranged by library system in this annual publication. Data reported include population, volumes added, total number of volumes, total number of periodicals, direct loans, interlibrary loans, total income, and total expenditures. A statewide summary reports aggregate data by size of home community and by number of hours open per week. For special libraries, the number of volumes and periodical titles held is reported. This publication also includes directory information for public, academic, and special libraries (see entry **542**).

PART TWO:

Subject-Related Reference Works

7.

Special Services and Operations

INTRODUCTION

The six preceding chapters have covered library-related reference works not devoted to specific subjects: universal and national indexing and abstracting services; bibliographies and library catalogs; current contents services; review publications; online data bases; lists of dissertations and theses; vocabularies and glossaries; lists of acronyms, initialisms, and abbreviations; thesauri; foreign-language handbooks; encyclopedias; yearbooks; manuals; biographical and membership directories; directories of libraries and archives; and sources of library statistics. Featured in this chapter are approximately 500 sources that concentrate on one or more library-related topics. The titles are arranged by subject—there are 103 sections in all, ranging from acquisitions to micrographics to women in librarianship—and subdivided by format.

Publications are included in this chapter on the basis of four criteria: *scope*—only reference sources that deal primarily, extensively, or exclusively with a library issue, development, process, or technique are covered here; *date*—the emphasis is on titles issued since 1970; *language*—references entirely in foreign languages and/or dealing exclusively with topics outside the interest of American librarians have been excluded; and *format*—processed materials and pamphlet-like publications (fifty pages or less) are generally omitted.

Since many of the subject-specific reference sources covered here deal with more than one topic, cross listings are provided. A complete list of all subject headings and "see" references used in this chapter is supplied in the Table of Contents.

Abstracting

For reference materials on abstracting see entries listed under the heading Indexing and Abstracting.

Academic Libraries and Librarianship

For reference materials on academic libraries and librarianship see entries listed under the heading College and University Libraries and Librarianship.

Acquisitions

BIBLIOGRAPHIC SOURCES

669 Library acquisitions: a classified bibliographic guide to the literature and reference tools. By Bohdan S. Wynar. 2d ed. Littleton, CO: Libraries Unlimited, 1971. 239p. LC 77–165064. ISBN 0–87287–035–9.

The compiler has provided an extensive list of citations to monographs, journal articles, and other materials that reflect standard acquisitions practices in all types of libraries. The guide is divided into five broad topics, and then subdivided further. The broad topics include organization and administration of acquisitions, publishing, and purchases. The subdivided categories cover more specific topics, including placing orders with vendors, discounts, gifts, exchanges, and approval plans. Lists of selection and verification aids are found in appropriate locations. Some of the entries have brief annotations and all provide standard bibliographic information. Entries are indexed by author, by subject, and, for the most important publications, by title.

HANDBOOKS AND MANUALS

670 Acquisitions: where, what, and how: a guide to the orientation and procedure for students in librarianship, librarians, and academic faculty. By Ted Grieder. Westport, CT: Greenwood, 1978. 277p. (Contributions in librarianship and information science, no. 22) LC–84762. ISBN 0–8371–9890–9.

This is a basic guide to the conduct of acquisitions work, with particular emphasis on acquisitions in an academic research library. It consists of two parts: the first, an "orientation" to the place of acquisitions work in libraries; the second, a manual of procedures for the conduct of acquisitions work. In the first part, the author reviews the place of acquisitions work in relation to other services and functions in the library, especially in the larger college or university environment. The second part, which comprises more than four-fifths of the publication, covers basic acquisition functions in a how-to-do-it fashion. Included are chapters on checking and how to prepare a checking manual, ordering and how to prepare an order manual, gifts and exchanges, planning and assigning staff responsibilities, recording statistics, preparing forms, explaining and defending operations, and establishing collection development policies. A subject index completes the work.

671 Books in other languages: how to select and where to order them. By Leonard Wertheimer. Ottawa: Canadian Library Assn., 1976. 129p. LC 77–364280. ISBN 0–88802–115–1.

The purpose of this work is to provide a list of selection aids and suppliers for the acquisition of non-English book titles. This information is provided for various countries and languages (including those of North American Indians). In most cases, the names and addresses of the major suppliers or vendors are identified, as well as the primary bibliographic resources that can be used for the identification and selection of non-English materials. Also included is brief information on the acquisition of records and tapes, large-print books, children's books, and nontraditional materials. Coverage tends to be uneven; entries for European countries and languages are well represented, but African and Middle Eastern countries and languages are not. For information which augments this work for Africa and the Middle East, see *The african book world and press* (entry no. **292**) and *A book world directory of the Arab countries, Turkey and Iran* (entry no. **293**).

672 Library acquisition policies and procedures. Ed. by Elizabeth Futas. Phoenix: Oryx, 1977. 406p. (A Neal-Schuman professional book) LC 77–7275. ISBN 0–912700–02–5.

Selected samples of acquisition policies and procedures in use by twelve public and fourteen academic libraries are reprinted in this work. In addition, partial selections have been included from fifty-six other acquisition policies. These deal with such specific categories as objectives, special formats, gifts, and weeding. Several documents of importance to library acquisitions are reproduced in the appendices: the Library Bill of Rights, Freedom to Read Statement, and Statement on Appraisal of Gifts, among others. An introductory chapter reports the results of a survey, conducted by the author, that supplies additional insights into library acquisition policies. The detailed subject index provides the reader with access to all policy statements dealing with specific topics.

673 Manuscript solicitation for libraries, special collections, museums, and archives. By Edward C. Kemp. Littleton, CO: Libraries Unlimited, 1978. 204p. LC 77–29015. ISBN 0–87287–183–5.

The object of this handbook is to explain how to conduct a systematic and practical program for the solicitation of manuscripts from potential donors. Chapters cover such topics as obtaining leads for sources of donations, maintaining correspondence, visiting potential donors, and appraising the collection when received. Examples and case studies are provided. Included in the appendices are examples of various documents, e.g., field notes, collection inventory samples, reminder files, and policy statements. Additional readings are noted in bibliographic citations for most chapters. The text is indexed by subject.

674 Practical approval plan management. By Jennifer S. Cargill. Phoenix: Oryx, 1979. 95p. LC 79–23389. ISBN 0–912700–52–1.

Intended as a manual for academic librarians involved in planning, designing, and operating approval plans, this work provides practical suggestions for implementing approval plan procedures and routines. It includes sample forms, contracts, and letters that can be adopted or adapted. Chapters cover such topics as vendors, bids and contracts, preparing profiles, and fiscal management. Some of the examples presented deal with services offered by specific vendors. A selected bibliography of additional readings is also included.

675 School library and media center acquisitions policies and procedures. Ed. by Mary M. Taylor. Phoenix: Oryx, 1981. 272p. LC 80–23115. ISBN 0–912700–70–X.

This is a compilation of acquisition and selection policies prepared by school library media centers. The policies included were selected from 233 sent to Taylor: of these, fifteen policies are presented in their entirety; thirty-three additional policies are extracted. Appropriate parts of the policies are organized by topic, such as: introductions, objectives, and selection criteria. Taylor's introduction provides a justification for the development of policies for collection development and acquisitions. Although examples of acquisition policies are included, the majority of the text concentrates on selection and collection development.

TERMINOLOGY SOURCES

676 German for libraries. By G. W. Turner. Rev. and ed. by A. J. A. Vieregg and J. W. Blackwood. Palmerston North, New Zealand: Massey Univ., 1972. 137p. (Massey University, library series, no. 5) LC 73–152603.
This guide to German grammar and bibliolinguistics is intended to assist librarians in ordering and cataloging German-language materials. For further information see entry **211**.

677 Manual of european languages for librarians. Ed. by C. G. Allen. New York: Bowker, 1975. 803p. LC 73–6062. ISBN 0–85935–028–2.
This publication provides basic language instruction for librarians who work with foreign-language materials. It is intended for catalogers, collection development and acquisition librarians, and bibliographers. For further information see entry **209**.

Administration and Management of Libraries

BIBLIOGRAPHIC SOURCES

678 Library management: a bibliography with abstracts. By Carolyn Shonyo. Springfield, VA: NTIS, 1977. 188p. NTIS/PS–76/1037/RC.
Part of the NTISearch series, this bibliography provides coverage of report literature from the NTIS collection of documents from 1964–1976. Each entry includes full bibliographic information and the NTIS document number. The bibliography consists of 188 entries. Topics cover various management subjects, including planning, operations analysis, management of acquisitions, personnel management, and management of library processing. Abstracts accompany each citation.

HANDBOOKS AND MANUALS

679 Managing the cataloging department. By Donald Leroy Foster. 2d ed. Metuchen, NJ: Scarecrow, 1982. 236p. LC 81–16694. ISBN 0–8108–1486–2.
Guidance is provided on optimal methods for the management and administration of cataloging departments. For further information see entry **805**.

680 Scientific management of library operations. By Richard M. Dougherty and Fred J. Heinritz, with Neal K. Kaske. 2d ed. Metuchen, NJ: Scarecrow, 1982. 286p. LC 81–18200. ISBN 0–8108–1485–4.
Substantially revised and updated, this second edition deals with a variety of management-related topics, including design of a library system, relationships between employees and the work environment, planning and implementing studies, cost analysis, time study, application of statistics, and use of standards. The authors' objective is to provide guidance for library managers and others in preparing, planning, and analyzing policies and procedures in order to achieve better cost economies and systems performance. The text is augmented by examples, illustrations, tables, charts, graphs, and bibliographies of selected additional readings.

681 **A simplified approach to implementing objectives-based management systems in library organizations.** By H. W. Handy. Las Cruces, NM: H. W. Handy, 1975. 175p.
The purpose of this manual is to provide guidance to individuals interested in implementing a management-by-objectives program in libraries. The approach is practical and is based on the results of the writer's own experience in working with libraries. The text uses a step-by-step approach, presenting examples of management-by-objectives plans with specific activities outlined. Chapter topics include basic principles of management by objectives, setting goals and objectives, evaluating staff performance, and strategies for introducing the system.

REVIEW PUBLICATIONS

682 **Advances in library administration and organization.** By Gerald B. McCabe, Bernard Kreissman and W. Carl Jackson. Greenwich, CT: JAI Pr., 1982– . Annual. ISBN 0–89232–213–6.
The first volume in this series of annual reviews on library administration and management was issued in 1982. Each annual volume is to deal with topics related to aspects of library management. For each topic, a state of the art review of the literature is provided. In the first volume, the following subjects are covered: continuity and discontinuity, microforms facilities, RLIN and OCLC, faculty status, automation, and construction of the Harvard library. Each article includes citations to key contributions in the literature.

African Studies Libraries

BIOGRAPHICAL SOURCES

683 **Directory of asian and african librarians in North America.** Chicago: Asian and African Section, Assn. of College and Research Libraries, American Library Assn., 1978. 35p.
Listed here are approximately 460 librarians working in some capacity with resources on Asia and Africa. For further information see entry **727**.

DIRECTORIES

684 **Directory of libraries and special collections on Asia and North Africa.** Comp. by Robert Collison. Hamden, CT: Archon, 1970. 123p. LC 71–16224.
Over 160 British libraries with subject strengths and special collections in the Orient, Middle East, and North Africa are described in this directory. For further information see entry **729**.

685 **Guide to federal archives relating to Africa.** Comp. by Aloha South. Waltham, MA: African Studies Assn., 1977. 556p. LC 77–412.
This guide was compiled by the National Archives and Records Service for the African Studies Association to identify the "known Africa-related records in the National Archives of the United States." The records, which include textual material, maps, sound recordings, and motion and still pictures, are located in the National Archives Building, the General Archives Division in the Washington National Records Center, Presidential Libraries, and the regional archives branches that are part of the Federal Archives and Records Centers.

Coverage of these holdings is comprehensive and thorough. Arrangement is alphabetical by name of the agency and then by subordinate agency. The entries are indexed by subject, place names, proper name, names of ships, and ethnic group names.

686   Guide to Washington, D.C. for african studies. By Purnima Mehta Bhatt. Washington, DC: Smithsonian Inst. Pr., 1980. 347p. (Scholars' guide to Washington, D.C., no. 4) LC 79–607774. ISBN 0–87474–238–2.

Identified in this directory are the holdings of various public and private institutions in the Washington, D.C. area that contain resource materials on the geographical, topical, and historical aspects of African resources. The institutions represented include libraries, embassies, associations, government agencies, international organizations, archives, and museums. Entries vary in length and depth, but those institutions with the most comprehensive collections are described in some detail. The strength of each collection is rated on a scale from A to D, thus providing the user with additional information on the quality of the holdings. Much of the data presented here was gathered first hand during visits to the institutions described. Entries focus on public service characteristics, such as hours of opening, policies regarding use, photocopying facilities, and interlibrary loan. Index access is by name of institution, collections of personal papers, subject strengths, and general subjects.

687   Handbook of american resources for african studies. Comp. by P. Duignan. Stanford, CA: Hoover Inst. on War, Revolution and Peace, Stanford Univ., 1967. 218p. (Hoover Institution bibliographic series) LC 66–20901.

Detailed descriptions are provided for the African holdings of ninety-five general libraries and archives, 108 church and missionary libraries and archives, ninety-five art and ethnographic collections, and four business archives. The entries vary in length, from a paragraph to several pages. Information in the longer entries is quite detailed and identifies the subject areas in which special collections are held. Of particular value are the notes on archival holdings that indicate the number of rolls of microfilm. Arrangement is by type of library and then alphabetically by name of the parent institution. A detailed index provides access by subject and by individuals whose papers are contained in archival collections. In spite of the age of this publication, it remains the most comprehensive guide to resources about Africa held by American libraries and archives.

688   The Scolma directory of libraries and special collections on Africa. Comp. by Robert Collison. Rev. by John Roe. 3d ed. Hamden, CT: Shoe String, 1973. 118p. LC 73–6539. ISBN 0–208–01332–6.

Compiled for the Standing Conference on Library Materials on Africa, this directory is intended to describe the African holdings of 141 libraries in the United Kingdom. The entries are arranged alphabetically by the name of the city or town in which each library is located. In London, libraries are grouped by postal district. Information is provided on name and address of the parent institution, telephone number, name of librarian, subjects covered, special collections or files held, services available, availability of materials, hours of opening, and publications. Subject access to the text is provided.

Afro-American Studies Libraries
DIRECTORIES

689 **Directory of afro-american resources.** Comp. by Walter Schatz. New York: Bowker, 1971. 485p. LC 71–126008. ISBN 0–8352–0260–7.

Now somewhat out of date, this 1971 directory identifies 2,100 organizations and institutions with Afro-American resource collections. Among those listed are libraries with major collections and civil rights organizations. Entries are arranged by state, city, and name of institution. An index to the holdings is also included.

Aging, Library Service To
BIBLIOGRAPHIC SOURCES

690 **A selected bibliography on the aging, and the role of the library in serving them.** By Mollie W. Kramer. Champaign: Graduate School of Library Science, Univ. of Illinois, 1973. 39p. (Occasional papers, no. 107) LC 73–622224.

Described in this annotated bibliography are books and articles concerned with the aging, including publications about the social and psychological needs of older citizens and about library service to this population group. Except for selected items from the *New York Times* and the *New York Post,* newspaper articles are generally not cited.

HANDBOOKS AND MANUALS

691 **Serving the older adult: a guide to library programs and information sources.** By Betty J. Turock. New York: Bowker, 1983. 294p. LC 82–20772. ISBN 0–8352–1487–7.

This manual covers the initiation and development of library and information services for older adults in various types of library and information agencies. Turock describes the unique information needs of older adults, providing instruction and examples to demonstrate how these needs can be met. The work is organized into four parts. The first provides a review and history of library information services for adults, along with background information about the older adult population. Part two describes methods and strategies for developing programs, including such topics as fundraising, using volunteers, and coordinating services with other community agencies. Part three presents model programs and practical examples for establishing such services as information and referral services, local history, genealogy, and oral history programs. Included in the final part are a bibliography and a directory of government, professional, and other agencies concerned with service to the older adult.

Agriculture Libraries
DIRECTORIES

692 **World directory of agricultural libraries & documentation centres.** Ed. by D. H. Boalch. Herpenden, England: The International Assn. of Agricultural Librarians and Documentalists, 1960. 280p. LC 60–3301.

Described in this directory are 2,531 agricultural libraries and information centers through-

179

out the world. The entries are arranged alphabetically by country, then by smaller geographic subdivisions, and finally by name of institution. All types of agricultural libraries are covered, including those in agricultural experiment stations, academic institutions, private firms, and state and national libraries. Information about each is brief. The name and address of the library is provided, with an indication of the date founded, number of volumes, staff size, and type of classification system used. The entries are indexed by subject and place name. Although now somewhat out of date, this is still the most extensive listing of libraries in the field of agriculture.

HANDBOOKS AND MANUALS

693 Primer for agricultural libraries. 2d ed. Wageningen, Netherlands: Centre for Agricultural Publishing and Documentation, 1980. 91p.

Intended to provide guidance in the operation of agriculture libraries, this manual presents basic information about the functions of library service: collection development, acquisition, classification and cataloging, and use of resources. Because exchange of publications can constitute a major means of acquisition in agricultural libraries, a section on the topic is included, with sample forms for requesting publications from various countries. Included in the several appendices are lists of current bibliographies, indexes and abstract journals, review sources, and major agricultural journals. The first edition was published under the same title in 1967.

Archives

Materials on archives also appear elsewhere in this guide. For bibliographies, directories, biographical and statistical sources covering archives in general, see the appropriate chapter in Part One. Included here are reference materials dealing with various aspects of archives as a subject.

BIBLIOGRAPHIC SOURCES

694 Archives in Australia. Comp. by Alan Ives. Canberra: Pearce Pr., 1978. 7v.

This extensive bibliographic survey of writings pertaining to archival studies in Australia is divided into several sections. Volumes 1 through 3 provide retrospective coverage of Australian writings on archives and manuscripts. Volume 4 cites current writings. Volume 5 lists current works written by "modest practitioners." Volumes 6 and 7 present historical coverage and include a directory of archives and manuscript collections in Australia. Taken together, these volumes constitute the most comprehensive bibliographical work and the most thorough directory source for archives in Australia.

695 Automation, machine-readable records and archival administration: an annotated bibliography. Comp. and ed. by Richard M. Kesner. Chicago: Society of American Archivists, 1980. 65p. LC 79–92994. ISBN 0–931828–22–8.

This international bibliography of 293 citations captures most of the literature that deals with automation and archives. For further information see entry **745**.

696 **Basic international bibliography of archive administration/Bibliographie internationale fondamentale d'archivistique.** Comp. by Michel Duchein. Munich: Verlag Dokumentation, 1978. 250p. (International review on archives/Revue internationale des archives, v. 25) ISBN 3–7940–3775–8.

This bibliography of monographs and journal articles, covering the time period from 1950 to the mid–1970's, is intended primarily for professional archivists, particularly those in developing nations. The work is limited largely to works in English, French, German, Italian, Spanish, and Russian. It is divided into eighteen chapters, each of which covers a broad topic, e.g., access to archival materials, preservation, laws and regulations, and training of archivists. Within each chapter, entries are arranged by the language of the publication. Subject and author indexes complete the volume.

697 **The history of archives administration: a select bibliography.** Comp. by Frank B. Evans. Paris: Unesco, 1979. 255p. (Libraries and archives: bibliographies and reference works, no. 6) LC 81–453351. ISBN 92–3–101646–6.

Extensive but not exhaustive, this international bibliography cites books and journal articles on the history of archives administration. The work is divided into four sections: an introduction to archives administration; an overview of the evolution of archives administration; a survey of archival agencies and programs; and a survey of international archival developments. The first section identifies basic readings on archival concepts, terminology, and principles, and on the nature and value of archives. The second section includes writings about archives in the ancient world, middle ages, and contemporary times. The third section, which accounts for approximately half of the book, is a country-by-country survey of writings on archival administration. The final section covers international archival developments, primarily archives of international organizations and activities of international archival associations. There is a detailed subject and author index that includes references to archival activities by country.

698 **Modern archives and manuscripts: a select bibliography.** Chicago: Society of American Archivists, 1975. 209p. LC 75–23058.

Although selective, this work provides extensive bibliographic coverage of writings on archival work during the past few decades. However, it is limited to materials in English and, further, covers only those writings emphasizing archival theory and practice in the United States. The bibliography is arranged in four broad sections, subdivided into thirty-three chapters, and further subdivided by a decimal classification system. The four broad chapters provide: an introduction to archives administration; survey of archival functions; an overview of American archival agencies and archives; and a review of international archival developments. The individual chapter bibliographies begin with a list of "Basic Readings," the most important writings on the topic of the chapter. Entries are not annotated and the bibliographic style makes considerable use of abbreviations. The bibliographic form does not include the name of the publisher, but other basic information is provided. Subject and author indexes are included.

699 **A select bibliography on business archives and records management.** Comp. and ed. by Karen M. Benedict. Chicago: Society of American Archivists, 1981. 134p. A total of 421 articles and eighteen books are cited in this annotated bibliography. For further information see entry **796**.

DIRECTORIES

700 **Children's authors and illustrators: a guide to manuscript collections in the United States research libraries.** Comp. by James H. Fraser. New York: K. G. Saur, 1980. 119p. (Phaedrus bibliographic series, no. 1) LC 79–24990. ISBN 0–89664–950–4.

The manuscript holdings of some of the major research libraries in the United States are identified and briefly described. For further information see entry **813**.

701 **Directory of business archives in the United States and Canada.** Chicago: Society of American Archivists, 1975. 34p. LC 79–2522.

The business archives of more than 100 American and Canadian firms are described in this source. For further information see entry **797**.

702 **Directory of jewish archival institutions.** Ed. by Philip P. Mason. Detroit: Wayne State Univ. Pr., 1975. 76p. LC 75–15504.

The holdings of major Jewish archival collections in the United States and abroad are described here. For further information see entry **942**.

703 **East, central and southeast Europe: a handbook of library and archival resources in North America.** Ed. by Paul L. Horecky. Santa Barbara, CA: ABC-Clio, 1976. 467p. (Joint Committee on Eastern Europe Publication series, no. 3) LC 76–28392. ISBN 0–87346–214–8.

This work is a basic reference tool for the study of essential collections on Europe available in major libraries, archives, and research institutions in the United States and Canada. For further information see entry **877**.

704 **Eastern Europe and Russia-Soviet Union: a handbook of west european archival and library resources.** By Richard C. Lewanski. New York: K. G. Saur; Detroit: Gale, distr., 1980. 317p. (Joint Committee on Eastern Europe Publication series, no. 9) LC 79–19520. ISBN 0–89664–092–2.

This directory identifies approximately 1,000 institutions in twenty-one western European countries that have significant holdings of archival materials on eastern Europe and the Soviet Union. For further information see entry **878**.

705 **Guide to ethnic museums, libraries, and archives in the United States.** By Lubomyr R. Wynar and Lois Buttlar. Kent, OH: Center for the Study of Ethnic Publications, Kent State Univ., 1978. 378p.

This is a guide to 828 ethnic museums, libraries, and archives in the United States that have collected materials on more than seventy ethnic groups. For further information see entry **875**.

706 **Guide to jewish archives.** Ed. by Aryeh Segall. Prelim. ed. Jerusalem: World Council on Jewish Archives; New York: National Foundation for Jewish Culture, distr., 1981. 90p.

International in scope, this work lists archives, libraries, and other institutions that have significant holdings of materials on the Jewish people. For further information see entry **943**.

707   A guide to manuscript sources for the history of Latin America and the Caribbean in the British Isles. Ed. by P. Walne. London: Oxford Univ. Pr. with the Inst. of Latin American Studies, Univ. of London, 1973. 580p. LC 73–165634.
Identified in the directory are major manuscript sources, with an inventory provided of manuscripts found in each collection. For further information see entry **953**.

708   Guide to the archives of international organizations. Part I, United Nations system: preliminary version. Paris: Unesco, 1979. 301p. PGI/79/WS/7.
This directory describes the archives of the United Nations and other international organizations in the United Nations family of agencies. For further information see entry **1187**.

709   International guide to library, archival, and information science associations. By Josephine Riss Fang and Alice H. Songe. 2d ed. New York: Bowker, 1980. 448p. LC 80–21721. ISBN 0–8352–1285–8.
In this directory of associations concerned with library and information science, archival work, and other closely-related fields, a total of fifty-nine international and 450 national associations are listed. For further information see entry **736**.

710   Library, documentation and archives serials. Comp. by Grazyna Janzing. Ed. by K. R. Brown. 4th ed. The Hague: International Federation for Documentation, 1975. 203p. LC 77–372703. ISBN 92–66–00532–0.
Nearly 1,000 serials in librarianship, information science, documentation, and archives are listed in this international directory. For further information see entry **948**.

711   Pan american directory of archives. Comp. by Gecia Vasco de Escudero. Ottawa: Public Archives of Canada for the Archives Committee of the Pan American Inst. of Geography and History, 1980. 35p.
Intended to complement rather than replace other directories of archives, this work arranges archival institutions in American nations by country. The archives in capital cities are listed first, beginning with national and governmental institutions. These are followed by university archives, religious archives, and private archives. Listings of archives for states or provinces follow those for the capital cities.

712   Scholars' guide to Washington, D.C. for latin american and caribbean studies. By Michael Grow and the Latin American Program of the Woodrow Wilson International Center for Scholars. Washington, DC: Smithsonian Inst. Pr., 1979. 346p. LC 78–21316.
This directory provides extensive coverage of the intellectual resources available in the Washington, D.C. area. For further information see entry **954**.

713   Slavic ethnic libraries, museums and archives in the United States: a guide and directory. Comp. by Lubomyr R. Wynar with Pat Kleeberger. Chicago: Assn. for

College and Research Libraries; Kent, OH: Program for the Study of Ethnic Publications, School of Library Science, Kent State Univ., 1980. 164p. LC 80–18034.
Described in this directory are libraries, museums, and archives collecting materials relating to fourteen Slavic groups. For further information see entry **876**.

714 Women's history sources: a guide to archives and manuscript collections in the United States. Ed. by Andrea Hinding. New York: Bowker, 1979. 2v. LC 78–15634. ISBN 0–8352–1103–7.
This guide identifies 18,000 collections related to women's studies found in 1,600 repositories in the United States. The listing, although not exhaustive, is extensive. The information provided about each collection covers the nature and size of the holdings as well as individuals represented in the holdings. A similar but more limited source is *Women religious history sources: a guide to repositories in the United States* (entry **715**).

715 Women's religious history sources: a guide to repositories in the United States. Ed. by Sister Evangeline Thomas. New York: Bowker, 1983. 400p. ISBN 0–8352–1681–0.
This source is similar to, but more limited than, *Women's history sources: a guide to archives and manuscript collections in the United States.* For further information see entry **714**.

HANDBOOKS AND MANUALS

716 Archival legislation, 1970–1980. New York: K. G. Saur, 1982. 447p. (Archivum: international review on archives, v.28) ISBN 3–5988–21228–3.
Reproduced in this compilation is legislation dealing with archives from fifty-one countries and Puerto Rico for the years 1970 through 1980. Arrangement is by country. The compilation was undertaken by the editorial board of *Archivum* and is the fifth in a series of publications on this topic. The previous four contain legislation for different areas of the world. In addition to presenting the legislation, the editors interpret worldwide patterns in archival legislation from the legislation included.

717 Archives administration: a manual for intermediate and smaller organizations and for local government. By Michael Cook. Folkstone, Kent: Dawson, Cannon House, 1977. 258p. LC 77–378944. ISBN 0–7129–0749–1.
While the author provides readers with practical, step-by-step information about the various phases of contemporary archival practice, the emphasis of the manual is on archival operations appropriate to small or medium sized archives, sometimes to the exclusion of topics relating to larger archives. The text applies primarily to archives found in small businesses, local governments, colleges and universities, and hospitals.

718 Archives and manuscripts: an introduction to automated access. By H. Thomas Hickerson. Chicago: Society of American Archivists, 1981. 60p. LC 81–52113. ISBN 0–931828–29–5.
An overview of computer applications to archive and manuscript collections is provided in this handbook. For further information see entry **753**.

719 Religious archives: an introduction. By August R. Suelflow. Chicago: Society of American Archivists, 1980. 56p. LC 80–17159. ISBN 0–913828–20–1.

This is a basic manual for planning and providing services in an archives of religious materials. For further information see entry **823**.

Art Libraries

BIOGRAPHICAL SOURCES

720 Art Libraries Society of North America: directory of members. Washington, DC: Art Libraries Society of North America, 1982– . Annual. LC 83–642049. ISSN 0737–3287.

In this membership directory of the major associations of art libraries in the United States, approximately 1,000 members are listed alphabetically. Entries contain the member's name, office address, telephone number, home address and telephone number, and special areas of interest.

DIRECTORIES

721 Directory of art libraries and visual resource collections in North America. Comp. by Judith A. Hoffberg and Stanley W. Hess for the Art Libraries Society of North America. New York: Neal-Schuman; Santa Barbara, CA: ABC-Clio, distr., 1978. 298p. LC 78–61628. ISBN 0–918212–05–7.

Approximately 1,300 libraries, museums, galleries, art schools, colleges, and universities are grouped into two categories. The first lists art libraries by state and province; the second covers visual resource collections. These two sections have separate subject indexes to special collections and an index to subscription series of visual resource collections. A combined index to institutions in both sections is also provided. Entries for the libraries contain the name, address, and telephone number of the library; the name of the director; type of library and date founded; hours of opening; availability of materials; services (e.g., reference, photocopying, interlibrary loan); publications; special programs, such as group tours; size of collection; subject emphases; and special collections. Similar information is provided for visual resource collections.

722 Directory of art libraries in Europe or libraries with important art holdings: a preliminary list. Paris: IFLA Round Table of Art Librarians, 1979. 62p. LC 80–152469.

The geographical coverage of this work includes continental Europe, but excludes the United Kingdom and the Republic of Ireland. The scope statement indicates that libraries with fewer than 1,000 art volumes have been excluded, unless they are devoted to "a very specific subject." National libraries, because they are all considered to have important art collections, are also omitted. There are approximately 600 libraries listed. Arrangement is alphabetical by country and then by city, according to the English spelling of the place names. Because the directory is not indexed, this is the only means of access to the entries. Institution names are in the spelling of the country of origin, with cyrillic names transliterated using the Library of Congress system. Entries contain the name, address and telephone number, name of the library director, hours of opening, and an indication of the holdings on art subjects.

723 Fine arts library resources in Canada. By the Resources Survey Division, National Library of Canada. Ottawa: National Library of Canada, 1978. 2v. (Research collections in canadian libraries, no.6) ISBN 0–660–10132–7 (v.1). ISBN 0–660–10133–7 (v.2).

All significant fine arts collections in Canada are covered in this listing. Entries are arranged by name of institution and contain information on collection strengths; collection policies; specialized holdings; slide, picture and photograph collections; and public access. The data were obtained with assistance from the Art Libraries Committee of the Canadian Association of Special Libraries and Information Services.

724 German art libraries/Deutche kunstbibliotheken. Comp. by Horst J. Tummers. Ed. by the Association of Art Libraries. Munich: K. G. Saur, 1975. 101p. LC 76–451919. ISBN 3–7940–3424–4.

Major German art libraries in selected cities are described in this directory. Entries include name and address, hours of opening, a brief summary of the history of the library, detailed descriptions of the holdings and special collections, and a bibliography of publications published by or about the library. The text is in German with English summaries.

HANDBOOKS AND MANUALS

725 Art library manual: a guide to resources and practice. By Philip Pacey. New York: Bowker, 1977. 423p. LC 77–70290. ISBN 0–8593–5054–1.

The intent of this manual published in association with the Art Libraries Society is to present basic information about the operation of art libraries. The work consists of twenty-four chapters contributed by separate authors. Each of these contains general background information, accompanied by practical suggestions based on experience. Most deal with types of art materials or resources for obtaining them. For example, there are chapters on museum and gallery publications, sales catalogs, exhibition catalogs, and trade literature. Also covered in the volume are abstracting and indexing services, microforms, sound records, and photographs. The emphasis is on the problems associated with acquiring, organizing, conserving, and utilizing these types of materials. Additional information is found in the appendices. The first identifies libraries and other organizations serving as sources of information. The second is a bibliography of writings on the conservation of materials. This work was sponsored by the Art Libraries Society (ARLIS), a British association. The majority of contributors are British, but the text is relevant to art librarians in any country; issues and problems are addressed in a universal fashion.

Asian Americans in Librarianship

For reference materials on Asian Americans in librarianship see entries listed under the heading Chinese Americans in Librarianship.

Asian Studies Libraries

BIBLIOGRAPHIC SOURCES

726 Asian libraries and librarianship: an annotated bibliography of selected books and periodicals and a draft syllabus. By G. Raymond Nunn. Metuchen, NJ:

Scarecrow, 1973. 137p. LC 73–6629. ISBN 0–8108–0633–9.
This is an annotated bibliography of 353 books and periodicals dealing with libraries and librarianship throughout Asia. For further information see entry **80**.

BIOGRAPHICAL SOURCES

727 Directory of asian and african librarians in North America. Ed. and comp. by Henry Scholberg. Chicago: Asian and African Section, Assn. of College and Research Libraries, American Library Assn., 1978. 35p. LC 78–112126.
Listed here are approximately 460 librarians working in some capacity with resources on Asia and Africa who are also members of the Asian and African Section of the Association of College and Research Libraries. Information about each is brief, including only name, title, and address. A name index is provided.

DIRECTORIES

728 Directory of east asian collections in north american libraries. New Haven, CT: Committee on East Asian Libraries, Assn. for Asian Studies, 1977– . Annual. LC 77–649994.
This brief directory lists approximately ninety East Asian collections in the United States and Canada. The countries covered include China, Japan, Korea, and Vietnam. Arrangement is alphabetical by name of the institution. Entries specify the name and address of the institution, name of the collection, and names and titles of staff members. There is a personal name index.

729 Directory of libraries and special collections on Asia and North Africa. Comp. by Robert Collison. Hamden, CT: Archon, 1970. 123p. LC 71–16224.
Over 100 British libraries with subject strengths and special collections in the Orient, Middle East, and North Africa are described in this directory. All types of libraries are listed, including special libraries. Arrangement is by the city or town in which the library is located. Entries include the name and address of the library, hours of opening, services offered, and policies regarding public access. The indexes provide additional access by subject and by names of special collections. This directory was compiled at the behest of the Sub-Committee of Oriental Libraries (SCONUL).

Associations: Library, Archival and Information Science

For information on individual associations see specific subject-related areas in this chapter.

BIBLIOGRAPHIC SOURCES

730 A bibliography of IFLA conference papers, 1968–1978. Comp. by Ismael Abdullahi. Copenhagen: IFLA Clearinghouse, The Royal School of Librarianship, 1979. 86p. ISBN 87–7415–069–3.

Listed in this bibliography are papers presented at the 34th to the 44th IFLA conferences. Chronological, subject, and author access is provided through the indexes. Copies of the papers can be obtained from the IFLA Clearinghouse at the Royal School of Librarianship, where they are stored.

731 ALA publication checklist, 1979– : a list of materials currently available from the American Library Association. Comp. by the staff of the ALA Headquarters Library. Chicago: American Library Assn., 1979– . Annual. LC 79–643470. ISSN 0193–810X.

This checklist provides bibliographic data for every publication currently available from the American Library Association and its units. For further information see entry **94**.

732 FID publications: an 80 year bibliography, 1895–1975. The Hague: FID, 1975. 94p. LC 76–350239. ISBN 92–66–00531–2.

The most significant publications from the International Federation for Documentation's first eighty years are identified here. For further information see entry **71**.

DIRECTORIES

733 Directory of library associations in Canada/Répertoire des associations de biliothèques au Canada. Ottawa: Library Documentation Centre, National Library of Canada, 1974– . Annual. LC 76–645552. ISSN 0380–1187.

This alphabetical list of approximately fifty library associations in Canada provides information on name, mailing address, telephone, date founded, objectives, size of membership, officers, length of term, names of committees, and publications. The scope of the directory is rather broad; it includes associations of archivists and alumni groups. However, some relevant groups are not included, such as publishers organizations, staff associations, and unions. Indexing is by geographical location, subject, name of the association, and acronym of the organization.

734 Handbook of national and international library associations. By Josephine R. Fang and Alice H. Songe. Prelim. ed. Chicago: American Library Assn., 1973. 326p. LC 73–5619. ISBN 0–8389–3143–X.

This title is superseded by the second edition *International guide to library, archival, and information science associations.* For further information see entry **736**.

735 International Federation of Library Associations and Institutions: directory. The Hague: IFLAI, 1931– . Annual.

This directory identifies all member library associations and associate member institutions and individuals. The brief entries include the name, address, and telephone number of member institutions and a list of officers. Also provided are a list of IFLAI officers and information about the association.

736 International guide to library, archival, and information science associations. By Josephine Riss Fang and Alice H. Songe. 2d ed. New York: Bowker, 1980. 448p. LC 80–21721. ISBN 0–8352–1285–8.

In this directory of associations concerned with library and information science, archival work, and other closely-related fields, a total of fifty-nine international and 450 national associations are listed. This represents an increase of 153 over the first edition, published by the American Library Association under the title *Handbook of national and international library associations* (entry **734**). Coverage extends to 178 countries, an increase of seventy-seven from the previous edition. Arrangement is alphabetical by country and then by name of association. Entries contain official name, acronym, address, names and titles of major officers, number of staff, major fields of interests, languages used, historical data structure and goals of the organization, financial status, and the most recent budget prior to publication of the directory. Special features include a list of official acronyms, a bibliography covering the years 1975–1980, a list of official journals and selected newsletters of the associations (with bibliographic information), an alphabetical list of the official names of associations, a roster of chief officers, and a chart of comparative statistical information on the associations for the period 1976–1980.

Audiovisual Services and Nonprint Materials
BIBLIOGRAPHIC SOURCES

737 Media in the library: a selected, annotated bibliography. By Evelyn H. Daniel with Karen A. Stiles. Syracuse, NY: ERIC-IR, 1978. 93p. ED 168 590.

A total of 496 items published between 1970 and 1978 are included in this bibliography. The citations chosen are intended to be of interest to school library media personnel, educational technologists, and students. Although most items are not annotated, a brief description is provided when the title is ambiguous. Approximately 100 of the entries are marked with an asterisk to signify that the item is "particularly important." Arrangement of the bibliography is by topic, such as selection of materials and equipment, media and teaching, and research. Although not limited to ERIC documents, a substantial number of the entries can be found in the ERIC data base.

738 Nonbook materials: a bibliography of recent publications. Ed. by Hans Wellisch. College Park: College of Library and Information Services, Univ. of Maryland, 1975. 131p. (Student contribution series, no. 6) LC 75–620053.

Cited in this annotated bibliography are 600 items concerned with the treatment of nonbook materials in libraries. The coverage extends to various forms of media, including audiorecords, clippings and ephemeral materials, maps, pictures, realia, and trade catalogs. Entries are arranged by type of materials and indexed by author and institution.

BIOGRAPHICAL SOURCES

739 AECT human resources directory. Washington, DC: AECT, 1982– . Annual.

Personal and institutional members of the Association for Educational Communications and Technology are listed in this annual directory. Information given for personal members includes address, telephone number, and type of position. In some instances, members have listed home addresses; in others, work addresses and position. Information about the organization is also included: the constitution and bylaws, names of members of committees, names and addresses of national affiliates and state affiliates, and suppliers of audiovisual supplies who were exhibitors at the most recent AECT national conference. Prior to 1981, this directory was published under the title, *AECT membership directory.*

HANDBOOKS AND MANUALS

740 Media equipment: a guide and dictionary. By Kenyon C. Rosenberg and John S. Doskey. Littleton, CO: Libraries Unlimited, 1976. 190p. LC 76–2554. ISBN 0–87287–155–X.

This work is intended as a guide for persons who purchase and use audiovisual equipment. For further information see entry **1015**.

Authors

BIOGRAPHICAL SOURCES

741 Librarian authors: a bibliography. By Rudolf Englebarts. Jefferson, NC: McFarland, 1981. 276p. LC 80–28035. ISBN 0–89950–007–2.

This work contains biographical sketches of 109 librarians, living and deceased, who have gained prominence as authors. The criteria for inclusion extends to authorship of works either in librarianship or outside the professional literature. A separate section provides selective bibliographies of the most significant writings of these authors. Although the majority of librarians listed are American, there are also prominent British, French, German, Indian, Italian, and Norwegian librarians covered. The biographical articles range from one to two pages in length and emphasize both professional and personal aspects of the life of the individual. The sketches are grouped chronologically, then alphabetically. There are three chronological categories, covering the years 1600–1800, 1800–1950, and 1950–1980. Individuals are placed in each category according to the period when they lived and made their most significant contributions. Some photographs are included. Indexing is by personal name, subject, institution, and selected publication titles.

Automation in Libraries

BIBLIOGRAPHIC SOURCES

742 An annotated bibliography of automation in libraries and information systems, 1972–75. Comp. by Maxine MacCafferty. London: Aslib, 1976. 147p. LC 77–350378. ISBN 0–85142–079–8.

This work is continued by *An annotated bibliography of automation in libraries, 1975–1978.* For further information see entry **743**.

743 An annotated bibliography of automation in libraries, 1975–1978. Comp. by Ainslie Dewe. London: Aslib, 1980. 76p. LC 80–514859. ISBN 0–85142–132–6.

The most recent in a continuing series of bibliographies concerned with library automation, this compilation cites monographs, periodical articles, and reports published between 1975 and 1978. Most of the entries are from the English-language literature, although important items in French and German are also listed. The bibliography tends to emphasize the aspects of automation that deal with library operations, e.g., circulation control, serials, and business applications. In general, the series has excluded citations to articles on commercially-available online systems, except when they have applicability to library automation. Earlier editions include *An annotated bibliography of automation in libraries and information systems, 1972–75* (entry **742**), *An annotated bibliography of library automation, 1968–1972* (entry **744**), and *Bibliography of library automation, 1964–1967 (entry **746**).

744 An annotated bibliography of library automation, 1968–1972. Comp. by Lynne Tinker. London: Aslib, 1973. 85p. LC 74–170581. ISBN 0–85142–050–8.
This work is continued by *An annotated bibliography of automation in libraries and information systems, 1972–1975* and *An annotated bibliography of automation in libraries, 1975–1978*. For further information see entry **743**.

745 Automation, machine-readable records and archival administration: an annotated bibliography. Comp. and ed. by Richard M. Kesner. Chicago: Society of American Archivists, 1980. 65p. LC 79–92994. ISBN 0–931828–22–8.
This international bibliography of 293 citations captures most of the literature that deals with automation and archives. Entries are annotated and indexed by author, journal name, and subject. The work also includes a chart showing the approximate output of articles on automation and archives and notes that, since 1972, approximately twenty-five articles a year have appeared. Many of these articles are not listed in indexing and abstracting services. Thus, this bibliography serves a unique function.

746 Bibliography of library automation, 1964–1967. Comp. by C. F. Cayless and Hilary Potts. London: British National Bibliography, 1968. 107p. LC 78–399413. ISBN 0–900220–00–7.
This title is continued by *An annotated bibliography of library automation, 1968–1972*, *An annotated bibliography of automation in libraries and information systems, 1972–1975*, and *An annotated bibliography of automation in libraries, 1975–1978*. For further information see entry **743**.

747 A directory of computer software applications: library and information sciences, 1970–March 1978. Springfield, VA: NTIS, U.S. Dept. of Commerce, 1978. 71p. LC 80–601076.
More than 400 research reports that identify and describe computer software applications for library or information service use are listed in this bibliography. Examples of the type of computer software applications covered include circulation control, serials, data base construction, and management information systems. All of the cited items are available from the National Technical Information Service. Many of the documents identified here were produced as the result of government-sponsored projects and thus are available for use in the public domain. Although complete bibliographic information is presented, the entries are not annotated. Also, the amount of software documentation varies among the publications, so it is difficult to determine how much detail is provided in the sources listed. Nevertheless, there are many software packages listed that could have wider application than the original installation, and the purpose of this work is to disseminate information about them.

748 Serials automation in the United States: a bibliographic history. By Gary M. Pitkin. Metuchen, NJ: Scarecrow, 1976. 148p. LC 76–18116. ISBN 0–8108–0955–9.

In this specialized, annotated bibliography, articles covering serials automation published between 1951 and 1974 are cited. Arrangement is by publication date. Following the entry are three "descriptors" which identify the subject content of the article. The first is concerned with "applications" and includes such topics as binding information, holdings information, ordering, and routing. The second identifies the type of library. The third provides an indication of the institution, e.g., institution name. In the appendix, an index by serials control function enables the user to identify all articles dealing with a particular function. There is also an author index.

DIRECTORIES

749 Directory of automated library and information systems in Australia. Ed. by Elizabeth Morrison and James Gilmore. Victorian ed. Melbourne: Victorian Assn. for Library Automation (VALA), 1978. 57p.

Automated library activities in Victoria are identified here. The directory is divided into three parts: "Applications"; "Libraries"; and "Processing Centres, Bureaux, Networks." The applications section groups institutions by type of applications, e.g., use of automation for acquisitions, cataloging, serials, and special listings. The other two sections are arranged by institution. Indexing is by library type and computers used.

750 Directory of music library automation projects. Comp. by Garrett H. Bowles. 2d ed. Philadelphia: Music Library Assn., 1979. 23p. (MLA technical reports, no. 2) LC 79–10768. ISBN 0–914954–14–8.

Based on data recorded on questionnaires sent to members of the Music Library Association, this directory describes 100 libraries utilizing automation for some type of library activity. For further information see entry **1063**.

751 Directory of operational computer applications in United Kingdom libraries and information units. Ed. by C. W. J. Wilson. 2d ed. London: Aslib, 1977. 196p. LC 77–372345. ISBN 0–85142–092–3.

The computer applications of 170 libraries and information centers in the United Kingdom are described in this directory. The entries include information about the purpose of the computer application, type of computer used, programming languages used, and amount of use received. Indexing is by named equipment, information systems, and data bases.

752 Minicomputers in libraries, 1981–82: the era of distributed systems. By Audrey N. Grosch. White Plains, NY: Knowledge Industry, 1982. 263p. LC 81–20763. ISBN 0–914236–96–2.

This is a combination handbook and directory. The directory portion, contained in a lengthy appendix, lists and describes installed systems. For further information see entry **759**.

HANDBOOKS AND MANUALS

753 Archives and manuscripts: an introduction to automated access. By H. Thomas Hickerson. Chicago: Society of American Archivists, 1981. 60p. LC 81–52113. ISBN 0–931828–29–5.

An overview of computer applications to archive and manuscript collections is provided in this handbook. Initial chapters deal with the basic characteristics of computer processing and technology. A separate chapter reviews the application of computer technology to archives from 1960 to the present. The final chapter deals with the design of automated processes for archival information retrieval. Augmenting the text are flow charts and sample forms. A brief glossary of terms is also included.

754 Choosing an automated library system: a planning guide. By Joseph R. Matthews. Chicago: American Library Assn., 1980. 119p. LC 80–17882. ISBN 0–8389–0310–X.

Aimed at librarians who need to select a computer-based automated system for library operations, this work assumes no background on the part of the reader and describes the process from the beginning phase through implementation. Among the topics covered are need analysis, selection of the system, developing the contract, installation, and implementation of the system. The functions of library service most suitable for automation are discussed in the appendices.

755 Developing computer-based library systems. By John Corbin. Phoenix: Oryx, 1981. 226p. (A Neal-Schuman professional book) LC 81–1232. ISBN 0–912700–10–6.

In this guide, the author defines the elements of computer-based systems and discusses the planning process for installing and operating an automated library system. Among the topics covered are requirements for a new system, evaluation and comparison, design specifications, software and vendor assistance, and installation of the system. Information is presented in a practical fashion, outlining specific steps to be followed throughout the process. A total of seventeen appendices provide samples that can be used in the planning and implementation process. For example, there is a sample report of a system evaluation and a sample proposal request for obtaining the service of a project consultant. A brief glossary, a selected bibliography, and a subject index are also included.

756 Library automation handbook. By Dennis Reynolds. New York: Bowker, 1983. 304p. ISBN 0–8352–1489–3.

This work focuses on the planning, purchasing, installing, and maintaining of an automated system for library use. Reynolds discusses such basic steps as the vendor's role and cost expectations for automating library services. In addition, a detailed analysis is provided for current technology, including commercial systems currently on the market. The development of machine-readable data bases and online public catalogs are also addressed.

757 The library manager's guide to automation. By Richard W. Boss. 2d ed. White Plains, NY: Knowledge Industry, 1983. 165p. ISBN 0–86729–052–8.

Presented in this manual is basic information about the application of automation to various

library processes, including acquisitions, cataloging, serials control, and online information retrieval. Boss provides guidelines for planning and implementing automated processes
in various types of libraries and for selecting appropriate hardware and software. He also
covers such topics as risk assessment, budgeting, and staff training. The manual assumes
little or no experience with computer technology on the part of the reader. The previous
edition was published under the same title in 1979.

758   Microcomputers and libraries: a guide to technology, products and applications.
By Mark E. Rorvig. White Plains, NY: Knowledge Industry, 1981. 135p. LC
81–12326. ISBN 0–914236–67–9.

This basic guide covers microcomputer hardware and software appropriate to library
applications. Rorvig also identifies library functions most suitable for microcomputer
applications. He uses examples and case studies of library applications to augment the
textual descriptions. In another useful section, the author provides profiles of vendors,
comparing products, capabilities, costs, and support services. Similar information about
microcomputers in smaller installations is available in Betty and Marie Costa's *Micro
handbook for small libraries and media centers* (Littleton, CO: Libraries Unlimited, 1983.
216p.).

759   Minicomputers in libraries, 1981–82: the era of distributed systems. By Audrey
N. Grosch. White Plains, NY: Knowledge Industry, 1982. 263p. LC 81–20763.
ISBN 0–914236–96–2.

This is a combination handbook and directory. The handbook portion of the work gives the
reader an overview of the present and future directions of system development in libraries
and, within this context, provides basic information about available hardware and software
for distributed computing. The author discusses sixteen-bit minicomputer systems and mid-
range computers, indicating their capabilities and limitations. Also covered are specific
computer systems and library and information system applications of minicomputers, with
specific examples of operational systems. The directory portion, contained in a lengthy
appendix, lists and describes installed systems. It is indexed by subject. Another appendix
reviews peripheral devices available for typical systems. There is also a glossary of terms
and a bibliography of selected readings. Subject and system name indexes complete the
work.

Awards and Prizes

HANDBOOKS AND MANUALS

760   Literary and library prizes. 10th ed. New York: Bowker, 1980. 651p. LC 59-11370.
ISBN 0-8352-1249-1. ISSN 0075-9880.

Information on more than 450 American, Canadian, English, and international literary
prizes and library awards through November, 1979 is provided in this edition. Arrangement
is by the country in which the prize is awarded, then by name of award. In the case of awards
given in the United States, the listing is further subdivided by type of award. Information
provided for each award includes the sponsoring organization, founding date, requirements,
and criteria for selection, as well as the names of the recipients, titles of the winning works,
and publishers. All told, more than 13,000 winners, awards and sponsors are listed. Names
of awards, recipients, sponsors, and discontinued awards are indexed.

Bibliographic Instruction

BIBLIOGRAPHIC SOURCES

761 Bibliographic instruction in academic libraries: a review of the literature and selected bibliography. By Jacquelyn M. Morris. Syracuse, NY: ERIC-IR, 1979. 47p. ED 180 505.

Not exhaustive, but representative, this bibliography covers 174 significant journal articles on bibliographic instruction in academic libraries up to near the time of publication. Six broad categories of articles are included: general materials on bibliographic instruction; planning and implementation of a bibliographic instruction program; methods of instruction; articles providing samples of materials; descriptive information about specific programs; and articles appearing in foreign languages. Access to the citations within these broad topics is by specific subject headings. Entries are generally not annotated, but in some instances, when titles are not descriptive, a brief description is provided.

762 The education of users of library and information services: an international bibliography, 1926–1976. Comp. by Peter J. Taylor, Colin Harris, and Daphne Clark. London: Aslib, 1980. 135p. (Aslib bibliography series, no. 9) ISBN 0–85142–121–0.

In this extensive bibliography on library user education, approximately 1,600 relevant publications are identified. A shorter, annotated bibliography of selected items precedes the longer, unannotated list. The compilation was prepared by consolidating the contents of several existing bibliographies and, thus, represents a more comprehensive treatment than a number of the earlier works. The coverage is international. Index access is by author.

763 Library instruction: a bibliography. Comp. by Deborah L. Lockwood. Westport, CT: Greenwood, 1978. 166p. LC 78–20011. ISBN 0–313–20720–8.

This is the most extensive list of current materials on library instruction. Cited are 933 papers, conference proceedings, chapters of books, journal articles, monographs, annual reports, and other types of materials, most of which were published in 1970 or later. Coverage is limited to items published in English that are available either commercially or through the ERIC system. Entries are organized into three major categories: general works, including directories of library instruction programs; materials emphasizing library instruction in specific types of libraries, subdivided by type of library; and the literature describing and evaluating the use of individual teaching methods and formats, such as tours, lectures and classes, and course-integrated instruction. A name index completes the work.

DIRECTORIES

764 A directory of bibliographic instruction programs in New England academic libraries. Comp. by Joan Stockard. Chicago: New England Chapter, Assn. of College and Research Libraries, American Library Assn., 1978. 185p.

A total of 115 academic libraries in New England with active programs of bibliographic instruction are listed in this directory. Contained in the entries are the name of the institution and library, its address and telephone number, information about the institution and the bibliographic instruction program, the audience to whom the program is directed, methods of publicity, subject focus, supporting materials available, documentation, and name of a contact person.

765 List of library instruction clearinghouses, directories and newsletters. Ed. by William Prince, Linda Lester, and James Ward. Chicago: Bibliographic Instruction Section, Assn. of College and Research Libraries, American Library Assn., 1981. 10p.

This directory identifies forty clearinghouses, directories, and newsletters oriented toward bibliographic instruction programs in libraries. The coverage is international, including the United States, Canada, the United Kingdom, and Australia. Arrangement is first by category (e.g., clearinghouse), then geographical. Entries contain the name of the clearinghouse (or if a newsletter, the title of the newsletter), address, and name of a contact person.

766 Southeastern bibliographic instruction directory: academic libraries. Tucker, GA: Southeastern Library Assn., 1978. 349p.

Bibliographic instruction programs in 349 academic libraries that are members of the Southeastern Library Association are identified in this directory. The academic libraries listed responded to a survey conducted in 1975 and updated in 1977. Entries are numbered and specify the name of the institution, enrollment, nature of the collection, degree programs at the institution, and the bibliographic instruction methods utilized. The information is indexed by methods and materials used and subjects or topics covered in instruction. Some of the libraries listed have deposited their instructional materials with the Southeastern Bibliographic Instruction Clearinghouse, in Nashville, Tennessee.

HANDBOOKS AND MANUALS

767 Bibliographic instruction: a handbook. By Beverly Renford and Linnea Hendrickson. New York: Neal-Schuman, 1980. 192p. LC 80–12300. ISBN 0–918212–24–3.

This work focuses on the planning and implementation of various types of bibliographic instruction programs. The types of programs covered include orientation programs, printed guides, materials for bibliographic instruction courses, and computer-assisted instruction. The volume also addresses such topics as analyzing user needs, stating goals and objectives, planning the step-by-step process required to meet the goals and objectives, and justifying the value of the program. Although intended for academic libraries, some of the content is applicable in other types of libraries.

768 Bibliographic instruction handbook. Chicago: Policy and Planning Committee, Bibliographic Instruction Section, Assn. of College and Research Libraries, American Library Assn., 1979. 66p.

This work consists of a variety of materials relevant to the implementation of a program in bibliographic instruction, including the ACRL bibliographic instruction guidelines, a needs assessment checklist, a model program timetable, a model set of objectives, examples of modes of instructions, a glossary of bibliographic instruction terms, a pathfinder (selected bibliography) on bibliographic instruction, and a sample evaluation sheet for students taking a bibliographic instruction course. The model programs and objectives are designed to provide practical guidance for individuals initiating or implementing bibliographic instruction activities.

769 Learning the library: concepts and methods for effective bibliographic instruction. By Anne K. Beaubien, Sharon A. Hogan and Mary W. George. New York: Bowker, 1982. 269p. LC 82–4262. ISBN 0–8352–1505–9.

This is a step-by-step guide to the establishment and implementation of an academic bibliographic instruction program. Part I deals with setting objectives and selecting appropriate instructional modes. Part II, "Understanding the Research Process," covers research problem analysis, search strategy in the research process, and the research process in various disciplines. Part III addresses the methods and approaches for instructing people in the research process. Part IV provides instructions on the implementation of a bibliographic instruction program, including observations about the costs of a BI program. The final section deals with the benefits of BI programs and identifies trends for the future. Completing the work is a selected bibliography of additional readings.

770 Library instruction for librarians. By Anne F. Roberts. Littleton, CO: Libraries Unlimited, 1982. 159p. LC 82–13997. ISBN 0–87287–298–X.

This manual provides both theoretical and practical information on a wide range of bibliographic instruction activities. It includes applications for public and special libraries as well as school and academic libraries. Roberts provides suggestions for the adoption and implementation of bibliographic instruction programs, indicating the advantages and disadvantages of the several methods of instruction; covered are tours, course-integrated instruction, formal courses, mini-courses, and computer-assisted instruction. A general literature review and reading lists at the end of each chapter identify additional sources of information.

771 Teaching library use: a guide for library instruction. By James Rice, Jr. Westport, CT: Greenwood, 1981. 169p. (Contributions in librarianship and information science, no. 37) LC 80–21337. ISBN 0–313–21485–9.

This basic manual was prepared to provide guidance to librarians and others in the design and implementation of bibliographic instruction and other library use programs. Topics covered include planning; strategies for implementing orientation and instruction programs; testing and evaluation; and instruction through design of the library. Examples are used to illustrate the points in the text. In addition, each chapter includes a selected bibliography of other sources to which the reader can turn for additional information.

Bibliography

HANDBOOKS AND MANUALS

772 Manual of bibliography. By Arundell James Kennedy Esdaile. Rev. by Roy Stokes. 5th rev. ed. Metuchen, NJ: Scarecrow, 1981. 397p. LC 81–9088. ISBN 0–8108–1462–5.

A basic manual of descriptive bibliography, this work was first published in 1931 and has been revised periodically since then. The fifth edition was issued in 1981. The intended audience includes librarians, rare book bibliographers, and students of literature. The manual contains chapters on the elements fundamental to an understanding of descriptive bibliography. Among the topics covered are parts of a book, typography, illustration, binding, and collation. A concluding chapter deals with the description of books in considerable detail, with examples. Also included are a brief glossary of terms and a subject index.

773 Principles of bibliographical description. By Fredson Bowers. Princeton, NJ: Princeton Univ. Pr., 1949. New York: Russell and Russell Reprint, 1962. 505p.

The standard manual treating the principles and practice of analytical bibliography, this work provides detailed instructions for precise bibliographic description of incunabula, as well as for early English and American books. The author covers in depth the requirements of bibliographic description for books of different time periods and forms. A separate chapter deals with hand-printed books, and then multiple chapters are devoted to books of the 16th–18th century and the 19th–20th century. Typical of the topics covered for each of these time periods are: description of the title page, collation, plates and insets, typography, illustrations and indices, and binding. Examples of detailed bibliographic description are used throughout to illustrate applications. An appendix presents a digest of the formulary used for description, includes sample descriptions, and provides some applications of formulary notation to incunabula. The text is indexed by subject.

774 Systematic bibliography: a practical guide to the work of compilation. By A. M. Lewin Robinson. 4th ed. New York: K. G. Saur, 1979. 135p. LC 79–40542. ISBN 0–85157–289–8.

The author describes the basic principles and provides practical guidelines for the inexperienced person undertaking the compilation of an enumerative bibliography. Among the topics covered are how to collect material, form of entry, annotating the bibliography, and physical layout. Also addressed is designing the work to facilitate retrieval of information. Some attention is given to the use of computers as a tool for both compilation and retrieval. Examples from noted bibliographies are used to illustrate the author's major points, and reproductions of several bibliographies are included with the text.

TERMINOLOGY SOURCES

775 Abbreviations and technical terms used in book catalogues and in bibliographies. By Frank Keller Walter. Boston: Boston Book, 1915. 167p. LC 18–10870.

These several hundred abbreviations found in bibliographic citations in dealers' catalogs and other bibliographies are drawn from the following languages: English and a variety of West European languages. For further information see entry **196**.

Bibliometrics

BIBLIOGRAPHIC SOURCES

776 Bibliometrics: a bibliography and index. By Alan Pritchard and Glenn R. Wittig. Herts, England: ALLM Books, 1981– . v.1– . v.1, **1894–1959.** LC 81–166825. ISBN 0–9506784–0–6.

This is the first in a projected three-volume bibliography intended to provide comprehensive coverage of the literature concerned with bibliometrics. For the purpose of this work, the authors have defined bibliometrics as "the application of mathematics and statistical methods to books and other media of communication" or "quantitative treatment of the properties of recorded discourse and behaviour appertaining to it." They have listed 624 studies that either use or describe methods of statistical analysis relating to various forms of printed communication, particularly journal and monograph literature, citation studies, and indexing/abstracting services. The literature covered in the bibliography is limited largely to

English-language titles. About two-thirds of the citations are to the journal literature; the other one-third are to monographs. Arrangement is chronological by time period and then by publication date. Special features include an appendix listing references contained in each item, a citation index, and an index to authors, editors, subjects of study, and modes of study. The compilers intend to publish a second volume covering 1960–1969 and a third volume covering 1970–1979.

HANDBOOKS AND MANUALS

777 Literature and bibliometrics. By David Nicholas and Maureen Ritchie. Hamden, CT: Shoe String, 1978. 183p. LC 77–20135. ISBN 0–208–01541–8.

This guide to bibliometric applications in library and information science, and other disciplines as well, includes definitions of terms and a discussion of applications of bibliometrics, including collection development, weeding and obsolescence, and studies of circulation. Also provided is a review of statistical methods applied to bibliometrics. Examples are taken primarily from a major research project conducted at the University of Bath, the "Design of Information in the Social Sciences (DISISS)."

Black Studies Resources

For reference materials on black studies resources see entries listed under the heading Afro-American Studies Libraries.

Blacks in Librarianship

BIOGRAPHICAL SOURCES

778 Directory of the Black Caucus of the American Library Association. 2d ed. Chicago: Black Caucus, American Library Assn., 1978. 140p. LC 75–316663.

Names of persons active in the Black Caucus of the American Library Association are listed in this directory under four categories: alphabetical, by name, with home addresses; alphabetical, by name, with library or work address; by type of library; and by geographical location. No biographical information is included. Although somewhat dated, the directory can be used to identify prominent black librarians.

779 Southeastern black librarian. By Dorothy May Haith. Huntsville, AL: Information Exchange System for Minority Personnel, 1976. 60p. LC 76–151097.

This directory identifies approximately 600 black librarians who resided or worked in nine states in the Southeast in 1976. The directory is not exhaustive and has not been updated since this first edition. However, it is useful for the identification of black librarians, more current information about whom can then be found in other directories. The entries, arranged by name and indexed by geographical location, specify position at the time of compilation, business address, name(s) of educational institutions attended, and degrees earned.

HANDBOOKS AND MANUALS

780 Handbook of black librarianship. Comp. and ed. by E. J. Josey and Ann Allen Shockley. Littleton, CO: Libraries Unlimited, 1977. 392p. LC 77–21817. ISBN 0–87287–179–7.

This compendium of information about Black Americans and librarianship consists of thirty-seven essays and resource lists organized into seven sections. The topics covered include significant books and periodicals for black collections, Afro-American resources, and vital issues in black librarianship. A chronology of significant events in librarianship from 1808–1977 that relate to blacks is included in one of the sections. Another provides statistics on library services to blacks and on black librarians. Separate chapters serve as directories of undergraduate library school departments in predominantly black graduate library schools; libraries of public library systems serving predominantly black communities; black academic libraries; libraries named for Afro-Americans; black-owned bookstores; and black book publishers.

Budgeting, Financing and Bookkeeping
BIBLIOGRAPHIC SOURCES

781 Financial aspects of library and information services: a bibliography. By Alan Cooper. Loughborough, England: Center for Library and Information Management, 1980. 117p. ISBN 0–904924–23–8.
Cited in this bibliography are 850 books and articles published in English between 1969 and 1979 that deal with the financing of libraries and information centers. Arrangement is by type of library or type of activity and indexing is by author.

HANDBOOKS AND MANUALS

782 Budgeting techniques for libraries and information centers. By Michael E. D. Koenig. New York: Special Libraries Assn., 1980. 71p. (Professional development series, v.1) LC 80–27698. ISBN 0–87111–278–7.
This basic manual briefly describes various budgeting systems, including PPBS and zero-based budgeting. Also covered, in a clear and practical fashion, are the various steps involved in a library's budget process. Koenig provides suggestions and guidance for readers inexperienced in budget preparation. A bibliography and glossary of terms complete the work.

783 Keeping track of what you spend: the librarian's guide to simple bookkeeping. By Brian Alley and Jennifer Cargill. Phoenix: Oryx, 1982. 96p. LC 81–11289. ISBN 0–912700–79–3.
This manual emphasizes practical methods of monitoring and reviewing the encumberance and expenditure of library funds. The day-to-day procedures necessary for an internal financial system are described. The methods included here are appropriate for libraries ranging in size from very small to quite large. They are explained in terms that do not require a prior knowledge of bookkeeping. The authors include a number of sample forms that can be adapted to most libraries' specific needs.

784 Zero-base budgeting in library management: a manual for librarians. By Ching-chih Chen. Phoenix: Oryx, 1980. 293p. LC 80–12055. ISBN 0–912700–18–1.

The purpose of this manual is to provide library managers with a basic background on the concept and the implementation of zero-base budgeting. However, it also provides useful information on other types of budgets. The first quarter of the book deals with budgeting in general and zero-base budgeting in particular. Chapter 1, "Fundamentals of Budgeting," covers the uses of the budget and the various types of budgets used by libraries. Subsequent chapters describe the nature of zero-base budgeting, use of decision packages, follow-up controls, and advantages and disadvantages of zero-base budgeting. The remaining three quarters of the book provides examples of the use of zero-base budgeting in seven different institutions. Among these are the Oregon State Library, the library of Ryerson Polytechnical Institute in Toronto, and the library of Arthur D. Little, Inc. A glossary of terms and a selected bibliography complete the work.

Buildings

BIOGRAPHICAL SOURCES

785 Library buildings consultant list. Chicago: Library Administration and Management Assn., American Library Assn., 1976– . Biennial.

This list identifies about sixty consultants who meet the minimum set of qualifications established by the Buildings and Equipment Section of LAMA and who have submitted an application for inclusion. Thus, while the list is not necessarily exhaustive, inclusion does indicate that persons have met stringent criteria. Entries specify the name and address of the individual, affiliation at of the time of publication, school and date of library school degree, library building experience (with a list of the five most recent building projects), type of expertise offered, type of services offered, geographical limitation, availability, and fees.

HANDBOOKS AND MANUALS

786 Book theft and library security systems, 1981–82. By Alice Harrison Bahr. White Plains, NY: Knowledge Industry, 1981. 150p. LC 80–26643. ISBN 0–914236–71–7.

Existing electronic security systems for libraries are described in this handbook. For further information see entry **1158**.

787 Design of the small public library. By Rolf Myller. New York: Bowker, 1966. 95p. LC 66–20401.

Practical guidance for persons planning and designing small public libraries is provided in this manual. Heavily illustrated, the work deals in a clear and simple fashion with the problems faced in planning, constructing, and furnishing the small library. Separate sections describe design possibilities for various service areas of the library. Although several years old, the basic elements identified here for planning the small public library are still valid.

788 Designing and space planning for libraries: a behavioral guide. By Aaron Cohen and Elaine Cohen. New York: Bowker, 1979. 250p. LC 79–12478. ISBN 0–8352–1150–9.

Based on seminars conducted by the authors, an architect and a behaviorist, this guide deals with those aspects of interior design that affect or condition the behavior of library users. Among the topics covered are behavioral aspects of space; lighting, power, and energy; and acoustics. A section on "Who Does What" provides brief statements about the responsibilities of each part of the team, including consultants, engineers, and architects, indicating what might be expected and how reasonable fees should be calculated. The text is supplemented by photographs, drawings, color samples, and numerous tables providing data on such topics as lighting, space requirements, and sound absorption. A selected bibliography identifies sources of additional information.

789 Libraries designed for users: a planning handbook. By Nolan Lushington and Willis N. Mills, Jr. Syracuse, NY: Gaylord, 1979. 289p. LC 78–27114. ISBN 0–915794–29–2.
User convenience serves as the focus for this handbook on planning public library buildings for communities of 100,000 population or less. The authors discuss in depth lighting, site location, parking, planning facilities for the handicapped, and use of graphics. The importance of knowing community needs and the role of the library in the community is covered, as are suggestions for obtaining this information. Separate chapters deal with the design of service areas for children and adults and the design of the school library/media center. The roles of consultants and architects are also addressed, with pointers on how to improve the librarian-consultant working relationship. Information is presented in a non-technical fashion, with examples and case studies to illustrate points. A particularly useful feature of the book is the inclusion of checklists of items to consider in planning service areas. The work concludes with a bibliography of additional references and a subject index.

790 Library buildings of Britain and Europe. By Anthony Thompson. London: Butterworths, 1963. 326p. LC 64–9681.
This work provides an overview of the library building process, with examples of library buildings from diverse locations in Britain, western Europe, and the United States. It has the most extensive collection of detailed descriptions of library buildings available in any single source. The book is divided into two parts. In Part 1, "Synthesis: The Creation of a Building," the author discusses the planning process, site location, allocation of space for library functions, exterior and interior design and construction, equipment and furniture, and data for determining the capacity of the building. Part 2 is a survey of libraries of various types, with photographs, floor plans, and a standard set of categories by which all of the buildings are discussed. Included are storage facilities, national libraries, public libraries, and libraries in colleges, universities, and elementary or secondary schools. Indexing is by subject and by name of institution.

791 Media center facilities design. Comp. and ed. by Jane Anne Hannigan and Glenn E. Estes. Chicago: American Library Assn., 1978. 117p. LC 78–9336. ISBN 0–8389–3212–6.
Guidelines for planning and designing school library/media centers are presented in this work. The text is organized into eight parts, each dealing with a separate phase of the planning process. Chapters are contributed by various individuals chosen for their experience with the particular phase. Topics covered include the student viewpoint of library facilities, steps in the planning process, application of guidelines and standards, design of

the facility, patterns of organization, and remodeling. Photographs and diagrams are included, as are charts and checklists for use by facility planners. A selected bibliography and subject index complete the volume.

792 Planning academic and research library buildings. By Keyes D. Metcalf. New
York: McGraw-Hill, 1965. 431p. LC 64–7868.
This detailed manual describes in depth the various phases required for planning and constructing large structures to house academic and research libraries. The work consists of seventeen chapters, each of which deals with a separate phase or aspect of the building process. Topics covered include traffic problems, accommodations for readers and staff, housing the collection, lighting and ventilating, and furniture and equipment. Throughout, examples are used together with diagrams and floor plans. Appendices provide sample building programs, formulas and tables, equipment that should not be overlooked, a bibliography, and a glossary of terms relevant to building planning. There is a detailed subject index as well.

793 Planning and design of library buildings. By Godfrey Thompson. 2d ed. New York:
Nichols, 1977. 189p. LC 77–137. ISBN 0–89397–019–0.
Intended for persons unfamiliar with the planning and design of library buildings, this work is organized into twenty chapters, each providing practical, detailed information. Chapters address such topics as reading areas, furniture and fittings, circulation control, lighting, and security and protection. The book is heavily illustrated with drawings, floor designs, photographs, and some diagrams indicating the dimensions required for shelf height and width. References are made to standards for space, seating, etc. A table at the end provides metric equivalents for distance and weight measures used in the United States. A lengthy bibliography is also included. The emphasis is on British practice, but much of the content is universally applicable.

**794 Planning barrier free libraries: a guide for renovation and construction of librar-
ies serving blind and physically handicapped readers.** Washington, DC: National
Library Service for the Blind and Physically Handicapped, Library of Congress,
1981. 61p. LC 80–607821. ISBN 0–8444–0352–0.
This guide addresses the renovation or construction needed for libraries to be part of the National Library Service for the Blind and Physically Handicapped network. Topics covered include the functional program, the architectural program, and renovations. Each of these are further subdivided and include specific recommendations relating to the main theme of the publication. Appendices provide minimum space and personnel required, restroom requirements, a flow diagram, an accessibility checklist, a timetable for construction of a new building, and a timetable for the renovation of a building. Drawings are used to illustrate the text.

795 Sign systems for libraries: solving the wayfinding problem. Comp. and ed. by
Dorothy Pollel and Peter C. Haskell. New York: Bowker, 1979. 271p. LC 79–11138.
ISBN 0–8352–1149–5.
Methods of planning and designing signs for libraries are described and illustrated in this manual. For further information see entry **1165**.

Business and Economics Archives and Libraries

BIBLIOGRAPHIC SOURCES

796 A select bibliography on business archives and records management. Comp. and ed. by Karen M. Benedict. Chicago: Society of American Archivists, 1981. 134p.

A total of 421 articles and eighteen books are cited in this annotated bibliography. Arrangement is alphabetical by author, with indexing by title and subject. Titles selected for inclusion cover a broad range of topics, including conservation, fire protection, business history, appraisal, acquisitions, and business records.

DIRECTORIES

797 Directory of business archives in the United States and Canada. Chicago: Society of American Archivists, 1975. 34p. LC 79–2522.

The business archives of more than 100 American and Canadian firms are described in this source. Entries are arranged alphabetically by name of the firm and specify the address and telephone number of the archive, the name of the archivist or person in charge, and the contents of the archives. Date of establishment and numerical information on the holdings are also included. The directory is not indexed.

798 Directory of economic libraries in Canada. Ed. by Irene Lackner and Gerald Prodrick. London, Canada: School of Library and Information Science, Univ. of Western Ontario, 1980. 282p. LC 82–198662. ISBN 0–7714–0230–9.

Approximately 450 libraries with significant collections of economics materials or significant information services in economics are listed in this work. Included are both public and private institutions. Arrangement is alphabetical by name of the library or parent institution. Entries contain name, address, telephone number, name of the director or person in charge, hours of service, policies regarding use of the collection, services available, subject areas covered, names of any special collections, an indication of any automation activities, cooperative projects, library publications, and statistical information about the size of staff and collection. Indexing is by province and city, personal name, subject, and type of library.

HANDBOOKS AND MANUALS

799 Manual of business library practice. Ed. by Malcolm J. Campbell. Hamden, CT: Shoe String, 1975. 186p. LC 75–20223. ISBN 0–208–01359–8.

Intended to provide an introduction to the sources and services offered by business libraries, this handbook consists of twelve chapters written by eight authors. Each chapter deals with a separate aspect of business library practice. For example, chapters cover the structure of business information, the administration of the business library, and listings of company information sources. Thus, the work serves as both a manual of practice and a guide to the most useful information literature. The sources covered and the examples used were chosen with commercial libraries in mind and are based largely on British experience.

Cataloging and Classification

BIBLIOGRAPHIC SOURCES

800 "Classification literature." Appears in **International classification: journal on theory and practice of universal and special classification systems and thesauri/
Zeitschrift zur theorie und praxis universaler und spezieller klassifika-
tionssysteme und thesauri.** Munich: Verlag Dokumentation, 1974– . 2 per year. LC
77–649204. ISSN 0340–0050.

This work provides abstracts of monographs, journal articles, conference proceedings,
guidelines, standards, and reports dealing with all aspects of classification of documents.
Coverage is international, with emphasis on European languages. Entries are in English and
German. The approximate number of items abstracted per year is 500. Arrangement is by
type or form of publication, e.g., journal articles, standards.

HANDBOOKS AND MANUALS

801 **Anglo-american cataloguing rules.** Prep. by The American Library Association,
The British Library, The Canadian Committee on Cataloguing, The Library Association, and The Library of Congress. Ed. by Michael Gorman and Paul W. Winkler. 2d
ed. Chicago: American Library Assn.; Ottawa: Canadian Library Assn., 1978. 620p.
LC 78–13789. ISBN 0–8389–3210–X.

This basic manual presents the rules for descriptive cataloging agreed to by the national
libraries of the United States, Canada, and the United Kingdom. The rules, commonly
referred to as AACR2, are intended to provide guidelines for descriptive cataloging for
English-speaking nations. The current set of rules is a revision of the first edition, published
in 1967. The objectives of the second edition are 1) to reconcile differences which existed
between the North American and British texts published in 1967; 2) to include amendments
and changes approved since 1967; 3) to include proposed amendments under discussion at
the time of the revision, and; 4) to expand the applicability of the rules to English-speaking
countries other than the United States, Canada, and the United Kingdom. The rules are
intended for use by general libraries for the creation of cataloging information. They are not
designed for specialized libraries or archives, but these institutions can use them as the basis
for their rules. The rules are divided into two parts. Part I, "Description," covers the general
rules for descriptive cataloging and includes rules for various types of materials, e.g.,
books, music, and sound recordings. Part II, "Headings, Uniform Titles, and References,"
addresses choice of access points, headings for persons, geographic names, headings for
corporate bodies, uniform titles, and references. Appendices cover capitalization, abbreviations, and numerals. There is also a glossary and a detailed index.

802 **The concise AACR2: being a rewritten and simplified version of Anglo-american
cataloguing rules, second edition.** Prep. by Michael Gorman. Chicago: American
Library Assn.; Ottawa: Canadian Library Assn.; London: The Library Assn., 1981.
164p. LC 81–3496. ISBN 0–8389–0325–8.

Prepared by one of the editors of the AACR2, this work is intended to "convey the essence
and basic principles of the *Anglo-american cataloguing rules* (AACR2) without many of
that comprehensive work's rules for out-of-the-way and complex materials." The same rules
and practices are followed, but this concise version tends to highlight those types of

materials most commonly found and refers the user to the full text for more detailed explanations. The organization is the same as the full set of rules. However, the appendices include only a section on capitalization and a glossary of terms. This compilation is intended for catalogers and others who do not require the extensive coverage and detail found in the primary work. It will be of most value to catalogers in small libraries.

803 Examples illustrating AACR2: Anglo-american cataloguing rules, second edition. By Eric J. Hunter and Nicholas J. Fox. London: The Library Assn., 1980. 184p. LC 81–164472. ISBN 0–85365–951–6.

This handbook was compiled on behalf of the Cataloguing and Indexing Group of The Library Association, with financial assistance from The British Library Bibliographic Services Division. A total of 383 examples are provided to illustrate the application of the rules for descriptive cataloging included in AACR2. These examples are intended to show the options available for interpretations of specific rules or to illustrate specific cataloging problems which arise in the use of AACR2. The examples appear in alphabetical order, by main entry of the work, and in some cases are accompanied by sample title pages or other text from the original. Various types of media are covered, although printed monographs are emphasized. A detailed subject index appears at the beginning of the work, providing references to all examples that illustrate rules concerned with each subject. Appendices cover such topics as added entries, cross references, and layout when paragraphing is not used.

804 Handbook for AACR2: explaining and illustrating Anglo-american cataloguing rules, second edition. By Margaret F. Maxwell. Chicago: American Library Assn., 1980. 463p. LC 80–17667. ISBN 0–8389–0301–0.

This guide to AACR2 uses examples to explain the application of most of the rules for descriptive cataloging. Each example presented here includes a full catalog entry. Also, in many instances, copies of the half or full title page are presented as well. Rule numbers are used to key the examples to the rules in AACR2. Where there are possible options in the interpretation of the rules, the author follows Library of Congress practice. Supplementing the text in the main body of the work, three appendices cover additional topics. The first comments on cataloging practice as shown in the figures used to illustrate the text. The second provides various lists, such as geographical names, names of U.S. presidents, and British sovereigns. The third contains an alphabetical list of examples used to illustrate AACR2. There is also a detailed subject index.

805 Managing the catalog department. By Donald Leroy Foster. 2d ed. Metuchen, NJ: Scarecrow, 1982. 236p. LC 81–16694. ISBN 0–8108–1486–2.

Guidance is provided on the optimal methods for the management and administration of cataloging departments. The content does not deal with the technical aspects of cataloging and classification, but rather with those responsibilities and problems normally dealt with by the administrator of a cataloging department. Included among the topics covered are staffing the department, training and evaluation, working out staff relationships, research and development within the department, and departmental tools. The manual approaches the topic of management in a practical fashion, using examples based on experience. A brief, selected bibliography on management is included. A subject index completes the work.

TERMINOLOGY SOURCES

806   German for librarians. By G. W. Turner. Rev. and ed. by A. J. A. Vieregg and J. W. Blackwood. Palmerston North, New Zealand: Massey Univ., 1972. 137p. (Massey University, library series, no. 5) LC 73–152603.
This guide to German grammar and bibliolinguistics is intended to assist librarians in ordering and cataloging German-language materials. For further information see entry **211**.

807   Glossary of cataloging terms. New Delhi: Indian Standards Inst., 19??. IS 769–1959.
This work is related to and partially superseded by *Indian standard glossary of classification terms.* For further information see entry **808**.

808   Indian standard glossary of classification terms. By Manak Bhavan. New Delhi: Indian Standards Inst., 1964. 110p. IS 2550–1963.
This work defines terms and shows relationships between terms through a classified arrangement. Although oriented toward classification of library materials, the terms and definitions deal with concepts of classification in general. Examples are provided to illustrate the concepts defined. In some cases, obsolete usage is included but is so defined. The work is arranged in twenty-three chapters organized by means of a classified system, with an alphabetical index providing access to the numbered entries. An earlier, related publication is *Glossary of cataloging terms* (entry **807**).

809   Manual of european languages for librarians. Ed. by C. G. Allen. New York: Bowker, 1975. 803p. LC 73–6062. ISBN 0–85935–028–2.
This publication provides basic language instruction for librarians who work with foreign-language materials. It is intended for catalogers, collection development and acquisition librarians, and bibliographers. For further information see entry **209**.

YEARBOOKS

810   Cataloger's and classifiers' yearbook. Chicago: Division of Cataloging and Classification, American Library Assn., 1929–1945. Annual. LC 29–22649.
The work is a continuation of proceedings of the Catalog Section of ALA (later known as the Division of Cataloging and Classification). The volumes typically include a directory of officers, names of committee members, reports of the committees, and in some volumes the text of papers presented at conferences. The work was discontinued after the 1945 volume.

Censorship

For reference materials on censorship see entries listed under the heading Intellectual Freedom.

Chicanos

For reference materials on Chicanos see entries listed under the heading Hispanic American Librarians and Librarianship.

Children and Young Adults, Library Service To

BIBLIOGRAPHIC SOURCES

811 **Media and the young adult: a selected bibliography, 1973–1977.** Ed. by Bernard Lukenbill and Elaine P. Adams. Chicago: Media and Young Adult Subcommittee, Research Committee, Young Adult Services Division, American Library Assn., 1981. 328p. LC 81–7977. ISBN 0–8389–3264–9.

This is an annotated bibliography of 587 research studies dealing with young adults and their needs. Citations are taken from the fields of education, sociology, psychology, psychiatry, mass communication, and marketing. Annotations are detailed and informative. The bibliography supplements an earlier work titled *Media and the young adult: a selected bibliography, 1950–1972.*

812 **Professional literature on library work with children.** Prep. for the International Federation of Library Associations by the Committee on Library Work with Children. Comp. by Annie Moerkercken van der Meulen and Oda le Maire. Rev. ed. The Hague: Bureau Book and Youth, NBLC, 1972. 56p. LC 74–190669.

In this highly selective international bibliography of the most important works on library service to children, fourteen countries are represented. Subject experts in each country submitted from ten to fifty titles. The bibliography is organized topically and then alphabetically by the country of origin of the works. Among the topics covered are history and organization of libraries, literature, the creating of books, children's reading, and book reviewing. The table of contents is printed in English, French, German, and Russian. Titles appear in the original language, with Russian titles transliterated into the Roman alphabet. The subjects are arranged by the English term, but include the equivalent in the other three languages. A list of countries and a list of persons selecting the titles is appended at the end of the volume.

DIRECTORIES

813 **Children's authors and illustrators: a guide to manuscript collections in the United States research libraries.** Comp. by James H. Fraser. New York: K. G. Saur, 1980. 119p. (Phaedrus bibliographic series, no. 1) LC 79–24990. ISBN 0–89664–950–4.

The manuscript holdings of some of the major research libraries in the United States are identified and briefly described. However, coverage is not complete and a number of major collections are not represented. The information contained in the entries is similar to that found in the *National union catalog of manuscript collections*; there is a description of the major components of each collection and, when possible, information on the number of pieces held in the collection.

814 **Guide to children's libraries and literature outside the United States.** Comp. by Amy Kellman with International Relations Committee, ALSC. Chicago: American Library Assn., 1982. 32p. LC 81–20597. ISBN 0–83893–254–1.

Institutions and organizations that can supply information about research collections on children's literature outside of the United States are identified in this directory. It is intended as a guide for the individual interested in children's literature who plans to travel abroad. The organizations identified are those in a position to provide access to research collections. Arrangement of entries is by continent, then by country, and finally by name of organization. Also included is a selection of books that provide background information on children's literature collections abroad that should be read prior to departure. Practical information about planning the trip is presented. The geographical coverage is somewhat uneven; some countries are better represented than others, and some are not included at all.

815   Resources for young people: a guide to national and local collections in the A.C.T.
By Belle Alderman. Canberra, Australia: Canberra College of Advance Education, 1982. 230p.

The subject strengths of eighty-six resource collections located in the Australian Capital Territory (A.C.T.) are identified in this directory. The information was obtained through personal visits to all institutions covered. The emphasis is on specific subject collections of materials for children and young people as well as general collections strong in this area. Listed are government and non-government schools at all levels, archival and research centers, libraries, associations, foundations, and institutes. Entries for each institution specify scope of the collection, history, funding, collection size, formats included, collection strengths, policies, method of organization and storage, public access regulations, and services and promotion. The information is indexed in detail by subject.

816   Special collections in children's literature. Ed. by Carolyn W. Field, National Planning for Special Collections Committee, ALSC. Chicago: American Library Assn., 1982. 257p. LC 81–20565. ISBN 0–83890–345–2.

This guide identifies resources on children's literature in 267 American and Canadian libraries. The listing is restricted to institutions that are publicly available and that include material for research on children's literature. Descriptions of the special collections are provided in some detail, specifying the nature and size of the holdings. These special collections include holdings of comic books, manuscripts, realia, and oral or visual histories. Private collections and general browsing collections are excluded. Entries are arranged alphabetically by subject. An appendix lists relevant articles, monographs, and bibliographies. There is also a list of authors and illustrators represented in other major collections not found in the main directory. This work updates an earlier directory published by Bowker in 1969 under the same title.

YEARBOOKS

817   Children's library yearbook. Comp. by the Committee on Library Work with Children of the American Library Association. Chicago: American Library Assn., 1929–1932. Annual. LC 29–12747.

The bulk of this work consists of articles about aspects of work with children. In addition, there are reports of committees, statistics, and a directory of children's librarians who were members of ALA during the time covered by the *Yearbook*. Other features of interest are salary statistics for children's librarians, a list of library schools specializing in work with children, and bibliographies of works on children's books and reading. This work was published for four years.

Chinese Americans in Librarianship

BIOGRAPHICAL SOURCES

818 Directory of chinese american librarians. Comp. by the Chinese American Librarians Association. Oak Park, IL: Chinese Culture Service, 1977. 36p. LC 77–373584.

Included in this directory is brief biographical information about nearly 400 librarians of Chinese ancestry who are employed in the United States. The information was supplied through questionnaires and subsequent follow-up research. Entries specify name, position, address, areas of specialization, degrees held, and the person's name in Chinese symbols. The directory is not complete, and there is no indication of the percentage of Chinese American librarians it actually represents.

Church, Synagogue and Theological Libraries

BIBLIOGRAPHIC SOURCES

819 Church and synagogue library resources. Comp. by Rachel Kohl and Dorothy Rodda. 2d ed. Bryn Mawr, PA: Church and Synagogue Library Assn., 1975. 16p. (CSLA guide no. 1) LC 75–1178. ISBN 0–915324–08–3.

Listed in this annotated bibliography are basic resources to be used in planning and operating a church or synagogue library. The bibliography deals with the topics much as a manual would; the various functions and procedures for operating a library are identified, and then bibliographic citations are provided to publications that explain how to carry them out. Among the topics covered are: selection of periodicals, selection and acquisition of nonbook items, technical processing, publicity, and use of directories. The choice of items is highly selective. The work is aimed at volunteers who staff a smaller church or synagogue library.

DIRECTORIES

820 A world directory of theological libraries. By G. Martin Ruoss. Metuchen, NJ: Scarecrow, 1968. 220p. LC 68–12632.

Although dated, the work may still be used to identify major theological libraries throughout the world. Additional information can be obtained in national directories to bring the content up to date. A total of 1,779 theological libraries are listed, arranged alphabetically by geographical location. Information is brief, but covers name and address of the parent institution, date library was founded, whether or not it has open stacks, holdings, predominant language, characteristics of the collection, policies regarding use of the collection, size of staff, type of classification system used, and an indicat the collection, policies regarding use of the collection, size of staff, type of classification system used, and an indicat the collection, policies regarding use of the collection, size of staff, type of classification system used, and an indication of the forms of material in the collection. The entries are indexed by name of institution and by religious affiliation. An introductory section provides a survey of theological libraries at the time the directory was prepared.

HANDBOOKS AND MANUALS

821   Church library handbook. By LaVose Newton. Rev. ed. Portland, OR: Multnomah
Pr., 1972. 67p. LC 76–189488.
This practical manual describes in non-technical terms the basic functions of a church
library, including acquisitions, processing, and public service. Also included are a glossary
of terms, a highly abridged selection of Dewey Decimal numbers, and a subject guide. The
final half of the book consists of accession sheets and financial record sheets intended to be
used by the church librarian.

822   Library manual for missionaries. Prep. by members of Christian Librarians' Fellowship. Ed. by Clara Ruth Stone. Springfield, OH: Christian Librarians' Fellowship,
1979. 138p. LC 79–116205.
Designed for persons without formal library education who will be working in libraries in
bible schools, bible colleges, or seminaries, this manual includes both an overview of the
functions and services of libraries and specific coverage of such activities as selection,
cataloging, filing, and planning. Examples are used to illustrate and checklists are included
when appropriate. The explanations avoid excessive use of technical terms, although a
glossary of basic library terminology is included in an appendix. Other appendices contain a
bibliography of reference sources, a general bibliography, a list of publishers and library
suppliers, and a sample materials selection policy.

823   Religious archives: an introduction. By August R. Suelflow. Chicago: Society of
American Archivists, 1980. 56p. LC 80–17159. ISBN 0–913828–20–1.
This is a basic manual for planning and providing service in an archives of religious
materials. The fundamental elements of archival work are identified and explained in a
practical manner. Topics covered include budgeting, facilities, staff, acquisition of materials, processing of materials, public service, and exhibits. In addition, a separate chapter
discusses the history of archives and the role they play in society. Appendices provide
examples of record forms that can be used. A brief bibliography augments the text.

**824   Running a library: managing the congregation's library with care, confidence,
and common sense.** By Ruth S. Smith. Greenwich, CT: Seabury, 1982. 122p. ISBN
0–8164–2413–6.
Produced in cooperation with the Church and Synagogue Library Association, this manual
on the operation of the church or synagogue library covers such topics as administration,
budgeting, income from supplementary sources, space planning, staffing the library,
acquisitions, and evaluation of services. Practical suggestions are included. The work is
directed to lay persons who are assigned the responsibility of managing the congregation's
library.

825   A theological library manual. By Jannette E. Newhall. London: Theological Education Fund, 1970. 162p. LC 70–594222. ISBN 0–902908–00–4.
The manual is aimed at persons with minimal formal library education who are placed in
charge of libraries in theological seminaries of various denominations. The depth of
coverage is greater than that found in the *Church library handbook* (see entry **821**). The
focus is on basic functions of library service, including acquisitions, cataloging and

classification, serials, preservation, and planning library facilities. Numerous examples and some diagrams and illustrations are provided. The manual deals particularly effectively with cataloging and classification problems, especially as they relate to non-English language materials. Specialized classification systems are described. Special features include a brief glossary of library terms; a directory of library supply houses, book vendors, and library associations; and a bibliography of related readings.

Collection Development

BIBLIOGRAPHIC SOURCES

826 Collection development and acquisitions, 1970–80: an annotated, critical bibliography. By Irene P. Godden. Metuchen, NJ: Scarecrow, 1982. 138p. LC 81–18530. ISBN 0–8108–1449–4.

A total of 345 entries covering collection development and acquisitions in all types of libraries are listed and annotated in this selective bibliography. Annotations are largely descriptive but include some evaluative and critical observations. Indexing is by author, title, and subject. Arrangement is by broad topic and then by subtopic. For example, one topic deals with the selection process, and subtopics cover collection development policies, reviews and reviewers, and censorship. The first section of the bibliography identifies the current and best texts and monographs in collection development, as judged by the author.

HANDBOOKS AND MANUALS

827 Guidelines for collection development. Ed. by David L. Perkins. Chicago: American Library Assn., 1979. 78p. LC 79–16971. ISBN 0–8389–3231–2.

The four sets of guidelines presented in this work were developed by the Collection Development Committee of ALA's Resources and Technical Services Division. They are practical formulations created to provide guidance to librarians faced with collection development information needs. The four guidelines cover the formulation of collection development policies; evaluation of the effectiveness of library collections; review of library collections; and allocation of library materials budgets. Each of the guidelines provides specific suggestions for achieving the stated objectives. The guidelines are presented in outline form and are accompanied by annotated bibliographies identifying additional literature on collection development.

828 Oral history: from tape to type. By Cullom Davis, Kathryn Back and Kay MacLean. Chicago: American Library Assn., 1977. 141p. LC 77–4403. ISBN 0–8389–0230–8.

This work provides general instruction and practical guidance in the practices and procedures required for developing an oral history collection. For further information see entry **1091**.

829 Weeding library collections—II. By Stanley J. Slote. 2d rev. ed. Littleton, CO: Libraries Unlimited, 1982. 198p. LC 81–20724. ISBN 0–87287–283–1.

The philosophy, process, and procedures of weeding or deselection of materials from libraries are covered in this manual. The author devotes roughly a third of the book to five approaches that can be used to identify core and peripheral manual. The author devotes roughly a third of the book to five approaches that can be used to identify core and peripheral literature. In addition, Slote presents his own step-by-step method for weeding collections. Procedures are described in a practical fashion, and some examples of forms are provided for additional assistance. The emphasis is on weeding public library collections; relatively little attention is given to special, school, or academic libraries, particularly to research libraries. The result is that the user cannot generalize from the information provided here to deal with many of the deselection problems faced by other types of libraries.

TERMINOLOGY SOURCES

830 Manual of european languages for librarians. Ed. by C. G. Allen. New York: Bowker, 1975. 803p. LC 73–6062. ISBN 0–85935–028–2.
This publication provides basic language instruction for librarians who work with foreign-language materials. It is intended for catalogers, collection development and acquisition librarians, and bibliographers. For further information see entry **209**.

College and University Libraries and Librarianship

Materials on college and university libraries also appear elsewhere in this guide. For bibliographies, directories, biographical and statistical sources covering academic libraries in general, see the appropriate chapter in Part One. Included here are reference materials dealing with various aspects of college and university libraries and librarianship as a subject.

BIBLIOGRAPHIC SOURCES

831 Bibliographic instruction in academic libraries: a review of the literature and selected bibliography. By Jacquelyn M. Morris. Syracuse, NY: ERIC-IR, 1979. 47p.
Not exhaustive, but representative, this bibliography covers 174 significant journal articles on bibliographic instruction in academic libraries. For further information see entry **761**.

832 The relegation and storage of material in academic libraries: a literature review. By L. Guilder, et al. Loughborough, England: Centre for Library and Information Management (CLAIM), Department of Library and Information Studies, Loughborough Univ., 1980. 77p. (CLAIM reports, no. 3) ISBN 0–904924–24–6.
This literature review is concerned with remote storage of materials in academic libraries. For further information see entry **1174**.

DIRECTORIES

833 Academic library facilities for the handicapped. By James L. Thomas and Carol H. Thomas. Phoenix: Oryx, 1981. 568p. LC 81–14020. ISBN 0–912700–95–5.
The equipment and facilities available to handicapped users in academic libraries in the United States and its territorial possessions are specified in this directory. For further information see entry **911**.

834　Directory of academic library consortia. By Donald V. Black and Carlos A. Cuadra. 2d ed. Santa Monica, CA: SDC, 1975. 437p. LC 77–55571.

Approximately 300 consortia or networks of academic libraries are listed in this directory. For further information see entry **1073**.

835　A directory of bibliographic instruction programs in New England academic libraries. Comp. by Joan Stockard. Chicago: New England Chapter, Assn. of College and Research Libraries, American Library Assn., 1978. 185p.

A total of 115 academic libraries in New England with active programs of bibliographic instruction are listed in this directory. For further information see entry **764**.

836　Southeastern bibliographic instruction directory: academic libraries. Tucker, GA: Southeastern Library Assn., 1978. 349p.

Bibliographic instruction programs in 349 academic libraries that are members of the Southeastern Library Association are identified in this directory. For further information see entry **766**.

HANDBOOKS AND MANUALS

837　The administration of the college library. By Guy R. Lyle. 4th ed. New York: Wilson, 1974. 320p. LC 74–18427. ISBN 0–8242–0552–9.

After distinguishing between college and university libraries, Lyle concentrates on the organization, practices and procedures, and administration of college libraries. He includes organization charts depicting possible options for organizing the college library. Each chapter provides a list of references.

838　Planning academic and research library buildings. By Keyes D. Metcalf. New York: McGraw-Hill, 1965. 431p. LC 64–7868.

This detailed manual describes in depth the various phases required for planning and constructing large structures to house academic and research libraries. For further information see entry **792**.

839　Public, school, and academic media centers: a guide to information sources. By Esther R. Dyer. Detroit: Gale, 1981. 237p. (Books, publishing and libraries information guide, v.3) LC 74–11554. ISBN 0–8103–1286–7.

In this guide to the literature, only materials current and easily available are listed. For further information see entry **1141**.

840　University library administration. By Rutherford D. Rogers and David C. Weber. New York: Wilson, 1971. 454p. LC 75–116997. ISBN 0–8242–0417–4.

Major topics and issues in university library administration are treated in this work. The authors provide an overview of those aspects of university library service they believe are most important to library administration. Their approach does not require extensive experience or background. Topics covered include program planning with the assistance of staff, faculty, students, and others; personnel policies; organization of the library's services; budgeting and fiscal management; collection development; technical processing; reader's services; measurement and evaluation of services; automation; and building planning. Appendices include examples of personnel evaluation forms, acquisition policies in university libraries, purchase agreements, and floor plans. Selected references are added at the end of each chapter and the text is indexed by subject.

STATISTICAL SOURCES

841 ALA survey of librarian salaries. Prep. by Mary Jo Lynch, et al. Chicago: Office for Research and Office for Library Personnel Resources, American Library Assn., 1982. 108p. LC 82–11537. ISBN 0–8389–3275–4.
Salary statistics for full-time professional librarians in thirteen different library positions were compiled from a January 1982 survey of 1,400 randomly selected public libraries serving populations of 25,000 or more and academic libraries not belonging to the Association of Research Libraries. For further information see entry **1097**.

842 ARL annual salary survey. Washington, DC: Assn. of Research Libraries, 1975/76– . Annual. LC 76–640547. ISSN 0361–5669.
Salary information for institutions that are members of the Association of Research Libraries is reported here. For further information see entry **1098**.

YEARBOOKS

843 College and reference library yearbook. Comp. by a Committee of the College and Reference Section, American Library Association. Chicago: American Library Assn., 1929–1931. Annual. LC 20–12503 rev.
This yearbook provides a combination of topical survey articles and news or statistics about college and university libraries. One issue has a section on academic library buildings; another contains a bibliography of college library administration in the United States. This work was published for only three years.

Communications Studies

BIBLIOGRAPHIC SOURCES

844 Communication research in library and information science: a bibliography on communication in the sciences, social sciences, and technology. By Thomas J. Waldhart and Enid S. Waldhart. Littleton, CO: Libraries Unlimited, 1975. 168p. LC 75–5551. ISBN 0–87287–111–8.
This bibliography focuses on the communication systems that exist among scientists, social scientists, and others in the research information cycle. Both studies of direct or personal communication and studies of communication through the medium of the literature are included. The time period covered by the citations is from 1964 to 1973, a period of considerable activity in this area of study. A total of 1,288 books and articles from a variety of subject fields are listed. A major strength of this work is its coverage of literature found outside the normal journals in library and information science. The arrangement of the entries is topical, including such headings as bibliometric analysis, author collaboration, literature growth and obsolescence, communication barriers, and information exchange

groups. In addition, there are a number of discipline-oriented studies identified. Although entries are not annotated, each includes "mini-indicators" that offer some descriptive information about the content of the work. Author and subject indexes are provided.

Comparative Librarianship

BIBLIOGRAPHIC SOURCES

845 A handbook of comparative librarianship. By Silvia Simsova and Monique MacKee. Rev. and enl. ed. New York: Shoe String, 1975. 548p. LC 74–14856. ISBN 0–208–01355–5.

This work combines the features of a handbook and a bibliographic guide. The handbook portion is superseded by *A primer of comparative librarianship.* For further information on both sections of this title, see entry **847**.

HANDBOOKS AND MANUALS

846 International handbook of contemporary developments in librarianship. Ed. by Miles M. Jackson. Westport, CT: Greenwood, 1981. 619p. LC 80–27306. ISBN 0–313–21372–0.

The historical development and the current state of library service in various countries throughout the world are treated in this work. Separate authors (over fifty) are responsible for articles on the various countries. These articles examine conditions affecting the various types of library service, as well as the state of the library profession in the country or countries examined. Many of the articles include lengthy bibliographies. Coverage extends to six countries in Africa, eight in the Middle East, nine in Asia, nine in Europe, plus Oceana, Canada, Mexico, the United States, and the Caribbean.

847 A primer of comparative librarianship. By Sylvia Simsova. Hamden, CT: Shoe String, 1982. 95p. LC 82–147199. ISBN 0–85157–431–X.

The *Primer* replaces the "manual" portion of the 1975 *Handbook of comparative librarianship* (entry **845**). It deals with such topics as conducting a literature search and planning comparative studies of librarianship. The portion of the 1975 handbook not replaced by the *Primer* is a guide to sources of information about librarianship in various countries. The chapters in that section are divided by region and sub-region. Entries include a wide range of publications (articles and monographs, annual reports, theses, and other types of sources). The list is not exhaustive, but was compiled largely as a result of efforts by students enrolled in courses in comparative librarianship, augmented by the author's own collection.

Computerized Library Services

For reference materials on computerized library services see entries listed under the heading Automation in Libraries.

Conservation of Library Materials

BIBLIOGRAPHIC SOURCES

848 A conservation bibliography for librarians, archivists, and administrators. By Carolyn Clark Morrow and Steven B. Schoenly. Troy, NY: Whitson, 1979. 271p. LC 79–64847. ISBN 0–87875–170–X.

This bibliography covers the literature of conservation of materials from 1966 until the late 1970's. The listing is divided into two parts. The first contains the compilers' choices of the most important items and is annotated. The second section is more comprehensive in its coverage of the literature and contains only bibliographic references. A total of 1,367 unique titles are cited in the two sections. The compilers have drawn on the journal literature, monographs, conference proceedings, and other resources and have listed publications appearing in the literature of a variety of fields, including chemistry and micrographics as well as librarianship and archival work. The topics covered include conservation administration, protection against environmental hazards and disasters, handling microforms, and general conservation techniques.

849 The conservation of archival and library materials: a resource guide to audio-visual aids. By Alice W. Harrison, et al. Metuchen, NJ: Scarecrow, 1982. 190p. LC 82–652. ISBN 0–8108–1523–0.

Approximately 500 audiovisual items dealing with the conservation of archival and library materials are listed and described in this selective bibliography. The focus is on the past twenty-five years. Included are films, filmstrips, and other formats that address conservation topics. Not all conservation topics are represented by audiovisual materials, and the authors have identified LC subject headings for which no materials were found. The arrangement is alphabetical by title. There is a subject index. Also included is a directory of producers and distributors of the materials.

850 Conservation of library materials: a manual and bibliography on the care, repair and restoration of library materials. By George Martin Cunha and Dorothy Grant Cunha. 2d ed. Metuchen, NJ: Scarecrow, 1972. 2v. LC 77–163871. ISBN 0–8108–0427–1 (v.1). ISBN 0–8108–0525–1 (v.2).

This two-volume work stands as the basic source on the conservation of library materials. Volume 2 consists of an extensive bibliography designed to accompany the manual (volume 1). For further information see entry **853**.

851 Library and archives conservation: 1980s and beyond. By George Martin Cunha and Dorothy Grant Cunha with Suzanne Elizabeth Henderson. Metuchen, NJ: Scarecrow, 1983. 2v. LC 82–10806.

This work (not yet published at the time of this writing) will update *Conservation of library materials: a manual and bibliography on the care, repair and restoration of library materials* and provide an overview of developments within the past fifteen years. For further information see entry **853**.

852 A selective bibliography on the conservation of research library materials. By Paul N. Banks. Chicago: Newberry Library, 1981. v.p.

Listed in this classified bibliography are 1,200 books, journal articles, and other materials in English concerned with the conservation and preservation of library materials in libraries and archives. Most of the materials cited were published in the 1960's and 1970's.

HANDBOOKS AND MANUALS

853　**Conservation of library materials: a manual and bibliography on the care, repair and restoration of library materials.** By George Martin Cunha and Dorothy Grant Cunha. 2d ed. Metuchen, NJ: Scarecrow, 1972. 2v. LC 77–163871. ISBN 0–8108–0427–1 (v.1). ISBN 0–8108–0525–1 (v.2).

This two-volume work stands as the basic source on the conservation of library materials. Volume 1 provides instructions on the conservation of all types of library materials. Volume 2 consists of an extensive bibliography designed to accompany the manual. Nearly 5,000 references to journal articles and monographs concerned with conservation are cited but not described. Coverage is international and includes many titles in languages other than English. Arrangement is by subject and corresponds to the subject categories in Volume 1. There is an author index. These two volumes are to be updated in 1983 by another major two volume work titled *Library and archives conservation: 1980s and beyond* (entry **851**). This update will provide an overview of developments within the past fifteen years and offer guidance in conservation management, preventative and restorative conservation techniques, and disaster planning. It will consist of more than 5,800 new citations, covering the English-language literature up through June, 1981.

854　**Conservation treatment procedures: a manual of step-by-step procedures for the maintenance and repair of library materials.** By Carolyn Clark Morrow. Littleton, CO: Libraries Unlimited, 1982. 191p. LC 82–181. ISBN 0–87287–294–7.

Book repair and maintenance procedures are described in a non-technical, step-by-step fashion in this basic manual. Photographs are included to illustrate each procedure. Several topics are covered, including book repair, book maintenance, and protective encasement. The treatment of each topic follows a standard format: identification of the options available, a list of equipment and supplies required, a description of the procedure, and any special instructions required for a specific activity. An appendix provides a decision-making checklist for book repair; a list of suppliers for equipment, tools and supplies; a test for manual dexterity; and a selected bibliography.

855　**Library and archives conservation: 1980s and beyond.** By George Martin Cunha and Dorothy Grant Cunha with Suzanne Elizabeth Henderson. Metuchen, NJ: Scarecrow, 1983. 2v. LC 82–10806.

This work (not yet published at the time of this writing) will update *Conservation of library materials: a manual and bibliography on the care, repair and restoration of library materials* and provide an overview of developments within the past fifteen years. For further information see entry **853**.

856　**Planning for library conservation: a needs assessment manual.** Prep. by Howard P. Lowell, et al. Denver: Colorado State Library, 1981. n.p.

Intended as a "self-assessment guide" for the conservation of library materials, this work provides the reader with step-by-step instructions to determine the conservation needs of the library and to establish a program to meet those needs. Among the topics treated are reasons for the deterioration of materials, environment conditions required for preservation, and staff training. Questions are used to form a checklist of points to be considered. Also included in the volume are sample forms for identifying conditions within the building that affect conservation, a list of suppliers of materials used in conservation, guidelines for library binding, instructions for surface cleaning items, and a bibliography of additional items on conservation of library materials.

857   Preserving library materials: a manual. By Susan G. Swartzburg. Metuchen, NJ: Scarecrow, 1980. 282p. LC 80–11742. ISBN 0–8108–1302–5.
Current state of the art information on the conservation and preservation of all types of library and archival materials is presented in this manual. The author has identified basic conservation problems and provides practical guidelines for dealing with them. Topics covered in the work include how to deal with insects and rodents, environmental factors (such as temperature and humidity), bookbinding, conservation of paper, conservation of photographic materials, preservation of reprographic reproductions, and care of paintings, prints, maps, and manuscripts. Several appendices augment the manual. These include such documents as the Library Binding Institute Standard for Library Binding and a self-inspection form for libraries from the National Fire Prevention Association; a selected list of periodicals; a rather extensive glossary of terms related to preservation and conservation; and a bibliography of more than fifty pages, with some annotated items. The text is indexed by subject.

Consortia

For reference materials on consortia see entries listed under the heading Networks and Consortia.

Continuing Education

BIBLIOGRAPHIC SOURCES

858   Continuing library education as viewed in relation to other continuing professional education movements. By Elizabeth W. Stone. Washington, DC: ASIS, 1974. 694p. LC 74–21737. ISBN 0–87715–108–3.
The textual portion of this work compares continuing education in librarianship with continuing education in other professions. It incorporates examples and documents from various professions, including medicine, nursing, and psychology. A substantial part of the book consists of an annotated bibliography of writings on continuing education, in library and information science as well as in other professions. The bibliography extends from pages 339–694, and it is one of the most comprehensive compilations on the subject.

859   Continuing professional education in librarianship and other fields: a classified and annotated bibliography, 1965–1974. Comp. by Mary Ellen Michael. New York: Garland, 1975. 211p. LC 75–8998. ISBN 0–8240–1085–X.
This work identifies significant literature on continuing education in librarianship and related fields for a ten-year period (from 1965 through 1974). The bibliography is divided

into three sections. The first section lists 285 articles, monographs, and reports on continuing education in the United States. The second part lists forty-five items concerned with continuing education in other countries. The third section identifies 117 items from other fields considered by the compiler to be of interest and relevant to the main topic. Arrangements within topics is alphabetical by author and the entries are indexed by author. The annotations are largely descriptive rather than evaluative.

DIRECTORIES

860 1979 directory of continuing education opportunities for library, information, media personnel. Comp. by CLENE, Inc. 4th ed. New York: K. G. Saur, 1979. 292p. LC 78–645522. ISBN 0–89664–064–7. ISSN 0162–847X.
This directory, produced by the Continuing Library Education Network and Exchange (CLENE), was prepared to identify forthcoming and ongoing continuing education opportunities for librarians and for persons in related professional fields. The directory is divided into several sections. Section I identifies continuing education opportunities by the topics covered. This is the main entry and the one that provides the most information about the programs. It specifies sponsorship, frequency, type of delivery system, credit, level, enrollment requirements, and name of a contact person. Section II provides a guide to the location of continuing education programs by geographical area (city and state). Section III is an index by primary producer. Section IV presents an alphabetical list of instructors and a list of instructors by content area. Section V summarizes statistics on continuing education. Although the continuing education opportunities identified here as forthcoming have all taken place, the directory continues to have value because many of the listed workshops or other short courses are held on an ongoing basis. In addition, the directory enables interested persons to identify instructors or organizations that have produced or sponsored continuing education programs. The first edition was issued by CLENE in 1976.

861 Staff development in libraries: a directory of organizations and activities, with a staff development bibliography. Comp. by Staff Development Committee, Library Administration and Management Division, American Library Association. Chicago: American Library Assn., 1978. 34p. LC 79–108854.
A total of fourteen organizations active in staff development are listed in this directory. Entries for the organizations specify organizational objectives, sources of funding, and availability of their training materials to the public. A short annotated bibliography of items on library staff development, grouped by topics, is also provided.

HANDBOOKS AND MANUALS

862 Library staff development and continuing education: principles and practices. By Barbara Conroy. Littleton, Co: Libraries Unlimited, 1978. 296p. LC 78–18887. ISBN 0–87287–177–0.
This manual draws on basic principles and theory to develop practical guidelines for building a strong staff development and continuing education program. The manual presents the user with a set of ideas, procedures, and guidelines for action. In addition, problems and issues are discussed, and possible solutions or options are suggested. The work is organized into three broad sections and subdivided by chapters (called guidelines). The

broad topics cover planning, implementation, and evaluation. Guideline topics include determining administrative responsibilities; locating and selecting educational staff; involving the learners; providing facilities, equipment, and materials; and implementing learning activities. Each guideline is followed by a selected bibliography; a general bibliography is included at the end. There is also a glossary of terms. The manual is designed to apply to a variety of situations and thus can be used to plan a staff development program within an individual library or for a statewide library association.

863   Planning library workshops and institutes. By Ruth Warncke. Chicago: American Library Assn., 1976. 178p. (ALA public library reporter series, no. 17) LC 75–43835. ISBN 0–8389–3178–2.

Detailed, practical instructions on the planning of library-sponsored workshops and institutes are provided in this manual. The work begins with the basic question of who is responsible for the production and planning of the workshop and indicates the advantages and disadvantages of the involvement of different types of institutions or associations. Chapters on planning and financial responsibility are also included. In the latter, a useful checklist of possible expenses is provided. The strengths and weaknesses of various workshop formats are assessed. The process of evaluating the workshop or institute is also covered. The work concludes with a discussion of possible methods of disseminating information from the workshop.

Copyright

BIBLIOGRAPHIC SOURCES

864   "Selected, annotated bibliography on photocopying of copyrighted works, 1970–1976, with a special sub list on the Williams and Wilkins vs. U.S. case." By Peri L. Schuyler and Jerry Kidd. In **Copyright and photocopying: papers on problems and solutions, design for a clearinghouse, and bibliography.** Ed. by Laurence B. Heilprin. College Park: College of Library and Information Services, Univ. of Maryland, 1977. pp. 85–158. (Student contribution series, no. 10) LC 77–620028. ISBN 0–911808–14–0.

The last seventy-three pages of Heilprin's work consist of an annotated bibliography of monographs, government publications, news reports, and journal articles from 1970 to 1976 that deal with photocopying copyrighted works. Some items are published by international organizations and have an international orientation. A few are in non-English languages and, although the annotations are all in English, the titles of foreign language items are not. The listing is particularly useful for historical material on copyright issued during the debate over changes in American copyright law brought about by major advances in technology.

865   Technology and copyright: sources and materials. Ed. by George P. Bush and Robert H. Dreyfuss. Mt. Airy, MD: Lomond, 1979. 552p. LC 79–65635. ISBN 0–912338–17–2.

This source book includes an annotated bibliography and reprints of significant publications pertaining to "the debate centering on the provisions of the Copyright Law relating to technology and copyright." For further information see entry **870**.

HANDBOOKS AND MANUALS

866 Applying the new copyright law: a guide for educators and librarians. By Jerome
K. Miller. Chicago: American Library Assn., 1979. 152p. LC 79–4694. ISBN
0–8389–0287–7.

This handbook contains information about the copyright law as it applies to librarians and to
teachers. It includes a useful history of events leading up to the current law, information
about securing protection of an individual's intellectual property through copyright, the
process of obtaining permission to make copies, and an analysis of the basic issue resolved
by the current copyright law.

867 Copyright, Congress and technology: the public record. Ed. by Nicholas Henry.
Phoenix: Oryx, 1978–79. 5v. LC 78–23747. ISBN 0–912700–13–0.

Following a brief introduction, each volume presents public documents, arranged in
chronological order, that were generated in revising the U.S. Copyright Act. In a sense, this
is a "legislative history"; the actual text of public documents relating to fundamental
copyright issues are reprinted, with index access provided. The various volumes cover
different time periods, beginning with 1958. Volume 4 includes documents dealing with the
anticipated future of information technology.

868 Copyright handbook. By Donald F. Johnson. 2d ed. New York: Bowker, 1982. 381p.
LC 82–4218. ISBN 0–8352–1488–5.

Included in this handbook is basic information on the provisions of the current copyright
law, updated to reflect changes, interpretations, and clarifications of the law. References to
court decisions and interpretations by the Copyright Office are provided, as are guidelines
for "fair use" and for interlibrary transactions. Other topics covered include registration,
ownership, exclusive rights, and infringement remedies. The first edition was published
under the same title in 1978.

869 General guide to the Copyright Act of 1976. By Marybeth Peters. Washington, DC:
Copyright Office, Library of Congress, 1977. v.p.

This volume was prepared as a training manual for staff members of the Copyright Office
and was later used for training sessions outside of the Office. Although major elements of the
law are summarized, the text does not constitute an "official summary." However, the work
does cover the basic aspects of the copyright law, with references to relevant sections of the
law and a summary of pertinent points in many of the sections. There is also a list of official
source materials on copyright law revision.

870 Technology and copyright: sources and materials.. Ed. by George P. Bush and
Robert H. Dreyfuss. Mt. Airy, MD: Lomond, 1979. 552p. LC 79–65635. ISBN
0–912338–17–2.

This source book includes an annotated bibliography and reprints of significant publications
pertaining to "the debate centering on the provisions of the Copyright Law relating to
technology and copyright." The bibliography, found in Part I, is arranged by subject. The
topics covered include the various technologies, such as microforms and video, and the
types of institutions that must interpret copyright applications. The reprints of pertinent
publications include articles, public documents, and the decision of the Williams and

Wilkins case. Although neither the bibliography nor the reprint section is exhaustive, the volume does provide balanced coverage of the issues at stake. Included at the end of the work are a list of periodicals cited and indexes by name, subject, and court case.

871 U.S. copyright documents: an annotated collection for use by educators and librarians. By Jerome K. Miller. Littleton, CO: Libraries Unlimited, 1981. 292p. LC 80–24768. ISBN 0–87287–239.

Except for interpretations that have been published since the cutoff date, all basic documents pertaining to the copyright question, based largely on the Copyright Revision Act of 1976 and the 1977 Ammendment, are reproduced in this handbook. Included are the act; the amendment; the House, Senate, and Conference committee reports; regulations of the Copyright Office; and selected other documents dealing with copyright. The compiler has edited out certain duplicative portions in the committee reports and integrated the documents in a way that brings a sense of continuity and order to the compilation. In addition, he has interjected comments that clarify points of the law or points made in the documents. The work concludes with a detailed subject index.

Data Base Services

For reference materials on data base services see entries listed under the heading Online Information Services.

Deselection

For reference materials on deselection see entries listed under the heading Collection Development.

Disadvantaged, Library Service To

DIRECTORIES

872 Directory of outreach services in public libraries. By the Office for Library Service to the Disadvantaged, American Library Association. Chicago: American Library Assn., 1980. 632p. ISBN 0–8389–3242–8.

Over 400 outreach programs sponsored by public libraries located in thirty-three states are described in this directory. The cut-off date for inclusion is March 31, 1978. The programs listed differ in nature and the descriptions vary in degree of detail provided. Entries generally contain the title of the program, a brief description of its scope and operation, a statement of objectives, the name and address of the contact person, size of professional staff, identification and description of the sources of funding, identity of the group to which the program is directed, staff development activities, members of the program advisory committee, the program's content areas, an indication of materials developed for use in the program, demonstrated results of the program, and the name of any cooperating agencies. Types of programs range from children's service activities to programs designed to meet special needs of the handicapped, alcoholics, or prisoners. The index provides subject access.

Document Delivery

DIRECTORIES

873 Document retrieval: sources and services. Ed. by Barry W. Champany and Sharon
M. Hotz. 2d ed. San Francisco: Information Store, 1982. 171p.

Suppliers able to provide requestors with the documents they ask for at the fastest possible
speed are listed in this directory. The scope is international, covering over 170 suppliers in
the United States and fifteen other countries. The suppliers are listed in one of the following
categories: libraries providing a document retrieval service that extends beyond the immedi-
ate service community; information centers of non-profit organizations, such as trade
associations (including those providing document delivery to non-member users); and
commercial enterprises (firms providing document delivery as a business). The term
document is defined in this work as any type of nonbook item, including microforms.
However, many of the suppliers listed also provide requestors with books as well. Arrangement is alphabetical by name of supplier. Entries specify name, address, telephone, telex
numbers, name of contact person, types of materials supplied, time required to fill an order,
the medium for ordering (e.g., telephone, mail, or electronic mail), and rates. Also noted is
who is responsible for copyright compliance. Indexing is by geographical location, subject,
and type of material.

Education for Librarianship

For reference materials on education for librarianship see entries listed under the
heading Library Education.

Educational Media

For reference materials on educational media see entries listed under the heading
Audiovisual Services and Nonprint Materials.

Employee Rights

For reference materials on employee rights see entries listed under the heading
Personnel Policies, Salaries, Benefits and Employee Rights.

Ethnic Studies Libraries

BIOGRAPHICAL SOURCES

874 Directory of ethnic studies librarians. Comp. by Beth J. Shapiro. Chicago: Office
for Library Service to the Disadvantaged, American Library Assn., 1976. 104 leaves.
LC 77-374207. ISBN 0-8389-5487-1.

Biographical information on ethnic studies librarians in the United States is provided in this
directory. Entries specify name, address, employer, position held, and areas of responsibility or interest. Additional access to the entries is provided in the index by subject,
geographic location, name of institution, and type of employment.

DIRECTORIES

875 Guide to ethnic museums, libraries, and archives in the United States. By Lubomyr R. Wynar and Lois Buttlar. Kent, OH: Center for the Study of Ethnic Publications, Kent State Univ., 1978. 378p.

This is a guide to 828 ethnic museums, libraries, and archives in the United States that have collected materials on more than seventy ethnic groups. Entries are arranged by ethnic group and each contains the name, address, and telephone number of the organization, names and titles of key personnel, date founded, size of staff, publications, nature of the collection, and some general comments about the institution. Each ethnic grouping is preceded by a brief bibliographic essay that identifies major subject catalogs or other private resources relating to the collections. Indexing is by institutional name and location.

876 Slavic ethnic libraries, museums and archives in the United States: a guide and directory. Comp. by Lubomyr R. Wynar with Pat Kleeberger. Chicago: Assn. of College and Research Libraries; Kent, OH: Program for the Study of Ethnic Publications, School of Library Science, Kent State Univ., 1980. 164p. LC 80–18034.

Described in this directory are libraries, museums, and archives collecting materials relating to fourteen Slavic groups. Arrangement is alphabetical by name of the ethnic group and then by name of the institution. Each entry covers the history of the institution, its objectives, major activities, facilities, publications, programs, and services.

European Studies Libraries

DIRECTORIES

877 East, central and southeast Europe: a handbook of library and archival resources in North America. Ed. by Paul L. Horecky. Santa Barbara, CA: ABC-Clio, 1976. 467p. (Joint Committee on Eastern Europe Publication series, no. 3) LC 76–28392. ISBN 0–87346–214–8.

The purpose of this work is "to provide scholars, librarians, students, and researchers with a basic reference tool for the study of the essential collections available in major libraries, archives and research institutions in the United States and Canada, by outlining the profiles of these collections and offering broad guidance to their subject and area contents." The countries defined by the work as east, central, and southeast Europe include Albania, Bulgaria, Czechoslovakia, East Germany, Greece, Hungary, Poland, Romania, and Yugoslavia. Profiles of forty libraries and archives having important collections in these areas are included; the descriptive text was prepared by library or faculty representatives from the individual institutions. Each entry indicates collection strengths and special collections held by the institution. Particular emphasis is placed on holdings in the social sciences and humanities.

878 Eastern Europe and Russia-Soviet Union: a handbook of west european archival and library resources. By Richard C. Lewanski. New York: K. G. Saur; Detroit: Gale, distr., 1980. 317p. (Joint Committee on Eastern Europe Publication series, no. 9) LC 79–19520. ISBN 0–89664–092–2.

This directory identifies approximately 1,000 institutions in twenty-one western European countries that have significant holdings of archival materials on eastern Europe and the

Soviet Union. Covered are colleges and universities, libraries, museums, and archives. Collections in the humanities and social sciences are emphasized. Arrangement is alphabetical by name of country, then by geographical location, and then by name of institution. Entries contain name and address, name of director, date of establishment, subject strengths and special holdings, type of catalog used, availability of photoduplication services, hours of opening, policies regarding circulation of materials, and publications from the institution. A useful feature is the list of bibliographic publications that cover the holdings individually or as a group.

879   Scholars' guide to Washington, D.C.: central and east european studies. By Kenneth J. Dillon. Washington, DC: Smithsonian Inst. Pr., 1980. 350p. (Scholars' guide to Washington, D.C., no. 5). LC 80–607019.

The first section of this work deals with resource collections in the Washington, D.C. area, including libraries, archives, museums, galleries, music and film collections, map collections, and data banks. Each entry specifies name, address, telephone number, characteristics of the collections, subject strengths, special collections held, and policies regarding public access. The second section provides a listing of Washington-based organizations that have an interest in central and eastern Europe. These are identified as potential sources of additional information. Indexing is by name and subject.

Evaluation

For reference materials on evaluation see entries listed under the heading Library Evaluation, Measurement and Research.

Exhibits

For reference materials on exhibits see entries listed under the heading Public Relations, Programs and Exhibits.

Fee-Based Information Services

DIRECTORIES

880   The directory of fee-based information services 1980–81. Ed. by Kelly Warnken. Woodstock, NY: Information Alternative, 1980. 94p. LC 76–55469. ISBN 0–936288–00–0.

More than 200 fee-based information services in the United States and other countries are grouped into the following categories: information brokers, information retailers, freelance librarians, information specialists, information consultants, indexers, independent librarians, and institutions providing library and information services for a fee. Arrangement is alphabetical by state or province and then by company name. Entries include name, address, and telephone number of the company or person, names of key individuals, subject specialization, services available, hourly fees, and scope of services. Indexing is by names of individuals, companies, and subject.

HANDBOOKS AND MANUALS

881　Fee-based information services: a study of a growing industry. By Lorig Maranjian and Richard W. Boss. New York: Bowker, 1980. 199p. (Information management series, no. 1) LC 80–20176. ISBN 0–8352–1287–4.

A combination handbook and directory, this work provides a description of fee-based information services and discusses major considerations in establishing such services: marketing, information gathering techniques, and the economics of the industry. In addition, there are profiles presented of the larger fee-based services, a case study of FIND/SVP, and discussion of related issues, such as the relationship of this industry to libraries. A directory of fee-based information services in the United States, Canada, and the United Kingdom is included in the appendix. The work also contains a selected bibliography of current monographs and articles on the subject.

882　The information brokers: how to start and operate your own fee-based service. By Kelly Warnken. New York: Bowker, 1981. 154p. LC 81–10170. ISBN 0–8352–1347–1.

Aimed at persons interested in becoming information brokers, this handbook covers the basic elements of the business, indicates the first steps in beginning as an information broker, describes how to identify and attract clients, and summarizes the types of services that can be offered. In addition, the financial aspects of the business are addressed.

Festschriften

BIBLIOGRAPHIC SOURCES

883　Beitrage aus deutschen festschriften auf dem gebiet des buch und bibliothekswesens 1947–1965. By Hedda Knoop-Busch. Göttingen, Federal Republic of Germany: Evangelischen Bibliothekar-Lehrinstitut, 1970. 67p. (Arbeiten aus dem Evangelischen Bibliothekar-Lehrinstitut Göttingen, no. 3) LC 72–363415.

In this bibliography, fifty-eight festschriften are arranged in alphabetical order by the name of the person honored. Subject contents are analyzed in a separate classified section; a total of 645 papers from the festschriften are identified here. There is also an author index to the papers. Bibliographic entries are in the language of the original paper, and most of the papers are in German.

884　Index to festschriften in librarianship. By J. Periam Danton. New York: Bowker, 1970. 461p. LC 75–88796. ISBN 0–8352–0261–5.

This volume indexes 3,300 articles from 283 publications, covering the years from 1864 to 1966. It is continued by *Index to festschriften in librarianship 1967–1975*. For further information see entry **885**.

885　Index to festschriften in librarianship 1967–1975. By J. Periam Danton and Jane F. Pulis with Patiala Khoury Wallman. Munich: Verlag Dokumentation; New York: R. R. Bowker, distr., 1979. 354p. LC 79–321196. ISBN 3–598–07034–9.

This volume and its predecessor, *Index to festschriften in librarianship* (entry **884**), provide extensive international coverage of festschriften in librarianship and related fields published through 1975. The first volume indexes 3,300 articles from 283 publications, covering the years from 1864 to 1966. The second volume indexes 6,000 articles from 136 additional festschriften issued through 1975 in twenty-six countries. Arrangement is alphabetical by author, and the entries are indexed by subject. The second volume also includes an introductory chapter on the history, development, and bibliographic control of festschriften in the field of librarianship as well as citations to review articles of festschriften in librarianship.

Filing Rules

HANDBOOKS AND MANUALS

886 ALA filing rules. Prep. by Filing Committee, Resources and Technical Services Division, American Library Association. Chicago: American Library Assn., 1980. 50p. LC 80–22186. ISBN 0–8389–3255–X.

This work is a successor to *ALA rules for filing catalog cards,* 2d edition, published in 1968, which in turn was a revision of *A.L.A. rules for filing catalog cards,* published in 1942. Because the current filing rules employ different principles for filing than the two preceding works, this volume is not considered by the Filing Committee (the committee responsible for its publication) as a new edition, but rather as a new work. The new rules are intended to be less complicated than previous rules and are also intended to apply to the arrangement of any bibliographic records, regardless of which rules were used for the creation of the records. Rules are limited in number and briefly stated. There are few exceptions and few options. The rules use the "file-as-is" principle: "character strings (one or more characters set off by spaces, dashes, hyphens, diagonal slashes, or periods) to be considered for filing should be considered in exactly the form and order in which they appear." The use of this concept makes the filing rules more easily adaptable to machine readable data bases. The filing rules are divided into two parts: general rules, those which apply commonly; and special rules, those which apply to situations that occur infrequently. The general rules are divided further into two categories: order of characters and access points. Explanations of each of these are provided, with examples. The special rules apply to abbreviations; initial articles; initials, initialisms, and acronyms; names and prefixes; nonroman alphabets; numerals; relators used in name headings; and terms of honor and address. The two appendices present examples regarding modified letters and special characters and articles appearing in the nominative case in several foreign languages. Numerous figures, tables, and examples add to the explanation of the rules. A glossary and index complete the work.

Film Libraries

HANDBOOKS AND MANUALS

887 Film library techniques: principles of administration. By Helen P. Harrison. New York: Hastings House, 1973. 277p. (Studies in media management; communication arts books) LC 73–5615. ISBN 0–8038–2294–4.

In this detailed manual, the author characterizes the functions served by film libraries and briefly traces the history of this type of library service in a variety of institutional settings. The remainder of the book treats such basic elements of film library service as selection and acquisition, film handling and retrieval, cataloging, information retrieval, space usage, staffing, and copyright. Information is based on British experience and procedure, although most is applicable to North American film libraries. The work concludes with a selected bibliography of additional sources.

Financial Aid

DIRECTORIES

888 Financial assistance for library education. Chicago: Standing Committee on Library Education, American Library Assn., 1969– . Annual. LC 73–649921. ISSN 0569–6275.

This annual directory identifies scholarships, fellowships, assistantships, and other forms of financial aid available to students who plan to attend library school in the United States or Canada. It includes financial aid opportunities sponsored by individual schools, state agencies and associations, and individual libraries as well as national awards. The majority of the listings apply to programs leading to the master's degree, although some are available for other levels. The directory is updated annually and published in the fall prior to the academic year when the awards are effective. However, because many of the awards have early deadline dates, copies of the directory should be requested as early as possible.

Friends of the Library

DIRECTORIES

889 A directory of friends of libraries groups in the United States. Comp. by Sandy Dolnick. Chicago: Friends of Libraries Committee, Public Relations Section, Library Administration Division, American Library Assn., 1978. 297p. LC 79–112075.

This directory identifies approximately 2,100 public library and academic library friends organizations. It is organized in two sections. The first describes seven statewide friends groups; the second lists friends of libraries organizations by state and city. Entries for both public and academic libraries are included under the city of location. Information is brief; only the name and address of the library are specified in the entries.

HANDBOOKS AND MANUALS

890 Find out who your friends are: a practical manual for the formation of library support groups. Ed. by H. Barrett Pennell, Jr. Philadelphia: Friends of the Free Library of Philadelphia, 1978. 66p.

Prepared as a how-to instruction manual for developing a strong friends of the library group, this work begins by considering the fundamental purposes of friends groups and then covers the various facets of organizing and maintaining such a group. Among the topics explored are selecting a steering committee, electing board members, establishing objectives, planning, incorporating, recruiting members, cooperating with the library staff, finances, and public relations. The book is based on the experiences of the Philadelphia Friends group and is applicable to various types and sizes of libraries. Included with the textual information are more than fifty pages of forms, sample letters, and documents, such as the bylaws of the Philadelphia Friends group.

Genealogists, Library Service To
HANDBOOKS AND MANUALS

891 Library service for genealogists. Ed. by J. Carlyle Parker. Detroit: Gale, 1981. 362p.
LC 80–26032. ISBN 0–8103–1489–4.

Unlike guides to genealogical research, which are usually directed toward the interested
genealogist, this manual is aimed at librarians interested in establishing genealogical library
service. The author identifies the library's role in providing genealogical service to the
public and indicates policies and procedures for establishing the service. Chapters deal with
specific problems faced by librarians in serving genealogists, including collection development, reference and interlibrary loan, locating vital records and reading old handwriting.
Each of the chapters includes useful and sometimes lengthy bibliographies that augment the
text. Also provided are case studies and sample requests that indicate the steps reference
librarians would follow to find the correct information. A detailed subject index completes
the volume.

Gifts and Exchange
HANDBOOKS AND MANUALS

892 Gifts and exchange manual. By Alfred H. Lane. Westport, CT: Greenwood, 1980.
136p. LC 79–7590. ISBN 0–313–11389–5.

Intended as a how-to manual of procedures, this work indicates "what should be done to
cope effectively with gifts to a library and to maintain an exchange program that will be
useful and productive but will entail the least possible complications." Topics covered
include the economics of exchange, exchange records, international exchanges, paper work
involved in exchanges, gifts to libraries, estimating and appraising gifts, records of gifts,
gift policies, soliciting gifts, disposition of unwanted material, and rare books and manuscripts. Several appendices provide additional useful information, such as IRS deduction
guidelines, a list of appraisers, the ACRL statement on appraisals, sample gift policy
statements, and a number of sample forms. A subject index is included.

Government and Administrative Libraries
DIRECTORIES

893 Canadian library directory: federal government libraries. Ottawa: National
Library of Canada; Information Canada, 1974. v.1. n.p.

This is the first part in a 1974 series of directories of Canadian libraries. It lists 234 libraries
in the federal government of Canada. The arrangement is alphabetical by the name of the
library. Entries specify name and address of the library, name of the director, hours of
opening, policies regarding use, services available, size of staff, collection size by type of
material, subject strengths, special collections, and publications of the libraries. Excluded
from the compilation are embassy libraries, penitentiary libraries, patient and medical
libraries located in hospitals, libraries in Indian schools, and recreational libraries of the
Canadian military forces. Index access is provided by geographic location, personal name,
subject, and automated operations. The directory is bilingual, printed in English and
French.

894 **Federal library resources: a user's guide to research collections.** Comp. by Mildred Benton. New York: Science Assoc., 1973. 111p. LC 72–94002. ISBN 0–87837–002–1.

Issued in 1973, this directory provides then current information about 163 research collections in U.S. federal government agencies. Particular emphasis is placed on those libraries that have extensive or unique research collections. Entries contain name and address of library, director's name, agency affiliation, hours of opening, a description of services offered, and information about the nature of the collection and the resources available. Indexing is by subject of collections and names of individuals. An expanded and updated edition is scheduled for publication in 1983.

895 **Guide to government department and other libraries and information bureaux.** 23d ed. London: Science Reference Library, British Library, 1978. 92p. LC 79–305718. ISBN 0–906654–16–8.

In this 1978 directory, libraries located in British government agencies, at home and abroad, are selectively listed. It includes 500 national libraries, institutes, international organizations, tourist agencies, social science and science libraries, and other related organizations. University and public libraries are excluded. Entries are classified by Dewey number and contain name and address, type of library, holdings, hours of opening, public access, loan policies, copying facilities, and a list of publications. Index access is provided by parent organization.

896 **World directory of administrative libraries: a guide to libraries serving national, state, provincial and lander-bodies: prepared for the sub-section of administrative libraries.** Ed. by Otto Simmler. Munich: Verlag Dokumentation, 1976. 475p. (IFLA publications, no. 7) LC 77–356471. ISBN 3–7940–4427–4.

More than 300 libraries serving national or sub-national levels of government are listed in this directory. Those included provide information service to administrative and legislative agencies within the levels of government represented. Coverage does not extend to the municipal level. Arrangement of entries is by country and then by size within each country. Entries specify the name of the library, an English translation of the name, the telephone and telex numbers, the type of collection, holdings, size of staff, name of library director, and a list of special services offered. Additional access is provided in the index by name of library (alphabetically arranged under country), name of library director, city, and a comparison of the official and English names. Because of an error made in the indexing, users must add 74 to every page number found in the index.

897 **Worldwide directory of federal libraries.** Ed. by Judith Bettelheim. Orange, NJ: Academic Media, 1973. 411p. LC 72–75955. ISBN 0–87876–029–6.

Arrangement in this 1973 directory of 2,248 libraries, information centers, and reference collections operated by the United States government, at home and overseas, is by branch of government, subdivided by major and subordinate agencies. Excluded from coverage are libraries operated by the government of the District of Columbia. The information contained in the entries includes name, address, telephone number of the library, name of librarian, number of staff members, number of holdings, subjects covered, special collections, interlibrary loan, copying services, and conditions for use of the library. Indexing is by name of personnel, agency, and geographical area. Although the directory is several years old, it still can be used successfully to identify federal libraries and can be updated by using more recent sources.

Government Publications

BIBLIOGRAPHIC SOURCES

898 Government documents in the library literature, 1909–1974. By Alan E. Schorr. Ann Arbor: Pierian Press, 1976. 110p. LC 77–70340. ISBN 0–87650–071–8.
This extensive bibliography identifies monographs and articles dealing with government publications at all levels for the time period noted in the title. The list is organized into four broad categories, covering U.S., state, United Nations, and League of Nations publications. Each of the categories is subdivided further. Items are included selectively for the period 1909 to 1920 and then comprehensively from 1921 on. Bibliographies of monographs and articles on government publications published subsequent to 1974 can be found in issues of *Government publications review* (entry **899**).

899 Government publications review. New York: Pergamon, 1971– . 6 per year. LC 81–5510. ISSN 0277–9390.
Bibliographies of monographs and articles on government publications published since 1974 are presented in this journal to update Schorr's *Government documents in the library literature, 1909–1974.* For further information see entry **898**.

BIOGRAPHICAL SOURCES

900 Directory of government document collections & librarians. 3d ed. Prep. by Government Documents Round Table, American Library Association. Ed. by Jane M. Mackay and Barbara L. Turman. Washington, DC: Congressional Information Service, 1981. 674p. LC 81–177268. ISSN 0276–959X.
In addition to providing information about the document holdings of 2,700 American libraries, this work lists names, titles, and telephone numbers of approximately 4,000 librarians, educators, government officials, and association officers who are involved with government publications. For further information see entry **901**.

DIRECTORIES

901 Directory of government document collections & librarians. 3d ed. Prep. by Government Documents Round Table, American Library Association. Ed. by Jane M. Mackay and Barbara L. Turman. Washington, DC: Congressional Information Service, 1981. 674p. LC 81–177268. ISSN 0276–959X.
Information about the documents holdings of 2,700 American libraries is found in this directory. In addition, the work lists names, titles, and telephone numbers of approximately 4,000 librarians, educators, government officials, and association officers who are involved with government publications. Entries are arranged geographically by state and then alphabetically by city and library. The information provided includes name of institution; name, address and telephone number of library; section responsible for documents; major categories of documents collected and relative size of collection; subject areas of exceptional

strength; issuing sources for depository items; issuing sources of documents collected in strength that are non-depository; names of staff members working with documents; and data on such library policies as public access, circulation, and interlibrary loan. Several indexes are included: library names, types of document collections, special collections, library school instructors who teach government documents courses, names of persons or agencies responsible for administering state documents programs, personal names, and key people in various types of government document activity. Two previous editions of this directory were issued, one in 1978 and the other in 1974.

902 Government depository libraries. Washington, DC: Joint Committee on Printing, U.S. Congress, 1982. 131p. LC 79–2860. ISSN 0148–5253.

This directory of the current libraries designated as depositories for U.S. government publications is revised irregularly (approximately every three years). Arrangement is geographical by state. Entries contain the Congressional district number, name of the city, name of the library, address and telephone number, and year designated as a depository. Where library names differ from that of the institution, each is listed. In addition to the directory information, the current text of the act governing U.S. depositories is reprinted. This directory is never completely up-to-date, of course, because new depositories are added constantly.

HANDBOOKS AND MANUALS

903 Administration of government documents collections. By Rebekah M. Harleston and Carla J. Stoffle. Littleton, CO: Libraries Unlimited, 1974. 178p. LC 74–81960. ISBN 0–87287–086–3.

Procedures for acquiring, processing, and organizing government publications are covered in this manual. Particular emphasis is placed on collections of federal documents. Chapters deal with such topics as record keeping, acquisition sources and procedures, processing, filing, shelving, inventory, weeding, binding, transferring or reclassifying documents, and cataloging by systems other than the SuDocs system. Throughout the manual, examples are used as well as sample cards and sample records. The information presented here is generalizable to both depository and non-depository libraries, and much of it can be applied to collections of documents at all levels of government.

904 From press to people: collecting and using U.S. government publications. By Yuri Nakata. Chicago: American Library Assn., 1979. 212p. LC 78–26306. ISBN 0–8389–0264–2.

The intent of this manual is to emphasize reference service and the delivery of public documents to users. It is designed as a tool for the beginning documents librarian, and it can also be used by the librarian not familiar with U.S. government documents. The initial chapters provide basic background information on government printing and the federal depository library system. Subsequent chapters cover organization and arrangement, collection development, use of the *Monthly catalog,* cataloging and classification, technical report literature and machine readable data bases, reference sources, and records and routines. Appendices deal with the classification system of the Superintendent of Documents, instructions to depository libraries, and guidelines for the depository library system. The text is indexed by subject.

905 Organizing a local government documents collection. By Yuri Nakata, Susan J. Smith and William B. Ernst, Jr. Chicago: American Library Assn., 1979. 61p. LC 79–12197. ISBN 0–8389–0284–7.

The result of a project sponsored by the Illinois Regional Library Council, this manual addresses the needs expressed by librarians who attended documents workshops and covers the treatment of municipal and other local government publications. The topics treated are acquisitions, organization, cataloging and classification, reference service, and publicity. The manual is replete with examples, sample forms and cards, and other resources of use in practice. Several appendices reproduce various forms, including a sample resolution for an ordinance requiring the deposit of documents with the library and a sample checklist of local documents. A selected bibliography of local government publications is appended at the end of the work.

906 State publications and depository libraries: a reference handbook. By Margaret T. Lane. Westport, CT: Greenwood, 1981. 573p. LC 80–24688. ISBN 0–313–22118–9.

The characteristics of state document depositories are discussed in depth in this work. The first part deals with the general characteristics of state depository library legislation and the relationship between libraries and state publications. Further discussions involve state library agencies and document distribution centers. Much of the material introduced here synthesizes what the author has found to exist or should exist in the various states. Part II presents a survey of the literature, followed by a lengthy bibliography of writings on state publications. The last part provides a state-by-state summary of information about depository libraries, including general information about state publications and citations to depository legislation. A model depository law and indexes by subject, author, and title of publications identified in the text complete the volume.

Grants and Proposal Writing

DIRECTORIES

907 Federal programs for libraries: a directory. Ed. by Lawrence E. Leonard. 2d ed. Washington, DC: State and Public Library Services Branch, Office of Libraries and Learning Resources, U.S. Office of Education, 1979. 72p.

This directory provides pertinent information about federal library and library-related funding programs. Covered in the 1979 edition are nine library funding programs and seventy-two additional programs offering possible library funding. Specified in each entry are the name of the program, name, address, and telephone number of the sponsoring agency, program characteristics, requirements for eligibility, type of grant, amount available for the fiscal year, range and average amount of current awards, application deadline, and public law and program number under which the program functions. Entries are indexed by applicant eligibility, authorizing legislation, CFDA number, name of federal agency, and subject. Also included is a list of sources providing information about library funding. The 1979 edition is now out of date, in part because of changes in funding patterns at the federal level. However, some of the information is still valid and, in addition, it can be used to suggest the names of agencies or programs that might offer funding for library purposes.

HANDBOOKS AND MANUALS

908 Grant money and how to get it: a handbook for librarians. By Richard W. Boss. New York: Bowker, 1980. 138p. LC 80–17880. ISBN 0–8352–1274–2.

Aimed at librarians seeking funding from private or public sources, this manual includes information about sources from which grant money is available, resources that can be used to identify potential donors, the basic elements of proposal writing and submission, how to negotiate changes, and how to learn from rejections. Several appendices cover such topics as names of foundations active in library support, state directories of foundations, sources of federal funding, and federal regional centers. Also included are a glossary of terms used in fundraising, a bibliography, and a subject index.

909 Grants for libraries. By Emmett Corry. Littleton, CO: Libraries Unlimited, 1982. 240p. LC 82–20886. ISBN 0–87287–262–9.

This manual was prepared to provide guidance in proposal writing, particularly for federal funds. Federal programs for each type of library are discussed in the first four chapters; together, these chapters provide a history of direct federal support for school media programs, college and university library programs, public library programs, and information science. In each of these chapters, examples of successful proposals are cited, with an indication of the type of information expected in the applications. The fifth chapter describes the various steps to take in developing a proposal. Private or foundation giving is discussed next; this chapter also identifies useful sources from which information about foundation grants can be obtained. There are eight appendices that provide supplementary information. One describes how to use the *Catalog of federal domestic assistance* for information about federal grants. Others abstract 113 library or library-related federal programs, summarize successful applications awarded under the Library Research and Demonstration program, and provide a model proposal. Also included is a bibliography of basic sources on the topic.

Handicapped, Library Service To

BIBLIOGRAPHIC SOURCES

910 Library services for the blind and physically handicapped: a bibliography, 1968–1978. By Jane Pool. Washington, DC: National Library Service for the Blind and Physically Handicapped, Library of Congress, 1979. 73p.

Using citations taken from standard indexes, the compiler has prepared a comprehensive bibliography of publications about library service to the blind and physically handicapped. The time period covered by the citations is ten years, from 1968 to August, 1978.

DIRECTORIES

911 Academic library facilities for the handicapped. By James L. Thomas and Carol H. Thomas. Phoenix: Oryx, 1981. 568p. LC 81–14020. ISBN 0–912700–95–5.

The equipment and facilities available to handicapped users in academic libraries in the United States and its territorial possessions are specified in this directory. The entries are arranged geographically, by state and institution, and indexed by institution. Although not all academic institutions are included, only very small colleges appear to be systematically overlooked. A significant amount of information is provided about each library: physical accessibility, e.g., whether or not there is an entrance at ground level, the space between stacks, and the width of the doors; special equipment availability, e.g., Kurzweil reading machine, large print typewriters, and Braille writers; and special services for handicapped users. This work should help handicapped students to choose the college or university they wish to attend.

912 Library resources for the blind & physically handicapped: a directory of NLS network libraries and machine-lending agencies. Washington, DC: National Library Service for the Blind and Physically Handicapped, Library of Congress, 1982. 110p. LC 76–640140. ISSN 0364–1236.

All regional and sub-regional libraries for the blind and physically handicapped are described in this directory. Entries for the fifty-six regional and 104 sub-regional libraries include the name, address, and telephone number of the library, an in-WATS telephone number, area served, librarian's name, hours of opening, nature of the book collection, special collections, and special services offered by the library. There is also a note indicating whether or not the library has a machine-lending agency. The print is in large type to enable the visually impaired to read it more easily. Appended to the directory is statistical information on the readership, circulation, and budget of the libraries.

913 Library services for the visually and physically handicapped in Australia: a directory. Canberra: National Library of Australia, 1977. 27p. ISBN 0–642–99103–0.

Approximately forty libraries providing service to visually or physically handicapped persons in Australia are identified in this directory. Excluded are university libraries, since blind students attending universities in Australia are largely served by the local state organizations for the blind. Brief information on the specific services offered to the handicapped is presented for each library.

HANDBOOKS AND MANUALS

914 Hospital libraries and work with the disabled in the community. By Mona E. Going. 3d ed. London: Library Assn., 1982. 324p. ISBN 0–85365–723–3.

This work includes chapters that deal with library service to persons with various handicaps. For further information see entry **1041**.

915 Improving library service to physically disabled persons: a self-evaluation check-list. By William L. Needham and Gerald Jahoda. Littleton, CO: Libraries Unlimited, 1983. 135p. LC 82–16200. ISBN 0–87287–348–X.

This work was prepared to provide librarians with a tool to use in evaluating the facilities and services offered by their library to physically disabled users. A substantial part of the book consists of self-evaluation checklists oriented toward specific types of libraries. The check-lists are presented in the form of questions, followed by a paragraph or more outlining a desirable course of action for the library. In addition to the checklists, there are a general introduction to the process of evaluating library service for disabled persons, a list of resources (including organizations) addressing library service to disabled persons and, in several appendices, a sample policy on library service for physically disabled persons, standards and legislation related to library service to this population, references to user studies and community surveys, and a list of regional and subregional libraries for the blind and physically handicapped.

916   Library and information services for handicapped individuals. By Kieth C. Wright. Littleton, CO: Libraries Unlimited, 1979. 196p. LC 78–26472. ISBN 0–87287–129–0.

This manual "is intended to provide an overview of the major handicapping conditions and identify the kinds of library services needed by handicapped individuals." The introductory chapters deal with the types of handicaps and the current legal situation relating to the handicapped. Subsequent chapters discuss individual handicaps and indicate library needs, standards for library service (where they exist), appropriate reading materials, and some practical guidelines for providing service. The handicaps covered are the blind and visually impaired, deaf and hearing impaired, mentally handicapped, aging, and physically handicapped. Special features include a glossary of acronyms, a list of organizations providing services to the handicapped, a bibliography of sources of materials and information, and a subject index.

917   Planning barrier free libraries: a guide for renovation and construction of libraries serving blind and physically handicapped readers. Washington, DC: National Library Service for the Blind and Physically Handicapped, Library of Congress, 1981. 61p. LC 80–607821. ISBN 0–8444–0352–0.

This guide addresses the renovation and construction needed for libraries to be a part of the National Library Service for the Blind and Physically Handicapped network. For further information see entry **794**.

918   Serving physically disabled people: an information handbook for all librarians. By Ruth A Velleman. New York: Bowker, 1979. 392p. LC 79–17082. ISBN 0–8352–1167–3.

This work provides information for libraries seeking to meet the library needs of physically disabled persons. It covers government requirements on physical accomodations and identifies names and addresses of professional and volunteer agencies, government agencies, independent living centers, and centers for special education where physically disabled persons can be served.

Hispanic American Librarians and Librarianship

BIBLIOGRAPHIC SOURCES

919   Library services and materials for Mexican Americans: a selected topics bibliography of ERIC documents. Las Cruces: New Mexico State Univ., 1977. 57p. ED 152 477.

There are ninety-three items on library services to Mexican Americans, published from 1946–1976, cited in this bibliography. Items listed are taken from entries that appeared in *Current index to journals in education* and *Research in education*. Among the subjects covered in the listing are children's literature, reference service, Spanish American literature, and Spanish-language periodicals.

BIOGRAPHICAL SOURCES

920   **Quien es quien: a who's who of spanish-heritage librarians in the United States.**
By Arnulfo D. Trejo and Kathleen L. Lodwick. Tucson: Bureau of School Services,
College of Education, Univ. of Arizona, 1976. 29p. (Graduate Library School mono-
graph, no. 5) LC 77–621461.

Biographical information is provided for 245 "Spanish-heritage librarians in the United
States" and "librarians in Puerto Rico." To be listed, individuals must have completed a
degree in library science. Entries indicate name, education, date of birth, where library
degree was awarded, fluency in Spanish, area of specialization, experience, memberships in
professional organizations, other biographical directories where the individual is included,
publications, honors received, home address, present position, and place of employment.
The work is not comprehensive.

DIRECTORIES

921   **Guide to hispanic bibliographic services in the United States.** By the staff of the
Hispanic Information Management Project and the National Chicano Research Network. Ann Arbor: Survey Research Center, Univ. of Michigan, 1980. 207p.

This directory identifies a total of seventy-six ongoing bibliographic services of various
types serving the Hispanic population in the United States. Many of the listed services are
libraries, but some are resource centers, museums, publishers, and even bibliographic
projects. Entries are arranged alphabetically by name of the organization or project and
contain the following information: name, address, telephone number, institutional affiliation, date founded, hours of opening, name of director, staff size and composition,
organizational characteristics, subject collections, types of materials, bibliographic access,
automated services provided, member networks, library services, publications, and names
of major libraries located in close geographical proximity. Also included is a separate listing
of special collections on Hispanics in the United States.

History of Libraries

For reference materials on history of libraries see entries listed under the
heading Library History.

Hospital Libraries

For reference materials on hospital libraries see entries listed under the heading
Medical, Hospital and Patient Libraries.

Indexing and Abstracting

BIBLIOGRAPHIC SOURCES

922   **Indexing and abstracting: an international bibliography.** By Hans H. Wellisch.
Santa Barbara, CA: ABC-Clio, with the American Society of Indexers, 1980. 308p.
LC 80–11907. ISBN 0–87436–300–4.

This extensive, annotated bibliography on indexing and abstracting contains 2,383 entries.

The coverage extends from 1856 through 1976, and through 1979 for monographs. Prior to 1950, coverage is inclusive; subsequent to 1950, the coverage is more selective. Cited are monographs, articles, and conference papers. The material is arranged in a systematic, taxonomic fashion, providing an insight into the structure of the literature. Topics covered include indexing languages, indexing systems, index production, name indexes, subject indexes, users and use studies, abstracting techniques, and abstracting and indexing services. The work is indexed by author and by subject. Of particular note are the informative, lengthy annotations and the detailed introduction that carefully outlines the scope and coverage of the work. Both are models for similar bibliographic works.

BIOGRAPHICAL SOURCES

923 NFAIS membership directory. Philadelphia: NFAIS, 1981– . Biennial. 71p.
Listed in this directory are forty-three NFAIS-member organizations involved in the production of indexing and abstracting services. Arrangement is alphabetical by name of the organization; entries include address and telephone number, name of contact person, objectives of the organization, principle products and services and, in some cases, the logo of the organization.

DIRECTORIES

924 Education and training in indexing for document and information retrieval. By James D. Anderson. New York: Society of American Indexers, 1981. 147p. LC 82–105275.
Courses, workshops, and seminars offered in the United States and Canada that provide instruction in indexing are listed in this directory. For further information see entry number **972**.

TERMINOLOGY SOURCES

925 A glossary of indexing terms. By Brian Buchanan. Hamden, CT: Shoe String, 1976. 144p. LC 75–20312. ISBN 0–208–01377–6.
The vocabulary of indexing is enumerated and defined in this work, which includes about 400 terms. The glossary was intended to foster uniform use of indexing terminology and thus comprises a basic vocabulary. Proper names are excluded, and therefore specific indexing tools and most specific classification schemes are omitted. Abbreviations are listed at the beginning of the alphabetical sequence for each letter of the alphabet. Each entry includes the term, a basic definition with examples, and when necessary a fuller, more detailed explanation. Cross-references and related terms are used.

Information Analysis Centers

DIRECTORIES

926 Defense Documentation Center referral data bank directory. Alexandria, VA: Defense Documentation Center, 1972– . Annual.
Listed in this directory are approximately 300 institutions willing to provide service to the defense community in specialized areas of interest. These include special libraries, data

banks, laboratories, information analysis centers, and other types of institutions. Entries, arranged alphabetically by institution, specify name of the agency, name, address, and telephone number of key personnel, the agency's mission and responsibilities, subject categories covered, types of materials held, and policies governing public service or public access. Indexing is by subject and personal names.

927 Directory of federally supported information analysis centers. 4th ed. Washington, DC: National Referral Center, Library of Congress, 1979. 87p. LC 74–9567. ISBN 0–8444–0128.
More than 100 federally-supported information analysis centers are identified in this directory. The centers listed fall largely into the sciences and the social sciences. Entries contain name of the center, address, telephone number, name of director, beginning date, size of staff, mission of center, scope of activities, holdings, publications, services offered, and conditions of use. The information is indexed by personal name, location, organizational name, and subject. The first edition of this directory was published in 1968.

Information Brokers

For reference materials on information brokers see entries listed under the heading Fee-Based Information Services.

Information Retrieval

For reference materials on information retrieval see entries listed under the heading Online Information Services.

Insurance for Libraries
HANDBOOKS AND MANUALS

928 Insurance manual for libraries. By Gerald E. Meyers. Chicago: American Library Assn., 1977. 64p. LC 77–24524. ISBN 0–8389–0236–7.
Written for library directors, trustees, and library personnel, this manual deals with the essential elements of a library's insurance needs and is based on the concept of risk management. The components of an appropriate insurance plan are also identified. Information is provided to enable responsible officials to appraise costs and needed coverage for library materials, the physical plant, and personal property. The manual suggests a method of measuring the effectiveness of the insurance program. Appendices contain sample forms that can be used by libraries of various sizes. Completing the work is a brief glossary of insurance terms covered in the text.

Intellectual Freedom
HANDBOOKS AND MANUALS

929 Censorship, libraries, and the law. Comp. by Haig Bosmajian. New York: Neal-Schuman, 1983. 240p. LC 83–2161. ISBN 0–918212–54–5.
This work contains the full text of court opinions in censorship cases involving school

libraries, as well as U.S. Supreme Court decisions cited by the lower courts. An introductory chapter by the compiler discusses the legal history of the banning of such works as *Catch–22* and *Slaughterhouse Five*. The foreword, by Nat Hentoff, deals with the First Amendment right to read and the role of librarians in defending that right.

930 Intellectual freedom manual. Comp. by the Office for Intellectual Freedom, American Library Association. 2d ed. Chicago: American Library Assn., 1983. v.p. ISBN 0–8389–3151–5.

The purpose of this work is to provide librarians with copies of the basic intellectual freedom documents and with practical advice to use when faced with a censorship problem. Among the documents included are the Library Bill of Rights, Statement on Labeling, and Freedom to Read Statement. Separate chapters deal with the types of censorship libraries might face and approaches to use to deal with them. Advice and guidelines are provided for the development of a selection policy as a method of preventing censorship problems before they arise. The second edition contains an added section concerning the organization of statewide support groups, coalitions, lobbying efforts, and options in strategy when conflicts arise at local or state level.

Interlibrary Loan and Photocopying

DIRECTORIES

931 A brief guide to centres of international lending and photocopying. 2d ed. Boston Spa, England: British Lending Library Division, IFLA Office for International Lending, 1979. 161p. LC 81–168803. ISBN 0–85350–172–6.

The purpose of this work is to identify libraries and other organizations providing international interlibrary loan and photocopying. This edition identifies 106 institutions in seventy-four countries. In the introductory material, the principles of international lending are stated, as agreed upon by the International Federation of Library Associations. Entries are arranged by country and contain the library or agency name, address, telex numbers, requirements for international lending, type of forms to be used, restrictions, type of postage preferred, and loan period. The information included here was obtain through a survey of international lending. Because not all nations responded, there are some gaps in the coverage.

932 Directory of interlibrary loan policies and photocopying services in canadian libraries. Comp. by the Committee on the Directory of Interlibrary Loan Policies and Photocopying Services in Canadian Libraries, Information Services Section, Canadian Library Association. Rev. ed. Ottawa: Canadian Library Assn., 1979. 88p. LC 80–467866. ISBN 0–88802–119–4.

Information on the interlibrary loan and photocopying policies of major Canadian libraries is presented here in parallel columns and covers the library symbol, library name, address, telephone number, telex and TWX numbers, loan policies (for monographs, theses, serials, and other formats), loan period, noncirculating items, eligible borrowers, charges, and method of payment. Also detailed are the photocopying policies of the libraries: turnaround time, price per exposure, minimum charge, time required to make microfilm copies, and cost for microfilm copies. Arrangement is by province and then by library. There is no index. The first edition of this directory was published in 1973.

933   **Directory of library reprographic services: a world guide.** Ed. by Joseph Z. Nitecki. 8th ed. Westport, CT: Meckler Publishing, 1982. 540p. ISSN 0160–6077.

Published under the sponsorship of the Reproduction of Library Materials Section of ALA's Resources and Technical Services Division, this work identifies photocopying departments in libraries of the United States and some other nations. In the current edition, 500 departments are covered. The main body consists of a geographical list of libraries, with an indication of the normal waiting time and the costs for various types of materials. There is also a list of libraries with the addresses to be used when placing orders. Appended to the main text is a glossary of terms, advice on requesting photocopy service, a sample request form, and a selected bibliography of materials on photocopying. A supplement, on microfiche, provides additional detailed information about selected libraries. The first edition of this directory was published in 1959.

934   **Interlibrary loan policies directory.** By Sarah Katharine Thomson. Chicago: American Library Assn., 1975. 486p. LC 74–32182. ISBN 0–8389–0197–2.

The interlibrary loan and photocopying policies of 276 major lending libraries in the United States are described in this directory. These include the national libraries; all state library agencies; and public, academic, and various types of special libraries. Entries are arranged by the National Union Catalog library location symbol. The information is detailed and includes the interlibrary loan address, photocopy address, telephone and teletype numbers, minimum charges for paper copy and microfilming, major non-circulating collections, policies on certain types of materials (such as serials and dissertations), and international lending policies. Because of the elapsed time, some of the information in this directory is out of date; thus, verification will be necessary before using the data in the directory.

935   **Symbols of american libraries.** Comp. and ed. by the Catalog Management and Publication Division, Library of Congress. 12th ed. Washington, DC: Library of Congress, 1980. 242p. LC 76–6640246. ISSN 0095–0874.

The identification symbols for libraries in the United States and Canada are listed in this directory. Included are symbols found in the *National union catalog, NUC books* and *NUC U.S. books*, the *NUC register of additional locations, New serial titles, Newspapers in microform*, the *National union catalog, pre–1956 imprints*, and symbols assigned by the National Library of Canada for Canadian libraries. Also listed are symbols assigned to libraries for state and local serials lists and regional union catalogs. The work is divided into two separate alphabetical lists. The first is by symbol and the second by name of the institution. Both lists carry the complete address of each institution. The first edition of the directory was issued in 1932, under the title *Key to symbols used in the Union catalog*. In 1942, the title changed to *Symbols used in the National union catalog of the Library of Congress* and in the late 1960's to the present title.

HANDBOOKS AND MANUALS

936   **AUSLOAN: australian inter-library loans manual.** Sydney: Reference Interest Group, Interloans Working Party and the Library Assn. of Australia, 1982. 53p. ISBN 0–86804–016–9.

Interlibrary loan procedures for Australian libraries are outlined in this manual. Both domestic and international interlibrary loans are covered. Useful as a practical guide to procedures. Also included is the text of the Inter-library Loan Code that was produced by the Australian Advisory Council.

International Exchange of Publications

DIRECTORIES

937 FID directory, 1977/1978– . The Hague: International Federation for Documentation, 1977– . Biennial.

Published until 1977 as the *FID Yearbook*, this biennial provides basic information about the International Federation for Documentation (FID). It identifies the officers, committees and committee members, regional commissions (with dates of establishment), and national and international members. The national members are listed by institutional name, with the address and telephone number of the institution, the name of the director, and a list of the services offered. National members consist of central documentation or library agencies in each country. For the United States, the agency is the U.S. National Committee for FID, which is part of the National Academy of Sciences-National Research Council. For the United Kingdom, the agency is Aslib. An additional list of affiliates, consisting of other organizations or individuals, is also included. A brief section called "Historical Facts" lists such information as names and dates of presidents and dates and locations of conferences and meetings.

938 Handbook on the international exchange of publications. Ed. by Frans Vanwijngaerden. 4th ed. Paris: Unesco, 1978. 165p. (Documentation, libraries and archives; bibliographies and reference works, no. 4) ISBN 92–3–101466–8.

The second part of this work is a directory of all institutions with national responsibility for international exchange. For further information see entry **939**.

HANDBOOKS AND MANUALS

939 Handbook on the international exchange of publications. Ed. by Frans Vanwijngaerden. 4th ed. Paris: Unesco, 1978. 165p. (Documentation, libraries and archives; bibliographies and reference works, no. 4) ISBN 92–3–101466–8.

Intended to facilitate the international exchange of publications among libraries and other institutions, this source reflects international agreements on these exchanges and provides lists of agencies that have national responsibility for international exchange. The fourth edition is divided into two parts. Part 1 describes the organization and management of international publication exchange. It includes a history of recent developments as well as the earlier agreements and protocols that led to international standardization of the exchange process. Part 2 is a directory of all institutions with national responsibility for international exchange. Entries specify name, address, and the activities and services of each institution listed. Previous editions appeared in 1950, 1956, and 1964.

Jail and Prison Library Service

HANDBOOKS AND MANUALS

940 Jail library service: a guide for librarians and jail administrators. By Linda L.

Bayley, Leni Greenfield and Flynn Nogueira. Chicago: American Library Assn., 1981. 114p. LC 81–2023. ISBN 0–8389–3258–4.

This manual is aimed at employees who provide library service in penal institutions. The authors identify some of the problems likely to be associated with work in this setting, including lack of administrative cooperation, limited resources, and need for security. Practical advice is offered to assist librarians with these problems.

941 Manual for prison law libraries. By O. James Werner. South Hackensack, NJ: Rothman, 1976. 120p. (American Association of Law Libraries publication series, no. 12) LC 75–37331. ISBN 0–8377–0110–4.

Practical information on the operation of a prison law library is provided in this manual. For further information see entry **962**.

Jewish Archives and Libraries
DIRECTORIES

942 Directory of jewish archival institutions. Ed. by Philip P. Mason. Detroit: Wayne State Univ. Pr., 1975. 76p. LC 75–15504.

This directory is published for the National Foundation for Jewish Culture. The holdings of major Jewish archival collections in the United States and abroad are described. Among those listed are the American Jewish Archives, Library of the Jewish Theological Seminary of America, and Hebrew Union College-Jewish Institute of Religion Manuscript Library. Entries indicate address and telephone number of each institution, holdings of the collections, and holdings lists issued by the libraries and archives. Subject and collection name indexes are provided.

943 Guide to Jewish archives. Ed. by Aryeh Segall. Prelim. ed. Jerusalem: World Council on Jewish Archives; New York: National Foundation for Jewish Culture, distr., 1981. 90p.

International in scope, this work lists archives, libraries, and other institutions that have significant holdings of materials on the Jewish people. The countries or regions represented are the United States, Canada, Australia, Israel, Great Britain, and the major European nations. Arrangement is first by country and then alphabetically by name of institution. Entries specify name, location, name of the director, form of governance, history and scope of the collection, and size of collection.

944 Guide to the jewish libraries of the world. Ed. by J. Fraenkel. London: World Jewish Congress, 1959. 64p. LC 63–2058.

In this international directory, approximately 200 libraries with extensive Jewish collections are listed and described. Both Jewish and non-Jewish libraries are included. Arrangement is geographical by country and then by city or town. Entries provide name and address; name of librarian; size of staff; number of volumes, manuscripts, and periodicals; subjects covered; number of volumes in Yiddish; and types of catalogs. Although information in the directory is quite dated, it still can be used to identify libraries with historically strong Jewish collections.

Journals in Library and Information Science
DIRECTORIES

945 Author's guide to journals in library and information science. Ed. by Norman D. Stevens and Nora B. Stevens. New York: Haworth, 1980. 183p. (Author's guide to journals series) LC 80–20964. ISBN 0–917724–13–5.

The purpose of this work is to identify and describe potential sources for journal publication in the fields of library and information science. Approximately 200 journals are listed, together with information about the characteristics of the journals, their policies, subject emphases, and percentage of unsolicited manuscripts published. Stevens' introduction provides prospective authors with guidelines for submitting papers for publication. A glossary of terms is also included and indexing is by subject.

946 The directory of library periodicals. Comp. by Mary Adele Springman and Betty Martin Brown. Philadelphia: Graduate School of Library Science, Drexel Inst. of Technology, 1967. 192p. (Drexel Library School series, no. 23) LC 67–24822.

Approximately 800 library periodicals are listed in this 1967 directory (150 more than included in the 1957 edition). The scope is limited to the United States. While newsletters and publications issued by individual libraries are covered, annual reports and book lists are not. Arrangement is alphabetical by sponsoring institution and then by title. Entries specify name of sponsoring institution, title of publication, editor, address of editor, frequency, subscription rate, and first published dated. There is a title index. Although dated, this directory is still useful; it can identify numerous periodicals not currently listed elsewhere, many of which are no longer published.

947 Library and library related publications: a directory of publishing opportunities in journals, serials, and annuals. By Peter Hernon, Maureen Pastine and Sara Lou Williams. Littleton, CO: Libraries Unlimited, 1973. 216p. LC 73–84183. ISBN 0–87287–068–5.

Major library and information science journals, irregular serials, annuals, and monograph series offering potential publishing opportunities are listed in this 1973 directory. The publication is divided into three major parts: library periodicals; annuals, irregular series, monographic series; and library-related periodicals. Within each section, the entries are listed by title and contain information on the type of articles accepted, style requirements, approximate length of acceptable manuscript, length of time required for evaluation, royalties, characteristics of a typical contribution, and editorial orientation. Also included are the address, subscription rate, circulation, frequency of publication, and name of the editor. The information is indexed by subject and title.

948 Library, documentation and archives serials. Comp. by Grazyna Janzing. Ed. by K. R. Brown. 4th ed. The Hague: International Federation for Documentation, 1975. 203p. LC 77–372703. ISBN 92–66–00532–0.

Nearly 1,000 serials in librarianship, information science, documentation, and archives are listed in this international directory. Also included are journals from such fields as automation, reprography, and micrographics, when they clearly relate to the other targeted fields.

This is the most extensive listing of periodicals in these fields currently available. All serial titles listed are in the roman alphabet, and some have English translations of the titles. Entries are arranged first by country, then alphabetical by title. Serials published by international organizations are listed separately, prior to the country listings. Similarly, abstracting, indexing, and current awareness services are found in a separate section. Entries vary in length, but typically include title, acronym, sub-title, translated title in parenthesis for transliterated titles, a note on former titles and dates, sponsoring body or publisher, address, and subscription address when different than publisher's address. The directory also indicates the date the title was first published, frequency, subscription prices, and sources that index the title. Concluding the volume are a separate list of titles that have ceased publication and an index by title.

949 **Library periodicals directory: a selected list of periodicals currently published throughout the world relating to library work.** Comp. by Paul A. Winckler. Brookville, NY: Graduate Library School, Long Island Univ., 1967. 76p. LC 67–7215.

Although dated, this directory of periodicals can be used for information on journals no longer published and, hence, no longer listed in current sources. Over 300 journals published throughout the world prior to 1967 are listed. Arrangement is by broad subject categories and then by title of the journal. Entries vary in length, with some providing little more than the title, date, frequency, place, and publisher. Others include a brief annotation describing the journal and sources where it is indexed. The directory itself has a title index.

950 **A selected list of newsletters in the field of librarianship and information science.** Comp. by J. R. Sharp. Ed. by M. Mann. Boston Spa, England: British Library Lending Division, 1981. 53p. (The British Library research and development reports, no. 5630) LC 81–180960. ISBN 0–905984–72–2.

This publication identifies 117 English-language "newsletters" from throughout the world that deal with librarianship and information science. The list is not comprehensive. Certain types of newsletters are excluded, for example, specialized newsletters issued by divisions of national library associations and those covering geographical areas of less than national scale. Entries contain title, publisher and address, ISSN, volume and date of first issue, volume and date of last issue in 1979, subscription rate, frequency, whether or not it carries advertising, and format. There is also a note on the nature of the contents. The directory identifies many titles not covered in the other lists of library and information science periodicals.

HANDBOOKS AND MANUALS

951 **Subjects of articles sought by editors of library and information science periodicals.** Comp. and ed. by Kenneth I. Taylor. Villanova, PA: Graduate Dept. of Library Science, Villanova Univ., 1978. 122p.

The intent of this publication is to identify the subject interests of 102 state, regional, national, and international journals in library and information science. The information reported is based on the results of a survey of the library press and reflects responses from the editors of the journals. The work is divided into three parts: Part I provides a frequency count of the subjects selected by the responding editors; Part II lists 143 subjects suggested by

---

librarians, library educators and others, and the periodicals interested in the subjects; Part III profiles each of the journals, indicating subjects desired, publishing objectives, whether or not unsolicited manuscripts are welcome, and name and address of the editor.

Latin American Studies Libraries

DIRECTORIES

952 Directory of libraries and special collections on Latin America and the West Indies. By Bernard Naylor, Laurence Hallewell and Colin Steele. London: Athlone Pr., 1975. 161p. (University of London Institute of Latin American Studies monographs, no. 5). LC 75–325909. ISBN 0–485–17705–6.

A total of 146 libraries in the United Kingdom that have major holdings of materials on Latin America and the West Indies are described in this directory, published for the Institute of Latin American Studies. Arrangement is alphabetical by the city in which the library is located, and then by name of library. Entries include name, address, telephone and telex numbers, subject emphasis of holdings, size of collection, hours of opening, policies concerning use, and policies concerning loans. A useful appendix contains the names of other organizations concerned with Latin America. An integrated index covers subject, location, named collections, acronym, and name of institution.

953 A guide to manuscript sources for the history of Latin America and the Caribbean in the British Isles. Ed. by P. Walne. London: Oxford Univ. Pr., with the Inst. of Latin American Studies, Univ. of London, 1973. 580p. LC 73–165634.

Identified in the directory are major manuscript sources for this area of the world, with an inventory of manuscripts found in each collection. Arrangement is by geographical area. England constitutes one major category (arranged by county, with a separate section for London); Wales, Northern Ireland, and the Republic of Ireland the other categories. Entries describe the holdings of each manuscript collection. The information is indexed by subject.

954 Scholars' guide to Washington, D.C. for latin american and caribbean studies. By Michael Grow and the Latin American Program of the Woodrow Wilson International Center for Scholars. Washington, DC: Smithsonian Inst. Pr., 1979. 346p. LC 78–21316.

This directory provides extensive coverage of the intellectual resources on Latin America and the Caribbean available in the Washington, D.C. area. It is divided into two parts, the first of which is a directory of resource collections. The second part identifies public and private organizations that can serve as potential sources of information or provide assistance to researchers. The directory of resource collections includes libraries, archives, museums, music collections, map collections, film collections, and data banks. The directory of organizations covers associations, cultural exchange and technical assistance organizations, U.S. government agencies, Latin American and Caribbean embassies, international organizations, research centers and information offices, and academic programs. Entries vary in length and coverage, but for the most part provide detailed information about each collection or organization: name, address, telephone number, hours of opening, areas of strength, and policies regarding public access and services. Sufficient detail is supplied to enable serious researchers to obtain a clear notion of the resources and facilities available. Appendices cover local periodical publications and other media and local bookstores. Indexes provide access by institutional or organizational name, personal papers, library subject strengths, and general subjects.

Law Libraries

BIBLIOGRAPHIC SOURCES

955 Law firm libraries, a selective, annotated bibliography, 1959–1978. By Carol W. Christensen. Austin: Tarlton Law Library, Univ. of Texas School of Law, 1978. 40p. (Tarlton Law Library legal bibliography series, no. 17) LC 80–621541.

The journal articles and monographs cited here provide guidance for the establishment and operation of law libraries in law firms. Arrangement is alphabetical by main entry. Topics covered include: planning a library; insurance; acquisitions, cataloging, and circulation; and treatment of such materials as pamphlets, forms, microforms, and photocopies. Annotations are brief.

BIOGRAPHICAL SOURCES

956 Biographical directory of law librarians in the United States and Canada. Saint Paul: West Pub., 1964– . Irreg. LC 64–5056.

Published for the American Association of Law Librarians by West Publishing Company, this work provides brief biographical sketches of law librarians currently active in American and Canadian libraries. Included are law librarians from law school libraries, private law firm libraries, and government agencies. Biographical information identifies position, place of employment, and previous positions held.

DIRECTORIES

957 Directory: International Association of Law Libraries. Marburg, Germany: International Assn. of Law Libraries, 1974– . Irreg. LC 75–645282. ISSN 0376–8430.

In this country-by-country list, over 600 member libraries from sixty-two countries are identified. Only brief directory information is provided: name and address of the library and name of the librarian. Access is through a unified index of personal members, institutional members, and institutional representation.

958 Directory of law libraries. New York: Commerce Clearing House, 1964– . Biennial. LC 76–647024.

The major domestic directory of law libraries, this work was issued until 1964 under the title *Law libraries in the United States and Canada* (entry **961**). It focuses on American and Canadian law libraries, but also includes a few libraries from other parts of the world if they meet criteria for AALL membership as noted below. U.S. and Canadian coverage includes institutional members of the American Association of Law Libraries (AALL), law libraries where one or more employees is a member of the AALL, and unaffiliated law libraries with collections of 10,000 volumes or more. Arrangement is by geographical location and entries contain the name of the library, address, name of librarian, size of collection, and phone number. Indexing is by personal name. Also included are a list of AALL chapter officers and the text of the association's constitution and bylaws.

959 Directory of law libraries in Australia and Papua New Guinea. Sydney: Butterworth, 1979. 73p. LC 80–470400.
In this directory, seventy-five law libraries in Australia and Papua New Guinea are listed by political jurisdiction and then by name of library. Larger political jurisdictions are subdivided by city. Entries contain name, address, telephone and telex number, staff size, policies regarding use, loan policy, interlibrary loan policy, photocopying, hours of opening, system of classification used, and type of catalog (e.g., dictionary, divided).

960 Directory of law libraries in the British Isles. Ed. by Barbara Mangles. London: British and Irish Assn. of Law Librarians, 1976. 150p. LC 77–357536.
A total of 370 law libraries in the British Isles are listed in this directory. Arrangement is by geographic location. Entries contain name, address, telephone and telex numbers, hours of opening, types of loans, size of collection, type of facilities, services available, collection strengths, and policies regarding use of the collection. Indexing is by name of library.

961 Law libraries in the United States and Canada. New York: Commerce Clearing House, 19??–1963. Biennial.
This title is continued by *Directory of law libraries.* For further information see entry **958**.

HANDBOOKS AND MANUALS

962 Manual for prison law libraries. By O. James Werner. South Hackensack, NJ: Rothman, 1976. 120p. (American Association of Law Libraries publication series, no. 12) LC 75–37331. ISBN 0–8377–0110–4.
Practical information on the operation of a prison law library is provided in this manual. The text is directed largely toward individuals with little or no background in law or librarianship. The basic elements of library service are covered, including staffing, facilities, equipment, and the acquisition, cataloging, and use of legal materials. Additional information leading to further assistance, either through consultants or other resources, is provided. Appended to the main body of the work is a bibliography of recommended books, a list of major publishers of legal materials, a directory of library supply houses, and the text of the *Gilmore vs. Lynch* case.

Legislation

For reference materials on legislation see entries listed under the heading Library Legislation.

Library Education
BIBLIOGRAPHIC SOURCES

963 Audiovisual materials in support of information science curricula: an annotated list with subject index. By Irving M. Klempner. 2d ed., rev. and exp. Syracuse, NY: ERIC-IR, 1977. 76p. ED 148 365.
This is an annotated bibliography of 451 audiovisual sources that can be used in the teaching of information science or information retrieval courses. The items cover a wide range of topics relating to different aspects of information science, such as logic, linguistics,

psychology, and technology. Included are films, filmstrips, slides, and videotapes. Annotations are descriptive and indicate where the sources can be obtained. There is a list of names and addresses of audiovisual producers that also identifies locations for obtaining items. A detailed subject index provides the user with access to the list. The first edition was issued under the same title in 1971.

964 **International guide to films on information sources.** 3d ed. The Hague: International Federation for Documentation, 1979. 36p. (FID Publication, no. 577) LC 81–107256. ISBN 92–66–00577–0.

Over 100 films, filmstrips, and slide/tape presentations that cover library and information resources in nine languages are identified in this brief bibliography. The listing only covers items produced after 1970 and does not cite titles noted in previous editions. Subject coverage includes automation, cataloging and classification, and use of information sources. Each entry supplies title of the item, date, country of origin, distributor, length of film or number of frames in filmstrips, and a brief annotation. A language/title index indicates items available in each language. There is also a general subject index. Previous editions were published in 1971 and 1973.

965 **A working bibliography of commercially available audiovisual materials for the teaching of library science.** By Irving Lieberman with Corinne McMullan and Bruce McMullan. 2d ed., rev. and exp. Syracuse, NY: ERIC-IR, 1979. 115p. LC 81–181107.

The citations included in this bibliography cover topics spanning the range of the library education curriculum. A variety of audiovisual formats are represented: films, filmstrips, slides, audio and video tapes, overhead transparencies, and charts. The materials are divided into seven broad categories, including reference, selection of materials, and automation of library processes. Entries contain bibliographical information and descriptive annotations. The work concludes with a title index and an alphabetical list of producers and distributors represented in the bibliography. The first edition of this bibliography was issued in 1970.

BIOGRAPHICAL SOURCES

966 **A directory of library schools and lecturers in librarianship in Australia, 1978.** Comp. by Edward R. Reid-Smith. Wagga Wagga, N.S.W.: Dept. of Library and Information Science, Riverina College of Advanced Education, 1978. 216p.

In addition to information about courses of study offered in Australian library schools, included here is biographical information about ninety-one library school faculty members who were teaching in Australian library education programs at the time the directory was compiled. For further information see entry **970**.

967 **Directory of UK library school teachers.** Rev. and ed. by John J. Eyre and the Association of British Library Schools. 3d ed. London: Clive Bingley, 1972. 79p. LC 73–162876. ISBN 0–85157–145–X.

This work consists of three parts, the first of which presents a list of sixteen library education programs in the United Kingdom, with names of faculty members, and the name, address, and telephone number of each school. The second part contains an alphabetical directory of faculty members, with brief biographical information provided, mostly pertaining to their teaching, research interests, and publications. The third part of the directory is a list of subjects followed by the names of faculty members who teach in those subject areas. Although much out of date, this source can still be used for its descriptions of the schools and individual faculty members.

968 **Journal of education for librarianship: directory issue.** State College, PA: Assn. of Library and Information Science Educators, 1960– . Annual. LC 63–24347. ISSN 0022–0604.

The member and associate member institutions of the Association of Library and Information Science Educators are listed in this annual directory. An alphabetical list of all faculty members is included at the back, with an asterisk by the names of those persons who are members of ALISE. Members of ALISE who are not affiliated with one of the member schools are also listed. For further information see entry **974**.

DIRECTORIES

969 **A directory of libraries and library training programmes in Thailand.** 3d ed. Bangkok: Unesco Regional Office for Education in Asia, 1974. 150p. LC 81–928575.

The current volume, arranged alphabetically by name of library, includes approximately 100 libraries of various types in Thailand. For further information see entry **328**.

970 **A directory of library schools and lecturers in librarianship in Australia, 1978.** Comp. by Edward R. Reid-Smith. Wagga Wagga, N.S.W.: Dept. of Library and Information Science, Riverina College of Advanced Education, 1978. 216p.

Information about forty-five courses of study at twenty-five library schools in Australia is presented in this directory. Also included is biographical information about ninety-one library school faculty members who were teaching in Australian library education programs at the time the directory was compiled. An earlier edition of this work was published in 1976 and included biographical information on forty faculty members.

971 **Directory of library science collections, 1977.** Comp. by Carol S. Nielsen. 2d ed. Chicago: Library Education Division, American Library Assn., 1977. 90p.

Information about the library science collections at forty-six schools accredited by the American Library Association and seventeen others which are not accredited is presented in this 1977 directory. Both American and Canadian schools are included. Arrangement is alphabetical by name of school, with separate listings for accredited and non-accredited schools. Each entry indicates the name of the school, address, telephone number, name of the librarian, types of degrees granted, budget for library science materials, number of volumes, number of periodical titles and other materials, special collections, interlibrary loan policy, photocopying policy, publications, and thesis requirements. Several tables at the end provide additional information about each school, such as seating capacity, access to computer terminals, and type of classification system used. The first edition of this directory was issued in 1975 under the title *Directory of library science libraries.*

**972	Education and training in indexing for document and information retrieval.** By James D. Anderson. New York: Society of American Indexers, 1981. 147p. LC 82–105275.
Courses, workshops and seminars offered in the United States and Canada that provide instruction in indexing are listed in this directory. Entries specify name of sponsor, address, contact person, instructors, course description, length of course, prerequisites, admission requirements, fees or tuition, frequency, topics covered, and titles of textbooks required. Also included in the volume are a classification of indexing concepts and procedures and a bibliography of textbooks used in indexing courses.

**973	Guía de escuelas y cursos en bibliotecología y documentación en America Latina.** 2d ed. Buenos Aires: Inst. Bibliotecologico, Univ. de Buenos Aires, 1979. 145p. LC 73–337332.
This directory identifies educational and training programs for librarians and information specialists throughout Latin America. More than fifty institutions are listed. Arrangement is by country and, for larger countries, by province. Entries describe specific courses available, admission requirements, size of school, academic resources, and the curriculum. An earlier version of this title was issued in 1973.

**974	Journal of education for librarianship: directory issue.** State College, PA: Assn. of Library and Information Science Educators, 1960– . Annual. LC 63–24347. ISSN 0022–0604.
The member and associate member institutions of the Association of Library and Information Science Educators (ALISE) are listed in this annual directory. The institutional membership includes all of the graduate programs accredited by the American Library Association and all of the graduate programs that are associate members. The institutional membership varies from year to year but, with the two categories combined, it is approximately 100. Arrangement is alphabetical by name of school, with a separate listing for member and associate member schools. Entries for each school provide the school's name, address, telephone number, name of the dean or director, and a list of all full-time, part-time, and summer school faculty members who taught during the year. Symbols by the names of each member of the faculty indicate up to five areas of specialization in their teaching. An alphabetical list of all faculty members is included at the back, with an asterisk by the names of those persons who are members of ALISE. Members of ALISE who are not affiliated with one of the listed schools are also listed.

**975	North american library education: directory and statistics, 1971–1973.** Ed. by D. Kathryn Weintraub and Sarah R. Reed. Bloomington: Graduate Library School, Indiana Univ., 1974. 123p. LC 68–8967.
This directory was issued as a report to the U.S. Office of Education under contract No. OE 0–73–5151 from 1963 until 1974. During this period, the title and publisher of the directory varied. The directory includes the names and addresses of all undergraduate and graduate library education programs in North America that have degree or diploma offerings or undergraduate minors. In addition, aggregate statistical information is presented, covering such topics as sources and amounts of funding, enrollments, degrees awarded, and placements. The directory information that identifies graduate and undergraduate programs now is covered in the *American library directory* (see entry **425**).

976 Répertoire des écoles des sciences de l'information. By Marcel Lajeunesse. Montreal: Assn. Internationale des Ecoles des Sciences de l'Information (AIESI), 1979. 134p. LC 80–365797.

In this directory, library and information science education programs in French-speaking countries (Algeria, Belgium, France, Morocco, Quebec/Canada, Senegal, Switzerland, and Tunisia) are described. Entries for each program contain the name, address, date founded, name of organization with which it is affiliated, director's name, names of teaching staff, student enrollment, type of training offered, diploma awarded, admission requirements, and length of program. In addition, the directory provides a comparative study of the training programs offered in the several countries. The organization responsible for the compilation and publication of the directory was founded in 1977 by deans and directors of some of the programs listed.

977 World guide to library schools and training courses in documentation/Guide mondial des écoles de bibliothécaires et documentalistes. 2d ed. Paris: Unesco; London: Clive Bingley, 1981. 549p. LC 81–165089. ISBN 0–85157–309–6.

Described in this directory are education programs in librarianship and documentation offered in eighty-seven countries. The languages of the directory are English and French. The introductory information appears in both. However, entries for specific schools appear only in one or the other. Arrangement is by country, with separate entries for each school within a country. Entries provide name, address, parent institution, date founded, main fields of study in the program, teaching levels and levels at which diplomas are awarded, admission requirements, length of program, course offerings, and some other general comments about the program. Coverage for the United States and Canada includes only graduate level programs, and each entry indicates whether or not the school has accreditation from the American Library Association and is a member institution of the Association of Library and Information Science Educators. An earlier edition of this directory was published in 1972 and described library education programs in twenty-six fewer countries than the current edition.

STATISTICAL SOURCES

978 Association of Library and Information Science Educators library education statistical report. State College, PA: Assn. of Library and Information Science Educators, 1980– . Annual. LC 82–21092.

This is the most extensive compilation of statistical information on North American library education available. At present, it covers a three-year period of time. However, some of the data reported extend back as far as seven years. The data are compiled by a committee of the Association of Library and Information Science Educators. Statistical information is collected in the fall term of the year prior to the publication date. Some of the data reported cover the year prior to collection date, and some cover the academic year in which the data are reported. The document is divided into five broad categories: faculty, students, curriculum, income and expenditures, and continuing education. Data are reported in detail for each of these area and cover such topics as faculty salaries, enrollment, placements, income from federal and other outside sources, and number of continuing education programs sponsored. Tables are not indexed; however, there is a table of contents which lists all tables included.

979 North american library education: directory and statistics, 1971–1973. Ed. by D. Kathryn Weintraub and Sarah R. Reed. Bloomington: Graduate Library School, Indiana Univ., 1974. 123p. LC 68–8967.

In addition to names and addresses of undergraduate and graduate library education programs in North America, aggregate statistical information is presented, covering such topics as sources and amounts of funding, enrollments, degrees awarded, and placements. For further information see entry **975**.

Library Evaluation, Measurement and Research

BIBLIOGRAPHIC SOURCES

980 Directory of library research and demonstration projects: 1966–1975. Prelim. ed. Washington, DC: U.S. Office of Education, 1978. 117p. LC 79–601743.

All library research and demonstration projects funded by the U.S. Office of Education from 1966 to 1975 are listed in this bibliography. Areas covered include library cooperation, library education and training, service to special target populations, and use of new technology. Each project is described briefly in a resume or abstract. Index access is available by subject, name of institution, name of principal investigator, and grant/contract number. Four appendices provide summary statistical information about the programs.

981 LIST: library and information services today: an international registry of research and innovation. Ed. by Paul Wasserman. Detroit: Gale, 1971–1975. Annual. LC 71–143963. ISSN 0075–9821.

This work (no longer published) identifies research projects in progress between 1971 and 1975 in various fields of library and information science throughout the world. For further information see entry **76**.

982 Performance measures and criteria for libraries: a survey and bibliography. Comp. by Pamela Noble and P. L. Ward. Brighton, England: Public Libraries Research Group, 1976. 94p. (PLRG occasional paper, no. 3) LC 77–374476. ISBN 0–9503801–2–1.

All aspects of library performance measurement are covered in this bibliography except mechanized retrieval systems, library automation, operations research, and cost studies. Lengthy descriptive comments about the measures are included.

983 R & D projects in documentation and librarianship. The Hague: International Federation for Documentation (FID), 1971– . Quarterly. ISSN 0301–4436.

This serial identifies and provides brief accounts of work in progress internationally in various facets of librarianship, information science, and documentation. For further information see entry **31**.

984 Radials bulletin. London: Library Assn., 1974– . 2 per year. LC 77–648394. ISSN 0302–2706.

This serial identifies research projects (approximately 500 per year) in librarianship, information science, and documentation initiated in the United Kingdom. For further information see entry **40**.

985 Research methods in library science: a bibliographic guide with topical outlines. By Bohdan S. Wynar. Littleton, CO: Libraries Unlimited, 1971. 153p. LC 79–168376. ISBN 0–87287–018–9.

This bibliography of works about library research and research applications is current only through the early 1970's. After a review of the research process in general, a total of 782 items are cited (some with brief descriptive annotations) in seven chapters, covering historical research, statistical applications, experimental research, surveys and case studies, content analysis, studies in reading, and studies in management theory. The chapters are subdivided into categories dealing with methodology and applications.

HANDBOOKS AND MANUALS

986 A data gathering and instructional manual for performance measures in public libraries. By Ellen Altman, et al. Chicago: Celadon, 1976. 171p.

Basic instructions in gathering and analyzing data for performance measures in public libraries are provided in this manual. Some of the measures could also be adapted for use in other types of libraries. The data gathering techniques covered by the authors are directed toward specific measures of performance: materials availability, library use, availability and patterns of information, and use of materials, equipment and facilities. A separate chapter deals with analyzing the data. The authors employ a step-by-step approach to describe the data collection process. Brief introductory sections review the value and purpose served by gathering the data. Sample forms are provided as models for gathering.

987 Evaluation techniques for school library media programs: a workshop outline. By Blanche Woolls, David Loertscher and Donald Shirey. Pittsburgh: Graduate School of Library and Information Sciences, Univ. of Pittsburgh, 1977. 85p.

Although this manual covering the evaluation of school library/media programs was designed to be used in a workshop setting, it can also be used independently. The authors provide an evaluation of existing instruments of measurement and evaluation; consideration of other measures of quality, such as interviews, observation, and best professional judgment; and a brief introduction to applicable methods of statistical analysis. Appendices include sample evaluation forms, a sample evaluation program, and a selected bibliography.

988 The measurement and evaluation of library services. By F. W. Lancaster. Washington, DC: Information Resources Pr., 1977. 395p. LC 77–72081. ISBN 0–87315–017–X.

Although written originally as a textbook, Lancaster's work serves equally well as a state-of-the-art handbook on the evaluation and measurement of various facets of library service. Separate chapters deal with catalog use, reference service, collection evaluation, evaluation of document delivery capabilities, library surveys, and automated systems. The text is presented in narrative form, supplemented by numerous examples of measurement techniques and research results. Following each chapter is a basic list of references on the topic covered in the chapter.

989 Measuring the quality of library service: a handbook. By M. G. Fancher Beeler, et al. Metuchen, NJ: Scarecrow, 1974. 208p. LC 74–12107. ISBN 0–8108–0832–7. Intended to instruct librarians in the measurement of library service, this handbook is divided into three parts. Part I identifies specific techniques of measurement and provides a citation to and description of works describing the techniques. Examples of questionnaires and other measurement instruments are included. In some instances, forms are reproduced to illustrate the characteristics of measurement instruments. Part II provides recommendations for action based on some of the measurement examples reported in Part I. Part III contains an annotated bibliography of background materials relevant to the topic, current to the early 1970's. A subject index completes the volume.

990 Output measures for public libraries. By Douglas Zweizig and Eleanor Jo Rodger. Chicago: American Library Assn., 1982. 100p. LC 82–1720. ISBN 0–8389–3272–X.
This manual was developed by the Goals, Guidelines and Standards Committee of the ALA Public Library Association to assist librarians in collecting data that describe library services to the community (output measures). The output measures covered include: circulation per capita, in-library materials use per capita, library visits per capita, program attendance per capita, reference transactions per capita, reference fill rate, title fill rate, subject and author fill rate, browsers' fill rate, registration as a percentage of population, turnover rate, and document delivery. For each of the output measures, the authors review the purpose of the measure and the procedures to obtain and analyze the data.

991 A systematic process for planning media programs. By James Liesner. Chicago: American Library Assn., 1976. 166p. LC 76–3507. ISBN 0–8389–0176–X.
In this manual for planning school library/media programs, an important evaluation component is included. The process consists of nine steps, based on the principles of PPBS. Among the procedures required are a survey of client perceptions of current service, a review of resource requirements for specific levels of service, and periodic evaluation of the achievements, direction, and needs of users. These procedures are described in detail, and appendices provide sample planning instruments.

YEARBOOKS

992 Library and research yearbook/Bibliotek og forskning aarbok. Oslo: Norske Forskningbibliotekarers Forening and the Norsk Bibliotekarlag, 1954–1974. LC 55–32676. ISSN 0405–993X.
This yearbook reports on library activities and library research in Scandanavian countries. For further information see entry **226**.

Library History
BIBLIOGRAPHIC SOURCES

993 ABHA: annual bibliography of the history of the printed book and libraries. Ed. by Hendrik D. L. Vervliet. The Hague: Martinus Nijhoff, 1970– . Annual. LC 74–641084. ISSN 0303–5964.
This international bibliography lists monographs, journal articles, exhibition catalogs,

dissertations, and auction and booksellers catalogs dealing with various aspects of books and libraries with emphasis on the history of the printed book, libraries and publications that characterize library collections. For further information see entry **65**.

994 American library history: a bibliography. By Michael H. Harris and Donald G. Davis, Jr. Austin: Univ. of Texas Pr., 1978. 260p. LC 77–25499. ISBN 0–292–70332–5.

In this extensive bibliography of writings on American library history, from earliest times through 1976, a total of 3,260 entries are included. Although not exhaustive, the bibliography is intended by the compilers to be as comprehensive as possible. The items included are those that were consciously written as library history. Arrangement is by broad topic, such as "Predecessors of the Public Library," or "Education for Librarianship." Each broad topic constitutes a separate chapter, and it is preceded by a bibliographic essay that provides the compilers' perspective on the literature of the topic. The entries are not annotated, but provide full bibliographic information. However, frequently used journal titles are abbreviated. A list of abbreviations is found in the front of the volume. There are author and subject indexes.

995 British library history: bibliography 1973–1976. Ed. by Denis F. Keeling. London: Library Assn., 1979. 200p.

This extensive bibliographic effort is an ongoing project of a committee of the Library History Group. The volume noted above is preceded by *British library history: bibliography 1969–1972* (entry **996**) and by *British library history: bibliography 1962–1968* (entry **997**). It includes not only those works written as library history, but also other historical materials that refer to libraries. Numbering is sequential in the volumes, and to date there is a total of 2,335 citations. Entries are annotated and are arranged by broad topic, with numerous cross references. Indexing is by author and subject.

996 British library history: bibliography 1969–1972. Ed. by Denis F. Keeling. London: Library Assn., 1975. 150p. NUC 80–221630. ISBN 0–85365–417–4.

This volume is continued by *British library history: bibliography 1973–1976*. For further information see entry **995**.

997 British library history: bibliography 1962–1968. Comp. by a Committee of the Library History Group. Ed. by Denis F. Keeling. London: Library Assn., 1972. 164p. LC 73–155203. ISBN 0–85365–345–3.

This volume is continued by *British library history: bibliography 1969–1972* and *British library history: bibliography 1973–1976*. For further information see entry **995**.

998 A guide to research in American library history. By Michael H. Harris. 2d ed. Metuchen, NJ: Scarecrow, 1974. 274p. LC 74–17113. ISBN 0–8108–07744–0.

The main body of this work consists of an annotated bibliography of American library history sources. It is divided into twelve sections, each topical in nature and covering works under such topics as "The Public Library," "Types of Library Service," and "Biographies of Librarians and Library Benefactors." The first section of the guide is comprised of three parts; each deals with a different aspect of library history. The first is an essay on the state of the art of library history; the second, an essay on the philosophy and methods of research in library history; and the third, a brief, annotated bibliography of the primary resources used in the study of library history. Author and subject indexes are provided.

HANDBOOKS AND MANUALS

999   American library development, 1600–1899. By Elizabeth W. Stone. New York: Wilson, 1977. 367p. LC 77–7881. ISBN 0–8242–0418–2.

A chronology of more than 1,300 events in the development of American libraries and librarianship is presented in this publication. The work begins with a fifty-three page chronological chart identifying events in library history in eight parallel columns. The categories represented by the columns are private, special, and government libraries; technical services; legislation; publications; professional activities; buildings; and miscellaneous. Following the chronological chart, each of the items identified in the chart is explained in one or two paragraphs. The arrangement for this explanatory section is also divided into the eight sections. The information in both sections is indexed by author, title, and subject. When appropriate, the source of the information is cited, and a full bibliographic citation is found in the bibliography at the conclusion. About 1,000 titles are listed in the bibliography.

1000   A chronology of librarianship. By Josephine Metcalfe Smith. Metuchen, NJ: Scarecrow, 1968. 263p. LC 67–12062.

Arranged by date, beginning with the 1st century A.D., this work provides brief descriptions of approximately 2,400 historical events in the history of libraries, librarianship, book production, and other related topics. The majority of the entries are from the 19th and 20th centuries, and particular emphasis is placed on librarianship in the United States. The last date recorded is in 1959. Entries follow a standard pattern, with the date listed first and then a brief description of the event. Many entries carry a brief citation to sources that are identified in a lengthy bibliography at the end of the work. The text is indexed by subject, persons, institutions, and titles.

1001   Indian library chronology. By P. S. G. Kuman. New Delhi: Metropolitan, 1977. 692p. LC 77–904708.

About 10,000 events in Indian library history and related fields (e.g., history of the book) are chronicled in this work. The time period covered extends from 3,000 B.C. to 1975. Entries indicate the year, and each item is numbered for each year. The type of information presented includes the publication of important works, the dates of major conferences, information about personal achievements, and passage of significant legislation. Some of the entries are detailed, but most are brief.

Library Instruction

For reference materials on library instruction see entries listed under the heading Bibliographic Instruction.

Library Legislation

HANDBOOKS AND MANUALS

1002 **American library laws.** Ed. by Alex Ladenson. 4th ed. Chicago: American Library Assn., 1973. 1,992p. LC 73–14863. ISBN 0–8389–0158–1. **First supplement, 1973–1974.** Chicago: American Library Assn., 1975. 244p. ISBN 0–8389–0158–1. **Second supplement, 1975–1976.** Chicago: American Library Assn., 1977. 264p. ISBN 0–8389–0253–7. **Third supplement, 1977–1978.** Chicago: American Library Assn., 1979. 240p. ISBN 0–8389–0304–5.

The basic volume and subsequent supplements present the texts of federal and state library legislation passed during specified time periods. The basic volume covers legislation up through the last day of 1972. The titles of each of the supplements indicate the inclusive dates of coverage. The text itself is reproduced from a photocopy of published versions of federal and state legal codes. Arrangement is first federal legislation, then state legislation subdivided by type of library or by subject (e.g., depository legislation, state aid to libraries). A detailed index provides access to legislation by individual titles, state, and subject.

1003 **Public library law: an international survey.** New Delhi: Metropolitan, 1971. 624p.

The work provides a country-by-country account of public library legislation. In the case of some countries, it only indicates the date of the first library law. In others, such as the United States and the United Kingdom, a much more detailed account is provided. For India, in-depth coverage of public library legislation is presented for each state.

1004 **Public library law and the law as to museums and art galleries in England and Wales, Scotland and Northern Ireland.** By A. R. Hewitt. 5th ed. London: Assn. of Assistant Librarians, Library Assn. 1975. 109p. LC 76–362404. ISBN 0–900092–25–4.

Major changes in library legislation in the United Kingdom came about subsequent to the fourth edition of this work, and those changes are reflected in this edition. The author begins with a brief characterization of extant public library law in the United Kingdom at the time of this work. Also included is the text of the Public Libraries and Museums Act of 1961 and extracts from the Local Government Act of 1972 that pertain to public libraries, museums, and art galleries. Finally, there is a summary of legislation arranged by such topics as finance, staff and by-laws, and land and buildings. Earlier editions of this work were published in 1932, 1947, 1955, and 1965.

Library Statistics

All statistical reports covering academic, public, school, and special libraries in general are listed in Chapter 6, of this guide. Library salary surveys are listed in this chapter under the heading Personnel Policies, Salaries, Benefits and Employee Rights. Included here are reference materials dealing with library statistics as a subject.

BIBLIOGRAPHIC SOURCES

1005   Statistics of libraries: an annotated bibliography of recurring surveys. By John Carson Rather and Nathan M. Cohen. Washington, DC: Office of Education, U.S. Department of Health, Education, and Welfare, 1961. 50p.

Over 150 library statistical sources that were issued as recurring surveys in the early 1960's are listed and described in this bibliography. The citations are divided into two sections. The first section covers forty-four national and regional statistics, grouped by type of library (including library education). The second section arranges 112 surveys alphabetically by state. Entries supply author, title, imprint, frequency of publication, and a relatively brief annotation. The annotations were prepared with the item in hand and do not reflect changes that might have occurred from earlier editions or issues. Further, the entries do not include the beginning date of publication, but only reflect the current edition. The index, characterized as "partly alphabetical and partly classified," covers such topics as bookmobiles and education for librarianship. The classified section includes a breakdown by topic under type-of-library headings. This bibliography was the most comprehensive of its type up through the time period covered and is still useful for identifying retrospective statistical series.

HANDBOOKS AND MANUALS

1006   Library data collection handbook. Ed. by Mary Jo Lynch. Chicago: Office for Research, American Library Assn., 1982. 228p. LC 82–147483.

This work, commissioned by the National Center for Education Statistics, is similar in purpose to the 1966 *Library statistics: a handbook of concepts, definitions, and terminology* (entry **1007**). It updates and expands upon the earlier *Handbook* by presenting a system of data collection that can be used in all types of libraries and by providing definitions of terms essential to the system.

1007   Library statistics: a handbook of concepts, definitions, and terminology. Prepared by the staff of the Statistics Coordinating Project; Joel Williams, Director. Chicago: American Library Assn., 1966. 160p. LC 66–22724.

This work was prepared to provide a basis for the standardized reporting of library statistics for various types of libraries. It came into being as a result of the cooperative effort of several organizations concerned with the reporting of library statistics. The approach used is to present statistical reporting procedures by type of library (and also for library education), and then characterize the various types of statistical information to be collected (e.g., population served, hours of service, library holdings, circulation, interlibrary loan transactions, reference service transactions, physical facilities, income, and expenditures). At the end of the volume is an extensive glossary of terms used in statistical surveys. Also included is a selected bibliography. This work served as the standard guide for the compilation and reporting of library statistics until 1982, when the *Library data collection handbook* (entry **1006**) was published.

Library Suppliers and Vendors

DIRECTORIES

1008 "Annual buyer's guide issue." Appears annually in **Library journal.** New York: Bowker, 1876– . LC 4–12654. ISSN 0363–0277. Monthly.

The August issue of *Library Journal* includes a directory of library suppliers and vendors for various types of products and services. Listed are suppliers of book shelving, plastic book jackets, bookmobiles, and a wide variety of other items. Entries specify the name, address, and telephone number of the company and a list of the products and services that they supply. They are arranged alphabetically by name of the company, with product access available through the index.

1009 **Directory of library suppliers used by australian libraries.** Prep. by Committee of the Acquisitions Special Interest Group, Library Assn. of Australia (A.C.T. Branch). Canberra: Acquisitions Special Interest Group, Library Assn. of Australia, 1982. 61p. ISBN 0–86804–024–X.

Vendors for books, periodicals, and other library materials and supplies are listed in this directory. The entries are arranged by geographical location and indexed by company name and subject specialization. A list of agencies represented by the suppliers is also included. The suppliers listed are not restricted to Australia; many are located in various parts of the world, particularly Europe and North America.

1010 **Information industry market place: an international directory of information products and services.** New York: Bowker, 1979– . Annual. LC 81–643678. ISSN 0000–0450.

The addresses and key personnel for the suppliers of a wide range of information products and services are identified in this directory. The listing is divided into seven sections, the largest of which is titled "Information Production." This section identifies approximately 400 data base publishers responsible for producing machine-readable data bases and print publications. Arrangement is alphabetical by name and entries contain address, telephone number, names of key personnel, types of products offered, subjects covered, frequency of update, method of access, and scope of the services provided. A second section identifies telecommunications networks, library networks and consortia, and online vendors. The third section lists more than 100 information analysis centers, government-sponsored clearinghouses, and other organizations that collect, analyze, evaluate, and process raw data for subsequent use. There is also a list of information brokers. These two listings are classified by subject and service. A fourth section lists manufacturers of terminals, consultants, and other support services. Section five identifies information-related organizations and online user groups in the United States. The sixth section contains an annual calendar of training sessions, conferences, and other activities, with short descriptions of each. The final section cites periodicals, reference works, and newsletters in the information field. A general geographical index and a "name and numbers" index provide access to all of the sections.

1011 **Information sources: the annual directory of the Information Industry Association.** Ed. by Faye Henderson and Fred Rosenau. Washington, DC: Information Industry Assn., 1977– . Annual. LC 77–642173. ISSN 0148–1053.

This directory lists companies holding membership in the Information Industry Association and producing various types of information products. Arrangement is alphabetical by name of the company. The entries contain a list of services, products, publications, resources, and consultation available from each IIA-member firm, as well as address, telephone number, names of key executives, a list of trade and brand names produced or sold, and product descriptions. Each entry is on a separate page and many of the entries include the company logo. There is also a listing of international offices or affiliates, arranged by country. An index by subject or type of product is included and a "name and numbers" section lists personal names, affiliation, location, and telephone number of key executives from member companies.

1012   International subscription agents: an annotated directory. Chicago: Resources and Technical Services Division, American Library Assn., 1978. 125p.

Vendors and subscription agents who accept orders for international subscriptions to periodicals and serials are listed alphabetically in this directory. For further information see entry **1160**.

1013   LRMP 1980– : library resources market place. New York: Bowker, 1980– . Annual. ISSN 0000–0442.

More than 4,500 organizations and persons providing products and services for libraries are listed in twenty-five sections grouped under eight broad categories: publishers, audiovisual producers and distributors, periodicals and agents, book dealers, library equipment and materials suppliers, organizations and schools, library services, and library awards. Entries are brief and contain name, address, telephone number of the organization, and key personnel. Personal and organization name indexing is provided.

HANDBOOKS AND MANUALS

1014   Guide to magazine and serial agents. By Bill Katz and Peter Gellatly. New York: Bowker, 1975. 239p. LC 75–26616. ISBN 0–8352–0789–7.

This work is intended to assist librarians in determining the best serials or periodicals agent for their library. For complete information see entry **1161**.

1015   Media equipment: a guide and dictionary. By Kenyon C. Rosenberg and John S. Doskey. Littleton, CO: Libraries Unlimited, 1976. 190p. LC 76–2554. ISBN 0–87287–155–X.

This work is intended as a guide for persons who purchase and use audiovisual equipment. It is divided into two parts, a guide and a dictionary. The guide section provides specific criteria and checklists for the evaluation and selection of media equipment. Guidance on the use of equipment is also offered, and references are made to terms defined in the dictionary. The dictionary, which consists of more than half of the work, defines approximately 400 media equipment terms, especially those terms that might be found on advertising issued by the manufacturers. Some of the terms are accompanied by illustrations. Also included are the names of some organizations that can supply additional information.

Library Technicians

HANDBOOKS AND MANUALS

1016   Introduction to library services for library technicians. By Barbara E. Chernik. Littleton, CO: Libraries Unlimited, 1982. 187p. LC 81–15663. ISBN 0–87287–275–0.

This general introduction to libraries covers personnel structure, materials, resources, library services in various types of libraries, automation, and networking. It also includes a section on the role of the library media technical assistant (LMTA) in the library. Charts, photographs, and sample forms illustrate the procedures and practices discussed in the text. Although originally intended as a textbook, Chernik's work can be used as a manual for new LMTAs in a library to provide basic background information and specific instruction in some of their responsibilities.

1017   Introduction to public services for library technicians. By Marty Bloomberg. 2d ed. Littleton, CO: Libraries Unlimited, 1977. 278p. LC 76–45779. ISBN 0–87287–126–6.

Intended as a manual for library media technical assistants (LMTA), this work provides guidance and practical suggestions for various types of public services. It is based on the assumption that many library public service tasks currently or formerly performed by professional staff members can and will be performed by technical assistants. It begins with an overview of the role of the LMTA in the library, particularly in public service activities. Next are discussed specific public service functions technical assistants might perform in public services, e.g., patron registration, collection control (discharging materials, reserve books, fine collection, etc.), and interlibrary loan. A substantial portion of the book is devoted to reference sources and services in various subject areas. There are also a glossary of terms, an appendix covering the format of Library of Congress and Sears subject headings, and a list of abbreviations.

1018   Introduction to technical services for library technicians. By Marty Bloomberg and G. Edward Evans. 4th ed. Littleton, CO: Libraries Unlimited, 1981. 363p. LC 81–798. ISBN 0–87287–228–9.

Aimed at persons who are employed or preparing to work as technical assistants in technical service library units, this manual provides clear and practical descriptions of the various facets of technical services, including acquisitions, bibliographic verification, and gifts and exchange work. The current edition incorporates automation and computer applications, where relevant. The authors have also grouped technical services skills that can be acquired through experience, through in-service training, and through formal classroom instruction. This listing is intended to provide the reader with a sense of the educational preparation needed to perform various tasks in a technical services unit of a library.

1019   Library technical assistant's handbook. By Mildred V. Borkowski. Philadelphia: Dorrance, 1975. 400p. LC 74–84484. ISBN 0–8059–2071–4.

This detailed manual describes the processes and tasks library technical assistants might be assigned, including acquisitions, cataloging and processing, circulation, shelving and retrieval, reference and bibliography, and audiovisual media. Each of these topics is subdivided into brief descriptive chapters. For example, under acquisitions, the tasks described include selection of materials, publishers and jobbers, library filing, searching and verifying, order work, periodicals and other serials, and non-book materials. Examples and illustrations are used to augment the text.

Local Studies Library Service

HANDBOOKS AND MANUALS

1020 Local history collections: a manual for librarians. By Enid T. Thompson. Nashville, TN: American Assn. for State and Local History, 1978. 99p. LC 77–28187. ISBN 0–910050–33–3.

This manual describes how to collect, preserve, and utilize materials to form a local history collection. Discussed in the manual are the types of materials that constitute documents of local history; collection procedures; questions of ownership and other legal issues; conservation of local history documents (particularly the most effective means of preserving different types of materials); cataloging, storage, and retrieval; and training and utilizing volunteer help. Special local history projects are described, including the development of an oral history program and a file of community resource persons. Numerous photographs supplement the text. Appendices provide the reader with names of relevant organizations, sources of supplies, and addresses of useful publications. A selective bibliography completes the work.

1021 Local studies librarianship. By Harold Nichols. London: Clive Bingley, 1979. 128p. LC 79–309470. ISBN 0–85157–272–3.

The concept of local studies library service involves the acquisition of materials for the contemporary as well as historical study of a local area. The concept is not new, but the use of the term is recent. This manual applies the basic elements of librarianship to the development of a local studies collection. Topics covered include acquisitions, storage and preservation, classification, cataloging, indexing, assistance to readers, publications programs, and publicity. Although British practice is reflected in the volume, concepts are applicable to the development of a local studies collection anywhere. A brief bibliography supplements the text. Indexing is by subject.

Mail, Books By

DIRECTORIES

1022 Books by mail: a handbook for libraries. By Choong H. Kim. Westport, CT: Greenwood, 1977. 416p. LC 76–15335. ISBN 0–8371–9029–0.

The third section of this handbook is a directory of seventy-five books by mail programs in the United States and Canada. For further information see entry **1023**.

HANDBOOKS AND MANUALS

1023 Books by mail: a handbook for libraries. By Choong H. Kim. Westport, CT: Greenwood, 1977. 416p. LC 76–15335. ISBN 0–8371–9029–0.

This manual and directory on books by mail library service is divided into three sections.

The first consists of a manual outlining in a practical, step-by-step approach the procedures to be used in planning and implementing a books by mail program. Topics covered in this section include preparation of mail catalogs, collection development, determining reading interests, and cost-effectiveness analysis. The second section is comprised of case studies of books by mail service from nine libraries. The third section is a directory of seventy-five books by mail programs in the United States and Canada. Entries provide substantial data about each of the programs listed. In addition to the name and address of the library and the name of the program director, the following information is supplied: area served, users and uses, collection, the type of catalog used, procedures and operation, and self evaluation. Statistical information on expenditures and circulation is also included for some programs.

Management of Libraries

For reference materials on management of libraries see entries listed under the heading Administration and Management of Libraries.

Manuscripts

For reference materials on manuscripts see entries listed under the heading Archives.

Map Libraries

DIRECTORIES

1024 Directory of canadian map collections/Répertoire des collections de cartes canadiennes. Comp. by Lorraine Dubreuil. 4th ed. Ottawa: Assn. of Canadian Map Libraries, 1980. 144p. ISBN 0–969068–21–2.
A total of 111 map libraries in Canada are identified in this directory. More than half of the collections listed are in academic libraries. Arrangement is alphabetical by province, then city, and then name of institution. Entries are in English, except when French is the most common language used for the name of the institution. Entries supply the name of library, name and title of person in charge, telephone number, size of staff, size of collection by map categories, areas of specialization, subject specialization, depository agreements, primary constituency served, policies regarding loans, hours of opening, types of facilities, classification and cataloging schemes used, shelf list, and a list of publications. Also included are an alphabetical list of map collections and an alphabetical list of the names of persons in charge. First issued in 1968, this directory identifies more Canadian map collections than *Map collections in the United States and Canada* (see entry **1026**).

1025 Map collections in Australia: a directory. Comp. and ed. by N. M. Rauchle. 3d ed. Canberra: National Library of Australia, 1980. 141p. LC 81–156964. ISBN 0–642–99205–3.
This publication consists of two directories, one identifying map collections in Australia and the other map sources in Australia. The directory of map collections is divided into three sections. Section I identifies the principal mapping authorities in Australia and outlines the responsibility of the governments of the Commonwealth and the States for mapping. Section

II lists approximately 300 map collections. For each collection, information is provided on name, address, number of printed map sheets, manuscripts map sheets, map reference books, aerial photographs, atlas volumes, landsat imagery, map specilization, major map specialization, main subject area covered, facilities, and policies regarding public access and written inquiries. Arrangement of the collections is alphabetical by state or territory. Section III covers private map collections. There are only a limited number listed and, for the most part, they have restricted access. The second part of this work contains the directory of map sources. It is divided into two sections, the first of which, "Map Reference Material," lists catalogs, brochures, guides, and atlases. The second includes map publishers, both public and commercial. Entries provide addresses and information about the types of maps available from the publisher. There is an index covering the map collections listed in Part I, Sections II and III.

1026   Map collections in the United States and Canada: a directory. Comp. by David K.
         Carrington and Richard W. Stephenson. 3d ed. New York: Special Libraries Assn.,
         1978. 230p. LC 77–26685. ISBN 0–87111–243–7.

A total of 747 major map collections in the United States and Canada are listed in this work. Included are map collections in academic and public libraries, museums, special libraries, and archives. Entries are arranged alphabetically by state or province, then by city. Data included in the entries were derived from questionnaires sent to the collections. Entries contain the name, address, telephone number, name of the person in charge, size and growth of the collection, major subject and geographical area specializations, date established, number of personnel, period of time emphasized by the collection, type of cataloging and classification system used, hours of opening, seating capacity, and number of users served per month. The first edition of this work was issued in 1954, the second in 1970.

1027   World directory of map collections. Comp. by the Geography and Map Libraries
         Sub-section, International Federation of Library Associations. Ed. by Walter W.
         Ristow. Munich: Verlag Dokumentation, 1976. 326p. LC 76–381150. ISBN
         3–7940–4428–2.

Described in this 1976 directory are 285 map collections from forty-six countries. Arrangement is alphabetical by name of country. Each entry contains up to sixteen categories of information; among these are name, address, telephone number, size of collection, subject specialization, policies regarding public access, and exchange policies. Entries are written in English, regardless of the country in which the collection is located. Coverage of the United States, Great Britain, West Germany, and Canada constitutes about forty percent of the entries, even though these nations are represented by separate national directories. The work is not indexed nor does it have a table of contents.

HANDBOOKS AND MANUALS

1028   Map librarianship. By Harold Nichols. 2d ed. London: Clive Bingley, 1982. 272p.
         LC 82–126289. ISBN 0–85157–327–4.

The basic elements of map librarianship are described in this manual. The intent is to cover the competencies required to operate a successful map library. The following subjects are addressed: the content of current map collections, acquisition of current and historical maps, storage and retrieval, options for classification and cataloging, identifying and dating historical maps, and preservation. Numerous practical examples are provided and sources for the acquisition of maps are supplied. A bibliography of additional readings is also included. The concepts presented emphasize British practice, although the bibliography draws from both British and American writings.

1029 Map librarianship: an introduction. By Mary Larsgaard. Littleton, CO: Libraries Unlimited, 1978. 330p. LC 77–28821. ISBN 0–87287–182–7.

Aimed at persons with little or no experience in map librarianship, this manual provides extensive information on the acquisition of current and historical maps, map classification, map cataloging (with some attention to computer applications), and the care and repair of maps. In the latter section, various types of damage and repair problems are dealt with individually. Additional coverage is given to public relations, reference service, and the administration of map libraries. Numerous examples are provided throughout to illustrate the author's points. Several appendices provide useful information for map libraries. Among these are a sample acquisition policy, a list of selected periodicals containing reviews of maps, a form for requesting free maps, sources of state highway and state geological maps, and a glossary of map terms. A lengthy bibliography, a supplemental reading list, and a subject index complete the volume.

Marine Transport Libraries

DIRECTORIES

1030 Marine transport: a guide to libraries and sources of information in Great Britain. By D. N. Allum, R. V. Bolton and D. S. Buchanan. London: Reference, Special and Information Section, Library Assn. and Marine Librarians' Assn., 1974. 63p. LC 76–350668. ISBN 0–85365–018–7.

Collections of marine transport materials are described in this directory. The coverage includes government libraries, public and academic libraries, company libraries, international organizations, and museums. The work is divided into two parts. The first covers seventy-two major collections and provides detailed information about each. Entries contain name, address, telephone number, name of librarian or information officer, size of staff, numerical data on holdings, hours of opening, areas of subject specialization, special collections, and services offered. Another 130 organizations that also have collections, but less substantial ones, are treated briefly in a separate listing; only the name, address, and telephone numbers are supplied. Name and subject access is provided in the index.

Measurement

For reference materials on measurement see entries listed under the heading Library Evaluation, Measurement and Research.

Media Centers

For reference materials on media centers see entries listed under the heading School Libraries/Media Centers.

Medical, Hospital and Patient Libraries

BIBLIOGRAPHIC SOURCES

1031 **Health sciences librarianship: a guide to information sources.** By Beatrice K. Basler and Thomas G. Basler. Detroit: Gale, 1977. 186p. (Books, publishing, and libraries information guide, v.19) LC 74–11552. ISBN 0–8103–1284.0.

In this annotated bibliography, 550 titles dealing with the policies, procedures, and administration of health science libraries are cited. These include books, pamphlets, annual reports, technical reports, videotapes, some chapters of books, and other materials. The entries are arranged into thirteen broad subject headings and indexed by specific topics. Materials are covered through 1975, but a substantial number of the titles were published prior to 1970.

1032 **Hospital and welfare library services: an international bibliography.** Comp. by Eileen E. Cumming. London: Library Assn., 1977. 174p. LC 77–368705. ISBN 0–85365–139–6.

The bibliography is an outgrowth of a discussion held by the IFLA Sub-committee of Hospital Libraries. It includes 2,164 citations taken from the literature of various languages and countries through 1972. The primary emphasis is on library service to hospital patients. Entries are arranged chronologically and then alphabetically within each time period. They are in the original language, with an English translation for those items originally published in foreign languages. There are indexes by author, subject, and geographical area covered.

1033 **Sourcebook on health sciences librarianship.** By Ching-chih Chen. Metuchen, NJ: Scarecrow, 1977. 490p. LC 76–11781. ISBN 0–1357–3519–X.

In this bibliography of the literature of health sciences librarianship, approximately 3,000 journal and non-journal references published between 1965 and early 1976 are cited. Entries are arranged under seventy-six subject terms covering topics most likely to be of interest to health science librarians. The treatment is extensive, but not exhaustive. The entries are not annotated. They are indexed by personal and corporate author. There is no subject index; access by subject is through the major subject terms. In the first section of the work, there is a review of articles appearing in the *Bulletin of the Medical Library Association* for the period from 1965 to 1976. This includes an analysis of citation patterns, subject coverage, and authorship. From this, the author derives some general observations about the production of literature on health sciences librarianship.

BIOGRAPHICAL SOURCES

1034 **Medical Library Association: directory.** Chicago: Medical Library Assn., 1950– . Annual. ISSN 0543–2774.

This directory lists the current membership of the Medical Library Association (MLA), which presently totals approximately 5,000 persons and institutions. The arrangement is alphabetical for personal members and geographical for institutional members. Personal entries contain the name, address and, where applicable, professional certification. Institutional member entries include the name and address of the institution and the name of the institutional representative.

DIRECTORIES

1035   **Directory of health science libraries in the United States, 1979.** Ed. by Alan M. Rees and Susan Crawford. Cleveland: Cleveland Health Sciences Library, Case Western Reserve Univ., 1980. 355p. (Health sciences information series) LC 80–65893.

Compiled as the result of a comprehensive survey of health sciences collections, this directory identifies 420 health sciences libraries in the United States. It includes hospital libraries, medical school libraries, libraries sponsored by medical societies, and libraries of health systems. All of the major collections are identified, as well as many of the small installations. Arrangement is geographical by name of city. Entries supply name and address of the library, name of library director, numerical data on library holdings, types of online access, size of staff, sponsoring organization, and services offered. Indexing is by name of organization. Earlier versions of this title were issued in 1970 and 1974.

1036   **Directory of major medical libraries in the United States.** Miami: U.S. Directory Service, 1978. 64p. LC 78–112692. ISBN 0–916524–07–8.

More than 1,000 medical libraries in the United States are listed in this directory. Included are those associated with university hospitals, medical centers, medical research laboratories, medical schools, departments of health, health education centers, educational societies, medical associations, experimental institutions, scientific institutions, and educational societies. An attempt was made to represent all collections of 5,000 titles or more in urban areas and collections of 2,500 or more in smaller population areas. Information provided is brief, listing only name and address of the library. Arrangement is by state and then locality.

1037   **Directory of major medical libraries worldwide.** Miami: U.S. Directory Service, 1978. 171p. LC 78–112608. ISBN 0–916524–08–6.

A companion volume to the *Directory of major medical libraries in the United States* (entry **1036**), this work identifies 2,800 medical libraries in 1,500 urban centers in 108 countries. The coverage is similar to that presented in the companion volume and, for the United States, the same libraries are listed. Arrangement is alphabetical by country, except for Australia, Brazil, Canada, and the United States, where arrangement is by locality and then alphabetical. Library names and place names in non-Roman alphabets are transliterated. Entries are brief and include only the name and address of the library.

1038   **Directory of medical and health care libraries in the United Kingdom and the Republic of Ireland.** Comp. by W. D. Linton. 5th ed. London: Library Assn., 1982. 228p. LC 77–354104. ISBN 0–85365–536–7.

All of the principal British medical libraries, and many of the smaller ones as well, are described in this directory. In addition, a number of other libraries are listed, but no significant information is provided about them. A requirement for inclusion was a minimum of twenty-five current subscriptions to periodicals in 1975. In all, 600 health science libraries (including dental, veterinary, and pharmaceutical libraries) are identified. Geographical coverage extends to England (with a separate listing for libraries in London), Wales, Scotland, Northern Ireland, and the Republic of Ireland. The entries include the name, address, telephone number, staff size, hours of opening, conditions, of access, subject strengths, special collections, volume count, services available, photocopying, and type of classification system. Entries are indexed by personal name, institutional name, type of library, geographical location, and name of special collections. Earlier editions were published in 1957, 1965, 1969, and 1977 under the title *Directory of medical libraries in the British Isles.*

1039   Medical Library Association: directory. Chicago: Medical Library Assn., 1950– . Annual. ISSN 0543–2774.
This directory lists the current membership of the Medical Library Association (MLA), which presently totals approximately 5,000 persons and institutions. For further information see entry **1034**.

HANDBOOKS AND MANUALS

1040   Handbook of medical library practice. Ed. by Louise Darling. 4th ed. Chicago: Medical Library Assn., 1982. 330p. ISBN 0–686–97361–5.
The purpose of Darling's work is "to serve as a practical manual reflecting accepted current methods for organizing and providing service from information resources to users of health sciences libraries of all types, large and small, clinical and research, academic, professional, and commercial." It is designed to provide basic information to new recruits to health science librarianship and to more experienced librarians who need a ready reference source. In a break with the earlier patterns of publication, the fourth edition is to be published in three volumes. These volumes will be interrelated, with cross references from one to another. Emphasis is on American practice, although there is a chapter on British medical libraries. In Volume 1, *Public services in health science libraries,* specific aspects of public services are discussed, including circulation policies, procedures, and problems; interlibrary loan/document delivery; reference services policies and practices; online searching and search techniques; and the teaching role of the library. A separate chapter deals with research in health sciences libraries. The two subsequent volumes will address technical services and administration of health science libraries. Previous editions of this work were published in 1943, 1956, and 1970.

1041   Hospital libraries and work with the disabled in the community. By Mona E. Going. 3d ed. London: Library Assn., 1982. 324p. ISBN 0–85365–723–3.
Each chapter in this manual deals with a separate aspect of library service to hospital patients and the disabled. Topics covered include mentally handicapped patients, disabled children, psychiatric patients, elderly patients, and the deaf and visually handicapped. Also provided are guidelines for developing hospital library service. The information included here is applicable to hospitals of varying sizes, but particularly to small hospitals. Earlier editions of the work were published in 1963 and 1973.

1042   The librarian and the patient: an introduction to library services for patients in health care institutions. Ed. by Eleanor Phinney. Chicago: American Library Assn., 1977. 352p. LC 76–45178. ISBN 0–8389–0227–8.
This manual focuses on library service to hospitalized patients in diverse types of health care institutions. A useful introduction to the organization and structure of different types of health care facilities is provided, together with information dealing more specifically with

the role of the library in the health care environment. Also covered are such topics as the role of the patient in different institutions, the impact of that role on the library, materials selection and acquisition, and patient services. Information is presented in a practical, direct fashion. Examples are used to illustrate the ideas. Two particularly valuable features are the introductory summaries beginning each chapter and the selected topical bibliographies concluding each chapter.

1043   Library practice in hospitals: a basic guide. By Harold Bloomquist, et al. Cleveland: Case Western Reserve Univ. Pr., 1972. 344p. LC 79-175301. ISBN 0-8295-0227-0.

Intended for the person in charge of a hospital library, with limited or no experience, this manual uses non-technical terms, but deals with the basic elements of library service in a systematic fashion. The work is divided into three broad categories and then further subdivided into seventeen chapters, each written by a different contributor. Each chapter has a selected bibliography of further works for the person interested in going beyond the manual. The text is indexed by subject.

1044   Manual for librarians in small hospitals. Ed. by Collette C. Ford. 5th ed. Los Angeles: Biomedical Library, Univ. of California at Los Angeles, 1981. 86p.

Aimed at the inexperienced librarian in a small hospital, this manual provides guidance in the fundamental elements of library service. Included are administration, selection of materials, acquisitions, cataloging and classification, labeling, selecting journals, processing books and journals, interlibrary loan, reference service, circulation, MEDLINE, regional medical library services, and audiovisual materials. An appendix provides a list of reference books that might be used to constitute a basic hospital library collection. The first edition of this manual was issued in 1971, under the editorship of Lois Ann Colaianni and Phyllis S. Mirsky.

1045   Medical librarianship. Ed. by Michael Carmel. London: Library Assn., 1981. 372p. LC 81-162108. ISBN 0-85365-703-3.

Intended to provide guidance for librarians in health science and health care libraries, this manual emphasizes (from a British perspective) medical information needs of patients and of the general public, health literature and audiovisual media useful in health science libraries, management and planning of library services, publicity, continuing education, and reader services. It also covers serials, books, literature searching, and user instruction. Numerous concrete examples are used to illustrate contemporary library service. Each chapter is supported by selected bibliographies for further reading. In addition, a separate section reviews recent research in health science information and studies of health sciences libraries. A subject index completes the volume.

STATISTICAL SOURCES

1046   Annual statistics of medical school libraries in the United States and Canada. Ed. by Richard Lyders. Houston: Assn. of Academic Health Sciences Library Directors and Texas Medical Center Library, Houston Academy of Medicine, 1978– . Annual. LC 81-640259. ISSN 0196-6448.

Reproduced in this series are data for medical school libraries compiled from responses to questionnaires mailed to approximately 140 institutions in the United States and Canada. Response rates vary from year to year. Not all medical school libraries choose to participate and, thus, the compilation is not comprehensive. The data are divided into aggregate summary tables for all responding schools and rank order tables for individual medical school libraries. The tables reflect such categories as collection size, expenditures for different types of materials, personnel size and expenditures, interlibrary loans, and number of MEDLINE searches. The data are indexed by subject.

Mexican Americans

For reference materials on Mexican Americans see entries listed under the heading Hispanic American Librarians and Librarianship.

Micrographics

BIBLIOGRAPHIC SOURCES

1047   Microforms: 1973–May, 1980 (Citations from the NTIS data base). By Mary E. Young. Springfield, VA: NTIS, 1980. 191p. PB 80–811151.
Continuing an earlier NTIS search covering 1964–1973, this bibliography identifies report literature in the NTIS data base on the topic of microforms. A total of 211 items released from 1973 to 1980 are abstracted. Among the topics covered are microfilm and microfiche format standards and utilization of microformatted materials. Although not limited to reports with library or information center applications, a substantial number of the entries have that focus. The entries follow standard NTIS format: title, corporate author, sponsoring agency, NTIS subject categories, abstract and descriptors, report number, contract number, and other bibliographic information. Also included are a number of items listed in ERIC and available through the ERIC Document Reproduction Service.

1048   Micrographics, 1900–1977: a bibliography. By Michael R. Gabriel. Mankato: Minnesota Scholarly Pr., 1978. 286p. LC 79–101793. ISBN 0–933474–01–6.
This is an extensive bibliography of English-language writings on all aspects of micrographics. Gabriel claims to comprehensively cover all known references published from 1900–1977. More than 3,500 citations are listed. The bibliography is not annotated, but it does provide sufficient bibliographic information to enable the user to locate the items. Materials cited include monographs, journal articles, and reports as well as all ERIC and NTIS works through the time covered. The entries relate not only to library use, but also to micrographic publishing, business use of micrographics, and engineering use of micrographics. Citations are arranged into fifteen topics, with no cross references, and indexed by personal author only (thus excluding a sizeable number of corporate authored items).

DIRECTORIES

1049   Directory of ERIC microfiche collections. Bethesda, MD: ERIC Processing and Reference Facility, 1976– . Biennial.
The names and addresses of libraries and other institutions that have at least two years of ERIC microfiche holdings are listed in this work. Identified are approximately 720 collections, of which seventy five are located outside of the United States. Arranged geograph-

ically, by location of the collection, the entries specify institution name, address, telephone number, name of contact person, scope of collection, type of reading equipment available, hours of opening, and whether or not computer search services are available.

1050 International micrographics source book. New Rochelle, NY: Microfilm Publishing, 1976– . Annual. LC 80–645286. ISSN 0272–0310.

Various types of micrographics services and equipment available internationally are identified in this directory. Among the groups covered are micrographics publishers, equipment manufacturers, and associations concerned with micrographics. Information is divided into categories, e.g., micropublishers. Entries are arranged by name of company rather than by country or other geographical designation. Limited information is provided in the directory, frequently necessitating contact with the listed agency in order to obtain needed information. From 1976 through 1980, this source was published as the *International microfilm source book.*

1051 Microform market place. Westport, CT: Microform Review, 1974/75– . Biennial. LC 74–4811. ISSN 0362–0999.

In this biennial international directory of 400 micropublishers active in microformat publishing, arrangement is alphabetical by name of company and entries contain name, address, telephone number, names of key executives, and information on the major microform publishing activities of each company. A special feature is the calendar of forthcoming meetings and conferences related to micropublishing.

HANDBOOKS AND MANUALS

1052 The evaluation of micropublications: a handbook for librarians. By Allen B. Veaner. Chicago: Library Technology Program, American Library Assn., 1971. 59p. (LTP publication no. 17) LC 73–138700. ISBN 0–8389–3128–6.

This 1971 manual is intended to provide guidance in the evaluation of every aspect of micropublications except subject content. It deals with the technical aspects of roll film, microfiche, and micro-opaques as of the early 1970's. Designed initially to provide assistance to persons who review microforms for review media, it has more general applicability. Topics covered include film size and legibility; film polarity; film stock; film coatings; and archival permanence. Veaner provides step-by-step instructions on the evaluation process, beginning with the examination of advertising from the publisher and following a progressive process of evaluation. A brief bibliography is included and the work is indexed by subject.

1053 A microform handbook. By Dale Gaddy for the American Association of Community and Junior Colleges. Silver Spring, MD: National Microfilm Assn., 1975. v.p. LC 73–92621.

Some of the content of this manual is of a general nature and not subject to obsolescence. This includes providing information about the application of micrographics in industry, government, and education; describing the characteristics of the various microformats; identifying the major types of microform hardware, illustrating the operation of each; and designing an educational microform system. There are several special features included with this work, some of which are now out of date: a buyers' guide, a list of micropublishers, a list of periodicals and newsletters, and micrographic standards.

1054 Micrographics. By William Saffady. Littleton, CO: Libraries Unlimited, 1978. 238p. LC 78–1309. ISBN 0–87287–175–4.

This introductory manual deals with micrographics in the library environment. Because it was designed to provide guidance in working with various facets of micrographics, it is written with a minimum of technical jargon and makes extensive use of examples to illustrate concepts. The topics covered include types of microforms, source document microfilm, computer-output-microfilm (COM), micropublishing, bibliographic control, storage and retrieval, microform readers, and the future of microforms. The work is well illustrated and includes a selected bibliography as well as a lengthy list of references at the conclusion of each chapter. The text is indexed by subject.

1055 Micrographics: a user's manual. By Joseph L. Kish. New York: Wiley, 1980. 196p. LC 80–16798. ISBN 0–471–05524–7.

This manual was prepared to provide guidance for the information systems manager and technician in the selection and use of micrographic equipment. Although oriented toward business applications, much of the manual is relevant to libraries. Topics covered include micrographics hardware, source document micrographics systems analysis and design, computer-output-microfilm (COM), and the micrographics management program. Numerous photographs, drawings, and other illustrations augment the non-technical text. There is a brief glossary of micrographic terms and a subject index.

1056 Micrographics handbook. By Charles Smith. Dedham, MA: Artech House, 1978. 297p. LC 78–2561. ISBN 0–89006–061–4.

In this basic guide to the production and use of microforms, good use is made of photographs and other illustrations. Various types of equipment are described. Included in the appendix are data on microform supply costs, microform reduction ratios, storage capacity of various microformats, and examples of forms that can be used in microform production.

TERMINOLOGY SOURCES

1057 Glossary of micrographics. 6th ed. Silver Spring, MD: National Micrographics Assn., 1980. 33p. ISBN 0–89258–065–8.

The intent of this glossary is to standardize the use of terminology associated with micrographics and to provide an accurate guide to persons unfamiliar with the terms. Updating an earlier edition, which appeared in 1971, a total of ninety-two entries appear in the current edition; two-thirds are new terms. In addition to the textual definitions, there are a number of diagrams that help illustrate terms. Tradenames and trademarks are excluded, but were included in the previous edition. The first appendix is a selected bibliography of glossaries and dictionaries in fields related to micrographics that contain micrographics terms. The second appendix is a bibliography of all standards to which a reference is made in the text of the glossary.

1058 Thesaurus of micrographic terms. By Bernard James and Stiles Williams. 2d ed. Hatfield, MA: National Reprographic Centre for Documentation, Hatfield Polytechnic, 1972. 42p. LC 72–190862. ISBN 0–85267–033–8.

Intended primarily as the key word retrieval language for the National Reprographic Centre's micrographic information system, this thesaurus provides a controlled vocabulary for a field that impacts heavily on library and information science. No definitions or scope notes are provided.

Museum Libraries

DIRECTORIES

1059 **Slavic ethnic libraries, museums and archives in the United States: a guide and directory.** Comp. by Lubomyr R. Wynar with Pat Kleeberger. Chicago: Assn. of College and Research Libraries; Kent, OH: Program for the Study of Ethnic Publications, School of Library Science, Kent State Univ., 1980. 164p. LC 80–18034.
Described in this directory are libraries, museums, and archives collecting materials relating to fourteen Slavic groups. For further information see entry **876**.

HANDBOOKS AND MANUALS

1060 **Libraries for small museums.** By Marcia Collins and Linda Anderson. 3d ed. Columbia: Museum of Anthropology, Univ. of Missouri, 1977. 48p. (Miscellaneous publications in anthropology, no. 4) LC 76–353333. ISBN 0–913134–90–2.
Basic elements in the operation of any small library are contained in this manual. Particular emphasis is placed on problems peculiar to the museum library. Topics covered include planning, financing, acquisition of materials, processing and cataloging, circulation, maintenance of records, and reference assistance. The authors assume the user will be operating on a highly restricted budget; thus, suggestions are made to accomodate those circumstances. A bibliography of additional sources of information to be consulted is appended.

Music Libraries

BIBLIOGRAPHIC SOURCES

1061 **Music libraries, including a comprehensive bibliography of music literature and a select bibliography of music scores published since 1957.** By Lionel Roy McColvin and Harold Reeves. Rewritten, rev. and enl. by Jack Dove. London: A. Deutsch, 1965. 2v. LC 65–53118/MN.
Volume 2 consists of an extensive bibliography of music, including music scores, books on various aspects of music, and fiction with a connection to music. For further information see entry **1071**.

1062 **A selected bibliography of music librarianship.** By Don Phillips. Urbana: Graduate School of Library Science, Univ. of Illinois, 1974. 47p. (University of Illinois occasional papers, no. 113) LC 76–622538. ISSN 0073–5310.
In this annotated bibliography of 241 items concerned with music librarianship, coverage extends to books, anthologies, theses, and periodical articles written in English or translated into English between 1937 and 1973. Materials that deal with a specific music library or its holdings and studies of music bibliography are excluded. The annotations are critical as well as descriptive. Arrangement is by broad topic, subdivided by more specific subject. Among the areas covered in the bibliography are acquisitions, cataloging and classification, history, and public service in music libraries.

275

DIRECTORIES

1063 Directory of music library automation projects. Comp. by Garrett H. Bowles. 2d
ed. Philadelphia: Music Library Assn., 1979. 23p. (MLA technical reports, no. 2)
LC 79–10768. ISBN 0–914954–14–8.

Based on data recorded on questionnaires sent to members of the Music Library Association, this directory describes 100 libraries utilizing automation for some type of library
activity, ranging from use of OCLC, to locally developed information storage and retrieval
systems, to fully integrated bibliographic record systems. The majority reported are in
academic libraries and the most commonly-used system is OCLC. Arrangement of the
entries in the directory is by zip code. Entries contain the name and address of the music
library and brief information about the automated systems used. Indexing is by name of
institution, type of function, and type of system used. An earlier version of the directory was
published in 1973.

**1064 Directory of music research libraries, including contributors to the Interna-
tional inventory of musical sources (RISM).** Comp. by Rita Benton. Prelim. ed.
Iowa City: Univ. of Iowa, 1967–1979. 4v. LC 77–15798.

This is an extensive international directory of music libraries. Volume 1 covers the United
States and Canada; Volume 2 represents thirteen European countries (Austria, Belgium,
Switzerland, German Federal Republic, German Democratic Republic, Denmark, Ireland,
Great Britain, Luxembourg, Norway, Netherlands, Sweden, and Finland); Volume 3 covers
Spain, France, Italy, and Portugal; Volume 4 includes Australia, Israel, Japan, and New
Zealand. The volumes were published separately, but each contains much the same type of
information. All four list institutions contributing to *RISM (Répertoire international des
sources musicales)*, the major international bibliography of music scholarship, as well as
other major music libraries. The arrangement of the volume covering the United States and
Canada is alphabetical by state or province. A total of 295 U.S. and thirty-six Canadian
music libraries are listed. Entries contain name, address, telephone number, a brief description of the collection, size of collection, types of materials held, policies regarding public
access, services offered, and titles of publications issued by the library. Each entry also
supplies the *RISM* symbol that uniquely designates the library. The subsequent volumes
follow the same format and are arranged by country. They are indexed by country, by
collection, and by institution name.

1065 Music collections in american libraries: a chronology. Comp. by Carol June
Bradley. Detroit: Information Coordinators, 1981. 249p. (Detroit studies in music
bibliographies, no. 46) LC 81–2907/MN.

Descriptive information about 374 major music collections in the United States is presented
in this source. For further information see entry **1069**.

**1066 Music libraries, including a comprehensive bibliography of music literature
and a select bibliography of music scores published since 1957.** By Lionel Roy
McColvin and Harold Reeves. Rewritten, rev. and enl. by Jack Dove. London: A.
Deutsche, 1965. 2v. LC 65–53118/MN.

Volume 1 contains a directory of music holdings in British public and university libraries
and some overseas libraries. For further information see entry **1071**.

HANDBOOKS AND MANUALS

1067 **The development of library collections of sound recordings.** By Frank W. Hoffman. New York: M. Dekker, 1979. 169p. (Books in library and information science, v. 28) LC 79–23064. ISBN 0–8247–6858–2.

This guide focuses on the selection, acquisition, and organization of sound recordings, for both music libraries and general library collections. It includes practical suggestions for those with only limited familiarity with sound recordings. Priority is given to circulating collections rather than historical or archival holdings of recordings. Topics covered include collection development, audio reproduction equipment, preservation of recordings, arrangement, and classification. In addition, Hoffman has compiled a recommended core collection that emphasizes items likely to be found in a large library.

1068 **Manual of music librarianship.** Ed. by Carol June Bradley. Ann Arbor: Music Library Assn., 1966. 140p. LC 68–4808/MN.

This practical manual written in 1966 is directed toward persons responsible for administering a music library. The contents consist of thirteen chapters written by different authorities. Topics cover the basic elements involved in operating a music library, including acquisition of materials for public and academic libraries, classification and cataloging, circulation, dealing with sound recordings, and friends groups. Although several years old, this manual still has value because of its practical coverage of the basic facets of music librarianship.

1069 **Music collections in american libraries: a chronology.** Comp. by Carol June Bradley. Detroit: Information Coordinators, 1981. 249p. (Detroit studies in music bibliographies, no. 46) LC 81–2907/MN. ISBN 0–89990–002–X.

Descriptive information on 374 major music collections in the United States is presented in this source. Arrangement is chronological by date of establishment for each collection, from 1731 to 1978. Each entry supplies the current address of the collection, the nature of the holdings, whether or not there are any published catalogs of the collection, and the library code for the collection. Entries vary in length, depending on the size of the library. A versatile publication, this work can be used as a chronology, a directory, and a guide to resources. The information is indexed by institution and by topics of the collections.

1070 **Music librarianship.** By Malcolm Jones. London: Clive Bingley, 1979. 130p. (Outlines of modern librarianship) LC 80–320356. ISBN 0–85157–274–X.

In addition to presenting an overview of music librarianship, this manual provides specific, practical information on the operation of music libraries. Jones considers the treatment of various types of physical formats found in music libraries, including printed music, recorded music, and the literature of music found in books and periodicals. Also covered is the application of standard library processes (such as acquisitions and circulation) to music libraries. Useful examples are provided throughout.

1071 **Music libraries, including a comprehensive bibliography of music literature and a select bibliography of music scores published since 1957.** By Lionel Roy McColvin and Harold Reeves. Rewritten, rev. and enl. by Jack Dove. London: A. Deutsch, 1965. 2v. LC 65–53118/MN.

Volume 1 of this two-volume set serves as a survey of basic library functions in the music library. Reflecting British practice, the topics covered include staffing the library, selection and acquisition of materials, binding, storage, displaying materials, and classification and cataloging. The volume also contains a directory of music holdings in British public and university libraries and some overseas libraries. Volume 2 consists of an extensive bibliography of music, including music scores, books on various aspects of music, and fiction with a connection to music.

1072   **Organising music in libraries.** By Brian Redfern. London: Clive Bingley, 1978. 2v. LC 78–819. v.1, **Arrangement and classification.** 105p. ISBN 0–208–05144–2. v.2, **Cataloguing.** 151p. ISBN 0–208–01678–3.

This two-volume work focuses on various aspects of cataloging and classifying music materials. In the first volume, classification problems are considered, along with specialized classification schemes and the treatment of music in general schemes. Also covered are methods for arranging sound recordings. The second volume addresses problems associated with descriptive and subject cataloging. Redfern's work is particularly useful because of the special attention he pays to specific types of materials likely to be found in music collections.

Networks and Consortia

DIRECTORIES

1073   **Directory of academic library consortia.** By Donald V. Black and Carlos A. Cuadra. 2d ed. Santa Monica, CA: SDC, 1975. 437p. LC 77–55571.

Approximately 300 consortia or networks of academic libraries are listed in this directory. To qualify for inclusion, a consortium must include two or more autonomous members and be actively functioning. Entries give the name and date founded, geographical area served, names of participating libraries and the date they joined, purposes and objectives, current and projected activities, special services, conditions of participation, annual budgets, sources of funding, role and functions of advisory boards, publications, and location of headquarters. The information is indexed by location, consortia activities, and name of the consortia.

1074   **Directory of library networks and cooperative library organizations, 1980.** By Helen M. Eckard. Washington, DC: National Center for Education Statistics, 1980. 181p. S/N 82–21533. ISSN 0734–824X.

This directory provides information on 608 library networks or cooperatives in the United States. Inclusion in the directory is based on the requirements that 1) membership be largely composed of libraries; 2) cooperative activities extend beyond traditional interlibrary loan; 3) services extend beyond reciprocal borrowing; 4) operation is for the mutual benefit of the constituent members; 5) the scope be interinstitutional. Entries contain the name and address of the organization, any acronyms used, name of director, telephone and teletype numbers, the fiscal or operational year used by the organization, extent of computerization, number of paid staff members, and annual operating costs. There is a subject index.

1075   **Library networks, 1981–82.** Ed. by Susan K. Martin. White Plains, NY: Knowledge Industry, 1981. 160p. (The professional librarian series) LC 80–26710. ISBN 0–9114236–55–5.

This is both a directory and a state of the art review of current developments in computer-based library networks. The text section includes such topics as competition vs. cooperation, patron access to information, the National Periodicals System and its place in networking, implications of machine-readable data for improved access to information, and services of major computer utilities. An appendix provides directory information on thirty networks; entries, arranged alphabetically by name of network, supply network name, address, name and address of director, membership (names and addresses of member libraries), current status, and expected plans for the future. Also included are a glossary and bibliography.

TERMINOLOGY SOURCES

1076   **A glossary for library networking.** By Dataflow Systems, for the Network Development Office, Library of Congress. Washington, DC: Library of Congress, 1978. 39p. LC 78–17002. ISBN 0–8444–0270–2.

About 180 terms that relate to the specialized area of library networking are listed here. Emphasis is on terms of functional value to librarians, computer specialists, and telecommunications engineers involved in developing or operating library networks. Many of these terms are omitted from other glossaries or vocabularies or, if found elsewhere, lack the specialized definition given here. Cross-references are used extensively.

Newspaper Libraries

DIRECTORIES

1077   **Newspaper libraries in the U.S. and Canada: an SLA directory.** Ed. by Elizabeth L. Anderson. 2d ed. New York: Special Libraries Assn., 1980. 321p. LC 80–25188. ISBN 0–87111–265–5.

In this directory, information is provided on the libraries of 314 newspapers with a daily circulation over 25,000 in the United States and Canada. This represents only fifty-six percent of the 558 newspapers with a circulation that high. However, almost all of the newspapers (111 out of 117) with a daily circulation over 100,000 are listed. The entries are divided by country, arranged by state or province, and listed by city. The following information is provided: name of the newspaper, time of issue (e.g., m̄morning), address, circulation figures for March 31, 1979, telephone number of the library, name of person in charge of the library, public access, services available (e.g., copy machines, readers, reader/printers), hours of opening, microform holdings, indexes, special collections, availability of automated filing systems, and products for sale (e.g., photo reprints, library-produced directories). The indexing is by name of city, newspaper group, and personal names. A special feature of the directory is its reprinting of newspaper banners for many of the papers. An earlier edition of this work was published in 1976 and included 297 libraries.

HANDBOOKS AND MANUALS

1078   **The modern news library.** By Geoffrey Whatmore. Syracuse, NY: Gaylord, 1978. 202p. LC 78–16174. ISBN 0–915794–35–7.

This manual is intended as a basic introduction to the processes and procedures of news library service. Whatmore describes those characteristics of library service most common to news libraries, including immediacy, obsolescence, and the archival function. The author focuses on the day-to-day activities in a news library, offering practical recommendations of ways to provide information service in this setting. He discusses in some detail selection of press clippings, daily routines to be followed, organization and arrangement of the collection, subject organization, biographical information, handling special subjects, creation of finding aids, and computer indexing. The emphasis is on British news library practice and examples refer primarily to British libraries. Subject access is provided through the index.

Nonprint Materials

For reference materials on nonprint materials see entries listed under the heading Audiovisual Services and Nonprint Materials.

Online Information Services

BIBLIOGRAPHIC SOURCES

1079 Databases: a bibliography. By Yahiko Kambayashi. Rockville, MD: Computer Science Pr., 1981. 464p. LC 80–26672. ISBN 0–914894–64–1.

A total of 3,912 items published from 1970 to 1980 are included in this bibliography. The subjects covered include data base models, management systems, hardware architecture, design of data base systems, security, distributed systems algorithms, and information theory. Arrangement is topical, under 160 different headings. In addition, there is a subject table arranged by date of publication, a key-word-in-context (KWIC) index, and an author index.

1080 Information sciences: data and information handling, storing, retrieving and dissemination: a DDC bibliography. Alexandria, VA: Defense Documentation Center, 1972. 4v. AD–739 600 (v.1). AD–739 610 (v.2). AD–739 620 (v.3). AD–739 630 (v.4).

This bibliography identifies the unclassified report literature on information storage and retrieval issued by the Defense Documentation Center (DDC) from June 1955 to September 1971. Entries appear as reported in the DDC abstracting service. Subject content is not limited to military applications. The first volume lists materials on storage and retrieval techniques, thesaurus building, and information dissemination research. Other volumes focus on technical information centers, testing techniques, user studies, and reports of conferences and meetings. The entries are indexed by corporate author, monitoring agency, subject, title, and personal author.

1081 On-line information retrieval, 1976–1979: an international bibliography. By J. L. Hall and A. Dewe. London: Aslib, 1980. 230p. (Aslib bibliography, no. 10) LC 80–501218. ISBN 0–85142–127–X.

This international bibliography identifies 890 monographs, articles, and reports covering online retrieval of information. Excluded from coverage are items on automated catalog access and retrieval of online numerical data. Entries are in the original language and annotations are in English. Indexing is by personal author, report number, and subject/name. An earlier volume, *On-line information retrieval, 1965–1976* (entry **1082**), cites over 900 items on the topic.

1082   On-line information retrieval, 1965–1976. Comp. by J. L. Hall. London: Aslib, 1977. 125p. (Aslib bibliography, no. 8) LC 77–375084. ISBN 0–85142–094–X.
This work is continued by *On-line information retrieval, 1976–1979: an international bibliography*. For further information see entry **1081**.

1083   Online information retrieval bibliography, 1964–1979. By Donald T. Hawkins. Marlton, NJ: Learned Information, 1980. 175p.
More than 1,800 items dealing with the retrieval of information from bibliographic, numeric, and full-text data base systems are cited in this bibliography. The emphasis is on retrieval techniques, characteristics of retrieval systems, and retrieval system theory. In addition, there are citations to papers on chemical substructure searching, data base descriptions, and private online retrieval systems. A subject index completes the work.

1084   Online searching: a dictionary and bibliographic guide. By Greg Byerly. Littleton, CO: Libraries Unlimited, to be published in 1983. LC 83–853. ISBN 0–87287–381–1.
This work provides definitions for more than 1,200 terms related to online searching. It also includes a selected, annotated bibliography of 722 journal articles published between 1970 and June 1982 on the same topic. The bibliography citations are grouped into two major sections, "General Overview of Online Searching" and "Specialized Subject Areas and Databases of Online Searching," and further subdivided into specific topics. Byerly also includes a set of articles that instructs beginners how to conduct a search in selected subject areas on representative data bases. Completing the volume are indexes by subject, periodicals cited, and author.

DIRECTORIES

1085   Encyclopedia of information systems and services. Ed. by John Schmittroth, Jr. 5th ed. Detroit: Gale, 1983. 1,248p. LC 82–18359. ISBN 0–8103–1138–0.
A total of 2,500 organizations that produce and disseminate computer-processed information in more than sixty countries are described in this directory. The listing is restricted to organizations specializing in bibliographic, numeric, and full text information. Included are publishers, professional associations and societies, libraries, government agencies, commercial operations, and service bureaus. However, the list does not extend to manufacturers of hardware or non-computerized abstracting and indexing services. Entries specify name, address, telephone number, founding date, head of unit, size of staff, description of the system or service, scope and/or subject matter, sources of input into the system, storage media, publications, microform products and services, computer-based products, availability, and name of a contact person. Foreign names are translated into English. Additional access is provided through twenty-three indexes, including subject, personnel, geographic location, name of data base, software products, and library management systems. This work is supplemented by *New information systems and services* (entry **1086**), also published by Gale.

1086   New information systems and services: a periodic supplement. Ed. by Anthony T. Kruzas and John Schmittroth, Jr. Detroit: Gale, 1981– . ISBN 0–8103–0941–0.
This title is issued as a supplement to *Encyclopedia of information systems and services*. For further information see entry **1085**.

HANDBOOKS AND MANUALS

1087   The library and information manager's guide to online services. Ed. by Ryan E.
Hoover. White Plains, NY: Knowledge Industry, 1980. 270p. LC 80–21602. ISBN
0–914236–60–1.

This manual was prepared to provide library and information service managers with basic
background information about online services. The topics covered include types of data
bases available, producers and vendors of bibliographic online services, measurement and
evaluation, training the searchers, online user groups, and the future of online services. The
chapters are written at a level suitable for persons with limited or moderate experience. The
text is augmented with a number of photographs, drawings, forms, and other graphics to
illustrate Hoover's points. A glossary of online terms, a selected bibliography of additional
items related to the topic, and a subject index complete the volume.

1088   LISA online user manual. Oxford: Learned Information, 1982. 119p. ISBN
0–904933–350.

Designed as a user's guide for online searching in the data base *LISA (Library and
information science abstracts),* this manual describes how to conduct searches on DIALOG
and ORBIT and provides examples of searches on each system. In addition, it lists the 3,000
terms most frequently used for subject indexing in *LISA* (entry **118**). No proper nouns are
included. The terms are presented in a thesaurus format with the use of "BT" for broader
terms, "NT" for narrower terms, etc. Other lists in the manual identify periodicals indexed
in *LISA* and journal title abbreviations used.

**1089   Reference and online services handbook: guidelines, policies, and procedures
for libraries.** Ed. by Bill Katz and Anne Clifford. New York: Neal-Schuman, 1982.
581p. LC 81–11290. ISBN 0–918212–49–9.

Reproduced in this work are excerpts from the reference and online services policy manuals
of academic, public, and special libraries. For further information see entry **1139**.

Oral History Collections

DIRECTORIES

1090   Oral history collections. Comp. and ed. by Alan M. Meckler and Ruth McMullin.
New York: Bowker, 1975. 344p. LC 74–32128. ISBN 0–8352–0603–3.

Listed in this extensive directory are oral history collections found in various types of
libraries, historical societies, archives, government agencies, hospitals, and other types of
institutions. The directory is divided into two parts. The first part contains a name and
subject index to the holdings of the collections. It is arranged alphabetically and includes all
of the known references to oral history holdings in any of the institutions covered in the
volume. Brief information about the holdings, including the number of typescript pages, is
provided. A reference to the institution(s) with the collection(s) is noted. The second part
consists of a listing of institutions with oral history collections. The list is arranged by state
and then by name of institution. Entries indicate name, address, telephone number, persons
responsible for the oral history collection, general information about the collection,
accessibility to the public, and purpose of the program. At the end of the volume there is a

brief section on oral history collections outside of the United States, covering Canada, Israel, and the Republic of Ireland.

HANDBOOKS AND MANUALS

1091   Oral history: from tape to type. By Cullom Davis, Kathryn Back and Kay MacLean. Chicago: American Library Assn., 1977. 141p. LC 77–4403. ISBN 0–8389–0230–8.

Intended as a guide for small or beginning oral history programs, this work provides general instruction and practical guidance in the practices and procedures required to develop an oral history collection. Included throughout the work are examples of forms that can be used and step-by-step instructions for each phase of oral history program development. Also provided is a sample dialogue that can be used as a guide for oral history interviews. Topics covered include collecting, processing, disseminating, and managing oral history. Completing the volume are a glossary of terms, rules of style, and a list of additional sources.

Patient Libraries

For reference materials on patient libraries see entries listed under the heading Medical, Hospital and Patient Libraries.

Periodicals

For reference materials on periodicals see entries listed under the headings Serials Management; Journals in Library and Information Science.

Personnel Policies, Salaries, Benefits and Employee Rights

HANDBOOKS AND MANUALS

1092   Personnel policies in libraries. By Nancy Paton Van Zant. New York: Neal-Schuman, 1980. 334p. LC 80–11734. ISBN 0–918212–26–X.

Excerpts from the personnel policies of more than fifty academic and public libraries are brought together under topics typically found in the policy statements. Some of the topics include affirmative action and equal opportunity, tenure and grievance procedures, evaluation, working conditions, employee relations, professional conduct, and absences and terminations. In addition to the excerpts, four full policy statements are reproduced. Van Zant also reports on a survey of personnel policies in academic and public libraries; data derived from more than 600 respondents are analyzed and presented.

1093   Personnel utilization in libraries: a systems approach. Prep. by Myrl Ricking and Robert E. Booth. Chicago: American Library Assn. with the Illinois State Library, 1974. 158p. LC 74–8688. ISBN 0–8389–3155–3.

This work draws upon a study conducted by the Illinois Library Task Analysis Project that determined the tasks performed in libraries, regardless of job title. The result is a list of functions and tasks organized into eight distinctive categories: collection development, collection organization, collection preparation and maintenance, collection storage and retrieval, circulation, collection interpretation and use, management, and staff development. Within these functional categories, tasks are identified and arranged by three categories of personnel: professional, technical, and clerical. The allocation of tasks to each category reflects U.S. library practice. In addition to the task list, there are chapters describing task identification and analysis, assessment of the library's objectives, and a model for the task analysis process. Several appendices present excerpts from other resources relating to task analysis. Completing the work are a brief glossary of personnel management terms and a selective bibliography of additional readings.

1094   Professional and non-professional duties in libraries: a descriptive list compiled by a working party of the Research and Development Committee of the Library Association. 2d ed. London: Library Assn., 1974. 86p. LC 75–314112. ISBN 0–85365–307–0.

This handbook is designed to distinguish between professional and non-professional duties and responsibilities. The duties and allocation of responsibility to professional or non-professional positions reflect British library practice. However, the assignment of duties does not necessarily reflect the practice of any specific type of library. Nine broad categories of library duties are established and, within each category, individual duties are defined to be professional or non-professional. The categories are general administration; personnel management; public relations; selection and withdrawal of material; acquisition and disposal of materials; cataloging, classification and indexing; production, preparation, conservation, housing, and handling of materials and associated equipment; information work and assistance to readers; and lending function of the libraries. A total of 273 duties are identified and indexed by subject.

1095   Public libraries: smart practices in personnel. By Peggy Sullivan and William Ptacek. Littleton, CO: Libraries Unlimited, 1982. 95p. LC 82–15334. ISBN 0–87287–278–5.

This manual defines and describes methods and techniques of personnel practice in all sizes of public libraries. Drawing on their own experiences, the authors provide examples to illustrate suggested personnel practice. Among the specific topics covered are organizational structure and theory, salary and wage structure, benefits, budgeting, employee evaluation, grievance procedures, hiring, promotions, terminations, and staff development.

1096   Rights of the public employee. By Robert P. Dwoskin. Chicago: American Library Assn., 1978. 269p. LC 78–1658. ISBN 0–8389–0257–X.

Although not limited to the rights of library employees, this work evolved out of legal work done on behalf of a public librarian. It is a handbook to which any public employee can turn for guidance about employment rights under the law. Chapters deal with such topics as exclusion and dismissal from public service, freedom of expression, political activities, belief and association, due process rights, and public employee unions. Examples are drawn from the whole spectrum of public employment. While legal vocabulary is kept to a minimum, cases are cited and legal precedents are noted to illustrate the author's points. The text is indexed by subject.

STATISTICAL SOURCES

1097   ALA survey of librarian salaries. Prep. by Mary Jo Lynch, et al. Chicago: Office for Research and Office for Library Personnel Resources, American Library Assn., 1982. 108p. LC 82–11537. ISBN 0–8389–3275–4.

This work provides salary statistics for full-time professional librarians in thirteen different library positions, including directors, assistant directors, reference librarians, and documents librarians. The data were compiled from a January 1982 survey of 1,400 randomly selected public libraries serving populations of 25,000 or more and academic libraries not belonging to the Association of Research Libraries. These groups were chosen for study because their salary data are not included in other sources. Data in this volume are arranged by type of library and geographical region. For most job positions, figures are provided for low, mean, and high salaries. Following the salary tables are an analysis of the data, an article entitled "Employee Compensation and the Library Manager," an annotated bibliography of other sources providing salary information, an enumeration of ALA policies relating to salary issues, a selected bibliography of items on compensation and benefits, and information about the survey methods used in the study.

1098   ARL annual salary survey. Washington, DC: Assn. of Research Libraries, 1975/76– . Annual. LC 76–640547. ISSN 0361–5669.

Salary information for members of the Association of Research Libraries is reported here. Data includes salary range of librarians employed at ARL libraries; median and beginning professional salaries; average, median, and beginning salaries for individual libraries; beginning salaries for individual libraries in rank order; median salaries in rank order; summary of rankings of individual libraries for a five-year period; salaries compared to the *Consumer Price Index;* and distribution of salaries by frequency.

1099   SLA triennial salary survey. New York: Special Libraries Assn., 1983. 74p. LC 83–595. ISBN 0–87111–302–3.

This is the sixth survey of members salaries conducted by the Special Libraries Association. The first was conducted in 1959 and the previous five were published in issues of *Special libraries.* The current survey reports data for 3,255 respondents (thirty-six percent of SLA's membership as of April, 1982). The data are reported in seventy-eight separate tables, including salary distribution by sex, by type of institution, by number of professional employees supervised, by highest subject degree, and by job title. Some of the tables provide comparison data taken from the previous SLA salary surveys. Although not indexed, the survey has a detailed table of contents.

1100   Statistics of public libraries in the United States and Canada serving 100,000 population or more. Comp. by Rick J. Ashton. Fort Wayne, IN: Allen County Public Library, 1981. 9 leaves. LC 81–211358.

Included in the report are data for each library on size of population served, total budget, per capita total expenditures, appropriation for materials and for total salaries, salary of director, tenure of director, salary of assistant director, tenure of assistant director, and current salary for beginning professionals. For further information see entry **575.**

Photocopying

For reference materials on photocopying see entries listed under the heading Interlibrary Loan and Photocopying.

Picture Librarianship

HANDBOOKS AND MANUALS

1101 Picture librarianship. Ed. by Helen P. Harrison. Phoenix: Oryx, 1981. 542p. LC 81–11291. ISBN 0–89774–011–4.

The topic of picture librarianship is treated thoroughly in this work. Both British and American practice are represented. The first section of the manual is arranged topically, with chapters written by different contributors. Topics covered include pictures as information, history of picture libraries, photography and printing, sources for obtaining pictures, selection, processing, preservation and storage, arrangement and indexing, microforms, exploitation or utilization of pictures, and administration. The chapters are informative and provide practical guidance for librarians working with picture collections. The second section presents case studies and surveys of various types of picture libraries. A total of twenty-six libraries from Britain and North America are covered in descriptive essays of eight to ten pages each. A lengthy bibliography of additional readings is included, and the work is indexed by subject.

Planning Libraries

DIRECTORIES

1102 Directory of planning and urban affairs libraries in the United States and Canada, 1980. Ed. by Jean S. Gottlieb. Ottawa: Council of Planning Librarians, 1980. 120p. (CPL bibliography) LC 80–111867.

A total of 291 planning and urban affairs libraries are listed in the most recent edition of this directory. Arrangement is by state, by city, and then by library. Entries contain name, address, telephone number, contact person, numerical data on holdings, special strengths, publications, and hours of opening. The information is indexed by name of parent organization or agency and personal name. Earlier editions of this directory were published in 1969 and 1971 under slightly different titles.

HANDBOOKS AND MANUALS

1103 Planning and urban affairs library manual. Ed. by Mary L. Knobbe. 3d ed. Washington, DC: International City Management Assn., 1975. 122p. NUC 78–39529. ISBN 0–87326–015–5.

Prepared for persons without formal library education, and published for the Council of Planning Librarians, this manual describes library functions in a small urban affairs or planning agency library. Written without the use of technical vocabulary, it covers such topics as planning for space and equipment, developing the library collection (accompanied by a selected bibliography of basic books), classifying and cataloging, budgeting, and offering reference service. There are three appendices. The first is the International City

Manager Association's subject descriptor list, a thesaurus of recommended terms on local government. The second is a directory of organizations and public interest groups concerned with local government; brief information about each is presented. The third is a list of publishers active in planning, urban affairs, or local government. The manual is not indexed.

Preservation

For reference materials on preservation see entries listed under the heading Conservation of Library Materials.

Prison Libraries

For reference materials on prison libraries see entries listed under the heading Jail and Prison Library Service.

Prizes

For reference materials on prizes see entries listed under the heading Awards and Prizes.

Programs

For reference materials on programs see entries listed under the heading Public Relations, Programs and Exhibits.

Proposal Writing

For reference materials on proposal writing see entries listed under the heading Grants and Proposal Writing.

Public Libraries and Librarianship

Materials on public libraries also appear elsewhere in this guide. For bibliographies, directories, biographical, and statistical sources covering public libraries in general, see the appropriate chapter in Part One. Included here are reference materials dealing with various aspects of public libraries and librarianship as a subject.

BIBLIOGRAPHIC SOURCES

1104 **Fact book of the american public library.** Comp. by Herbert Goldhor. Urbana: Graduate School of Library and Information Science, Univ. of Illinois, 1981. 80p. (Occasional papers, no. 150) LC 82–621199. ISSN 0276–1769.

Provided here are references to statistical information about American public libraries from

1970–1978 that are in a machine-readable data base at the University of Illinois' Library Research Center. Cited in the data base are annual reports, journal articles, library surveys, monographs, dissertations, report literature, and other sources. Goldhor's "fact book" abstracts these sources. Entries are arranged alphabetically by topic under 138 subject terms.

1105   Public, school, and academic media centers: a guide to information sources. By Esther R. Dyer. Detroit: Gale, 1981. 237p. (Books, publishing and libraries information guide, v.3) LC 74–11554. ISBN 0–8103–1286–7.

In this guide to the literature, only materials current and easily available are listed. For further information see entry **1141**.

DIRECTORIES

1106   Directory of outreach services in public libraries. By the Office for Library Service to the Disadvantaged, American Library Association. Chicago: American Library Assn., 1980. 632p. ISBN 0–8389–32442–8.

Over 400 outreach programs sponsored by public libraries located in thirty-three states are described in this directory. For further information see entry **872**.

HANDBOOKS AND MANUALS

1107   ABC's of library promotion. By Steve Sherman. 2d ed. Metuchen, NJ: Scarecrow, 1980. 242p. LC 79–24232. ISBN 0–8108–1274–6.

This practical manual is intended for use in small and medium-sized public libraries. For further information see entry **1126**.

1108   Administration of the small public library. By Dorothy Sinclair. 2d ed. Chicago: American Library Assn., 1979. 156p. LC 79–12338. ISBN 0–8389–0291–X.

This revision of an earlier manual published in 1965 tends to place more emphasis on governance, finance, and planning functions, and less on services. All major administrative functions are addressed, including library objectives, policies, personnel administration, and interlibrary cooperation. A number of examples illustrate the points made. Each chapter is accompanied by a brief bibliography of selected additional readings. The book is directed toward new and inexperienced administrators of small public libraries, although the content is also appropriate for librarians of larger libraries and heads of branch libraries in larger systems.

1109   A data gathering and instructional manual for performance measures in public libraries. By Ellen Altman, et al. Chicago: Celadon, 1976. 171p.

Basic instructions in gathering and analyzing data for performance measures in public libraries is provided in this manual. For further information see entry **986**.

1110   Design of the small public library. By Rolf Myller. New York: Bowker, 1966. 95p. LC 66–20401.

Practical advice for persons planning and designing small public libraries is provided in this manual. For further information see entry **787**.

1111   Experiencing displays. By Rita Kohn. Metuchen, NJ: Scarecrow, 1982. 220p. LC 82–3187. ISBN 0–8108–1534–6.

This compendium of display ideas for school and public libraries is organized according to concepts or the shapes of physical objects (e.g., cylinders). For further information see entry **1128**.

1112   Handbuch des büchereiwesens. Ed. by Johannes Langfeldt. Wiesbaden: Harrassowitz, 1976. ISBN 3–447–01732–5.

This encyclopedic work covers the history and present conditions of public library services in Germany and German-speaking countries. For further information see entry **219**.

1113   Libraries designed for users: a planning handbook. By Nolan Lushington and Willis N. Mills, Jr. Syracuse, NY: Gaylord, 1979. 289p. LC 78–27114. ISBN 0–915794–29–2.

User convenience serves as the focus for this handbook on planning public library buildings for communities of 100,000 population or less. For further information see entry **789**.

1114   Library promotion handbook. By Marian S. Edsall. Phoenix: Oryx, 1980. 244p. (A Neal-Schuman professional book) LC 79–26984. ISBN 0–912700–15–7.

Aimed at the library director or public information officer, this work is primarily related to public library public relations activities. For further information see entry **1131**.

1115   Output measures for public libraries. By Douglas Zweizig and Eleanor Jo Rodger. Chicago: American Library Assn., 1982. 100p. LC 82–1720. ISBN 0–8389–3272–X.

This manual was developed by the Goals, Guidelines and Standards Committee of the ALA Public Library Association to assist librarians in collecting data that describe library services to the community (output measures). For further information see entry **990**.

1116   A planning process for public libraries. By Vernon E. Palmour, Marcia C. Bellassai and Nancy V. DeWath. Chicago: American Library Assn., 1980. 304p. LC 80–13107. ISBN 0–8389–3246–0.

Designed to be used in the planning and development of public library standards and services at the local level (in order to reflect local community library and information needs), this manual represents a significant effort by the Public Library Association and the authors. The emphasis is on meeting client needs by engaging in a broadly based planning effort that involves various segments of the local population. Guidelines are provided for the implementation of the planning process, including preparing to plan, and the collection and utilization of data. Included with the text are forms, tables, sample surveys, sample maps for the community profile, and a bibliography of additional source materials.

1117   Public libraries: smart practices in personnel. By Peggy Sullivan and William Ptacek. Littleton, CO: Libraries Unlimited, 1982. 95p. LC 82–15334. ISBN 0–87287–278–5.

This manual defines and describes methods and techniques of personnel practice in all sizes of public libraries. For further information see entry **1095**.

1118 Public library law: an international survey. New Delhi: Metropolitan, 1971. 624p.

This work provides a country-by-country account of public library legislation. For further information see entry **1003**.

1119 Public library law and the law as to museums and art galleries in England and Wales, Scotland and Northern Ireland. By A. R. Hewitt. 5th ed. London: Assn. of Assistant Librarians, Library Assn., 1975. 109p. LC 76–362404. ISBN 0–900092–25–4.

Major changes in library legislation in the United Kingdom came about subsequent to the 4th edition of this work, and those changes are reflected in this edition. For further information see entry **1004**.

1120 Rights of the public employee. By Robert P. Dwoskin. Chicago: American Library Assn., 1978. 269p. LC 78–1658. ISBN 0–8389–0257–X.

Although not limited to the rights of library employees, this work evolved out of legal work done on behalf of a public librarian. For further information see entry **1096**.

1121 School and public library media programs for children and young adults. By D. Philip Baker. Syracuse, NY: Gaylord, 1977. 412p. LC 76–54919. ISBN 0–915794–09–8.

Descriptions of exemplary public and school library media programs selected from across the country are presented in this source. For further information see entry **1150**.

1122 Weeding library collections—II. By Stanley J. Slote. 2d rev. ed. Littleton, CO: Libraries Unlimited, 1982. 198p. LC 81–20724. ISBN 0–87287–283–1.

The philosophy, process, and procedures of weeding, or deselection of materials from libraries, are dealt with in this manual, with emphasis on public library collections. For further information see entry **829**.

1123 Wheeler and Goldhor's practical administration of public libraries. Rev. by Carlton Rochell. New York: Harper, 1981. 464p. LC 79–3401. ISBN 0–06–13601–4.

This manual describes the basic components of public library service for various sized libraries. A total of twenty-one chapters are grouped into three broad sections: planning, management, personnel, finance, organization; administration of services to the public; and administration of support services. Written for the public library manager, the work includes history, theory, and practical guidance in the management of the types of service covered. Each chapter includes a bibliography of additional readings and there is a selected, annotated bibliography of significant related works provided at the end.

STATISTICAL SOURCES

1124 ALA survey of librarian salaries. Prep. by Mary Jo Lynch, et al. Chicago: Office for Research and Office for Library Personnel Resources, American Library Assn., 1982. 108p. LC 82–11537. ISBN 0–8389–3275–4.

Salary statistics for full-time professional librarians in thirteen different library positions were compiled from a January 1982 survey of 1,400 randomly selected public libraries serving populations of 25,000 or more and academic libraries not belonging to the Association of Research Libraries. For further information see entry **1097**.

Public Relations, Programs and Exhibits
BIOGRAPHICAL SOURCES

1125 **Library public relations workshop consultants.** Comp. by the Public Relations Section of the Library Administration and Management Association. Chicago: Library Administration and Management Assn., American Library Assn., 1982. 58p.

Listed in this directory are persons who have conducted a minimum of five public relations workshops or seminars within the past five years.

HANDBOOKS AND MANUALS

1126 **ABC's of library promotion.** By Steve Sherman. 2d ed. Metuchen, NJ: Scarecrow, 1980. 242p. LC 79–24232. ISBN 0–8108–1274–6.

Intended for use in small and medium-sized public libraries, this practical manual includes instructions on writing press releases and other news or feature items, preparing public service announcements for radio or television, and producing videotape or slide/tape presentations. Suggestions for cultivating support from prominent citizens and library users and developing support within the political community are also included.

1127 **Effective library exhibits: how to prepare and promote good displays.** By Kate Coplan. 2d ed. Dobbs Ferry, NY: Oceana, 1974. 176p. LC 74–4428. ISBN 0–379–00265–5.

Based on her long experience as Chief of Exhibits and Publicity at Enoch Pratt Free Library, Coplan has provided a detailed, illustrated manual on the preparation of exhibits in libraries. Many of the illustrations are photographs of successful library exhibits. Although the author's experience is largely in the public library, the suggestions offered are applicable to any type of library. The work begins with a rationale for exhibits and proceeds to discuss resources needed, exhibit preparation, use of lighting, use of silk screen techniques, captions, sources of free or inexpensive display materials, and numerous other topics. Also provided are a list of sources of supplies and equipment, a bibliography of related readings, and a subject index.

1128 **Experiencing displays.** By Rita Kohn. Metuchen, NJ: Scarecrow, 1982. 220p. LC 82–3187. ISBN 0–8108–1534–6.

This compendium of display ideas for school and public libraries is organized according to concepts or the shapes of physical objects (e.g., cylinders). Included with each display idea are objectives, recommendations for actions or activities to accompany the display, and suggestions for the preparation of the display. Photographs and drawings illustrate each display idea. In the appendices are forms for planning displays, photographs of additional displays, a glossary of terms, and a statement of display philosophy. The text is indexed by subject.

1129   Library display ideas. By Linda Campbell Franklin. Jefferson, NC: McFarland, 1980. 230p. LC 80–17036. ISBN 0–89950–008–0.

Practical ideas for library exhibits and displays, particularly in school libraries, are presented in this manual. After the introductory chapter, which covers such basics as obtaining the right supplies and equipment, Franklin describes month-by-month or topical ideas that can be used for exhibits. Each exhibit idea is accompanied by an illustration and construction instructions. Appendices include a month-by-month calendar of events and a list of manufacturers and distributors. A subject index concludes the work.

1130   Library programs: how to select, plan and produce them. By John S. Robotham and Lydia LaFleur. Metuchen, NJ: Scarecrow, 1976. 295p. LC 76–2033. ISBN 0–8108–0911–7.

This work describes methods for planning and implementing various types of programs, ranging from performing arts programs to workshops and automated programs. The work is divided into three sections. The first discusses the characteristics of various types of programs, including needed equipment, facilities, and ideas for possible programs. The second deals with finding and choosing the appropriate program for the library's needs. The third covers program planning and production. Practical suggestions and first-hand examples are provided throughout to elaborate on ideas presented. Appendices include sample book lists, a list of discussion films, a sample film program, sources for obtaining films, and sample flyers for publicity. A selected, annotated bibliography also is provided, as is a subject index.

1131   Library promotion handbook. By Marian S. Edsall. Phoenix: Oryx, 1980. 244p. (A Neal-Schuman professional book) LC 79–26984. ISBN 0–912700–15–7.

Aimed at the library director or public information officer, this work serves as a practical guide to library public relations activities. Included are such topics as using media for publicity and library exhibits and displays. First-hand examples and illustrations are also provided. While the information presented in this manual applies to various types of libraries, it is most related to public library activity.

1132   Marketing the library. By Benedict A. Leerburger. White Plains, NY: Knowledge Industry, 1982. 124p. LC 81–18132. ISBN 0–9144236–89–X.

Strategies for enlisting community support and attracting new users to all types of libraries are covered in this handbook. Included are practical suggestions for writing press releases, using newsletters and annual reports to market the library, developing special events and programs, establishing and maintaining relationships with other community groups, and lobbying for support with public officials.

1133   Poster ideas and bulletin board techniques: for libraries and schools. By Kate Coplan. 2d ed. Dobbs Ferry, NY: Oceana, 1981. 248p. LC 80–24971. ISBN 0–379–20333–2.

This compendium of ideas for posters and bulletin boards can be used by both public and school librarians. Illustrations, in black and white as well as color, are used to highlight points made in each chapter. Among the topics covered are use of color, design of "attention-getting bulletin boards," exhibits representing the seasons, and care and preservation of display materials. One long section focuses on display ideas and presents photographs of exhibits and bulletin boards for a variety of occasions. A list of sources of supplies is included, as are a selected bibliography of readings and a subject index. The first edition of this handbook was published by Oceana in 1962.

1134 68 great ideas: the library awareness handbook. Ed. by Peggy Barber. Chicago: American Library Assn., 1982. 68p. LC 82–11518. ISBN 0–8389–0376–2.
The sixty-eight ideas included in this handbook were selected, from several hundred submitted by all types of libraries throughout the United States, on the basis of their effectiveness in stimulating awareness of libraries among users and the general population. Examples include consumer awareness programs, direct mail campaigns, and a health awareness day. A separate entry is devoted to each idea; the entry contains an identification of the target audience, description of the idea, name of the organization from which the idea originated, and name, address, and telephone number of a contact person from whom the reader can obtain further information.

1135 You can do it: a PR manual for librarians. By Rita Kohn and Krysta Tepper. Metuchen, NJ: Scarecrow, 1981. 232p. LC 80–24217. ISBN 0–8108–1401–3.
Intended to provide practical information for the planning and implementing of library public relations programs, this manual is arranged in outline form and includes checklists or guidelines to be considered. Among the topics covered are use of signs, displays and exhibits, advertising and other use of the media, and staff self-inventory. Sample forms and suggested procedures are provided. There are two appendices, one presenting suggestions for giving a public speech and the second offering directions for writing a feature section on books for publication.

Rare Book Librarianship
HANDBOOKS AND MANUALS

1136 Rare book librarianship. By Roderick Cave. Hamden, CT: Shoe String, 1976. 168p. LC 75–29045. ISBN 0–208–01360–1.
Custodianship of rare books and the management a rare books collection are the main topics covered in this manual. In this respect, it is unlike the majority of items published on rare books; those are concerned with bibliography or the collection of the materials. Cave's work is intended to provide practical guidance to librarians responsible for rare book collections, particularly to individuals with limited previous experience in this area. The author uses examples from British practice, but they are generalizable to any country. The specific subjects addressed include acquiring rare books, processing, cataloging and classification, care and restoration, housing, organizing the collections for use, publicity and publications, and training rare book librarians. Several photographs and illustrations augment the text. A subject index is provided.

Reference Librarianship
BIBLIOGRAPHIC SOURCES

1137 The information interview: a comprehensive bibliography and an analysis of the literature. By Wayne W. Crouch. Syracuse, NY: ERIC-IR, 1979. 44p.

This annotated bibliography identifies materials concerned with the reference or informa-tion interview. The citations include articles, reports, dissertations and theses, conference proceedings, and parts of monographs. Abstracts are of variable length, but some are quite lengthy. Indexing is by subject and author. The listing is preceded by an introduction to the topic, summarizing what is known about the interview process and identifying some of the major aspects of the topic.

1138   **Reference service: an annotated bibliographic guide.** By Marjorie E. Murfin and Lubomyr R. Wynar. Littleton, CO: Libraries Unlimited, 1977. 294p. LC 76–54879. ISBN 0–87287–132–0.

Identified in this bibliography are 1,258 monographs, journal articles, reports, theses, and dissertations concerned with various aspects of library reference service. The bibliography covers the time period from 1876 through 1975 and is extensive but selective in coverage. Each item has a descriptive annotation as well as full bibliographic information. ERIC report citations include the document accession number. The bibliography is divided into fourteen chapters (and numerous sub-chapters), including history of reference service, theory and philosophy, reference service in each of the four major types of libraries, special types of reference service, the reference process, research in reference, and information retrieval. Entries are indexed by author and title. The only subject access is provided through the numerous cross references.

HANDBOOKS AND MANUALS

1139   **Reference and online services handbook: guidelines, policies, and procedures for libraries.** Ed. by Bill Katz and Anne Clifford. New York: Neal-Schuman, 1982. 581p. LC 81–11290. ISBN 0–918212–49–9.

Reproduced in this work are excerpts from the reference and online services policy manuals of academic, public, and special libraries. The policies, solicited during 1980 and early 1981, are taken from large and medium-sized libraries. The work is arranged in five sections. The first consists of articles addressing the need for service policy manuals. Among the items included is a reprint of RASD's policy guidelines, titled "A Commitment to Information Services: Developmental Guidelines, 1979." Part 2 presents excerpts from academic libraries' reference policy statements. Excerpts from public libraries' reference policies are included in Part 3. Part 4 provides excerpts from academic, public, and special libraries' online service policies. The final part offers the full service policies of an academic, public, and special library. These are presented as examples of model policies.

Research in Librarianship

For reference materials on research in librarianship see entries listed under the heading Library Evaluation, Measurement and Research.

Russian and Soviet Studies Libraries

DIRECTORIES

1140   **Scholars' guide to Washington, D.C. for russian/soviet studies.** By Steven A.

Grant. Washington, DC: Smithsonian Inst. Pr., 1977. 403p. (Scholars' guide to Washington, D.C., no. 1) LC 77–22563. ISBN 0–87474–484–9.

This directory identifies libraries, archives, museums, film and map collections, and other types of institutions and agencies in the Washington area that hold collections or make available information about the Soviet Union. The volume is divided into two part. The first identifies collections of materials; the second identifies organizations that can provide information on Soviet topics. Arrangement is by type of collection or institution. Entries contain name, address, and telephone number of the institution or agency, notes on the size and nature of the collection (including subjective comments on the quality of the collection), and a descriptive note on programs and activities sponsored by the institution.

Salaries and Benefits

For reference materials on salaries and benefits see entries listed under the heading Personnel Policies, Salaries, Benefits and Employee Rights.

Scholarships and Fellowships

For reference materials on scholarships and fellowships see entries listed under the heading Financial Aid.

School Libraries/Media Centers

Materials on school libraries/media centers also appear elsewhere in this guide. For bibliographies, directories, biographical, and statistical sources covering school libraries/media centers in general, see the appropriate chapter in Part One. Included here are reference materials dealing with various aspects of school libraries/media centers as a subject.

BIBLIOGRAPHIC SOURCES

1141 Public, school, and academic media centers: a guide to information sources. By Esther R. Dyer. Detroit: Gale, 1981. 237p. (Books, publishing and libraries information guide series, v. 3) LC 74–11554. ISBN 0–8103–1286–7.

In this bibliographic guide to the literature of various library media programs, only materials current and easily available to professionals are listed. The work is divided into six parts, including management, collection development, and facilities design. Among the specific subjects covered are copyright, legislation, intellectual freedom, networking, and cable regulations.

BIOGRAPHICAL SOURCES

1142 International Association of School Librarianship: membership directory. Kalamazoo, MI: International Assn. of School Librarianship, 19??– . Biennial.

Included in this directory of association members are individuals involved in various types of school library activity throughout the world. Entries specify members' position and

295

institutional affiliation. The number of entries in each biennial edition varies, but the listing in the most recent issue exceeds 500.

HANDBOOKS AND MANUALS

1143 Censorship, libraries, and the law. Comp. by Haig Bosmajian. New York: Neal-Schuman, 1983. 240p. LC 83–2161. ISBN 0–918212–54–5.
This work contains the full text of court opinions in censorship cases involving school libraries, as well as U.S. Supreme Court decisions cited by the lower courts. For further information see entry **929**.

1144 Evaluation techniques for school library media programs: a workshop outline. By Blanche Woolls, David Loertscher and Donald Shirey. Pittsburgh: Graduate School of Library and Information Sciences, Univ. of Pittsburgh, 1977. 85p.
Although this manual covering the evaluation of school library/media was designed to be used in a workshop setting, it can also be used independently. For further information see entry **987**.

1145 Experiencing displays. By Rita Kohn. Metuchen, NJ: Scarecrow, 1982. 220p. LC 82–3187. ISBN 0–8108–1534–6.
This compendium of display ideas for school and public libraries is organized according to concepts or shapes of physical objects (e.g., cylinders). For further information see entry **1128**.

1146 Handbook for school media personnel. By Philip M. Turner. 2d ed. Littleton, CO: Libraries Unlimited, 1980. 132p. LC 80–21152. ISBN 0–87287–225–4.
This work is concerned with the operation and management of a school audiovisual center. Practical suggestions are offered, based on the experience of the author and other media personnel in the field. Among the topics covered are equipment selection, maintenance, and distribution; production of instructional materials; training faculty to use both hardware and software; and communications with the faculty. Augmenting the text are such helpful items as pre-purchase checklists, examples of forms to be used with equipment maintenance, and a bibliography of additional resources.

1147 Library display ideas. By Linda Campbell Franklin. Jefferson, NC: McFarland, 1980. 230p. LC 80–17036. ISBN 0–89950–008–0.
Practical ideas for library exhibits and displays, particularly in school libraries, are presented in this manual. For further information see entry **1129**.

1148 Media center facilities design. Comp. and ed. by Jane Anne Hannigan and Glenn E. Estes. Chicago: American Library Assn., 1978. 117p. LC 78–9336. ISBN 0–8389–3212–6.
Guidelines for planning and designing school library/media centers are presented in this work. For further information see entry **791**.

1149   **The principal's handbook: on the school library media center.** By Betty Martin and Ben Carson. Syracuse, NY: Gaylord, 1978. 212p. LC 78–1957. ISBN 0–915794–22–5.

Intended for school principals, this publication attempts to define the role of the school library media center and to indicate the responsibilities and roles of various key individuals, including the principal, teachers, media specialist, and district media director. Additionally, the manual examines the goals and objectives of media programs, the difference between a traditional library and a media center, and the relationship of the media program to the school program. Procedures for evaluating media programs are suggested to the principal. Several appendices are included, for example, a list of 100 representative media center tasks, educational media program criteria, and a survey checklist of library services. Also provided are a bibliography and a subject index.

1150   **School and public library media programs for children and young adults.** By D. Philip Baker. Syracuse, NY: Gaylord, 1977. 412p. LC 76–54919. ISBN 0–915794–09–8.

Descriptions of exemplary library media programs selected from across the country are presented in this source. The main body of the work consists of a state-by-state account of selected school and public libraries, indicating the services offered, funding, staff size, target population, and program objectives. In all, fifty programs are covered and indexed by subject.

1151   **School librarian's encyclopedic dictionary.** By Fay Dix Marshall. West Nyack, NY: Parker, 1979. 248p. LC 79–10365. ISBN 0–13–793679–6.

Arranged alphabetically, this encyclopedia deals with topics in librarianship and the book world as they relate to school libraries. Curriculum-related topics, such as ancient history, and technical aspects of librarianship, such as cataloging, are covered. Articles vary in length from less than a column to several pages; some are lengthy and complex enough to be subdivided. A topical or broad subject area index pulls together related articles, such as those on audiovisual aids. Further access is available through a conventional subject index.

1152   **School library and media center acquisitions policies and procedures.** Ed. by Mary M. Taylor. Phoenix: Oryx, 1981. 272p. LC 80–23115. ISBN 0–912700–70–X.

This is a compilation of acquisition and selection policies prepared by school library media centers. For further information see entry **675**.

1153   **The school library media center.** By Emanuel T. Prostano and Joyce S. Prostano. 3d ed. Littleton, CO: Libraries Unlimited, 1982. 230p. ISBN 0–87287–286–6.

This manual places the operation and management of the school library media center within the context of the school's total educational program. Chapters cover such topics as facilities and furniture, equipment, and the budget. All facets of effective library media center management are discussed. Earlier editions of this work were published in 1971 and 1977.

1154   **The school library media program: instructional force for excellence.** By Ruth Ann Davies. 3d ed. New York: Bowker, 1979. 580p. LC 79–20358. ISBN 0–8352–1244–0.

Concerned with the role and function of the school library media center, Davies deals with such topics as the library media specialist's role as instructional technologist, curriculum programs supported by the library media program, and program evaluation techniques. Appendices provide media evaluation guidelines, instructions on how to use ERIC, facilities planning, a sample resource unit, a glossary of terms, and a bibliography. The text is indexed by subject. The 1973 and 1974 editions were published by Bowker under a slightly different title.

1155 Steps to service: a handbook of procedures for the school library media center. By Mildred L. Nickel. Chicago: American Library Assn., 1975. 124p. LC 74–19420. ISBN 0–8389–0161–1.

This practical manual is designed to present, in non-technical terms, the steps and procedures required to organize a school library media center. It is intended for the new professional and for the experienced librarian interested in evaluating existing services. Among the topics covered are selection, ordering, processing, circulation, and planning and implementing programs and service. A new edition is scheduled to be published in summer, 1983.

1156 A systematic process for planning media programs. By James Liesner. Chicago: American Library Assn., 1976. 166p. LC 76–3507. ISBN 0–8389–0176–X.

In this manual for planning school library/media programs, an important evaluation component is included. For further information, see entry **991**.

YEARBOOKS

1157 School library yearbook. Comp. by the Education Committee, American Library Association. Chicago: American Library Assn., 1927–1932. Annual. LC 27–26905.

During the period of publication, this yearbook carried a variety of information, including news items from state school library supervisors, information on teaching the use of the library, and standards for libraries in elementary and secondary schools and in teachers' colleges. Along with articles, each volume provides a directory of school librarians who were members of ALA and a directory of state school library supervisors. Statistics are included often also.

Security Systems
HANDBOOKS AND MANUALS

1158 Book theft and library security systems, 1981–82. By Alice Harrison Bahr. White Plains, NY: Knowledge Industry, 1981. 157p. LC 80–26643. ISBN 0–914236–71–7.

Existing electronic security systems for libraries are described in this handbook. Included is information about the distribution, operation, cost, installation, and special features of each of the systems currently available on the market. Cost comparisons are presented tabularly. The opinions of librarians who have installed specific systems are presented in an appendix.

Bahr proposes practical methods for conducting an inventory, sampling, and taking a census of the collection to determine and limit losses. The author also includes statistical information documenting the loss of library materials and the need for security systems.

Selection

For reference materials on selection see entries listed under the heading Collection Development.

Serials Management

BIBLIOGRAPHIC SOURCES

1159 Serials automation in the United States: a bibliographic history. By Gary M. Pitkin. Metuchen, NJ: Scarecrow, 1976. 148p. LC 76–18116. ISBN 0–8108–0955–9.

In this specialized, annotated bibliography, articles covering serials automation published between 1951 and 1974 are cited. For further information see entry **748**.

DIRECTORIES

1160 International subscription agents: an annotated directory. 4th ed. Chicago: Resources and Technical Services Division, American Library Assn., 1978. 125p. LC 77–2667. ISBN 0–8389–0259–6.

Over 200 vendors and subscription agents who accept orders for international subscriptions to periodicals and serials are listed alphabetically in this directory. For each, the following information is presented: name and address, geographic specialization, types of materials the dealer will supply, discounts, ratings by library users, and acquisition procedures. Entries are indexed by country of specialization.

HANDBOOKS AND MANUALS

1161 Guide to magazine and serial agents. By Bill Katz and Peter Gellatly. New York: Bowker, 1975. 239p. LC 75–26616. ISBN 0–8352–0789–7.

This work is intended to assist librarians in determining the best serials or periodical agent for their library. The authors attempt to present sufficient "background information concerning serials and their management to provide an understanding of the agent-library relationship and providing facts, details, and descriptions of the services and procedures of the major and selected smaller domestic and foreign serials subscription agents." The manual is divided into four parts. The first reviews the place of serials and periodicals in the library and the characteristics of periodical publishing. The second deals with the role of subscription agents and how to select them. Part III discusses serials management. The last part contains several checklists to be used in analyzing and locating serials agents and services. Also included is a directory of subscription agents that, because of the date of the publication, can no longer be considered accurate.

1162 Serial publications: their place and treatment in libraries. By Andrew D. Osborn. 3d ed. Chicago: American Library Assn., 1980. 486p. LC 80–116686. ISBN 0–8389–0299–5.

Written from an American perspective, this manual describes the basic functions of serials librarianship, including selecting, acquiring, checking, cataloging, storing, utilizing, and abstracting and indexing. The third edition has been updated to provide information about the application of computer processes, but it does not present sufficient detail to enable readers to rely solely on the information supplied here. Previous editions of the work were published in 1973 and 1955.

1163 Serials librarianship. By Ross Bourne. London: Library Assn., 1981. 272p. LC 81–129419. ISBN 0–85365–631–2.

The underlying assumption of the author in this manual is that serials must be treated differently and managed separately in a library because of the continuous and repetitive procedures to be followed. Based on this assumption, the author describes the basic functions of serials librarianship, including selecting and acquiring, checking, claiming, and cataloging. He also examines serial librarianship as it exists in various types of libraries. Among the other topics covered in the manual are bibliographic standards as they apply to serials, application of automation to serials librarianship, and education of serials librarians. Examples and observations tend to reflect British practice and experience.

1164 Serials: past, present and future. By Clara D. Brown and Lynn S. Smith. 2d rev. ed. Birmingham, AL: EBSCO Industries, 1980. 390p. LC 80–81267. ISBN 0–913956–05–8.

This manual provides a step-by-step description of the processes and procedures involved in serials work. Among the topics covered are created and using a "kardex" file for serials, claiming missing issues, and binding. Sample forms that apply to serials work are reproduced to be used by the readers. The first edition of this work was published by C. D. Brown in 1972 under the title *Serials acquisition & maintenance.*

Sign Systems
HANDBOOKS AND MANUALS

1165 Sign systems for libraries: solving the wayfinding problem. Comp. and ed. by Dorothy Pollet and Peter C. Haskell. New York: Bowker, 1979. 271p. LC 79–11138. ISBN 0–8352–1149–5.

Methods of planning and designing signs for libraries are described and illustrated in this manual. Major signage needed in various types of libraries is addressed in the twenty chapters written by several contributors. Discussed in the chapters are the language of signs, the role of the design consultant, signs for handicapped patrons, signs and the school media center, wayfinding in research libraries, coordinating graphics and architecture, and designing open-stack areas for the user. Numerous photographs and drawings are used to illustrate the text. An appendix provides technical and psychological considerations derived from the Institute of Signage Research. There is also an annotated, selective bibliography for further information on this topic and a general index accessing subjects, names, and locations.

1166 Signs and guiding for libraries. By L. Reynolds and S. Barrett. London: Clive Bingley, 1981. 158p. LC 80–140234. ISBN 0–85157–312–6.

Practical advice on the creation and placement of signs and other graphics in libraries is provided in this manual. The authors' approach is to present general principles concerned with signage and then provide examples of the application of those principles. Techniques for the preparation of signs are given, supplemented by numerous illustrations. Also included is information about types of materials which can be used in signs. The text is indexed by subject.

Slide Libraries

HANDBOOKS AND MANUALS

1167 Slide libraries: a guide for academic institutions, museums, and special collections. By Betty Jo Irvine and P. E. Fry. 2d ed. Littleton, CO: Libraries Unlimited, 1979. 321p. LC 79–17354. ISBN 0–87287–202–5.

The basics of organizing and servicing slide collections in libraries or other types of institutions are presented in this manual. Clear and detailed instructions are provided on such topics as acquisitions, production methods, storage and access systems, projection systems, and classification and cataloging. The text is augmented with numerous photographs, illustrations, forms, or other graphics. A lengthy bibliography is included and three directories are appended at the end of the work. One directory lists distributors and manufacturers of various types of equipment and supplies; another identifies sources of slides; and the third contains a directory of slide libraries. This work is revised from an earlier edition, published in 1974, and it includes information about machine indexing techniques, environmental controls, and preservation methods for slides not covered in the previous edition.

Spanish Heritage Librarians and Librarianship

For reference materials on Spanish heritage librarians and librarianship see entries listed under the heading Hispanic American Librarians and Librarianship.

Special Libraries and Librarianship

Materials on special libraries also appear elsewhere in this guide. For bibliographies, directories, biographical, and statistical sources covering special libraries in general, see the appropriate chapter in Part One. Specific types of special libraries are covered under other headings in this chapter. Included here are reference materials dealing with special libraries and librarianship as a subject.

HANDBOOKS AND MANUALS

1168 Handbook of special librarianship and information work. Ed. by L. J. Anthony. 5th ed. London: Aslib, 1982. 416p. LC 82–235080. ISBN 0–85142–160–1.

Drawing on British experience and practice, this detailed manual describes the operations and procedures of special library work. The focus is on current practices, particularly those which date from the previous edition (1975) to the early 1980s. The chapters, written by different contributors, cover such topics as computer-based information retrieval systems, networks, and the use of audiovisual materials in the special library. In addition to offering practical information, this work also provides a general overview of each area or topic covered. An extensive list of references is found at the end of each chapter. The chapters consist of new content rather than just a revision of chapters found in the previous editions. Thus, the earlier versions—published in 1955, 1962, 1967, and 1975—continue to have value.

1169 A sampler of forms for special libraries. By Social Science Group, Washington, D.C. Chapter, Special Libraries Assn. New York: Special Libraries Assn., 1982. 211p. LC 81–8747. ISBN 0–87111–262–0.

Forms used by a variety of special libraries for diverse purposes (acquisitions, cataloging, circulation control, reference, interlibrary loan, library statistics, and budgeting) were acquired, evaluated, selected, and finally published in this work. Many of the forms can be used or adapted for use by other types of libraries, so the value of this collection of forms is not limited to special libraries. Arrangement is by section, with each section preceded by descriptive information about the forms and their utilization. Also included are an annotated bibliography and an article by J. B. Kaiser on the "Mechanics of Forms Design," reprinted from *Forms design and control.* A subject index completes the work.

1170 Scientific and technical libraries: their organization and administration. By Lucille J. Strauss, Irene M. Shreve and Alberta L. Brown. 2d ed. New York: Becker and Hayes, 1972. 450p. (A Wiley-Becker-Hayes publication) LC 71–173679. ISBN 0–471–83312–6.

Practical information about the operation and administration of technical libraries is offered in this manual. Because of its limited scope, the content does not extend to all types of special libraries but only to those in the areas named in the title. Topics covered include acquisitions, organization of materials, technical processes, staffing and managing, budgeting, facilities, and services. An appendix includes a lengthy list of basic reference sources, current as of 1970. Although this list is now over a decade old, it still is useful; many of the cited titles have been brought out in more recent editions. An earlier edition was published in 1964 by Interscience.

1171 Special librarianship. By Wilfred Ashworth. New York: K. G. Saur, 1979. 120p. (Outlines of modern librarianship) LC 79–312159. ISBN 0–85157–227–4.

This brief manual describes the role and functions of special libraries, differentiating among types of special libraries. Separate chapters deal with such topics as the special library within the organization, information handling, and evaluation and promotion of special library services. Examples and bibliographic citations reflect a British orientation. A subject index completes the work.

1172 Special libraries: a guide for management: with revisions through 1974. By Jo Ann Aufdenkamp and others. Ed. by Edward G. Strable. New York: Special Libraries Assn., 1975. 74p. LC 74–19252. ISBN 0–87111–228–0.

Aimed at management personnel in corporations with special libraries, this manual was prepared to explain the nature of special libraries and information centers. In addition to describing the general characteristics of special libraries, various chapters provide explanations of library processes in non-technical terms. Topics covered include acquisition, organization, and dissemination of materials; staffing; space and equipment needs; and budgeting. An appendix reproduces a business user evaluation questionnaire. A list of additional readings is also provided.

STATISTICAL SOURCES

1173 SLA triennial salary survey. New York: Special Libraries Assn., 1983. 74p. LC 83–595. ISBN 0–87111–302–3.

This sixth survey of members salaries conducted by the Special Libraries Association reports data for 3,255 respondents which represents (thirty-six percent of SLA's membership as of April), 1982. For further information see entry **1099**.

Statistics

For reference materials on statistics see entries listed under the heading Library Statistics.

Storage

BIBLIOGRAPHIC SOURCES

1174 The relegation and storage of material in academic libraries: a literature review. By L. Guilder, et al. Loughborough: Centre for Library and Information Management (CLAIM), Dept. of Library and Information Studies, Loughborough Univ., 1980. 77p. (CLAIM reports, no. 3) ISBN 0–904924–24–6.

Concerned with remote storage of materials in academic libraries, this literature review cites items published between 1970 and 1978 in Great Britain, the United States, and Europe. Although the text of the review emphasizes British practice, the literature, observations, and applications are valid for any location.

Suppliers and Vendors

For reference materials on suppliers and vendors see entries listed under the heading Library Suppliers and Vendors.

Synagogue Libraries

For reference materials on synagogue libraries see entries listed under the heading Church, Synagogue and Theological Libraries.

Technical Services

BIBLIOGRAPHIC SOURCES

1175 **Library technical services: a selected, annotated bibliography.** By Rose Mary Magrill and Constance Rinehart. Westport, CT: Greenwood, 1977. 238p. LC 76–27130. ISBN 0–8371–9286–2.

A total of 1,274 journal articles, monographs, reports, newsletters, and other serials covering various aspects of library technical services are identified in this work. Because the citations were selected from a list at least twice as long, this bibliography represents items considered to be most valuable by the compilers. For the most part, the materials included were published within the ten years prior to publication of the bibliography, with emphasis placed on items issued since 1970. Annotations are descriptive and generally brief. The arrangement is topical and covers organization of technical services, acquisitions, maintenance, circulation, serials, and special materials. Within each of these broad categories are numerous subdivisions. Indexing is by personal names (including authors) and subject.

1176 **Management and costs of technical processes: a bibliographical review, 1876–1969.** By Richard M. Dougherty and Lawrence E. Leonard. Metuchen, NJ: Scarecrow, 1970. 145p. LC 72–14738. ISBN 0–8108–0320–8.

In this historical bibliography, an attempt has been made to provide comprehensive coverage of items relating to cost data, study methodologies, and work simplification in technical processes. Coverage is less comprehensive in other related areas. A total of 853 items are cited. Full bibliographic information is provided, but there are no annotations. The bibliography is arranged by subject, with numerous cross references, and indexed by personal and corporate author. An introductory chapter traces the development of cost studies in libraries.

HANDBOOKS AND MANUALS

1177 **Introduction to technical services for library technicians.** By Marty Bloomberg and G. Edward Evans. 4th ed. Littleton, CO: Libraries Unlimited, 1981. 363p. LC 81–798. ISBN 0–87287–228–9.

Aimed at technical assistants in technical services, this manual provides practical guidance in various facets of technical services. For further information see entry **1018**.

1178 **Managing the catalog department.** By Donald Leroy Foster. 2d ed. Metuchen, NJ: Scarecrow, 1982. 236p. LC 81–16694. ISBN 0–8108–1486–2.

This manual provides practical guidance on the optimal methods for managing the cataloging department. For further information see entry **805**.

Theater Libraries

DIRECTORIES

1179 **Performing arts libraries and museums of the world/Bibliothèques et musées des arts du spectacle dan le monde.** Prep. by the International Federation of Library Associations. Ed. by Cecile Giteau. 2d ed., rev. and enl. Paris: Edition du

Centre National de la Recherche Scientifique and Unesco, 1967. 801p. NUC 71–82779.
This extensive international directory identifies libraries and museums for the performing arts, primarily for the theater. Public and private collections from thirty-seven countries are listed by country, then by city or town, and finally by name of institution. Entries, which appear both in French and English, contain the name of the institution, name of the director and sponsor, hours of opening, types of assistance given users, history of the collection, nature and size of holdings, and publications issued by the institution. The information is indexed by subject and by names of collections and persons.

Theological Libraries

For reference materials on theological libraries see entries listed under the heading Church, Synagogue and Theological Libraries.

Thesaurus Construction and Use
BIBLIOGRAPHIC SOURCES

1180 Thesauri and thesaurus construction. Comp. by Maxine MacCafferty. London: Aslib, 1977. 191p. (Aslib bibliography, no. 7) ISBN 0–85142–102–4.
This bibliography, covering the period from January 1970 to June 1976, identifies 825 monographs, articles, and reports on thesauri and thesaurus construction. Coverage is international; items are cited in the original language. Indexing is by language of the article, name of organization, author, and subject.

1181 Thesaurus bibliography. Ed. by H. J. van der Aa. Amsterdam: Studiecentrum NOVI, 1977. 86p. LC 77–372637. ISBN 90–6298–073–2.
This is an extensive, although not exhaustive, bibliography on the development, application, use, and evaluation of thesauri. Coverage is international. Entries are taken from the literature of the 1960's and 1970's. Citations are in the original language, with non-Roman alphabets transliterated. Some of the titles of non-English publications are translated into English, especially those in east European or oriental languages. Arrangement is alphabetical by main entry. The entries are not annotated, but a note indicates the language of the work. A subject index is provided.

HANDBOOKS AND MANUALS

1182 Thesaurus construction: a practical manual. By Jean Aitchison and Alan Gilchrist. London: Aslib, 1972. 95p. LC 73–159779. ISBN 0–85142–042–7.
This work is intended to provide practical guidance in the construction of thesauri for information retrieval. The authors begin with a section on the place of the thesaurus in information system design. They then deal with features of the thesaurus in some detail. Covered in this section are such topics as standardization and control of terms, specificity and precoordination levels, and elements of structure and classification. The options for the presentation of thesauri are also treated (e.g., classified or alphabetical). The last major section is devoted to a step-by-step description of the techniques to follow in the construction of a thesaurus. Access to specific information about thesaurus construction is facilitated

by the extensive subdividing of the text and by a detailed subject index. Also included in the work is a bibliography of additional readings.

1183 **Thesaurus-making: grow your own word-stock.** By Helen M. Townley and Ralph D. Gee. London: Andre Deutsch, 1980. 206p. LC 81–125934. ISBN 0–233–97225–0.

The development of controlled vocabulary thesauri to be used in information retrieval is described in this basic manual. The authors have intended the work to be used by persons with limited experience who are working in an environment where they are essentially operating alone. The book begins with a chapter on theory and another on the environment in which a given thesaurus is used. Subsequent chapters serve as a practical guide to the development of a thesaurus and cover such topics as the filing sequence, assembling potentially useful words, thesaurus construction, use of compound phrases, evaluation and testing, and computer applications. Included in the appendices are the British and International Standards for mono-lingual thesauri, sources of package programs for the development of thesauri, some samples from various thesauri, a glossary, and a bibliography of additional readings. A subject index completes the volume.

Transportation Libraries

DIRECTORIES

1184 **Transportation libraries in the United States and Canada: an SLA directory.** Comp. by the Transportation Division, Special Libraries Assn. 3d ed. New York: Special Libraries Assn., 1978. 221p. LC 77–17615. ISBN 0–87111–233–7.

Information on 205 transportation collections in the United States and Canada is included in this directory. Coverage extends to all types of transportation, including air, motor vehicle, and rail. Arrangement is alphabetical by the name of the library. Entries supply name, address, telephone number, name of director, collection size, staff size, a brief description of the library, network affiliation, special collections, services provided to persons not affiliated, and publications of the library. Indexing is by subject, geographic area, and personal name. Previous editions were published in 1973 and 1968.

Trustees

HANDBOOKS AND MANUALS

1185 **The library trustee: a practical guidebook.** By Virginia G. Young. 3d ed. New York: Bowker, 1978. 192p. LC 78–13065. ISBN 0–8352–1068–5.

The intent of this work is to provide a manual that can be used by public library trustees as a guide to their responsibilities and duties. There are twenty-four chapters, written by various individuals who have served as library trustees or who can knowledgeably describe the responsibilities of trustees. Included are such topics as qualifications and appointments, the trustee's relationship with the librarian and staff, the trustee and the law, the trustee and finances, and the trustee and the political process. Advice is practical and, in some cases, exhortive. Several appendices are provided, including sample bylaws, instructions on how to form a friends group, and a checklist of budget considerations. A suggested reading list for library trustees and a subject index are also included.

U.S.S.R., Resources On

For reference materials on U.S.S.R. resources, see entries listed under the heading Russian and Soviet Studies Libraries.

United Nations Libraries

DIRECTORIES

1186 **Directory of United Nations information systems.** 2d ed. Geneva: United Nations Inter-Organization Board for Information Services, 1980. 2v. LC 81–120590.
This directory describes the various information services available through the United Nations, its subordinate units, and specialized agencies. It is written in English, French, and Spanish. Arranged by agency name, entries specify name of the information system, name, address, and telephone number of the parent agency, name of the director or other contact person, holdings of the collection or data base, and services offered by the unit. The information is indexed by subject, geographical area, and name of information system. The first edition was issued in 1978 under a slightly different title.

1187 **Guide to the archives of international organizations. Part I, United Nations system: preliminary version.** Paris: Unesco, 1979. 301p. PGI/79/WS/7.
This is the first of a projected three-part series that eventually will cover the United Nations, the archives of other international organizations in the United Nations family of intergovernment organizations, and other repositories that have holdings relating to international organizations. Part I covers the United Nations, fourteen specialized agencies, and a few selected organizations that traditionally have had a close relationship with the United Nations. All together, thirty-three organizations are treated in this work. Entries contain information about the agency's policy on access to the archives, facilities, and document reproduction; the nature of the archival holdings; reference sources available that provide access to the holdings; and special features of each archive. Indexing is by institutional name, subdivision of each organization, and personal names where personal papers are included in an archival collection.

University Libraries and Librarianship

For reference materials on university libraries and librarianship see entries listed under the heading College and University Libraries and Librarianship.

User Studies

BIBLIOGRAPHIC SOURCES

1188 **Index to user studies.** Comp. by FID Study Committee/Information for Industry (FIC/II). The Hague: International Federation for Documentation, 1974. 103p. LC 75–332032. ISBN 92–66–00515–0.
Over 200 studies of the users of libraries, information centers, and information generally are cited in this bibliography. Most of the studies listed were completed between the mid–1960's and the early 1970's. The entries, representing literature from twenty different countries,

include full bibliographic information and a brief descriptive annotation. Subject and author indexes provide additional access to the citations.

1189   User studies: an introductory guide and select bibliography. Ed. by Geoffrey Ford. Sheffield, England: Center for Research on User Studies, Univ. of Sheffield, 1977. 92p. (Occasional paper, no. 1) LC 78–318127. ISBN 0–906088–00–3. ISSN 0140–3834.

This work consists of an introductory guide to the diverse aspects of user studies and a selective, annotated bibliography providing bibliographic information on the 236 works on user studies mentioned in the text. Although some U.S. materials are cited, particularly studies from the American Psychological Association Project on Scientific Information Exchange in Psychology, the emphasis is primarily on British studies. The scope is not limited to studies of library use but extends to studies of information use in other settings as well, including book stores and bibliographic services.

Vertical Files

HANDBOOKS AND MANUALS

1190   The vertical file and its satellites: a handbook of acquisition, processing, and organization. By Shirley Miller. 2d ed. Littleton, CO: Libraries Unlimited, 1979. 251p. (Library science text series) LC 79–13773. ISBN 0–87287–164–9.

All aspects of work with vertical files and related files (such as clipping files) are covered in this manual. Specific subjects addressed include acquisitions, sources of vertical file materials, labeling, filing, weeding, and circulating of vertical file materials. Special attention is given to collections of vocational materials, local history materials, maps, pictures, and files on local community activities. The text is augmented by illustrations and indexed by subject.

Women in Librarianship

BIBLIOGRAPHIC SOURCES

1191   The role of women in librarianship 1876–1976: the entry, advancement, and struggle for equalization in one profession. By Kathleen Weibel and Kathleen M. Heim, with assist. from Dianne J. Ellsworth. Phoenix: Oryx, 1979. 510p. (A Neal-Schuman professional book) LC 78–27302. ISBN 0–912700–01–7.

This compilation of articles and other writings tracing the role of women in librarianship from 1876 to 1976 is accompanied by a comprehensive annotated bibliography of over 1,000 entries. The bibliography covers virtually every English-language item on the topic of women in librarianship, including letters to the editor that followed important articles. An updated bibliography covering the years 1977–1981 will be published as a continuing project of the ALA Committee on the Status of Women. The Committee has deposited with the American Library Association an archival collection of most of the items listed in the bibliography and the update; these can be accessed by persons interested in pursuing further study.

BIOGRAPHICAL SOURCES

1192 SHARE: sisters have resources everywhere: a directory of feminist library workers. Comp. and indexed by Carole Leita. 4th ed. Berkeley: Women Library Workers, 1980. 54p.

Biographical information on 117 feminist library workers throughout the United States is provided in this biographical source. The entries, arranged alphabetically by state to facilitate personal contacts on a geographical basis, include brief professional and personal information about each individual. The listing is indexed by name, subject interests, names of women's collections, and presses specializing in the publication of women's materials.

DIRECTORIES

1193 Directory of library and information profession women's groups. Comp. by Mary Mallory. Chicago: Committee on the Status of Women in Librarianship, American Library Assn., 1982. 24p.

National, state, and foreign groups actively involved with women's issues, particularly in the information professions, are described in this directory. Entries contain the name of the organization, purpose, type of membership, dates and locations of meetings, the name(s) of contact persons. Appendices include a list of activities of the organizations covered in the directory and a bibliography of 1981 publications on women in the information professions.

Workshops and Conferences

For reference materials on workshops and conferences see entries listed under the heading Continuing Education.

Young Adults

For reference materials on young adults see entries listed under the heading Children and Young Adults, Library Services To.

AUTHOR INDEX

The author index is arranged alphabetically, word by word. All characters or groups of characters separated by spaces, dashes, hyphens, diagonal slashes or periods are treated as separate words. Acronyms not separated by spaces or punctuation are alphabetized as though they are single words, while initials separated by spaces or punctuation are treated as if each letter is a complete word. Personal names beginning with capital "Mc," "M'" and "Mac" are all listed under "Mac" as though the full form were used. "St." is alphabetized as if spelled out.

Abdullahi, Ismael, **730**
Accademie e Biblioteche Italiane
 Direzione Generale, **370**
Adams, Elaine P., **811**
Agur, Ustus, **148**
Agyei-Gyane, L., **302**
Aitchison, Jean, **1182**
Alderman, Belle, **815**
Ali, Syed Irshad, **89**
Allen, C. G., **209**
Alley, Brian, **783**
Allum, D. N., **1030**
Alonso, Aníbal Salazar, **417**
Altman, Ellen, **986**
Aman, Mohammed M., **75**
American Association of Community and
 Junior Colleges, **1053**
American Library Association, **801**
 Association for Library Service to
  Children
  International Relations Committee,
   814
  National Planning for Special
   Collections Committee, **816**
 College and Reference Section, **843**
 Committee on Library Work with
  Children, **817**
 Education Committee, **1157**
 Headquarters Library, **94, 731**
 Library Administration and
  Management Association
  Public Relations Section, **1125**
  Staff Development Committee, **861**
 Office for Intellectual Freedom, **930**

 Office for Library Service to the
  Disadvantaged, **872**
 Resources and Technical Services
  Division
  Filing Committee, **886**
 Standing Committee on Library
  Education, **888**
Amos, Geraldine Odester, **299**
Anderson, Elizabeth L., **1077**
Anderson, James D., **972**
Anderson, Linda, **1060**
Anthony, L. J., **1168**
Art Libraries Society of North America,
 721
Ash, Lee, **276, 281, 430**
Ashton, Rick J., **549**
Ashworth, Wilfred, **1171**
'Associació de Bibliotecaries de
  Barecelona
  Vocalia de Cultura, **379**
Association Canadienne des Bibliothèques
  Reference Section, **4**
Association of Art Libraries (German
  Federal Republic), **724**
Association of British Library Schools,
  967
Aufdenkamp, Jo Ann, **1172**

Back, Kathryn, **1091**
Badough, Rose Marie, **97**
Bahr, Alice Harrison, **786, 1158**
Bakar, Ahmad Bakeri bin Abu, **325**
Baker, D. Phillip, **1150**

International Federation of Library
    Associations, **1179**
  Committee on Library Work with
    Children, **812**
  Geography and Map Libraries Sub-
    section, **1027**
Irvine, Betty Jo, **1167**
Ives, Alan, **694**

Jackson, Miles M., **846**
Jackson, W. Carl, **682**
Jahoda, Gerald, **915**
James, Bernard, **1058**
Janzing, Grazyna, **948**
Japan
  Ministry of Education, **168**
Japan Libraries Association
  International Exchange Committee, **324**
Japan Special Libraries Association,
    322–323
Jaques Cattell Press, **279, 396, 425**
Jennings, Margaret, **450**
Jōhō Kanri Kenkyu Iinkai, **167**
Johnson, Donald R., **868**
Jones, David J., **215**
Jones, L., **394**
Jones, Malcolm, **1070**
Jordan, Anne Harwell, **45**
Jordan, Melbourne, **45**
Josey, E. J., **780**
Jovanovic, Slobodan, **395**
Jurić, Sime, **176**

Kakoures, Georgios M., **164**
Kambayashi, Yahiko, **1079**
Kan Lai-bing, **320**
Kananov, P. H., **172**
Kaske, Neal K., **680**
Katz, Bill, **1139, 1161**
Kawabata, Julie, **519**
Keeling, Denis F., 995–997
Keller, Clara D., **96**
Kellman, Amy, **814**
Kent, Allen, **217**
Kent, Rosalind, **212**
Kern, Wilfried, **86**
Kesner, Richard M., **745**
Khosla, Raj K., **246, 248, 303, 308**
Khurshid, Anis, **89**

Khurshid, Zahirruddin, **90**
Kidd, Jerry, **864**
Kilgour, Frederick G., **98**
Kim, Choong H., **1023**
Kish, Joseph L., **1055**
Kiss, Jeno, **369**
Kleeberger, Pat, **876**
Klempner, Irving M., **963**
Klimowiczowa, I., **377**
Knobbe, Mary L., **1103**
Knoop-Busch, Hedda, **883**
Kocowski, Bronislaw, **221**
Koenig, Michael E. D., **782**
Kohl, Rachel, **819**
Kohn, Rita, **1128, 1135**
Korean Library Association
  Commission for Technology, **169**
Kosa, Geza A., **253, 255**
Kramer, Mollie, W., **690**
Krause, Friedhilde, **100–101**
Kreissman, Bernard, **682**
Kruzas, Anthony T., **1086**
Kuman, P. S. G., **1001**
Kunz, Fritz, **85**
Kunze, Horst, **220**
Kusbandarrumsansi, H., **321**

Lackner, Irene, **798**
Ladenson, Alex, **1002**
LaFleur, Lydia, **1130**
Lajeunesse, Marcel, **976**
Lancaster, F. W., **988**
Lancour, Harold, **217**
Landau, Thomas, **216, 267**
Lane, Alfred H., **892**
Lane, Margaret T., **906**
Langfeldt, Johannes, **219**
Lankage, Jayasiri, **177**
Larsgaard, Mary, **1029**
Laskeev, Nikolaj Alesandrovic, **100–101**
le Maire, Oda, **812**
Leach, Steven G., **50**
Lee, Joel M., **280, 462**
Leerburger, Benedict A., **1132**
Leita, Carole, **1192**
Lemaitre, Henri, **142**
Lengenfelde, Helga, **73**
Lengenfelder, Helen, **288**
Lenroot-Ernt, Lois, **427–428**
Leonard, Lawrence E., **907, 1176**

Ruckl, Gotthard, **220**
Rudkin, Anthony, **293**
Ruoss, G. Martin, **820**

Sabzwari, Ghaniul Akram, **250**
Saffady, William, **1054**
Salem, Shawky, **133**
Salimei, M., **372**
Salokoski, Juuso, **257**
Saunders, W. L., **241**
Saur, Klaus Gerhard, **286**
Sawoniak, Henry, **200**
Schatz, Walter, **689**
Schlachter, Gail A., 126–127
Schmittroth, John, Jr., **1085–1086**
Schoellkopf, Catharine, **477**
Schoenly, Steven B., **848**
Scholberg, Henry, **727**
Schorr, Alan Edward, **438, 898**
Schultz, Claire K., **208**
Schutze, Gertrude, **70, 72**
Schuyler, Peri L., **864**
Segall, Aryeh, **943**
Sehlinger, Peter J., **416**
Senalp, Leman, **134**
Shamsuddoulah, A. B. M., **316**
Shamurin, E. I., **143**
Shapiro, Beth J., **874**
Sharp, J. R., **950**
Shaver, Donna, **519**
Sherman, Steve, **1126**
Shirey, Donald, **987**
Shockley, Ann Allen, **780**
Shonyo, Carolyn, **678**
Shreve, Irene M., **1170**
Simmler, Otto, **896**
Simsova, Silvia, **845, 847**
Sinclair, Dorothy, **1108**
Slote, Stanley J., **829**
Smith, Charles, **1056**
SmitZih, Josephine Metcalfe, **1000**
Smith, Lynn S., **1164**
Smith, Ruth S., **824**
Smith, Susan J., **905**
Snow, Peter, **389**
Snyder, Patt, **447**
South African Academy of Science
    and Art
    Vaktalburo, **158**
South, Aloha, **685**

South Carolina Library Association, **527**
South Carolina State Library Board, **527**
Southeastern Library Association, **433**
Southwestern Library Association, **434**
Special Libraries Association
    Baltimore Chapter, **475**
    Connecticut Valley Chapter, **447**
    Transportation Division, **1184**
    Washington D. C. Chapter
        Social Science Group, **1169**
Springman, Mary Adele, **946**
Steele, Colin, **287, 952**
Stephenson, Richard W., **1026**
Stevens, Nora B., **945**
Stevens, Norman D., **945**
Stiles, Karen A., **737**
Stockard Joan, **764**
Stoffle, Carla J., **903**
Stokes, Roy, **772**
Stolk, H. A., **186**
Stone, Clara Ruth, **822**
Stone, Elizabeth W., **858, 999**
Strable, Edward G., **1172**
Straka, Josef, **83**
Strauss, Lucille J., **1170**
Strickland, J. T., **294**
Suchodolska, E., **377**
Suelflow, August R., **823**
Sullivan, Martha J., **281**
Sullivan, Peggy, **1095**
Surendar, Kumar, **305**
Suslova, I. M., **223**
Swartzburg, Susan G., **857**
Swiderski, Boleslaw, **222**
Szentirmay, Paul, **347**

Tagger, Mathilde A., **312**
Tait, H. F. C., **393**
Tait, James A., **393**
Taylor, Kenneth I., **951**
Taylor, L. J., **124, 243**
Taylor, Mary M., **675**
Taylor, Peter J., **762**
Tayyeb, R., **199**
Teinila, Teena, **257**
Tepper, Krysta, **1135**
Thomas, Carol H., **911**
Thomas, James L., **911**
Thomas, Sister Evangeline, **715**
Thomison, Dennis, 126–127

Yangyong, S., **329**
Young, Heartsill, **181**
Young, Mary E., **1047**
Young, Virginia G., **1185**

Zell, Hans, **292**
Zhdanova, G. S., **175**
Zidouemba, Dominique, **295**
Zweizig, Douglas, **990**

TITLE INDEX

The title index is arranged alphabetically, word by word. All characters or groups of characters separated by spaces, dashes, hyphens, diagonal slashes or periods are treated as separate words. Acronyms not separated by spaces or punctuation are alphabetized as though they are single words, while initials separated by spaces or punctuation are treated as if each letter is a complete word. Numerals (including those identifying year dates) are alphabetized according to their word equivalents.

GEOGRAPHIC INDEX

This index provides access to the place of publication (imprint) and geographic scope (coverage) of each of the titles described in this *Guide*. The index terms follow a word-by-word alphabetical arrangement and refer the user to the appropriate entry by number.

Africa
　Coverage: **Directories**, 292–295, 684–688
　See also International; names of specific countries
Alabama
　Coverage: **Directories**, 433, 435–436; **Statistical sources**, 599–600
　See also United States
Alaska
　Coverage: **Directories**, 437–438
　See also United States
Alberta, Canada
　Coverage: **Directories**, 403; **Statistical sources**, 555
　See also Canada
Algeria
　Coverage: **Directories**, 976
　See also Africa; International
Arab Countries
　Coverage: **Bibliographies**, 78–79; **Directories**, 293; **Vocabularies and glossaries**, 133, 144, 159
　See also International; names of specific countries
Argentina
　Imprint: **Current contents**, 106; **Directories**, 411, 973; **Indexes and abstracts**, 1–2; **Vocabularies and glossaries**, 193
　Coverage: **Directories**, 411; **Indexes and abstracts**, 1–2
　See also International; Latin America
Arizona
　Coverage: **Directories**, 439; **Statistical sources**, 601
　See also Southwestern States; United States
Arkansas

Coverage: **Directories**, 440–441; **Statistical sources**, 602
　See also United States
Asia
　Coverage: **Bibliographies**, 80, 726; **Directories**, 684
　See also International; names of specific countries
Australia
　Imprint: **Bibliographies**, 694; **Biographical sources**, 253–255, 966; **Directories**, 331–342, 344, 749, 815, 913, 970, 1009, 1025; **Encyclopedias**, 215; **Handbooks and manuals**, 936; **Statistical sources**, 545
　Coverage: **Bibliographies**, 694, 742–744, 746, 776; **Biographical sources**, 253–255, 966; **Directories**, 330–333, 346, 694, 749, 913, 943, 959, 970, 1009, 1025; **Encyclopedias**, 215; **Handbooks and manuals**, 936; **Statistical sources**, 545; **Terminologies**, 775
　See also Commonwealth Countries; International; names of specific cities, states, and territories
Australian Capital Territory, Australia
　Coverage: **Directories**, 335, 815
　See also Australia; New South Wales, Australia
Austria
　Imprint: **Biographical sources**, 349; **Directories**, 349–350; **Handbooks and manuals**, 349; **Statistical sources,** 349
　Coverage: **Biographical sources**, 349; **Directories**, 349–350; **Encyclopedias**, 219; **Handbooks

751, 895, 931, 944, 950, 952–953,
960, 977, 1030, 1038, 1066;
Dissertations and theses, 124;
Handbooks and manuals, 240–241,
243, 717, 790, 802–803, 825, 914,
1004, 1021, 1028, 1041, 1045,
1070–1072, 1088, 1094, 1119, 1163,
1166, 1168, 1182–1183; **Indexes and
abstracts**, 37–41; **Review
publications**, 108–112; **Statistical
sources**, 564–570; **Thesauri**, 205;
Vocabularies and glossaries, 136;
Yearbooks, 228–232, 234
Coverage: **Acronyms**, 196–198, 200;
Bibliographies, 70, 72, 91–93, 832,
852, 982, 995–997, 1061, 1174, 1189;
Biographical sources, 263–267,
741; **Directories**, 348, 684, 895,
943, 953, 960, 1030, 1066;
Dissertations and theses, 124;
Handbooks and manuals, 245, 717,
777, 790, 793, 799, 825, 887, 914,
988, 1004, 1021, 1028, 1040–1041,
1045, 1070–1072, 1078, 1094, 1101,
1119, 1136, 1163, 1166, 1168, 1171,
1182–1183; **Indexes and abstracts**,
38–41, 44–45; **Review publications**,
108–111; **Statistical sources**, 568;
Thesauri, 205–206; **Vocabularies
and glossaries**, 131–137, 139–144,
146–179, 185; **Yearbooks**, 229–231,
234
See also Commonwealth Countries;
International; London, England;
Oxford, England; United Kingdom
Estonia
Imprint: **Vocabularies and glossaries**,
148
Coverage: **Directories**, 383;
Vocabularies and glossaries, 148
See also Europe; International; U.S.S.R.
Ethiopia
Imprint: **Directories**, 299–300
Coverage: **Directories**, 299–300
See also Africa; International
Europe
Coverage: **Acronyms**, 202;
Bibliographies, 68, 74, 832, 1174;
Directories, 283, 348, 703–704,
722, 878, 943, 1009; **Encyclopedias**,
218, 222, 224; **Foreign language

handbooks, 209, 213; **Handbooks
and manuals**, 693, 790; **Indexes and
abstracts**, 6, 11, 13, 15, 17, 19,
33–34, 38–39, 42, 62; **Review
publications**, 111–112;
Terminologies, 677, 775, 809, 830;
Yearbooks, 225
See also International; names of specific
cities, countries, and regions

Federal Republic of Germany
Imprint: **Acronyms**, 202;
Bibliographies, 73, 77, 87, 101, 696,
800, 883, 885; **Biographical
sources**, 259; **Current contents**,
107; **Data bases**, 117; **Directories**,
285–286, 288–289, 292, 361–364,
366–367, 724, 896, 957, 1027;
Encyclopedias, 218–220;
Handbooks and manuals, 1112;
Indexes and abstracts, 18–20;
Vocabularies and glossaries, 138,
149, 163
Coverage: **Bibliographies**, 87;
Biographical sources, 259;
Directories, 360–367;
Encyclopedias, 219; **Indexes and
abstracts**, 18–20
See also Europe; German Democratic
Republic; Germany; International
Fiji
Imprint: **Directories**, 345
Coverage: **Directories**, 345
See also Commonwealth Countries;
International
Finland
Imprint: **Biographical sources**, 257;
Directories, 354
Coverage: **Biographical sources**, 257;
Directories, 354; **Indexes and
abstracts**, 35–36; **Vocabularies and
glossaries**, 145
See also Europe; International;
Scandanavian Countries
Florida
Coverage: **Directories**, 433, 452–454;
Statistical sources, 609–610
See also Southeastern States; United
States
France

348

Imprint: **Bibliographies**, 697;
Directories, 283, 290, 294–295,
357, 708, 722, 938, 977, 1179, 1187;
Handbooks and manuals, 939;
Indexes and abstracts, 9–12;
Thesauri, 206; **Vocabularies and
glossaries**, 140, 142–143, 161, 184
Coverage: **Acronyms**, 196, 198, 200;
Bibliographies, 210, 742–744, 746;
Biographical sources, 741;
Directories, 355, 357, 976; **Indexes
and abstracts**, 9–10, 12; **Thesauri**,
204, 206; **Vocabularies and
glossaries**, 131–134, 136–137,
139–144, 146–147, 149–150,
152–156, 162
See also Europe; International; Paris,
France

Georgia
Coverage: **Directories**, 433, 455;
Statistical sources, 611–612
See also Southeastern States; United
States
German Democratic Republic
Imprint: **Bibliographies**, 66, 74,
85–86, 100; **Biographical sources**,
258; **Directories**, 358–359; **Indexes
and abstracts**, 13–17
Coverage: **Bibliographies**, 85–86;
Biographical sources, 258;
Directories, 358–360, 365;
Encyclopedias, 219
See also Europe; Federal Republic of
Germany; Germany; International
Germany
Coverage: **Acronyms**, 196, 198, 200;
Bibliographies, 77, 742–744, 746;
Biographical sources, 741;
Directories, 724; **Encyclopedias**,
218–220; **Foreign language
handbooks**, 211; **Handbooks and
manuals**, 1112; **Indexes and
abstracts**, 20; **Terminologies**, 676,
806; **Vocabularies and glossaries**,
131–134, 136–137, 139–144,
146–150, 152–156, 163
See also Europe; Federal Republic of
Germany; German Democratic
Republic; International; West Berlin,

Germany
Germany, Federal Republic of. *See* Federal
Republic of Germany
Ghana
Imprint: **Directories**, 301–302
Coverage: **Directories**, 301–302
See also Africa; Commonwealth
Countries; International
Great Britain. *See* United Kingdom
Greece
Imprint: **Vocabularies and glossaries**,
164
Coverage: **Vocabularies and
glossaries**, 164
See also International
Greenland
Coverage: **Directories**, 348
See also International
Guyana
Coverage: **Biographical sources**, 272
See also Caribbean; Commonwealth
Countries; International; Latin
America

Hamilton County, Indiana
Coverage: **Directories**, 463
See also Indiana
Hancock County, Indiana
Coverage: **Directories**, 463
See also Indiana
Hawaii
Coverage: **Directories**, 456–457;
Statistical sources, 613
See also United States
Hendricks County, Indiana
Coverage: **Directories**, 463
See also Indiana
Holland. *See* Netherlands
Hong Kong
Imprint: **Directories**, 320
Coverage: **Directories**, 320
See also Asia; International
Hungary
Imprint: **Directories**, 368–369; **Indexes
and abstracts**, 21–24; **Vocabularies
and glossaries**, 137
Coverage: **Acronyms**, 198; **Directories**,
368–369; **Indexes and abstracts**,
21–22, 24; **Vocabularies and
glossaries**, 137, 155

See also Europe; International

Iceland
  Coverage: **Directories**, 348; **Indexes and abstracts**, 35–36
  See also Europe; International; Scandanavian Countries
Idaho
  Coverage: **Directories**, 431, 458; **Statistical sources**, 614
  See also United States
Illinois
  Coverage: **Directories**, 459–461; **Statistical sources**, 615
  See also United States
India
  Imprint: **Bibliographies**, 88; **Biographical sources**, 246–248; **Directories**, 303–309; **Handbooks and manuals**, 244, 1001, 1003, 1118; **Indexes and abstracts**, 25; **Terminologies**, 187, 807–808
  Coverage: **Bibliographies**, 88, 742–744, 746, 776; **Biographical sources**, 246–247, 741; **Directories**, 303, 306, 308; **Handbooks and manuals**, 1001; **Indexes and abstracts**, 25; **Terminologies**, 807–808; **Vocabularies and glossaries**, 187
  See also Commonwealth Countries; Delhi, India; International
Indiana
  Coverage: **Directories**, 463–464; **Statistical sources**, 616
  See also United States
Indonesia
  Imprint: **Directories**, 321; **Vocabularies and glossaries**, 165
  Coverage: **Biographical sources**, 251; **Directories**, 321; **Vocabularies and glossaries**, 165
  See also Asia; International
International
  Coverage: **Acronyms**, 199–201; **Bibliographies**, 65–67, 69, 71, 73–76, 92, 97, 695–697, 730, 732, 745, 761–762, 800, 812, 845, 850–851, 859, 864, 883, 885, 922, 964, 981, 983, 993, 1032–1033,

1062, 1081–1082, 1180–1181, 1188; **Biographical sources**, 1142; **Current contents**, 104–106; **Data bases**, 117–118; **Directories**, 284–291, 692, 702, 706, 708–710, 734–736, 765, 814, 820, 873, 880, 896, 931, 933, 937–938, 942, 944–945, 948–951, 957, 977, 1010–1012, 1027, 1037, 1049–1051, 1064, 1085–1086, 1160, 1179, 1186–1193; **Encyclopedias**, 214, 217, 221; **Handbooks and manuals**, 244, 671, 716, 725, 760, 822, 846–847, 853, 855, 939, 1000, 1003, 1088, 1118; **Indexes and abstracts**, 2, 5–8, 11, 14, 16, 19, 22, 26, 30–34, 37–39, 43, 47–48, 51, 53, 57–58, 60, 62, 64; **Vocabularies and glossaries**, 138; **Yearbooks**, 233, 239
  See also names of specific foreign cities, continents, provinces, states, and territories
Iowa
  Coverage: **Directories**, 465, 467; **Statistical sources**, 617
  See also United States
Iran
  Coverage: **Directories**, 293, 310
  See also Arab Countries; International; Middle East
Ireland
  Coverage: **Bibliographies**, 91; **Directories**, 348, 386–387; **Yearbooks**, 228, 232
  See also Commonwealth Countries; International; Northern Ireland; Republic of Ireland; United Kingdom
Irish Republic. *See* Republic of Ireland
Islamic Republic of Pakistan. *See* Pakistan
Israel
  Imprint: **Directories**, 311–312, 706, 943; **Vocabularies and glossaries**, 150
  Coverage: **Directories**, 311, 943, 1090; **Vocabularies and glossaries**, 150
  See also International; Jerusalem, Israel; Middle East
Italy
  Imprint: **Biographical sources**, 260–261; **Directories**, 370–372; **Thesauri**, 203–204; **Vocabularies**

Biographical sources, 250;
Directories, 314–316
See also International
Papua New Guinea
Coverage: **Directories**, 959
See also Commonwealth Countries;
International
Paris, France
Coverage: **Directories**, 355–357
See also France
Pennsylvania
Coverage: **Directories**, 520–522, 524;
Statistical sources, 653
See also Pittsburgh, Pennsylvania;
United States
People's Republic of China
Imprint: **Directories**, 319
Coverage: **Directories**, 319
See also Asia; China; International
Peru
Imprint: **Directories**, 421
Coverage: **Directories**, 421
See also International; Latin America
Philadelphia, Pennsylvania
Coverage: **Directories**, 520
See also Pennsylvania
Philippines
Imprint: **Biographical sources**, 251;
Directories, 326
Coverage: **Biographical sources**, 251;
Directories, 326
See also International
Pittsburgh, Pennsylvania
Coverage: **Directories**, 523
See also Pennsylvania
Poland
Imprint: **Acronyms**, 200; **Directories**,
377; **Encyclopedias**, 221–222;
Indexes and abstracts, 32;
Vocabularies and glossaries,
153–154
Coverage: **Acronyms**, 198; **Directories**,
376–377; **Encyclopedias**, 222;
Vocabularies and glossaries, 146,
153–155
See also Europe; International
Prince Edward Island, Canada
Coverage: **Statistical sources**, 561
See also Canada
Puerto Rico
Imprint: **Directories**, 525

Coverage: **Biographical sources**, 920;
Directories, 525
See also Caribbean; International;
United States

Quebec, Canada
Coverage: **Directories**, 409; **Statistical
sources**, 548
See also Canada
Queensland, Australia
Coverage: **Directories**, 340
See also Australia

Republic of China. *See* Taiwan
Republic of Ireland
Coverage: **Directories**, 348, 953, 960,
1038, 1090
See also International; Ireland; Northern
Ireland
Rhode Island
Coverage: **Directories**, 477, 526;
Statistical sources, 654
See also New England; United States
Rhodesia. *See* Zimbabwe
Romania
Imprint: **Directories**, 378; **Indexes and
abstracts**, 33
Coverage: **Acronyms**, 198; **Directories**,
378; **Vocabularies and glossaries**,
155
See also Europe; International
Russia. *See* U.S.S.R.

St. Louis, Missouri
Coverage: **Directories**, 484
See also Missouri
St. Paul, Minnesota
Coverage: **Directories**, 481–482
See also Minnesota
Saskatchewan, Canada
Coverage: **Directories**, 410; **Statistical
sources**, 563
See also Canada
Scandanavian Countries
Coverage: **Data bases**, 116, 119;
Yearbooks, 226–227
See also International; names of specific
countries
Scotland

ABOUT THE AUTHORS

Gary R. Purcell is Professor, Graduate School of Library and Information Science, University of Tennessee. He is president-elect of the Reference and Adult Services Division of the American Library Association and past president of the Association of American Library Schools.

Gail A. Schlachter is Vice President and General Manager of ABC-Clio Information Services. She was the Assistant Library Director at the University of California at Davis, has served on the library school faculty at the University of Southern California, and is currently Reference Book Review Editor for *RQ*.

Charles Bunge is Professor of Library Science at the University of Wisconsin-Madison. He is a past president of both the Wisconsin Library Association and the Association of American Library Schools. Dr. Bunge is the recent recipient of the Isadore Gilbert Mudge Award.